# Global Stage

## Teacher's Book 3

Michelle Worgan



macmillan education

Macmillan Education
4 Crinan Street
London N1 9XW
A division of Springer Nature Limited

Companies and representatives throughout the world

Teacher's Book ISBN 978-1-380-00236-5
Teacher's Blended Pack ISBN 978-1-380-00234-1



Written by Michelle Worgan



First published 2019



Designed by emc design ltd
Front cover design and concept by 3CD
Cover adaptation by Roberto Martinez

The authors and publishers would like to thank the following for permission to reproduce their photographs: Matthew Hayes (p. 16), Lina Acosta Sandaal (p. 18)

The authors and publishers are grateful for permission to reprint the following copyright material: p. 11 Extract from 'Framework for 21st Century Learning' © 2017 Partnership for 21st Century Skills. Reprinted with permission; p. 17 Extract from 'Collaborative for Academic, Social, and Emotional Learning' © 2017 CASEL. Reprinted with permission.

Full acknowledgements for illustrations and photographs in the facsimile pages can be found in the **Language Book** ISBN: 978-1-786-32874-8 and **Literacy Book** ISBN: 978-1-786-32592-1.



Printed and bound in Mexico

This book was printed in November 2018 by:
Editorial Impresora Apolo, S.A. de C.V.
Centeno 150-6, Granjas Esmeralda,
Iztapalapa, C.P. 09810,
Ciudad de México, México.

2023 2022 2021 2020 2019
10 9 8 7 6 5 4 3 2 1

# Contents



macmillan education

| Speaking | Writing | International English | Literacy Book |
| --- | --- | --- | --- |
| | | | **Literacy Review:** Scanning; Cause and Effect; Sequence of Events; Main Idea and Details; Fact and Opinion; *st; tr; nd; ng* |
| **Conversation**<br>Asking for and offering help and advice<br>**Pronunciation**<br>/sk / and /gr/ | **Word Building**<br>Adverb endings<br>**Product**<br>A Book Report | | **Fantasy**<br>*The Beginning of Alice's Adventures*<br>**Informational Text**<br>*Learning and Your Brain*<br>**Reading Skill**<br>Skimming a text |
| **Presentation**<br>Describing biomes<br>**Pronunciation**<br>/pl/ and /cl/ | **Sentence Building**<br>Sequencers<br>**Product**<br>Writing Instructions | **US** *plastic wrap*<br>**UK** *cling film* | **Informational Text**<br>*Two Different Forests*<br>**Folk Tale**<br>*A New Friend*<br>**Reading Skill**<br>Understanding the author's purpose |
| | | | |
| **Conversation**<br>Buying a birthday present<br>**Pronunciation**<br>/pr/ and /dr/ | **Sentence Building**<br>Conjunctions: *and, but, so*<br>**Product**<br>Anecdotal Paragraph | **US** *allowance; bill; college*<br>**UK** *pocket money; note; university* | **Informational Text**<br>*The History of Money*<br>**Story**<br>*The $100 Bill*<br>**Reading Skill**<br>Identifying problems and solutions |
| **Presentation**<br>Describing a hobby<br>**Pronunciation**<br>/ð/ and /θ/ | **Sentence Building**<br>Time phrases and commas<br>**Product**<br>A Diary Entry | | **Informational Text**<br>*Teamwork Makes the Dream Work*<br>**Play**<br>*Late for the Show*<br>**Reading Skill**<br>Understanding the sequence of events |
| | | | |
| **Conversation**<br>Agreeing and disagreeing<br>**Pronunciation**<br>/θ/ and /ʧ/ | **Punctuation**<br>Using quotation marks and commas<br>**Product**<br>A Description | **US** *program; have a show; apartment*<br>**UK** *programme; do a show; flat* | **Informational Text**<br>*The Art of Sound*<br>**Poem**<br>*Beethoven's 9th*<br>**Reading Skill**<br>Understanding cause and effect |

| Speaking | Writing | International English | Literacy Book |
|---|---|---|---|
| **Conversation**<br>Talking about a menu<br>**Pronunciation**<br>/fr/ and /bl/ | **Outlining**<br>Using Headings<br>**Product**<br>Describing an experiment | **US** *trash can; server*<br>**UK** *rubbish bin; waiter/waitress* | **Story**<br>*Little Chef*<br>**Persuasive Text**<br>*Too Young to Cook?* True Stories of Young Chefs<br>**Reading Skill**<br>Scanning for specific information |
| | | | |
| **Presentation**<br>Describing a dream job<br>**Pronunciation**<br>/str/ and /tr/ | **Punctuation**<br>Using exclamation points and quotation marks<br>**Product**<br>Finishing a Story | **US** *fire truck; truck; student; named; exclamation point*<br>**UK** *fire engine; lorry; pupil; called; exclamation mark* | **Story**<br>*What Happens Next?*<br>**Informational Text**<br>*Animals to the Rescue*<br>**Reading Skill**<br>Making inferences and predictions |
| **Presentation**<br>An endangered animal<br>**Pronunciation**<br>/h/ and /w/ | **Word Building**<br>Synonyms<br>**Product**<br>A Concrete Poem | **US** *ocean floor*<br>**UK** *seabed* | **Persuasive Text**<br>*Coral Reefs*<br>**Fantasy**<br>*The Lost Camera*<br>**Reading Skill**<br>Identifying perspective |
| | | | |
| **Conversation**<br>Giving health advice<br>**Pronunciation**<br>/kw/ and /kr/ | **Spelling**<br>Simple past irregular verb forms<br>**Product**<br>A Letter to a Friend | **US** *have a fever, sick; clinic, shot*<br>**UK** *have a temperature, ill; health centre, injection* | **Informational Text**<br>*Take Your Medicine*<br>**Story**<br>*A Surprise Cure*<br>**Reading Skill**<br>Understanding main ideas and details |
| **Presentation**<br>Telling a story about something you made<br>**Pronunciation**<br>/br/ and /fl/ | **Paragraph Building**<br>Transition: words and phrases<br>**Product**<br>A Story | | **Informational Text**<br>*Moving Machines*<br>**Science Fiction**<br>*Searching for Sterling*<br>**Reading Skill**<br>Understanding facts and opinions |

| Unit | Reading 1 | Reading 2 | Reading Skill | Content Area | Social and Emotional Learning | Key Concept | Language Book |
|---|---|---|---|---|---|---|---|
| **Literacy Review** | Scanning; Identifying Cause and Effect; Sequence of Events; Final *st* and Initial *tr*; Identifying the Main Idea and Details; Identifying Fact and Opinion; Final *nd* and *ng* | | | | | | |
| **1 I Love Reading** page 8 | **Fiction** *The Beginning of Alice's Adventures* Fantasy | **Nonfiction** *Learning and Your Brain* Informational Text **Spelling** final *er* | Skimming a text | Science: Neuroscience | Self-Awareness: Label and recognize own and others' emotions | Why is reading important? | **Vocabulary** book genres and adjectives, school subjects **Grammar** simple past review, regular and irregular verbs, adverbs of manner |
| **2 What Lives Here?** page 24 | **Nonfiction** *Two Different Forests* Informational Text | **Fiction** *A New Friend* Folk Tale **Spelling** *ai* | Understanding the author's purpose | Science: Ecology | Responsible Decision-Making: Make decisions based on moral, personal, and ethical standards | How are plants, animals, and humans connected? | **Vocabulary** plants, animals, and nature **Grammar** comparatives and superlatives with adjectives and adverbs |
| **3 How Much Is It?** page 40 | **Nonfiction** *The History of Money* Informational Text | **Fiction** *The $100 Bill* Story **Spelling** *ar* | Identifying problems and solutions | History: Culture | Responsible Decision-Making: Identify problems when making decisions, and generate alternatives | Why do we need money? | **Vocabulary** money and math **Grammar** modals: *have to/don't have to, should/shouldn't, could* |
| **4 We Can Do It** page 56 | **Nonfiction** *Teamwork Makes the Dream Work* Informational Text **Spelling** *or* | **Fiction** *Late for the Show* Play | Understanding the sequence of events | Social Studies: Teamwork | Relationship Skills: Exhibit cooperative learning and working toward group goals | How does teamwork help us? | **Vocabulary** theater and time **Grammar** past progressive |
| **5 Make Some Noise** page 72 | **Nonfiction** *The Art of Sound* Informational Text **Spelling** *ou* | **Fiction** *Beethoven's 9th* Poem | Understanding cause and effect | Arts & Humanities: Music | Social Awareness: Respect others | What different types of sounds are in our world? | **Vocabulary** sounds and musical instruments **Grammar** *going to* for making plans |

| Unit | Reading 1 | Reading 2 | Reading Skill | Content Area | Social and Emotional Learning | Key Concept | Language Book |
|---|---|---|---|---|---|---|---|
| **6 That Looks Good** page 88 | **Fiction** *Little Chef* Story | **Nonfiction** *Too Young to Cook? True Stories of Young Chefs* Persuasive Text **Spelling** final *old* | Scanning for specific information | Arts & Humanities: Culinary Arts | Responsible Decision-Making: Implement problem-solving skills when making decisions, when appropriate | Why is food important? | **Vocabulary** kitchen and food **Grammar** verb patterns with infinitives and gerunds |
| **7 How Can We Help?** page 104 | **Fiction** *What Happens Next?* Story | **Nonfiction** *Animals to the Rescue* Informational Text **Spelling** final *ly* | Making inferences and predictions | Social Studies: Communities | Self-Management: Exhibit positive motivation, hope, and optimism | How can we help each other in a disaster? | **Vocabulary** emergencies and natural disasters **Grammar** relative clauses with *who* and *that* |
| **8 Under the Sea** page 120 | **Nonfiction** *Coral Reefs* Persuasive Text **Spelling** final *ight* | **Fiction** *The Lost Camera* Fantasy | Identifying perspective | Science: Marine Biology | Social Awareness: Identify social cues (verbal, physical) to determine how others feel | What is life like under the sea? | **Vocabulary** sea life and appearance **Grammar** simple present review, present progressive review, future with *will* |
| **9 What's the Matter?** page 136 | **Nonfiction** *Take Your Medicine* Informational Text **Spelling** *ur* | **Fiction** *A Surprise Cure* Story | Understanding the main idea and details | Science: Health & Medicine | Self-Management: Set plans and work toward goals | What do we do when we're sick? | **Vocabulary** illness and treatment **Grammar** simple past and past progressive with *when* review, past progressive with *while* |
| **10 Don't Push the Button** page 152 | **Nonfiction** *Moving Machines* Informational Text | **Fiction** *Searching for Sterling* Science Fiction **Spelling** *ough* | Understanding facts and opinions | Science: Engineering | Self-Management: Overcome obstacles and create strategies for more long-term goals | Does technology make our lives easier? | **Vocabulary** machines and materials **Grammar** comparatives review, modals review |

# Welcome to *Global Stage*

You have in your hands a complete language and literacy course that will support you and your students in developing their English skills, and their love of reading and the English language.

The **Language Book** contains the building blocks of language skills and systems. Students will focus on learning the language and how it works. Beautiful picture dictionary scenes, lively songs, and contextualized grammar sections support them in working out and learning new language. Photos and texts about children around the world will inspire them to explore thought-provoking questions about what it means to be a Global Citizen. Live-action videos will expose learners to other children using the language they are learning before they take their turn.

The **Literacy Book** contains a variety of fiction and nonfiction texts, as well as activities for learners to explore literacy concepts, develop reading skills, and respond to the texts they have read. As they work through the course, students will further develop their thinking skills, and they will build self-reflection skills, which will allow them to become increasingly more effective and independent learners.

Together, the **Language** and **Literacy Books** explore topics across the curriculum while exposing students to differences in American and British English through the International English feature.

### How to Use the Books Together

The **Language Book** and **Literacy Book** units are designed to provide a complete English language learning experience. There is no prescribed order for teaching the books: You may start with either book. You can choose to work through a whole unit and then move to the other book. Alternatively, you can start with the first **Literacy Book** reading, then move to the **Language Book**, then back to the second **Literacy Book** reading.

Used together, the two books cover the four skills, provide a solid foundation in vocabulary and grammar, and help train your learners to become competent users of English and independent thinkers.

## Pedagogical Philosophy

The goal of ***Global Stage*** is to support children in becoming competent and confident English speakers while also developing as self-directed, inquisitive learners and responsible global citizens.

### *Global Stage* starts with the child and looks out towards the world.

***Global Stage*** assumes that every learner comes to school with a wealth of knowledge, thoughts, and opinions about their lives and the world, and that this is the starting point for their continued learning. All units include moments for students to consider and share their experiences, as well as consider others' points of view. This not only validates their thoughts, priming them to be open to learning, but is also the basis for learning empathy, which is one of the goals of our Global Citizenship lesson.

We know that children learn best when they feel safe to express their emotions. This is why we have carefully interwoven a social and emotional learning strand into the course. When you read the texts with your class, you will find opportunities to pause and reflect on how the characters feel and why, as well as opportunities for the students to think about how they feel in their lives when they encounter similar situations. Building and strengthening the ability to reflect will support students in becoming considerate, thoughtful citizens of the world.

## *Global Stage* encourages self-reflection and a growth mindset to support children in increasing their academic achievement.

Every child has strengths they can build on, as well as areas they should develop and strengthen. We also know that what students and their teachers believe about intelligence influences academic achievement. A growth mindset is the belief that intelligence is not fixed, but rather can grow and continue to develop. Carol Dweck, who coined this term, and her colleagues demonstrated that a growth mindset empowers children to increase their academic achievement.

*Global Stage* supports students by helping them learn to reflect on their learning. Teachers can further support their students by focusing their praise on children's effort and improvement from where they start on their learning journey. This kind of feedback that focuses on growth reinforces the notion that children have the power to make progress by working toward it, encouraging students to view their progress and skills as something they can improve, rather than purely the result of their static abilities.

*Global Stage* includes various forms of review to support children in improving self-reflection skills: Our **Language Book** reviews, the Think It Over pages, are always open-ended, prompting students to think about what they have learned, how they have learned it, how they think they might learn better, and what they think they should continue to work on. When you do these lessons in class, you can take advantage of this social moment for students to hear from each other. One child may mention that they learned the most with the unit song, while another might recall a game or a story. Children will benefit from considering what has worked for them and for others, while also planning for how to continue to learn. These are also moments for you to praise the class for their effort, pointing out where they've made progress.

Our **Literacy Book** includes Think Together pages, a space for students to get used to reflecting on how they respond to texts, and how working with those texts might have enriched what they think about the Key Concept questions at the top of the page.

Finally, our **Student's App** on **Navio** allows learners to review the language and skills they have studied and receive instant feedback, as well as increasing challenges as they progress. Students will be supported in learning and improving their English, while having fun and working at their own pace.

Helping children notice where they are making progress will help them build their self-reflection skills and also encourage them to seek further challenge.

## *Global Stage* helps you teach beyond the test.

In ***Global Stage*** you will find a robust and engaging course. With its dual-book approach to language and literacy, and its focus on engaging the students and allowing them to develop their thinking and self-management skills, ***Global Stage*** supports children in learning beyond the language needed for doing well on tests.

Students are challenged to learn at a stimulating pace. They encounter a variety of topics and language points, as well as texts and ideas. But you and they have strong support every step of the way. Whether it is the way the **Language Book** sets up a speaking or writing task in incremental steps so the learner knows what to work on and the teacher can see where they need help, or the way thinking opportunities are woven into the two books, encouraging children not only to learn information but also get better at analyzing it, ***Global Stage*** supports students' long-term development. For example, throughout the six levels of ***Global Stage***, learners will be developing the ability to figure out the meaning of Words in Context. They will learn that words have many layers of meaning, and they will learn to develop strategies to figure out aspects of the meaning themselves, from the context in each text. Their goal won't be to learn the word, but rather to understand the overall meaning of the text, and to make an educated guess about what the word may mean in that context. This skill will help them become better readers, learners, and test takers throughout their academic lives in English and in whatever other language they happen to be studying.

## *Global Stage* supports children in developing 21st Century Skills.

In their widely accepted *Framework for 21st Century Learning*, which outlines their vision for student success in the new global economy, the Partnership for 21st Century Skills says that:

> *Learning and innovation skills increasingly are being recognized as the skills that separate students who are prepared for increasingly complex life and work environments in the 21st century, and those who are not. A focus on creativity, critical thinking, communication, and collaboration is essential to prepare students for the future.*

***Global Stage*** infuses these important skills into every unit in a way that challenges the children and enhances the learning objective in each lesson. Students are consistently given opportunities to think and discuss everything from readings and skills to grammar points and writing mechanics. This ensures they are actively communicating to form a solid and personalized understanding of English. Our Think Together lesson, in the **Literacy Book**, includes a cooperative learning activity where learners can practice collaborating in a structured way, building the skills to listen to others, participating responsibly, and contributing equally to the activity outcome. Finally, lessons like Take the Stage and Write About It encourage creativity as students plan and produce individual presentations, conversation role-plays, and texts and critical thinking as they are supported to organize their thoughts.

## Course Components

### Language Book

The **Language Book** contains seven lessons per unit:

- Two Vocabulary lessons. One includes a song and the other is linked to Global Citizenship themes and includes listening activities.
- Two Explore Language lessons with grammar presentation and practice.
- A speaking lesson (Take the Stage / Talk About It) that presents either a presentation or conversational skill and includes pronunciation practice.
- A writing lesson (Write About It) that explores writing mechanisms such as spelling and punctuation.
- A Think It Over lesson that focuses on self-reflection and getting students to think about how they learn.

Throughout ***Global Stage***, students are exposed to a simplified inductive approach to grammar, vocabulary, and skills. They are guided to look at language in context so that they can discover concrete patterns. When students are given an opportunity to figure out a concept for themselves, they are much more likely to develop a deeper understanding, appreciation, and retention of knowledge.

In addition, opportunities to review and recycle what they have learned are built into the course with the review lessons (Put It Together) after every two units. These communicative games help students enjoy revisiting and practicing target language. There is also a mid-year and an end-of-year play, so students can use the language they've learned in a practical context. The first play, *The Grassland Orchestra*, uses vocabulary and grammar structures from Units 1–5. The second play, *Into the Future* recycles vocabulary and grammar structures from Units 6–10.

## Literacy Book

There are two texts in each unit of the **Literacy Book**, which are fully explored in a series of lessons:

- A Get Ready to Read lesson introduces the unit topic and creates interest. It also includes the reading skill focus.
- A Reading lesson presents a fictional or nonfictional text.
- An Explore the Reading lesson includes post-reading comprehension and analysis activities as well as a spelling activity.
- Each unit ends with a Think Together lesson that draws the two readings together and explores the Key Concept for each unit.

In each unit, students encounter a reading skill and learn the use of the skill through practice in context. Learning these skills helps students read more quickly and effectively and gives them greater confidence, which in turn means they get more enjoyment from reading.

Each text includes a Words in Context feature where students are encouraged to figure out the meaning of words from their context, rather than learn the words as vocabulary.

The **Literacy Book**, develops Social and Emotional Learning (SEL) and Content and Language Integrated Learning (CLIL), while also including Visible Thinking Routines (VTR) and opportunities for Critical Literacy. Students are encouraged to work collaboratively by discussing and exploring ideas through Cooperative Learning Routines.

## Three-Stage Reading Approach

The goal of the reading lessons is to get students reading for pleasure and to absorb information, rather than focusing on the mechanics of language in the text. The teaching notes suggest a three-stage approach to achieve this:

- Stage 1 **Engage with the Text.** This stage should be purely about reading for enjoyment and might include a prediction question to keep students motivated to find the answer.
- Stage 2 **Analyze the Text and Features.** In this stage, students read the text once again, while you help them analyze the text through the embedded callout questions. These questions will strengthen students' ability to make sense of the text and encourage them to begin thinking critically about what they are reading.
- Stage 3 **Interact with the Text.** This stage is about encouraging students to become actively involved in the learning process. They may be asked to act out the reading, or do reconstruction or analysis activities. When students interact more deeply with the text, their reading comprehension and writing skills improve, as they develop a greater understanding of how texts are constructed.

## Spelling Patterns

Research shows that recognition and understanding of spelling patterns leads to improved reading. Both spelling and reading require students to make connections between how a word looks, how it sounds, and what it means. Knowing the spelling of a word helps students to create a more definite mental image, which supports them to read the word fluently.

The **Literacy Book** focuses on one letter combination in each unit, providing a logical framework for students to begin recognizing spelling patterns in words. Each pattern has been selected from curricula used in US schools. This structured approach to spelling has been shown to be far more effective in the long-term than getting students to learn long lists of words for a test.

Spelling pattern work in the **Literacy Book** is linked to one reading in each unit as part of the Explore the Reading lessons with further practice in the **Student's App** on **Navio**. Extension activities in the digital **ETB** encourage students to analyze the similarities and differences between words e.g. in word families.

Once students begin to recognize spelling patterns, they will have a strategy to approach spelling and reading new words with a similar structure.

**Spelling Pattern** *-er*

Listen and write. Then check your answers.

1 c________ 2 w________ 3 a________ 4 f________ 5 r________

Now find more words ending with *er* in the reading.

Together, the two books lay the foundation for an inductive approach to learning, encouraging students to recognize patterns and think critically through ordering, analysis, and categorization tasks.

The Unit 1 Walkthrough notes give more in-depth information about the purpose and learning outcomes for each activity, as well as further guidance on addressing core features such as visualization, inductive grammar, international English, reading skills, the reading strategy, Words in Context, and learning reflections.

## Student's App on Navio

The **Student's App** on **Navio** is where children all find their practice activities for the course. It expands on the topic and objectives found in the **Language Book** and **Literacy Book**. It includes automatically graded interactive exercises for each unit, which can be done in class or for homework, so that children receive immediate feedback. These exercises cover reading and listening skills, spelling practice, speaking skill and pronunciation practice, extended writing practice, as well as grammar and vocabulary.

The **Student's App** on **Navio** world also provides support and guidance for more introspective objectives such as reading comprehension, SEL and CLIL activities.

The **Student's App** on **Navio** transforms the clasroom-based lessons found in the **Language Book** and **Literacy Book** into an immersive, self-directed, game-like experience that students can do alone.

Using the **Student's App** on **Navio** with your students can take different forms:

Classroom study with **Language** and **Literacy Books** and Tap & Teach lessons.

- Study and practice alone in a computer lab with **Student's App**.
- Study and practice alone at home with **Student's App**.
- Study and practice with parents with **Student's App**.

Each gameplay produces data which is then sent to the teacher's gradebook, providing deeper insight into each student's strengths and weaknesses, and concrete data that can be quickly accessed to create more insightful feedback.

The activities on the **Student's App** on **Navio** are benchmarked to Cambridge English online practice, ranging from *Starters* for the lower levels to *Preliminary for Schools* for Level 6. This benchmarking covers both content and web app functionality, preparing students academically and equipping them for the practical experience of online testing.

## Teacher's Book

This Teacher's Book provides all the steps you need to bring each lesson of the **Language** and **Literacy Books** to life, including lesson objectives, warm up and cool down activities, and full answer keys. Audio and video scripts are at the back of the book, and Unit 1 contains a comprehensive walkthough, with clear explanations of the purpose of each activity and tips on how to make the most of them in class. The notes also remind the teacher of the additional support available through the Tap & Teach Lessons (TTL) for heads-up learning, the supplementary printouts in the Resource Bank, and extra practice students can do in class or at home.

## Teacher's App on Navio

The **Teacher's App** on **Navio** is your primary source for classroom resources and supplements, and is designed to work on both laptops and tablets. It includes Tap & Teach Lessons (projectable classroom lessons), the Resource Bank, the Test Generator, Student's Progress Tracker, the **Enhanced Teacher's eBook** as well as access to the Student's App.

### Tap & Teach Lessons (TTL)

Tap & Teach Lessons (TTL) are the course projectables. They contain tools for delivering dynamic and stimulating lessons, including class audio, videos, and interactive activities. If you use the TTL with an interactive whiteboard, you will be able to use all the standard features, such as highlighting and hiding content.

There are three different types of video in ***Global Stage***:

- **Song Videos** (optional). These appear in Lesson 1 of the **Language Book** and may be used to practice some of the set 1 vocabulary as well as features of rhythm and stress patterns in English.
- **Speaking Videos** (essential). These appear in Lesson 5 of the **Language Book** and feature a child or children modelling a presentation or conversation, which includes functional language. Students will analyze the language and use the video as a model when planning and preparing for their own presentation or conversation.
- **Reading Videos** (optional). These accompany one reading text of the **Literacy Book** per unit to engage students in the text visually and aurally. This method of digital storytelling helps students make connections to past experiences and apply critical thinking to the new information they are being given.

### Videos at Home: The Flipped Classroom Approach

If you are unable to watch the videos in class or you want to provide students with additional support, consider asking them to watch the videos at home before the lesson. This allows students to engage with the content in a way that suits them and allows them to pause and rewatch as many times as they want. It also offers parents the opportunity to watch the video with their child and support their learning.

If they watch the song or reading videos at home, give students a question or task to think about while they are watching. They will come to class feeling relaxed, confident, and prepared with ideas and observations to share. If students watch the speaking video at home, you could also have them do activities A and B from Take the Stage / Talk About It before the lesson. Watching the videos at home also frees up class time for collaborative and communicative activities.

### Resource Bank

The Resource Bank is where you can find:

- **Spelling Printouts.** Extra practice of the letter combinations covered in each unit of the **Literacy Book**.
- **Differentiated Writing Support.** Attractive writing templates for the Write About It pages in the **Language Book**. These include "Support" and "Challenge" options for students that need them.
- **Review Unit Support.** Extra practice for the review units at the start of each student book. These cover grammar, vocabulary, and literacy activities.
- **Grammar Printouts.** Extra practice for each grammar lesson in the **Language Book**.
- **Tests.** Unit, mid-year, and end-of-year tests.
- **Cambridge English Exam Materials.** Practice for students preparing for *Starters*, *Movers*, or *Flyers*.
- **Letters to Parents.**
- **Other Printouts.** Graphic organizers to aid Visible Thinking Routines and reading skills in the **Literacy Book**, as well as extra materials for Put It Together games and extension activities in the **Language Book**.
- **Videos and audio tracks** to support the course.
- **Curricula and Framework mapping documents.**

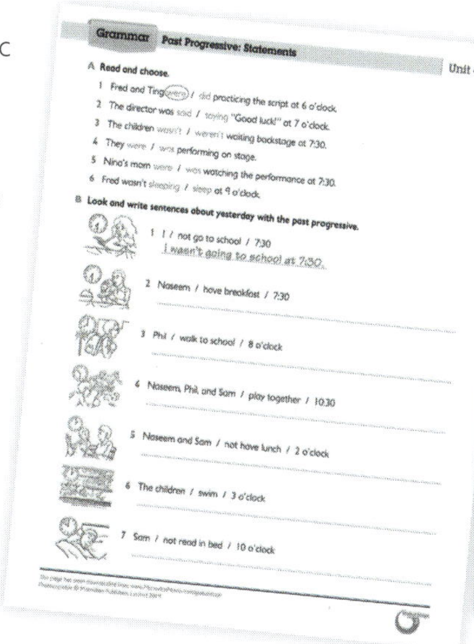


### Test Generator

The Test Generator contains the pre-written unit, mid-year, and end-of-year test activities, as well as extra activities that allow teachers to generate and edit new tests.

### Student's Progress Tracker

The Progress Tracker is an interactive gradebook that allows you to track your students' progress within ***Global Stage*** and the **Student's App** on **Navio**.

### Student's App on Navio

As the teacher, you have full access to the **Student's App** on **Navio** so you can assign homework and activities for your students, and explore the digital world yourself.

### Enhanced Teacher's eBook (ETB)

The digital **ETB** is an extended version of this **Teacher's Book**. In addition to teaching notes, it provides classroom management tips; ideas for differentiating activities; projects to support the Global Citizenship lessons, plus a range of activity and lesson extension features. These features include Social and Emotional Learning (SEL), Discussion, Genre, Video Focus, Critical Thinking, Creative Thinking, and Collaboration. The **ETB** also highlights key links between the **Language Book** and the **Literacy Book**.

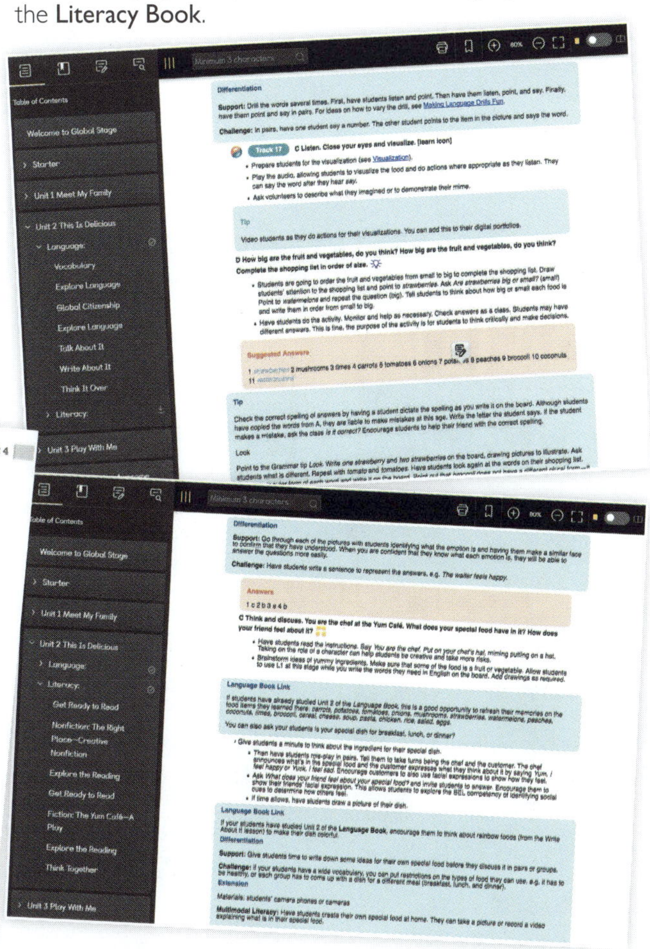

# Holistic Learning

While the success of students and schools may be measured in terms of tests and grades, ***Global Stage*** believes in taking a holistic approach by developing the whole child and preparing him/her to take on the challenges of global living. Through its subject matter and in its activity types, the course encourages students to develop thinking skills, engage in cooperative learning activities, develop social and emotional learning (SEL) skills, and gain an awareness of global citizenship.

## Global Citizenship Education

> *Global Citizenship Education (GCE) aims to empower learners to assume active roles, to face and resolve global challenges, and to become proactive contributors to a more peaceful, tolerant, inclusive and secure world.*
>
> —United Nations Educational, Scientific and Cultural Organization

The **Language Book** includes a Global Citizenship lesson in each unit, which has been designed to teach students about the lives of other children through the context of a listening activity. Discussion questions help them explore ideas and make connections to their own lives. The long-term objective is to prepare students for experiences outside of their everyday world and to fulfil aspirations to travel and study abroad.

In Level 3, lessons raise awareness about global issues through interesting and engaging topics designed to get students thinking about the things they can do as global citizens within their own communities. Key questions raised include: Why do communities need libraries?; How do people stay healthy?; Why is sea life important?; and Why do people invent new things? The Unit 1 Walkthrough notes for the **Language Book** provide guidance for teaching Global Citizenship lessons.

Matthew Hayes is a doctoral researcher at the Institute of Education in London under Douglas Bourn, Professor of Development Education. His research concerns Global Citizenship Education in English language textbooks.

### What is GCE?

What does the future hold for your students, many of whom will graduate well into the 2030s? From the environment to the economy, poverty to jobs, challenges abound. But whatever the future holds, there is one thing we can be certain of: the biggest challenges facing humanity are not constrained by national borders or language but are truly global in scale and character. These are global problems requiring global solutions, and those of us working in education have a unique responsibility and opportunity to prepare the next generation for these challenges. GCE offers a solution to these challenges and has emerged in recent years as a high-profile policy agenda in education systems all over the world.

With this in mind, GCE can be an effective toolkit for teachers wishing to prepare their students for the challenges and opportunities of the 21st century. The skills and values it espouses are essential if our students are to successfully navigate all the future holds. GCE is too important to languish on the fringes of the curriculum, competing for space as an arbitrary additional subject in an already overcrowded timetable or sandwiched into one-off school events. Just as Digital Literacy is moving beyond ICT and into every corner of the curriculum, GCE thrives best where it is embedded in mainstream curriculum subjects. Few subjects better provide the context and aspiration called for by GCE than the teaching of English as a second language.

There is much scope for creativity too. Although GCE is a declared target of the United Nations' Sustainable Development Goals, one of its virtues is that it is not owned or prescribed by any supranational organisation. There is no mandated curriculum and no accreditation body. The core concepts underpinning GCE have been traced back to some of our earliest history and are not only to be found in Western culture and philosophy. Arab scholars, for example, have written of the influence of medieval Muslim thinkers on GCE theory.

This democratic quality to GCE enables a wide variety of policy and practice, as GCE can be adapted to local contexts and cultures, and to your classroom. There are three broad themes in current GCE thinking and practice and as you work through this textbook, you will see these throughout the exercises and subject matter.

**Global orientation:** Often referred to as cosmopolitanism, this area of GCE cultivates a student's awareness of the world—its structures, cultures and politics—with a positive 'orientation'. Its focus is on tolerance and understanding, developing citizens that can comfortably and successfully navigate the world in all its variety.

**Global skills:** This area is about the competencies aspired to by global citizens. You may recognize it as closely related to "21st Century Skills" and "Life Skills", and it cultivates skills such as collaboration, creativity, critical literacy, and communication. This not only prepares students for success in a competitive global knowledge economy, but for lives as contributing global citizens able to identify and solve problems that are both local and global.

**Global conscientiousness:** This third theme runs through all aspects of GCE and is its most distinguishing feature. It is signalled through the word 'citizenship', denoting an individual's legal status as a member of a given community, with this status granting them certain rights and responsibilities. While historically this community has been restricted to the nation-state, *global* citizenship looks beyond the national to the global community of which we are all a part. Its rights and responsibilities are global in nature, calling each of us to action. This can take many forms and there should be no universal prescription of actions to be taken. It is being an *active* global citizen which is required of us. This means listening to our conscience and, when it identifies global injustice, being motivated by this to act.

Your selection of this high-level English language textbook means English is a leading subject in your curriculum and timetable. No doubt you acknowledge the English language as the *lingua franca* of the modern era, enabling your students to participate on a global scale—whether in work or life. As educators, then, what better context in which to use GCE to encourage your students to think beyond their immediate community, and be globally oriented, competent and conscientious. The English language may have an historical affinity to the West, but GCE recognises that it should not be a pedestal to promote one culture and education above any other. On the contrary, through embedding GCE in English language teaching we can encourage our students to question an unjust world and its imbalanced perspectives.

By using this textbook to teach English in a creative, forward-thinking and global way you will be providing your students with the skills and values to go out into the world and be truly active global citizens.

## Social and Emotional Learning (SEL)

> *Social and emotional learning (SEL) is the process through which children and adults acquire and effectively apply the knowledge, attitudes, and skills necessary to understand and manage emotions, set and achieve positive goals, feel and show empathy for others, establish and maintain positive relationships, and make responsible decisions.*
>
> —Collaborative for Academic, Social, and Emotional Learning

Research shows that SEL can positively affect students' connection to school, promote positive behavior, and lead to academic achievement. Helping students develop social and emotional skills lays the foundation for behaviors that will lead to positive personal development and professional success.

The five SEL areas are shown below.

| |
|---|
| **Self-Management** |
| The ability to recognize emotions, thoughts, strengths and weaknesses. This includes having confidence and optimism. |
| **Self-Awareness** |
| The ability to regulate emotions, thoughts and behaviors in different situations. This includes managing stress and working toward goals. |
| **Responsible Decision-Making** |
| The ability to empathize with others, to understand social norms, and to recognize resources and support in family, schools, and community. |
| **Relationship Skills** |
| The ability to establish and maintain healthy relationships. This includes active listening, cooperating, and handling conflict well. |
| **Social Awareness** |
| The ability to make good choices based on ethics, safety, and social norms. This includes considering the well-being of oneself and others. |

SEL is integrated into the **Literacy Book**, and a key concept area is addressed throughout the fiction text in each unit. As part of the reading strategy, students are guided to make connections between the SEL concept and the people and events in the text and, ultimately, to their own lives.

Lina Acosta Sandaál, MA, LMFT is the founder of Stop Parenting Alone, a parenting and therapy center in Miami in the USA. She is the parenting expert of a national morning show, and consults for MomsRising, a lobbying organization for family rights.

### What is SEL?

Your mouth is dry, and your heart is in your ears. Some of your students look frozen, while others wriggle in their chairs. No one is truly into the day's well-planned discussion. What is happening? Why is the lesson failing? The lesson is suffering the effect of emotions, social awareness, and self-judgment in the classroom. In every moment of a teacher's day, the mind, brain, and body flow through the interactions between the external information and the internal understanding and reflecting of the environment. So when I am asked what is SEL and why do we need it, my response is whether you intentionally teach it or not, you have been a model for SEL from the first day you stepped into a classroom.

The goal of integrating and implementing social and emotional learning into the curriculum is to build students' ability for self-awareness, self-management, social awareness, relationship skills, and decision making. Students attain these competencies by practicing ways to understand and manage emotions, build and manage relationships, and show care and concern for others. The Fetzer Group coined the term, and the word "learning" was intentional. Social emotional skills and development are not stagnant; they continue to grow and expand with each experience students have with caregivers, teachers, friends, and the culture/community at large. If you hold this in mind, that your students are learning through repetition how to be self-aware, how to manage emotions and focus, how to continue to build and manage relationships and practice decision making, then the task of social and emotional learning in your curriculum will not feel so difficult.

#### Why SEL Is Important to Your Classroom

It is an absurd task to attempt to separate what happens socially and emotionally to a student from what they are cognitively learning from your lesson. When you ignore how SEL and academic achievement work together you are only teaching a percentage of your student, and not the whole child. A majority of teachers understand that their students walk into the classroom full of emotions, thoughts, and experiences that hinder their academic achievement. Deficits in social and emotional development hamper students' ability to learn, which leads to them disrupting the classroom. A student who cannot manage their emotional state will become overwhelmed with fear and embarrassment if you ask them to speak to you in a language in which they are not fluent. Focus, cognitive flexibility, and decision-making are impacted when we have low self-awareness and management of our emotional states.

Recall the difficulty of writing emails at work when you have just had a fight with a loved one on the phone. When we have a strong emotional and social response, it is hard to focus on the task at hand. If it is difficult for an adult, imagine a young student. If your curriculum includes social and emotional learning, your students will be practicing skills to make those daily stressors less intrusive to their learning. Research supports this. Children in the HighScope Perry Preschool Study showed how social and emotional skills attained in preschool continued to bring positive outcomes to those students through age 40. HighScope moved "non-cognitive" skills to the forefront of their curriculum. Conversely, the Adverse Childhood Experiences Study (ACEs) showed that children who suffer adverse experiences and do not process those emotions fare poorly both in their mental and physical health. Social and emotional learning helps students thrive throughout their entire lives.

#### What Well-Accomplished SEL Looks Like

Now, stop and imagine your classroom in a group discussion: one of the students is playing with his lip while rocking slightly, another student is raising her hand as high as possible, hoping you will see that she wants to speak next, and another student is mumbling in response to the story you just read together. In a classroom that prioritizes SEL, all of these examples of self-management and relationship skills are accepted. Why? Because you understand that the student who is playing with his lips and rocking regulates his emotional and physical states this way, instead of standing up and disrupting the class. The student who knows to raise her hand and contain her emotions is making a responsible, self-aware decision in managing her excitement as to not interrupt her friend who is speaking.

Finally the student who is speaking slowly, quietly and under his breath is at last risking to discuss in a group because you have spoken to your students about what it means to feel scared, how to tolerate that fear, and how to work through it. Today you reap the benefit of that continued social-emotional message. How amazing that your quiet, observant student has made the decision to speak, experiences the safety to manage his fear and the opportunity to strengthen his relationships with his friends and you, his teacher.

## Content and Language Integrated Learning (CLIL)

Research has shown that content-based learning increases motivation as students see language being used in real-life contexts. The nonfiction texts in the **Literacy Book** include content from a range of different subject areas. They feature engaging topics and provide opportunities for thinking and discussion.

In Level 3, students will learn through science, history, social studies, and arts & humanities.

## Competencies

*Global Stage* incorporates five competencies that have been identified and linked to outcomes such as better academic performance and positive peer relationships. Relevant icons appear in the footers of each lesson, and the teaching notes in the **TB** and **ETB** highlight which activities are connected to each competency to allow for further exploration in the classroom.

| | |
|---|---|
| **Me** | Activities that develop social and creative skills and consider lifestyle choices. |
| **Act** | Activities that help develop a sense of social responsibility, mutual understanding, tolerance and ethical behavior. |
| **Think** | Activities that develop thinking skills to explain, infer, classify, discuss, notice, and discover. |
| **Learn** | Activities that foster learning autonomy and help develop learning strategies. |
| **Communicate** | Activities that promote interpersonal and collaborative skills to develop teamwork, leadership, empathy, and responsibility. |

## Self-Reflection

Self-reflection is an important part of any learning process. Research shows that without regular review and reflection time, much of a lesson can be forgotten. Self-reflection increases students' understanding of how they learn best, making future learning more effective and leading to improvements in achievement.

Self-reflection is a critical feature of *Global Stage*. Students are asked to reflect on their performances and written work in the Speaking and Writing lessons in the **Language Book** and to reflect more deeply about their learning in the end-of-unit lessons in the **Language Book** and **Literacy Book**.

The Think It Over lesson in the **Language Book** provides graphic organizers for students to respond to questions such as *What did I do? How did I learn?* and *What did I learn?* The purpose of these questions is to get students into the habit of self-reflection from an early age, helping them begin to learn how to learn.

In the My Reading Journal section of the Think Together lesson in the **Literacy Book**, students are asked to give a personalized response to the readings and reflect on the unit as a whole. They are encouraged to think critically about what they enjoyed and why, what they would like to learn more about, and to identify strengths and weaknesses.

In Level 3, both the **Language Book** and **Literacy Book** ask students to start making connections between what they enjoyed and what they learned. This prepares them for higher levels where they will be expected to understand how successes were achieved, how less successful experiences can be turned into learning experiences, and to find strategies for working through activities they find less enjoyable.

The Unit 1 Walkthrough notes for both books provide more information on making these lessons a valuable and successful experience.

# Learning Techniques

## Visible Thinking

Visible Thinking is a flexible research-based framework developed out of Harvard University for enriching classroom learning and fostering students' intellectual development. Some of its key goals are:

- To develop deeper understanding of content.
- To encourage greater motivation for learning.
- To develop learners' thinking and learning abilities.
- To develop learners' attitudes toward thinking and learning and their alertness to opportunities for thinking and learning.
- To create a shift in classroom culture toward a community of enthusiastically engaged thinkers and learners.

Visible Thinking employs thinking routines—short, easy-to-learn strategies that help extend and deepen students' thinking. These routines make it easier for you to see how the students are thinking and interpreting content: *Are students explaining things to one another? Are they offering creative ideas? Are they brainstorming and debating plans?* Visible Thinking encourages students to develop discussion skills and to find personal meaning in the content. This stimulates their continued interest and commitment to their own learning in the classroom.

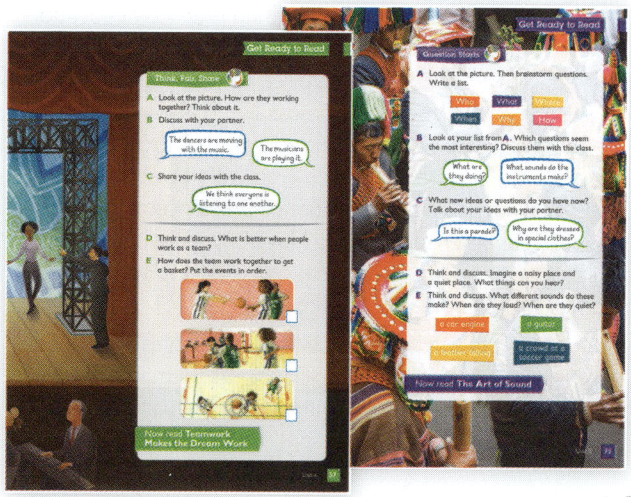

In Level 3, each opening lesson in the **Literacy Book** features one of three Visible Thinking Routines (VTR): See, Think, Wonder; Think, Pair, Share; or Question Starts. These routines stimulate students' curiosity and encourage them to make predictions, observations, and interpretations about the picture. They provide an opportunity for students to think about the overarching theme/topic of each **Literacy Book** unit and tie into a pre-reading activity to prepare students cognitively for what they are about to read.

### See, Think, Wonder

Students are asked what they see in the picture, then what they think about it, and finally what they wonder (or what questions they have) about it.

This routine works best when students are given time to think of ideas individually before sharing them with the class. In this way, students begin to use English meaningfully, although it is acceptable for them to use L1 to express more complex ideas.

### Think, Pair, Share

This routine encourages individual participation and can be used with all abilities and class sizes.

**Think**. Students are given time to think independently about the question that has been posed, forming ideas and questions of their own.

**Pair**. Students are grouped in pairs to discuss their thoughts. This step allows students to articulate their ideas and to consider those of others. They are encouraged to listen to each other and use phrases like *I agree/ disagree* and *Me, too*.

**Share**. Student pairs share their ideas with the whole class and give their reasons.

The benefit of using this routine for discussion questions is that students get to practice and learn through repetition, their ideas become more refined at each stage of the process, and they often feel more comfortable presenting ideas to a group with the support of a partner.

Think, Pair, Share is also used as a cooperative learning routine.

### Question Starts

Students look at the picture and think of some questions they would like to ask about it using the prompts Who? What? Where? When? Why? How? They then practice negotiation skills by working in groups and then as a class, sharing their questions, and deciding on the three they think are the most interesting or that they would most like to know the answer to. The third part of the routine asks students to discuss the picture again in pairs and to come up with new questions or ideas they have about the picture or the concepts it shows. They should be encouraged to move beyond what they see and to start thinking of ideas connected to some of the themes suggested by the picture.

The purpose of this routine is that it encourages students to think more deeply about a topic and gets them into the habit of questioning beyond what they see on the page.

For all three routines, it is important to scaffold students' responses by asking follow-up questions, e.g. *What makes you say that?* Example dialogues have been provided in the teaching notes to help you do this. Make sure you keep students' thinking visible by noting down and displaying their ideas to return to in the Think Together lesson.

VTRs provide a great way to engage learners at the start of a topic, but they can also be used at different points in the unit to keep students connected to the topic or as a way to reflect on what they have learned in a meaningful way.

## Cooperative Learning Routines

Teachers who use Cooperative Learning Routines can make a huge difference in achievement and engagement by providing opportunities for multiple students to participate and answer a question, instead of calling on just one student for the answer. Along with higher academic achievement, you will see a reduction in the gap between high- and low-achieving students, improved social skills, higher self-esteem, more enthusiasm for learning, a happier classroom climate, and decreased discipline problems. You will also see the emergence of leadership and conflict-resolution skills.

The following routines are used in Level 3 in both the **Literacy Book** and **Language Book**:

A **Round Robin** is where groups of four students have a limited time to take turns orally brainstorming as many different answers to a discussion question as they can within a limited time frame (one minute is recommended). A **Rally Robin** is the same but with pairs. A **Roundtable** is similar to a Round Robin, but students take turns writing down or drawing their ideas on a piece of paper, within their groups.

The **Three-Step Interview** takes the place of the traditional group discussion because each person in a group must produce and receive information. In the first two steps of this routine, students work with a student from a different group. They interview each other about a topic. Then, in the third step, students return to their original groups and take turns sharing what they have learned from their partners. You can also have them share ideas with the class.

**Numbered Heads Together** is a cooperative learning strategy that holds each student accountable for learning some material. Students are placed in groups and each person is given a number (from one to the maximum number in each group). The teacher poses a question and students "put their heads together" to figure out the answer. The teacher calls out a specific number to respond as spokesperson for the group. This strategy ensures that each member of a group knows the answer to a problem or question asked by the teacher. Because no one knows which number will be called, all team members must be prepared.

**Inside-Outside Circle.** You will need to make some space in the classroom for this routine. Students stand in concentric circles facing each other. Students in the outside circle ask questions, and those who are inside answer. On a signal, students rotate to create new partnerships. On another signal, students trade inside/outside roles.

Talking one-on-one with a variety of partners gives extensive practice in speaking and active listening skills. Interactions can be structured to focus on specific skills and/or target language.

**Chalk Talk** is useful for getting quieter or less-confident students to share ideas with peers. Write different categories on large sheets of paper and have groups of students silently brainstorm everything they can think of about that category, or any questions they have about it. Then have the groups rotate the pieces of paper until everyone has written on each category. Hang the pieces of paper up and give students time to review other students' ideas, add more ideas of their own, and write answers to any of the questions. Bring the class together to discuss any new ideas they have after reading each other's responses and to try to resolve any unanswered questions.

**Option Explosion.** Students discuss and share ideas to think of solutions to a problem, e.g. Alice is at the bottom of a big hole. There are doors in the hole, but all the doors are locked. How can she get out? Have students discuss their ideas in small groups. Each group can appoint a scribe. Then have students get into new groups with different students and think again (you could also do this stage with the whole class). This time they should try to think beyond the more obvious solutions and think of ideas that didn't come up during the first discussion making full use of their imaginations. They can combine their earlier ideas, or use them as a platform to jump off and explore new options. Remind students that this is fantasy, so crazy ideas are welcome!

### Tips for Setting Up Class Discussions

- Write the question(s) on the board, and give students a minute to reflect in silence.
- If there is more than one discussion question, deal with each in turn, giving students time to think and discuss in pairs or small groups. Help with new words and allow the use of L1 for more complex ideas.
- Help students structure their discussions by providing appropriate graphic organizers on the board or handing out templates for the groups to fill in.
- You will not always be able to ask everyone for their ideas. Be sure you choose different students each time, so no one feels left out.
- Have students share their ideas in teams, e.g. a team per table. Have each team choose a name or color. During each lesson or activity, one person will give the team's answers and responses. Record who the speaker is for each activity so everyone gets a turn.
- Give the speaker an object, such as a cardboard microphone, to remind students who will speak.
- Use the Cooperative Learning Routines to structure the discussions and share information discussed.
- When sharing ideas as a class, Group Time can provide a relaxed atmosphere, which may encourage students to contribute more. See the **Group Time** box for more suggestions.

### Group Time

Designate a particular area of the classroom for Group Time, free from distractions. Set out a circle of chairs, with no desks, so students can see each other clearly. You should also sit on a chair as part of this circle, so that it is clear your role is to encourage and facilitate discussion, rather than to lead it. At the beginning of the year have students discuss and agree on some rules for Group Time, e.g. one person speaks at a time; everyone listens to each other; students can disagree with each other, but must do so respectfully; Group Time is fun! Nominate a student to be the scribe and write up the rules the class decides on.

During Group Time, ask open-ended questions and encourage students to give reasons for their answers. Pass an object, such as a toy or a cushion, around so it is clear who is speaking. Encourage everyone to join in the discussion, but give students a safe word to use, such as "pass", if they need more thinking time. Let them know it's OK to need time to think and that you will come back to them. At the end of the Group Time discussion, praise students for their ideas.

## Visualization

Visualizations are used in the vocabulary lessons of each unit to encourage students to create mental images of the new words, using their senses combined with previous experiences. Visualizations provide a different way for students to engage personally with the language and help them learn new words.

Set up a visualization activity as follows:

- Take several deep breaths with students, slowly saying *breathe in, breathe out.*
- Count down slowly from ten to one using a calm voice.
- Say *Close your eyes and visualize*, pointing to your temples with both hands to demonstrate *imagining*. If students prefer to keep their eyes open, that's fine, too. The key is for them to feel calm and relaxed, so avoid using phrases like *You must keep your eyes closed* or *Don't Look!* which will restrict students.
- Play the audio track and encourage students to imagine or act out as prompted. Pauses have been included in the audio to give students time for reflection. They then repeat the word.
- After the visualization activity, give students time to share their images. They can do this through drawing, miming, or by describing their thoughts to a partner using L1.
- Emphasize that everyone's visualizations will be different and that all ideas are valuable.

Students may need additional support the first time you do this. Pause after each word or play the audio track through twice to give them a second chance to create images in their mind. When they share images, students will learn from one another and get ideas for the next time you do this activity.

The more regularly you do this, the more students will understand what is expected and the more they will get out of the activity. An optional visualization track is available in the TTL for the vocabulary in the Global Citizenship lesson.

### Words in Context

The Words in Context feature focuses on helping students apply strategies for dealing with words they do not know. The goal is not for students to learn the full meaning of a word, but rather to understand what the word means in that particular context. Students discover that words have many layers of meaning, and that they will build knowledge of words over time. Every time they encounter a word, they learn one aspect of the meaning of the word.

It can be helpful to introduce the following strategies into lessons:

- Look at each sentence containing a target word, encouraging students to **look at the pictures to guess the meaning**.
- **Use the words around the new words to guess their meaning**. Tell students to look for words that they know in the sentence that contains the new word and to use these to build a context for the sentence. They should be logical when working out the meaning of the new word by thinking about what would make sense in this context, e.g. students may be able to identify other words in the sentence that mean the same thing, or that are connected to the new word in some way.
- **Read the next words or sentence to get clues** to explain the meaning of a new words. Encourage students to read on whenever they encounter a word they don't know, as sometimes what comes after can provide clues such as definitions, examples, or context to help them understand the word.
- **Use the sentence or paragraph before to guess the meaning of the new words**. Remind students that they can sometimes look back to get useful information and a context that will help them to figure out the meaning of the new word.
- **Think about whether the word is an object, a person, a place, or an action to figure out the meaning**. Encourage students to look at the other words around the word to help them do this, e.g. in the sentence *In a basketball game, ten players are on the court,* the preposition *on* may give students a clue that a *court* is a place.
- **Use pictures/actions/events in the video to help discover meaning**. Have students look for pictures in the text or pause the video, and encourage students to look at the image on screen to figure out the meaning of the new word.
- **Think about how the two things are similar to help understand the words**. Tell students that sometimes a writer compares two things using the word *like*, e.g. in the sentence *The famous composer lifts his arms high, and brings them down like an eagle that flies*, students can try out the action and think about what type of creature makes a similar action (a bird), in order to understand what an eagle is.
- **Use negative sentences nearby to help decode the meaning of a new word**. Explain that negative sentences can sometimes help us to figure out the meaning of a new word by stating what it isn't.
- **Use L1 knowledge to establish meaning**. Have students try to find similar words in their own language.

### Multimodal Literacy

To become fully literate in today's world, students must become as proficient with the new literacies of search engines, web pages, email, instant messages, blogs, podcasts, e-books, wiki pages, digital photos, videos, and apps as they are with the traditional literacies of paper, pencil, and books.

However, students also need to learn new skills to enable them to use each of these technologies effectively, e.g. searching for key words and navigating a nonlinear reading pathway via hyperlinks. Students also need to develop and utilize critical-thinking skills for online reading. In an age when anyone may publish anything on the internet, it is more important than ever to equip students with the tools to critically evaluate source material.

Both the **Language Book** and the **Literacy Book** provide opportunities for developing higher-order thinking skills through activities that teach students to analyze, question, and to foster thoughtful discussion. In addition, the digital **ETB** includes Multimodal Literacy ideas for taking lessons beyond the book and integrating them with the students' own technologies. An example of this is a research project, where students are asked to find more information about a topic using both print and digital resources. Projects can be researched at home with parental support, or teachers can provide opportunities for small groups to collaborate together, culminating in a class presentation.

Students can also be encouraged to create using different technologies (including digital cameras, videos, apps) and to choose work to upload to their digital portfolios, which can be shared with parents.

#### Ideas for Introducing Multimodal Literacy Skills and Concepts

- **Encourage students to use *Global Stage's* digital resources.** The **Student's App** provides important early experiences of navigating an online interface in a controlled and safe environment.
- **Show how putting precise keywords into search engines can help you find better information.** If you have access to computers and are able to get online in school, give students a question to answer in pairs, but tell them they can only use one keyword. Discuss how successful they were, then have them repeat the activity with two and then multiple keywords. Elicit that using more keywords helps you be more specific and gives you better information to answer the question.
- **Highlight the importance of scanning for key information.** When you're teaching students how to scan reading texts for relevant information, explain how this is also a useful

skill for finding key information online. Every time you ask students to research something online, elicit what they need to look out for to scan effectively.

- **Have struggling readers teach more-confident readers.** When you introduce a new technology or skill in class, differentiate by teaching it to struggling readers first so that they become the experts, and then empower them to teach more-confident readers. That way everyone is given the chance to be good at something and no one gets left behind.
- **Use digital portfolios.** Digital portfolios replace traditional folders as a way to capture and store students' work. You can put students in charge of what gets included in their portfolio as a way to encourage independence, responsibility, and reflection. They enable you to:
  - Demonstrate oral skills through videos and audio recordings, alongside on-paper tasks.
  - Empower students struggling with writing and reading by giving them alternative ways to express themselves and demonstrate learning.
  - Share students' learning easily and frequently with parents, without organizing a time for them to come into class, and without risk of the work getting mislaid at home.

Digital portfolios also allow students to view their learning journey and become a valuable tool for self-reflection. The digital **ETB** provides suggestions for digital portfolios.

# Classroom Management

## Making Language Drills Fun

The **Language Book** audio contains language drills to practice the new language presented in each Vocabulary and Explore Language lesson. Drilling helps familiarize students with the language and encourages them to notice the correct pronunciation and rhythm. It also allows you to see which words or phrases will need further practice.

Drilling works by being repetitive, so it is important to add some variations to make it fun and keep students engaged. You can do this by having students say the words or phrases in different ways:

- **Volume**. Have students whisper and then get progressively louder, and then quieter again.
- **Emotion**. Have students use a happy voice and then repeat with sad, angry, tired, and excited voices.
- **Speed**. Have students speak very slowly, then get progressively faster, and then slower again.
- **Voices**. Have students imagine they are a lion, then have them repeat by imagining they are a mouse, a robot, a bird, and a frog. Even when speaking in these different styles, students should be encouraged to use the correct pronunciation and intonation.

Try not to overload students by asking too much at once. The first time you play the audio, have them focus on pronunciation. When you feel they are comfortable with this, encourage them to notice and replicate the correct intonation.

For grammar drills, focus on rhythm and chunks of language, not just individual words. After practicing the recorded sentences, you can encourage students to make new sentences with the target structure. Have the students build a substitution drill on the board starting with the original questions or sentences. Write the sentences on the board, leaving a line for the words you want to change and encourage them to call out suggestions, e.g. *I'm a ____________ reader.* Students could suggest *slow* or *careful*. Then have them practice saying the new sentences in pairs.

## Role-play in the Classroom

Performing role-plays in class is a great way for students to interact with the new language or stories and gain confidence using the language in a more informal way. Both the **Language** and **Literacy Books** offer many opportunities for role-play. For example, students can role-play the presentation dialogues in the Explore Language lessons, and they can role-play the stories in the **Literacy Book**. Some of the Talk About It lessons in the **Language Book** require students to plan and write a role-play conversation.

### Five Stepping Stones to Performance

- **Step 1** Put students into groups according to how many parts there are in the dialogue or story you are going to role-play. Vary the groups and encourage students to work with classmates they don't normally work with. Pair confident students with less-confident classmates. Allow students to assign themselves roles within their groups, as this will practice negotiating skills.
- **Step 2** If the conversation or story you wish to role-play is on audio or video, then play it first for students to follow. Discuss how the characters' voices differ, and encourage them to think about how the characters are feeling at key moments in the story. Have students notice sound effects and ask them what these add to the overall effect.

  Play it again, this time encouraging students to say their lines out loud along with the audio/video. Then have students focus on reproducing the intonation.
- **Step 3** Now, give students time to practice their role-play without multimedia. They can use the dialogue or the story in the book to help them remember their part. Encourage students to speak with expression and to try to think about intonation. Where appropriate, have them think about the type of voice their character has, e.g. a deep voice or a high, squeaky voice. Tell them to think about how their character is feeling and to include some suitable facial expressions and actions.

  You can challenge stronger students to continue the conversation or add embellishments to their character.

- **Step 4** When they are ready, pairs or groups can come to the front and perform their role-play for the class. Make sure everyone gets a chance to perform at some point during the course. Encourage students to video record each other's performances. These videos can be uploaded to their digital portfolios.
- **Step 5** You could organize an open event at the end of the term for parents. Have groups of students prepare and act out different stories from the **Literacy Book** or the plays from the **Language Book**. Give students extra practice time to give them confidence to perform in front of an audience. Encourage them to think about suitable sound effects to use in their performance (e.g. rustling paper for rain), or to source these through sound-effect apps. You could also get students and families involved in providing costumes and making props.

Tip Get students to vote on their favorite song from the **Language Book** and have them perform it together at the beginning of the open event. This will help dispel a lot of nerves and ensure a smoother performance when students come to act out the stories.

## Differentiated Learning

Even across one class, students differ in many ways; from age, energy, interests, adaptability, experience, and familiarity with the world outside the home, to emotional maturity, linguistic aptitude, and physical development. As a way of targeting learning to meet individual students' needs, the **ETB** lesson notes include below-level *Support* differentiation ideas to help students achieve the activity goal and above-level *Challenge* ideas to extend activities. For print users, the following are ways you can differentiate activity types:

### Vocabulary

**Support.** Check the meaning of each word by asking questions to confirm or help with understanding.

**Challenge.** Have students personalize the vocabulary by saying a sentence with one of the words.

### Language Drills

**Support.** Give students enough time to process each item on the recording and to listen to how each word is spoken. Break down the phrases into smaller chunks, gradually building up to the full sentence.

**Challenge.** Have students substitute words in the drill to make new questions and statements. Ask them to come up with wild and funny ideas!

### Conversations

**Support.** Give students plenty of time to prepare their conversations. Allow them to copy the phrases they want to use from B and write out the dialogue in full in their notebooks. They can read their dialogues several times until they feel comfortable enough to have a conversation without using their notebooks.

**Challenge.** Encourage students to add more turns in their conversation and to change the phrases they use each time they practice it.

### Writing

**Support.** Have students discuss their ideas with a partner before completing their plan. This will help them organize their thoughts into writing.

**Challenge.** Have more-confident students use the *Challenge* printout for their plan to encourage them to include additional information in their writing.

### Question Starts Visible Thinking Routine

**Support.** Students may find it hard to think of a variety of questions. Suggest example questions using each question word and write them on the board. Alternatively, ask students what they think they know about the picture. This will lead into an interesting discussion and should generate more questions.

**Challenge.** For every question generated, encourage students to provide a secondary question that links to the previous one; for example, *Who's the girl? And where's she from?*

### Reading Comprehension

**Support.** Have students work in pairs to answer questions. They can take turns to read a question aloud. Both students in the pair should look back at the reading to find the answer, then they can compare their answers together before writing them in their books.

**Challenge.** Have students answer the questions without looking back at the reading. They can use the reading to check their answers once they've finished.

### Discussions

**Support.** Give students a list of questions to think about and answer before they talk. Writing notes or answers first can help shy students or those lacking confidence.

**Challenge.** Encourage more-confident students to voice their opinions and ask them to report back to the class without any notes in front of them.

### Role-plays (in the **Literacy Book**)

**Support.** Play the audio while students perform the story. This way, students don't have to worry about their lines and can focus on interpreting each scene.

**Challenge.** Have students improvise the story, making their own changes to the dialogue.

# Games Bank

### 60 seconds
Put students in groups of three or four. Each student has 60 seconds to say as many things as they can that they learned in the lesson. They can mention anything they have learned, e.g. vocabulary, facts etc. Use the timer on the TTL and call out *Time!* when the time is up.

### Alphabet Game
Write the alphabet vertically in three or four columns on the board, with space next to each letter to write a word. Divide the class into two teams. Teams brainstorm words related to a topic starting with each letter of the alphabet (or as many as they can think of). Teams then take turns to say a word (give a 10 second time limit). Write each team's word in a different color next to the letter it starts with on the board. Letters cannot be repeated. If a team can say no more words, move on to the other team, until no one can say a word. Count the words in the different colors to see who scored the most.

### Backs to the Board
Have one student sit in a chair at the front of the classroom with their back to the board so they can't see it. Write a word on the board, and have the class give clues and definitions to help the students guess the word. Write some sentence prompts on the board to help students phrase their ideas, e.g. *It's something that you use … It's a person who …*

### Basketball
Place four containers at the front of the classroom and label them with four categories. Give students some scraps of paper which they can use to make paper balls. You are going to call out a statement, and students should throw their ball into the correct bin. You can have students play in two or three teams, standing in a line. The students at the front of each line throw, then go to the back of the line. Continue until every student has had a turn.

### Bingo
First brainstorm and write words from your chosen topic on the board. Have students draw a 3x2 grid in their notebooks and choose six of the words. To play, call out one of the words. If students have this word on their bingo boards, they should draw a cross in the relevant square of their grid. When a student has crossed all six squares, they call out *Bingo!* If all six words are correct, this student is the winner.

### Chain Game
Use chain memory games to practice the target language. Have students sit in a circle. One student says a sentence using the target language, e.g. *Yesterday, I went kayaking.* The next student repeats the sentence in the third person and adds another sentence, e.g. Student B: *Yesterday, she went kayaking and I read a comic book.* The next student has to say all the previous sentences in the third person and add their own. This continues until someone gets mixed up or can't remember what the last person said. That student says a new sentence and starts the chain again. Make sure students know that their sentences don't have to be true.

You can vary this game to suit the grammar structures you wish to practice, e.g. negatives (Student A: *I was eating dinner at 7:30.* Student B: *I wasn't eating dinner at 7:30. I was watching TV at 7:30.*) or questions and answers using the second person (Student A: *Last night I was sleeping. While I was sleeping, what were you doing?* Student B: *While you were sleeping, I was eating candy. While I was eating candy, what were you doing?* Student C: *While she was sleeping and you were eating candy, I was swimming in the sea.*)

You can also play this game in teams. The team that continues one chain for the longest time, wins!

### Change Places
Have students place their chairs in a big circle and sit down.

Version 1: give each student the name of one of three types of fruit, going round the circle, e.g. *strawberry, mango, watermelon, strawberry, mango, watermelon,* etc. Check everyone knows which fruit they are. Remove one chair so that one student is standing. To play, call out the name of one fruit. Students who are that fruit should stand up and change places with another student. The student who doesn't find a chair stands in the middle and chooses the next fruit. To get everyone standing up and moving, call out *Fruit Salad!*

Version 2: remove one chair so that one student is standing. Call out sentences and have students stand up and change places with another student if the sentence is true for them. The student who doesn't find a chair stands in the middle and says the next sentence. (If the sentence is true for them, they should also move.)

### Correct the Teacher
Call out lines from songs, stories, or dialogues, but make mistakes. When students hear a mistake, they raise their hands and call out *No!* Choose a student to correct the mistake.

### Describe It!
Students play in pairs. One student in the pair chooses a word and describes it. The other student has to guess the word. Students take turns to describe and guess. To make it more challenging, give pairs a time limit and see how many words they can guess correctly.

### Draw It!
Have a volunteer come to the front, and show him/her a word from the vocabulary set you wish to practice, or whisper it into his/her ear. The student draws the word on the board. Have students raise their hands and guess.

## Find Someone Who

Write prompts on the board and have students copy them into their notebooks. e.g. *Find someone who … went on vacation / who has more than two brothers and sisters / who wants to be a doctor when they grow up.* Then tell students to stand up and ask questions to find one person for each prompt and write down his/her name. Do one or two examples with students, first, e.g. *Did you go on vacation? How many brothers and sisters do you have?* The first person to find a match for all their questions is the winner!

You can vary this by having students write the prompts themselves, e.g. by writing sentences about what they were doing this morning and having them ask questions to find other students who were doing the same things as them at the same time.

## Gradient Line

Use one of the walls in your classroom to see how much students like different things. Place a happy face to represent *I love* at one end of the wall, and a sad face to represent *I hate* at the other end. Have the students stand up. Demonstrate by saying, for example, *I (love) reading comics* and moving to the relevant position along the wall. Then ask *How much do you like reading comics?* and encourage students to move. Repeat with other types of reading material.

## Jump!

Have students stand up behind their desks. Tell them you are going to call out some words. If those words are in the reading, they must jump. If the words are not in the reading, they should remain standing still. Call out key nouns and verbs from the reading, with other words in between.

## Mime It!

The same as *Draw It!* but students act out the word you give them.

## Never-Ending Sentence

Have students make up a story using one very long sentence in a chain. Demonstrate first with a few students. Give them a story starter and have them continue the story, each saying *and, but,* or *so* before adding a new sentence, e.g.:

Teacher: *Last summer I wanted a skateboard*
Student A: *so I walked to the shop*
Student B: *and looked at the skateboards in the window*
Student C: *but I didn't like the colors*
Student D: *so I went in the shop …*

Have students play again in groups. They can do this orally, or you could have them write down their sentences. Challenge the groups to see who can keep going to make the longest sentence.

## Odd One Out

Play in pairs. Write three or more words on the board. All the words except one should be connected to one another in some way. Students must look at the words and decide in their pairs which word is the "odd one out" and why, e.g. write *pineapple, strawberry, chocolate, lemon* on the board. *Chocolate* is the "odd one out" because it is not a fruit. Repeat with other words. At the end, invite pairs to say which words they have circled and why. Did everyone choose the same words? Sometimes there may be more than one possible answer, so reward students who can give reasons for their choices.

## Pass the Ball

Have students sit in a circle. Throw a ball to a student and have that student make a sentence or prediction using the target language when they catch the ball. That student then throws the ball to another student and the game continues.

## Pass the Paper

Put students into groups of approximately 10 students and have them work in pairs within these groups. Have enough sheets of paper for each pair in a group, e.g. if you have a group of 10, you will need five sheets of paper for that group. Write the name of a different lexical set at the top of each of the five sheets of paper. In their groups, each pair writes at least one new word belonging to the lexical set on their paper, before passing it to the next pair in their group. Continue having students write and then pass on their sheets of paper until each pair has written at least once on each of the five sheets of paper. Then have groups take turns reading out a different word from each sheet of paper. How many different words can the class remember for each lexical set?

## Pass the Whisper!

Have students stand in a line. Whisper a sentence or question using the target language to one student and have him/her pass it on until it reaches the student nearest the door. That student must say the sentence or question aloud. Repeat as required.

## Pelmanism

In pairs, have students make a set of pelmanism cards. For example, one student makes cards with verbs and the other makes cards with related nouns to practice verb–noun collocations. You could also use this game to practice vocabulary (matching words to pictures or words to definitions), or to explore connecting ideas in the **Literacy Book** (e.g. treatments and cures in Unit 9).

To play, put students in pairs or small groups and have them place all the cards face down on the table in random order. They take turns to take two cards, describe the cards, and decide whether they have a match. If the cards match, the student keeps them and takes another turn. If they don't match, the student must put them back on the table and the next student takes a turn. The student who finds the most matching cards wins.

## Physical Spelling

Read out a key word. Have students spell out the word and do actions at the same time: they should raise their arms for letters with stalks going up (e.g. b); fold arms for words with no stalk (e.g. c), and lower arms to sides for letters with stalks going down (e.g. p).

## Shark

Before the game starts, draw on the board a simple series of 10 steps leading down to water. On the top step, draw a stick figure. In the water draw a shark waiting with open mouth.

Use words from the lesson and draw a series of lines on the board, one for each letter. Have students raise their hands to guess the letters. For each correct guess, write the letter on the line. For each incorrect guess, erase the stick figure and draw it again one step nearer the shark. Write the wrong letters on the board so they are not repeated.

Students win if the word is completed before the stick figure reaches the shark—but they must continue saying letters, not shout out the word!

## Simon Says

Use this game to practice actions and imperatives. Give an instruction. If you say *Simon says* before the instruction, students should do it. If you don't say *Simons says*, students should stay still.

## Spinner Drawing Game

Assign a number from 1–6 to each part of a plant (e.g. stem, seed, petals, leaves, roots, pollen) and write this on the board. Give groups a spinner (downloaded from the Resource Bank) and have them spin to find out which part of the plant they should draw. The objective is to be the first person in the group to draw the complete flower. If students spin and get the same number twice, they have to wait until their next turn to spin again.

## Snowballs

Students write down something they learned on a piece of scrap paper and make it into a ball. On your signal, they throw their paper snowballs in the air. Then each learner picks up a different ball, opens it, and reads it out.

## Stand Up, Sit Down

Call out statements that practice the target language, e.g. *My mom is tall.* If the statement is true for students, they stand up. If it is not true, they stay sitting down. Alternatively, you can have students put their hands on their heads for true statements and keep their hands by their sides for false ones. You can play this game for any true/false statements. Have students take turns to come to the front and call out a statement.

## Twenty Questions

Students have to try to guess what you are thinking of by asking closed (yes/no) questions (a maximum of 20). If you have more than 20 students, consider having them think of questions in pairs.

## Unscramble

Write the target vocabulary on the board with all the letters scrambled. Tell students what vocabulary set they belong to, e.g. toys, food, or family. Have students work in pairs to unscramble them. You could turn this into a race or provide a time limit. If students find it difficult, give them the first letter of each word.

## Versus

Have students stand in a line in the middle of the classroom or in the corridor. Call out a series of two option questions using words from the vocabulary set you want to practice, pointing to the left or right for each option. Students choose their favorite by stepping to the left or right, according to their preference.

Alternatively, use actions instead of movements. Demonstrate as you call out, e.g. strawberries (hands on head) or apples (hands behind back).

## Who Said It?

Review dialogue and characters from readings. Make handwritten cards with a quotation from the reading. First, check that students remember the names of the characters in the target reading. Then hold up one of the cards, saying *What does it say?* and have the students read it aloud all together. Say *Who said it?* When they have answered for each sign, play the reading video or audio again to check answers. Alternatively, say the quotations aloud without writing them down.

## Word Tennis

In this game, pairs of students will pass words or sentences between them. Encourage them to say the words quickly, like a ball passing between tennis players.

Version 1: Students take turns to say words connected to a particular topic, e.g. *barbecue*:
Student A: *hot*
Student B: *burgers*
Student A: *food*
Student B: *cook*.

Version 2: Students take turns making verb–noun, verb–adjective, or verb–adverb combinations, e.g.:
Student A: *She built …*
Student B: *She built a house.*
Student A: *She built a tower*
Student B: *She built a hospital.*

A student who is unable to think of another word to go with that verb should put a new ball into play (as in a game of tennis) by saying a different verb, e.g. *We felt …*

## Yes/No Game

Write a big *Yes* on the left of the board and a big *No* on the right. Tell the students you will say sentences. If they agree with the sentence or think it is true, they point left and say *Yes!* If they disagree or think it is false, they point right and say *No!*

Alternatively, make the game into a TPR (Total Physical Response) game by assigning *Yes* to one side of the room and *No* to the other and having students move from one side to the other as you say each item.

# Language Review

## Vocabulary

### Lesson Objectives

- to review vocabulary: nature, weather, food, animals, adjectives, and action verbs

**Materials**
Audio Track 1

**A** TRACK 1 TB p. 213 **Listen and write. What's beautiful?**

- Have students look at the picture and say what they see. Encourage them to describe the picture in as much detail as possible. If necessary, write prompts on the board (e.g. *people, clothes, weather, place, nature*).
- Tell students they are going to listen to two boys talking. Ask a gist question: *What are they discussing?* Play the audio and have students point to the pictures as they listen. Then elicit the answer to the question (where to go / what to do).
- Students are now going to listen, unscramble, and write the nature words they hear. Play the audio again and pause to give students enough time to write. Display the answers on the board for students to check.
- Ask the comprehension question *What's beautiful?* and elicit answers. Play the audio again to check.

**Answers**
1 mountains 2 snow 3 waterfall 4 forest 5 lake
6 beach 7 rain 8 rainbow The rainbow is beautiful

**B Look and write.**

- Quickly review the names of the foods by asking students to say what they see in the pictures.
- Tell students they are going to do a crossword puzzle. Look at the example together. Point to the picture of the soup and ask *What's this?* Ask *Where do we write "soup"?* Show students how to look for the question number in the puzzle. Have them notice the columns labeled *Across* and *Down*. Write these words on the board and draw arrows to show what they mean.
- Have students complete the crossword puzzle individually. Allow a few minutes for this. Then check answers by projecting the completed puzzle onto the board using the Tap & Teach Lessons (TTL).

**Answers**
Across: 1 *soup* 6 chicken 7 tomato 8 eggplant
Down: 2 pineapple 3 peas 4 rice 5 spinach
6 corn

**C Look and match. Then complete. Use the words in the boxes.**

- Review the meaning of the words in the two boxes. Call out one of the animals (e.g. *chameleon*) and have students point to the picture in their books. Then review the adjectives by using gesture to demonstrate each one; for example, hold your hand up in front of you with a frightened expression on your face for *dangerous*.
- Say *Write the words from the boxes in the sentences.* Tell students to use the pictures and other words in the sentences to help them.
- Have students do the activity individually. Then check answers as a class, asking students to read their sentences aloud.

**Answers**
1 *snake*; dangerous 2 dinosaur; huge 3 bear; dirty
4 chameleon; tiny 5 penguin; slow 6 duck; soft

**D Find the verbs. Then choose four and make sentences with a partner.**

- Have students look at the word snake. Ask *Can you see any verbs?* Look at the example with the class. Remind students that verbs are actions or things we do.
- Tell students there are 12 verbs in the word snake. Have students find and circle the verbs.
- Tell students to work in pairs to write sentences using four of the verbs they found. Their sentences can be about anything they like.

**Answers**
*give*; drop; clap; bake; carry; dance; borrow; smile; travel; finish; pack; share and Students' own answers

**Practice** **Resource Bank:** Language Review Vocabulary Printouts
**Student's App:** Language Review Vocabulary Practice

## Explore Language

### Lesson Objectives

- **to review present progressive, comparative and superlative adjectives, and simple past**

**Materials**
Audio Track 2

**A Look and complete. What are they doing?**

- Students are going to review the present progressive. Have them look at the picture on p. 8. Ask *What is Ted doing? What is Jeff doing?* and elicit answers. Remind students we use *be* + *-ing* to say what is happening now.
- Then tell students to look at the picture to find out what each person is doing and complete the speech bubbles. Check answers as a class.

**Answers**
1 *'re painting* 2 'm swimming 3 'm kayaking
4 're sailing 5 's reading 6 're digging 7 's sleeping

**B** TRACK 2 TB p. 213 **Listen and complete.**

- Students are going to review comparative adjectives. To familiarize students with the context for the listening, have them look at the picture for one minute and try to remember as much detail as possible and then close their books. Ask the following questions: *How many people are painting pictures?* (three) *Where is the man sleeping?* (on the beach / under the umbrella) *What is the mom wearing on her head?* (sunglasses) *Is it raining, or is the sun shining?* (The sun is shining.) *What color is the kayak?* (yellow) *What color is Ted's baseball cap?* (purple) *How many children are sailing in the boat?* (two)
- Have students open their books. Tell them that they are going to listen to Ted, Sadie, and Jeff talking about watersports. Have students point to the characters in the picture. Ask *What watersports do you know?*
- Draw students' attention to the sentences. Play the first part of the audio and look at the example together. Elicit that we use comparative adjectives to compare two things.
- Then play the audio and have students complete the sentences individually. Check answers as a class. Ask students if they can remember why we add *more* to some adjectives. (We use *more* with adjectives that have two or more syllables.)

**Answers**
1 *faster* 2 slower 3 smaller 4 more exciting
5 more difficult 6 stronger 7 better
8 quieter; more interesting

**C Read and complete.**

- Students are going to review the simple past. Have students look at the text. Tell them to read it quickly (skim) to see what it is about. Give students up to one minute to read. Then ask them what they remember.
- Ask *Is the writer talking about today?* (No, it's about yesterday.) Ask *What verb forms do we use to talk about yesterday?* (simple past) Have students read the text again and write the verbs in the simple past. Then check answers.

**Answers**
1 *was* 2 saw 3 wasn't 4 played 5 ran 6 were
7 ate 8 went

**D Look at A. Complete.**

- Students are going to review superlative adjectives. Look at the example together. Ask *How do we know how big Ted's backpack is?* Tell students to look at the picture in A and find Ted. Have them identify the three backpacks and notice that Ted's is bigger than the others. Elicit that we use superlative adjectives to compare three or more things.
- Tell students to use the picture to compare the things in the sentences. They should use the adjectives in the box.
- Have students complete the activity individually. Then check answers as a class. Ask students if they can remember why we add *most* to some adjectives. (We use *most* with adjectives that have two or more syllables.) Can they remember why *curly* becomes *curliest*? (For adjectives that end in *y* we take away the *y* and add *iest*.)

**Answers**
1 *the biggest* 2 the smallest 3 the most beautiful
4 the longest 5 the curliest 6 the worst

**Practice** **Resource Bank:** Language Review Grammar Printouts
**Student's App:** Language Review Grammar Practice

# Literacy Review

## Fiction

### Lesson Objectives

- to review the reading skills of scanning, identifying cause and effect, and identifying the sequence of events
- to review phonics sounds *–st* and *tr–*

**Materials**
Audio Tracks 1 and 2

**A** TRACK 1 TB p. 229 **Scan the story. Answer the questions. Then listen and read.**

- Students are going to practice the reading skill of scanning. Have students look at the picture. Ask *What do you see? What do you think the story is about?* Tell students to use the pictures and title to predict ideas about the reading. Have students work in pairs to share their ideas.
- Have students look at the story extract and refer them to the three questions. Tell them that they don't have to read every word to answer the questions. Give students one to two minutes to scan the text. Then have them write the answers in their books.
- Then listen and read to check answers.

**Answers**
1 *Don't Move* 2 inside a tent in a forest
3 Mom and Suzie

**B Read and write *True* or *False*.**

- Ask a volunteer to read the example (1). Ask *Why is it false?* and have students find the answer in the reading. Then have students read the other statements and write if they are true or false.
- Check answers as a class. Encourage students to justify their answers by referring back to the text.

**Answers**
1 *False* 2 False 3 True 4 True 5 True

**C Read, think, and write.**

- Students are going to review the reading skill of identifying cause and effect. Tell students that a cause is why something happens. The cause is the reason. The effect is what happens. The effect is what changes.
- Draw students' attention to the activity. Look at the first sentence together. Say *A strong wind blew. What happened to the tent?* Then say *Suzie felt very alone. What made her feel this way?*
- Have students continue the activity individually. Then check answers as a class.

**Answers**
1 Our tent shook like a sail.
2 They were the only people on the trail.
3 She jumped.
4 The creature was hungry.

**D Put the events in order.**

- Students are going to review the reading skill of sequencing events. Remind students that a sequence is an order.
- Tell students to put the five sentences in order. Then check answers as a class. You could display the answers using the Tap & Teach Lessons (TTL).

**Answers**
4, *1*, 3, 2, 5

### My Reading Journal

**What do you think happens next? Write.**

- Students are going to make predictions about what happens next in the story. Brainstorm a few possible ideas with the class. Provide any language help when needed.
- Then have students choose an idea and write it in their books. Ask some volunteers to share their ideas with the class.

**Example Answer**
The animal finds and eats their food.

### Phonics *–st* and *tr–*

TRACK 2 TB p. 229

**Listen and unscramble. Then find more words ending with *st* and beginning with *tr* in the reading.**

- With books closed, play the audio and have students repeat each word. Ask *Which words do you remember?* Then have them open their books and look at the scrambled words. Play the audio again, pausing for students to write the words in their books.
- Have students look back at the reading to find more words ending with *st* and beginning with *tr*. Give them one or two minutes before checking answers as a class.

**Answers**
1 *fast* 2 train 3 nest 4 travel 5 trash 6 best
7 first 8 true
In the reading: forest; just; trees; trail

**Practice** **Resource Bank:** Literacy Review Reading Skills Printouts
**Students's App:** Reading Skills Practice; Phonics Practice

## Nonfiction

### Lesson Objectives

- to review the reading skills of scanning, identifying main idea and details and identifying fact and opinion
- to review phonics sounds *–nd* and *–ng*

**Materials**
Audio Tracks 3 and 4

**A** TRACK 3 TB p. 229 **Scan the reading. Answer the questions. Then listen and read.**

- Students are going to practice the reading skill of scanning for specific information. Have students read the three questions. Tell them to look at the reading to find the answers. Remind them not to read every word.
- Then listen and read to check answers.

**Answers**
1 *Mexico City* 2 the monarch butterfly
3 more than 4,000 km.

**B Read and answer.**

- Students are now going to scan for further information. Have them read the example question. Ask *Which words are important? What do we have to find out?* Then have them look back at the reading to find where the answer is (first paragraph).
- Give students two minutes to read the questions and underline the key words. This is a useful strategy for scanning.
- Then have students find the answers to the questions in the reading. Check answers.

**Answers**
1 *The butterflies arrive in Mexico every fall.*
2 The butterflies travel from North America.
3 It is about 97 km. from Mexico City.
4 The trees turn orange and their branches bend.
5 The monarchs start their journey home in the spring.

**C Think and write. What is the main idea? What are the details?**

- Students are going to review the reading skill of identifying the main idea and details. Tell students that the main idea gives the most important information. The details give extra information so you understand more.
- Have students look back at the text to identify the main idea. Have them compare their ideas in pairs and decide how best to express this together. Each student should then write their agreed sentence or sentences in the table.
- Then have students find three details in the text. Check answers by asking a few students about their ideas.

**Suggested Answers**
**Main Idea:** To describe the migration of the monarch butterflies / to describe what an amazing sight it is.
**Details:** Some monarch butterflies travel more than 4,000 km. from North America to escape the winter and to mate. It is a UNESCO World Heritage Site.
Scientists believe this place is important for the planet.
The site protects the trees from being cut down.
There are so many butterflies that the trees turn orange, and branches bend under the weight.
In spring, the forest fills with the fluttering of tiny wings, as the monarchs get ready to make the long journey home.

**D Read and write *Fact* or *Opinion*.**

- Students are going to review the reading skill of identifying facts and opinions. Elicit that a fact is a piece of information that is correct and true. An opinion is what someone thinks. It is what they believe.
- Look at the example together. Point out that the use of *beautiful* means it is an opinion. Say *Different people think different things are beautiful.*
- Give students a few minutes to read and decide whether the sentences are fact or an opinion. Check answers.

**Answers**
1 *Opinion* 2 Fact 3 Opinion 4 Fact 5 Fact

### My Reading Journal

**What's one thing you learned from the reading?**

This question focuses on personalization. Elicit ideas and write them on the board as a spidergram (or mind map). Have students choose one idea to write in their books.

**Example Answer**
I learned monarch butterflies travel more than 4,000 km.

### Phonics *–nd* and *–ng*

TRACK 4 TB p. 229

**Listen and complete with *nd* and *ng*. Then find more words ending with *nd* and *ng* in the reading.**

- Have students look at the beginnings of the words. Ask *Can we add* nd *or* ng *to these words?*
- Play the audio and have students repeat each word and write the endings.
- Have students look back at the reading to find more words with the two endings. Give them one or two minutes before checking answers as a class.

**Answers**
1 *send* 2 find 3 stand 4 wrong 5 thing
6 sing 7 strong 8 sound
In the reading: and; thousand; bend; amazing; something; spring; fluttering; long

**Practice** **Resource Bank:** Literacy Review Reading Skills Printouts
**Student's App:** Reading Skills Practice; Phonics Practice

UNIT 1
# I Love Reading

## Unit Overview

### Themes

The importance of libraries

The benefits of reading

### Synopsis

In this unit, students will explore why reading is important. They will learn about different types of books and how we can learn from them. They will discuss the benefits of sharing books, and also the benefits of libraries as places to learn and as social places. Students will plan and prepare a conversation recommending a book and write a book report.

## Language Book

**Vocabulary**
*adventure, biography, boring, complicated, exciting, famous, fantasy, interesting, novel, popular, science fiction*
p. 35

**Explore Language**
Simple Past: Regular and Irregular Verbs
p. 37

**Global Citizenship**
Why do communities need libraries?
*art, English, geography, health, history, math, music, P.E. (physical education), science, technology*
p. 39

**Explore Language**
Adverbs of Manner
p. 41

**Talk About It**
Conversation: asking for and offering help and advice
p. 43

**Write About It**
A Book Report
Word Building: adverb endings
p. 45

**Think It Over**
Review and Reflection
p. 47

Chapter Three

Chapter Four

## Literacy Book

### Think Together
Why is reading important?

p. 61

### Visible Thinking
Question Starts

p. 49

### Nonfiction
Informational Text: *Learning and Your Brain*

Words in Context: *lobes, workout, cells, fibers, messages, connecting, creative*

p. 57

### Fiction
Fantasy: *The Beginning of Alice's Adventures*

Words in Context: *sleepy, chased, fell, shelves, corner*

p. 51

### Reading Skill
Skimming a text

p. 55

### Spelling Pattern
*–er*

p. 59

## Language and Literacy Connections

The connecting theme in Unit 1 is learning and having fun through reading.

| | Language | Literacy |
|---|---|---|
| **Vocabulary** | **Set 1:** books and reading; adjectives<br>**Set 2:** school subjects | **Fiction:** exciting, interesting, novel, geography<br>**Nonfiction:** math, music, P.E. |
| **Grammar** | **Simple Past: Regular and Irregular Verbs**<br>Where did you go yesterday?<br>I went to the library.<br>We looked for books about robots.<br>**Adverbs of Manner**<br>I read quickly.<br>You really do read carefully! | **Fiction**<br>Alice sat by the river.<br>Alice got up, quickly, and chased after him. |
| **Skills** | **Pronunciation:** /sk/ and /gr/ | **Reading:** skimming a text<br>**Spelling Pattern:** *–er* |
| **International English** | | vest/waistcoat; center/centre; fiber/fibre; visualize/visualise |

# Lesson 1 Walkthrough: Vocabulary

This lesson introduces the theme of the unit and presents and practices the first vocabulary set.

## Warm Up

Warm Up activities are either language or topic-based. Their purpose is not to pre-teach new vocabulary, but to engage students, activate prior knowledge, and prepare students cognitively for the lesson ahead. The digital **Enhanced Teacher's eBook (ETB)** also contains Two-Minute Review activities to recall previously taught language or skills. These activities are quick to do, so time is not taken away from the rest of the lesson, and are easy to integrate into a classroom routine. You can choose to do both the Two-Minute Review and the Warm Up or just one or the other, to suit the needs of your class.

## Activity A Picture Dictionary Scene

**Activity A** presents the first lexical set (eight to twelve words) through a picture dictionary scene. This scene is designed to support learning by providing word–picture association. Alongside this, its purpose is to get students thinking about the unit topic, reviewing language, and making connections to their own world. The scene includes key characters from the corresponding **Literacy Book** unit and the previous unit of the **Language Book** for students to identify. This is to help students make connections between the two books, between units, and between the topics and characters, to show how communities work.

The new language is contextualized aurally in a dialogue. The audio includes at least six of the target vocabulary items to encourage students to explore the image and develop discrimination skills. Students should be encouraged to point to the pictures or words as they hear them mentioned. The process of listening, searching for, and finding vocabulary items helps students to engage with the target language. **Literacy Book** Links are highlighted in the digital **Enhanced Teacher's eBook** (ETB).

There is always a gist or comprehension question to focus students and help them understand the general meaning of the dialogue. The digital **ETB** provides further comprehension check questions to explore the picture and audio in more detail.

## Activity B Drill & Controlled Vocabulary Practice

**Activity B** is a drill and provides initial practice of all the target vocabulary. Pausing the audio will give all students enough time to say the words and enable you to give immediate feedback on pronunciation. For ideas on how to make language drills fun, see **TB p. 23**.

The listen and number task asks students to write numbers next to the vocabulary items in the picture in the order they hear them mentioned. This gets students thinking about the target language, which will help them to learn it.

## Activity C Visualization

**Activity C** is a visualization activity and offers a different pathway for students to interact with the target language. The audio prompts students to create their own mental images of the vocabulary and to do actions where appropriate. This personalized approach makes learning more meaningful and therefore more memorable. Students are not expected to articulate (in English) what they have visualized because sometimes this may be harder than the target word. However, a variety of pair-/class-work activities for exchanging ideas have been provided to give students a means for creative output. See **TB p. 21** for how to set up a visualization activity.

## Activity D Controlled Practice & Critical Thinking

**Activity D** provides further language practice by getting students to interact with the picture dictionary. Critical thinking skills are developed as students complete a categorization task such as a chart, graphic organizer, or Venn diagram, and sometimes more than one answer is possible.

## Activity E Song

**Activity E** is always a song connected to a unit theme and provides additional context for the target language: any words not in the dialogue in A will be contextualized here. There is a fill-in-the-blank activity, where students are encouraged to predict the answers before listening to check. The song allows students to have fun with the language and helps them to learn through rhythm, rhyme, and repetition. There is usually a link to a Social and Emotional Learning (SEL) competency.

The song is supported by an animated video with the lyrics displayed to encourage heads-up participation. When the song lends itself to it, encourage students to invent actions or movements to do while singing: a Total Physical Response (TPR) approach will help them to learn and retain the new language. Additional Video Focus ideas are provided in the digital **ETB**.

## Cool Down

The Cool Down is a final game or activity that provides an opportunity to wrap up the lesson. It reviews and reinforces the lesson objectives.

# Language

## Vocabulary

### Lesson Objectives

- to learn book genre vocabulary and adjectives: *adventure, biography, fantasy, novel, science fiction; boring, complicated, exciting, famous, interesting, popular*
- to sing a song about libraries

**Materials**
Audio Tracks 3 to 6; Video; a selection of book covers (Cool Down, CD)

### Warm Up

Write anagrams of the book titles from the picture in Lesson 1 on the board and have students work in pairs to unscramble them. Give students two or three minutes; for example, *bRoot kaMer* (*Robot Maker*); *The luCod piSh* (*The Cloud Ship*). Then ask students what they think the books are about.

**A** TRACK 3 TB p. 213 **Listen and find. Who gets books for Kareem?**

- Have students look at the picture and say what they see. Ask questions to prompt discussion: *What are these children doing? What books can you see? What's on the walls?*
- Tell students they are going to listen to Kareem and his friends talking about library books. Play the audio and have students point to the words or pictures as they listen.
- Ask the comprehension question *Who gets books for Kareem?* and elicit the answer. Play the audio again for students to check.

**Answer**
Millie, two other friends (Adam, and Lucy,) and ROBO find books for Kareem.

**B** TRACK 4 TB p. 213 **Listen, say, and number the pictures in A.**

- Play the audio and have students point to the pictures and say the words.
- Tell students to listen again and write numbers next to the words in the picture. Do the example together (interesting). If students need more time to write their answers, pause the audio.
- Check answers by calling out a number and having students call out the word. Alternatively, project the answers using the TTL.

**Answers**
1 *interesting* 2 science fiction 3 complicated
4 novel 5 popular 6 biography 7 exciting
8 fantasy 9 famous 10 adventure 11 boring

**C** TRACK 5 TB p. 213 **Close your eyes. Listen, visualize, and say.**

- Prepare students for the visualization (see TB p. 21).
- Play the audio, allowing students to visualize the ideas as they listen. Make sure students know not to speak until they hear the word *say*. Put your finger to your lips if necessary.
- Have students talk about their ideas in pairs. Then have some students share their ideas with the class.

**D** **Look and write.**

- Students are going to categorize the vocabulary. This encourages critical thinking, because students must group words in a logical or meaningful way. Point to the table and have students notice the examples.
- Tell students to write the words in the table. Then check answers as a class. You could project the answers using the TTL. Point out that *novels* and *biographies* are in the plural form here as they are count nouns and we're talking about them in a general sense. The other genres are used as adjectives, and we can use them with a noun, e.g. "fantasy stories," "science fiction books."

**Answers**
Kinds of books: *novels*, biographies, adventure, fantasy, science fiction
How to describe books: *interesting*, exciting, boring, complicated, popular, famous

**E** TRACK 6 TB p. 213 **Listen and complete. Then watch and sing.**

- Point to the song title *The Library*. Ask *What can you do in the library?* and elicit suggestions. Then play the song once, allowing students to listen and enjoy it.
- Explain to students that some parts of the words are missing and they have to complete them. Ask *Can you guess what words they are?* Encourage students to look at the first letter as a clue. Play the song again, this time pausing for students to write their answers.
- Check answers as a class.
- Play the song video and encourage students to sing and move to the music as they watch.

**Answers**
1 *novel* 2 adventure 3 exciting 4 fantasy 5 boring
6 famous 7 biography 8 interesting

### Cool Down

Bring in a selection of books from the five different genres, or project images of book covers onto the board. Assign each of the genres to an area of the classroom by placing signs on the walls. Show students a book cover and have them decide which genre it is and move to the appropriate area of the classroom. Tell students if they were correct. Any students who moved to a different area of the classroom sit down. Repeat with other book covers. The last students standing win.

**Practice** **Student's App:** Vocabulary Practice; Song Video

# Lesson 2 Walkthrough: Explore Language

The grammar lessons present and practice the target structures using a simplified inductive approach. This encourages the students to think about the patterns of language and to make and test assumptions through carefully staged and scaffolded activities. By laying the groundwork for the kinds of tasks they will do in higher levels, they are supported to become independent thinkers from the very beginning.

### Activity A Contextualized Presentation

**Activity A** presents the lesson's grammar focus through the context of a dialogue or story. Students listen and read, but the target language is not highlighted at this point. The gist or comprehension question gives students a reason to listen and supports them to understand the story. The digital **ETB** provides questions to check students' comprehension. If you don't use the **ETB**, ask simple comprehension questions to help students make connections with prior knowledge and personalize the scenario.

### Activity B Grammar Analysis Table

**Activity B** is a grammar table with sections for students to fill out, focusing on form. Most of the sentences come from the dialogue in Activity A; if they are not there, the answers will be filled in, with the key word(s) highlighted to provide a model. Students need to identify the sentences and copy the missing words, thereby drawing their attention to the grammar structure and to language patterns. The teacher's notes help you to scaffold the discussion for the first four units, after which students are encouraged to take the lead in identifying and discussing the grammar patterns and completing the table. However, the **ETB** provides additional Support notes, should you prefer to continue leading the grammar discussion.

Attached to the table is a language tip, pointing out additional information related to the grammar point that needs further support. There are three types of tip:

- **Remember** when students have most likely already seen this language feature, e.g. contractions.
- **Look** a new, additional piece of information about the grammar, e.g. a spelling pattern or anomaly.
- **Watch Out** highlights typical mistakes learners make.

### Activity C Inductive Analysis

**Activity C** is a continuation of the language analysis, as students are asked to focus on the meaning and usage of the grammar structure. Concise concept statements are given to explain how the language is used. Students have to think critically to choose between different options, which helps them to interact with the language. Encourage students to discuss their ideas in pairs before checking answers as a class. First language (L1) can be used to support this task when language in the concept statements is above level.

### Activity D Drill: Sentence Level

See **TB p. 40**.

### Activity E Controlled Practice: Written

See **TB p. 40**.

### Activity F Freer Practice: Communication

See **TB p. 40**.

## Explore Language

### Lesson Objectives

- to review the simple past: regular and irregular verbs
- to practice book genre vocabulary and adjectives

**Materials**
Audio Tracks 7 and 8

### Warm Up

Ask students if they do group projects at school and what they are about. If students don't do group projects, have them say what topics they are interested in studying.

**A** TRACK 7 TB p. 214 **Listen and read. What's Gavin's project about?**

- Remind students of the picture scene on pp. 10–11. Ask *What was Kareem's project about?* (robots) Tell students that they are going to listen to Kareem talking to a new friend, Gavin, about his project. Play the audio and have students follow the dialogue in their books.
- Ask the gist question *What is Gavin's project about?* and elicit the answer. Play the audio again for students to check. Ask if students can remember what Kareem read about (the first robot).

**Answer**
Gavin's project is about frogs.

**B Look at A. Complete.**

- Write or project the table onto the board. Tell students that the sentences they need are all in the dialogue.
- Look at the first question in the table. Ask *Is the question about the present or the past? What makes you say that?* Elicit that *yesterday* tells us the question is about the past. Explain that words like *yesterday* and *last week* tell us that we need the simple past.
- Refer students to the dialogue in A. Have students find the question and notice which word is missing in the table (go). Complete this together. Elicit that this verb is the base form, not the past form. Draw students' attention to the verb in orange. Ask *Which word do we need to make a question in simple past?* (did)
- Have students work in pairs to complete the rest of table. Check answers as a class. Encourage students to notice the regular and irregular forms. Elicit more regular and irregular verbs in the simple past.
- Review verb forms in the questions. Ask *Is the verb in the simple past?* (No, the auxiliary verb *do* is in the simple past; the main verb is the base form.) Point out that this is the same for negative sentences, e.g. *I didn't see you.*
- Review the short answer forms.
- Draw students' attention to the Grammar tip *Watch Out*. Ask students what they notice about the two forms of *read*. (They look the same.) Then say *I read my book in class every morning. / I read my book yesterday.* Write the two sentences on the board. Ask students how they know which form is being used; elicit *time words* and underline *every morning* and *yesterday*. Drill the different pronunciation of each form: /ri:d/ and /red/.
- If you feel that students need more guidance, the **ETB** provides a differentiation activity to help you support students as they explore the grammar table.

**Answers**
go; went; looked; Did; find; did

**C Think and discuss. Then choose.**

- Review the meaning of *now* and *before* with students. Draw a clockface with the current time on the board and elicit this is *now*. Then draw a clockface with the time showing five minutes before. Elicit this is *before*.
- Have students work in pairs to discuss the question. Refer them to the table in B for examples of verbs in the simple past. Then check the answer.

**Answer**
before now

**D** TRACK 8 TB p. 214 **Listen and say.**

- Tell students they're going to practice saying the structures. Play the audio, having students repeat each sentence chorally.
- For ideas on how to vary the drill, see TB p. 23.

**E Help Millie write in her diary. Look and complete.**

- Review what a diary is by asking *Do you write a diary? Why do people write diaries? Is a diary fiction or nonfiction?* Encourage students to share their ideas.
- Tell students that they have to help Millie complete a diary entry about her day at the library.
- Have students complete the activity individually. Remind them to use the dialogue in A and the table in B to help them. Check answers as a class.

**Answers**
1 *went* 2 looked 3 didn't want 4 didn't see
5 found 6 borrowed

**F Play a chain game. Talk about yesterday.**

- Brainstorm activities that students like to do and write them on the board. Elicit each verb or phrase in the simple past.
- Demonstrate the activity first, using the prompt from the page, and continue it with several students. Then divide the class into groups of three to play the game (see TB p. 25).

### Cool Down

Play *Mime It!* (see TB p. 26) by having students mime activities they did the previous day.

**Practice** **Resource Bank:** Grammar Printout
**Student's App:** Grammar Practice

# Lesson 3 Walkthrough: Global Citizenship

This lesson presents and practices the second vocabulary set, practices listening for gist and specific details, and gives students the opportunity to learn about the lives of other children around the world and to make connections with their own lives.

## Opening Question

The **opening question** takes the place of the Warm Up and is designed to activate interest and curiosity in the Global Citizenship topic by helping students to make connections to prior knowledge. Don't correct students at this point or give too much feedback, as the lesson is structured so that they develop ideas to discuss at the end of the class.

## Activity A Contextualized Vocabulary

**Activity A** presents the new vocabulary through eye-catching photos or pictures, to provide a real-world context. There is a contextualized listening activity which presents some of the target language through a dialogue or monologue. This listening activity provides an introduction to the Global Citizenship part of the lesson on the facing page. Students will be able to make connections between this audio and the audio for D and E.

## Activity B Drill & Controlled Vocabulary Practice

See **TB p. 34**.

## Activity C Controlled Vocabulary Practice: Written

**Activity C** is a fill-in-the-blank, matching, or read and circle activity to encourage students to think critically about the new vocabulary and to use it through controlled practice.

## Visualization

There is a visualization audio track for this vocabulary set on the TTL. See **TB p. 34**

## Activity D Listening for Gist and Main Idea

**Activity D** provides input for the Global Citizenship discussion at the end of the lesson. There are usually two speakers for each lesson who explore the Global Citizenship theme in connection to different countries around the world. Students listen for the main idea of the audio topic and answer a gist question.

Before they listen, give students some time to look at the pictures. You could let them find the countries mentioned on a world map and ask them what they already know about these countries to activate prior knowledge. Tell students to listen out for key vocabulary they recognize. Explain that thinking about these words in order will help them to understand what the listening is about and answer the gist question. Some of the new vocabulary from Activity A is always recycled here.

## Activity E Listening for Details

**Activity E** encourages students to listen out for specific details. Ask them how many of the questions they can answer from information they have remembered from D, but reassure them that this is not a memory test and that it doesn't matter if they don't remember. Then play the audio again, so they can listen and check their answers and answer any questions they missed.

Encourage further discussion and personal response to what they heard by analyzing the answers (e.g. why something was false) and having students talk about what they found interesting or surprising.

## Discussion Questions

**The discussion questions** address the key holistic learning concepts that run through the unit. Ultimately, the discussion can be done in pairs with some whole-class input at the end, although you may wish to have a whole-class discussion for the initial units to allow students to become familiar with the activity. The Global Citizenship strand at this level encourages students to think about how they can get involved in their community, and how their community can have an impact on the wider world, and on them.

There is usually one personalization question and one question that asks students to look further and see the bigger picture. Deal with each one in turn, giving students time to think and discuss in their pairs or small groups. Allow use of L1 for new words and more complex ideas as this will enable students to express themselves and develop a clearer understanding of the key concepts. You can also challenge students to provide sentences beyond their ability by translating words and phrases from L1 into English.

Bring the class back together to discuss the conclusions they have reached. Use graphic organizers on the board to present students' ideas. Revisit the opening question and see if students answer it differently now. In-depth ideas to help you structure each discussion as well as project ideas can be found in the digital **ETB**.

## Competencies

Icons in the teaching notes highlight which activities in the **Language Book** are connected to one of the five competencies: Me, Act, Think, Learn, and Communicate. For more information see **TB p. 19**.

## Global Citizenship

### Lesson Objectives

- to learn school subjects vocabulary: *art, English, geography, health, history, math, music, P.E. (physical education), science, technology*
- to explore how we can share books in the local community
- to practice listening for gist and details

**Materials**

Audio Tracks 9 to 11; Audio Track A; a globe or map (Activity D)

### Opening Question

Ask the opening question: *Why do communities need libraries?* Elicit ideas and encourage students to think about who goes to libraries and the different things they can do there. Remind them of the picture they saw in Lesson 1. Ask *Who was there? What did they do?*

**A** TRACK 9 TB p. 214 **Listen to Linda talk about her library. How does it grow?**

- Tell students they are going to listen to a girl named Linda talking about her library. Play the audio and have students point to the words or pictures as they listen.
- Ask the gist question: *How does it grow?* Elicit what students understand by *grow. Does the library get bigger?* Play the audio again for students to check.

**Answer**

The library grows because children and their parents give books they don't want anymore.

**B** TRACK 10 TB p. 214 **Listen, say, and number the pictures in A.**

- Play the audio and have students point to the pictures and say the words.
- Tell students to listen again and number the pictures in the order they hear them. Do the example together (science).
- Check answers by asking volunteers to call out the numbers and asking others to respond. Alternatively, project the answers using the TTL. Ask questions to check students understand each word.

**Answers**

1 *science* 2 math 3 history 4 geography 5 English 6 technology 7 art 8 music 9 health 10 P.E. (physical education)

TRACK A TB p. 214 **Visualization**

The TTL has a visualization audio track for this vocabulary set. (See TB p. 21.)

**C Read and complete.**

- Students are going to complete the sentences with the vocabulary from A. Look at the example together. Point out that students can use the words in the sentence to help them identify the missing word.
- Have students complete the sentences individually. Then check answers as a class.

**Answers**

1 *history* 2 geography 3 P.E. 4 English 5 science 6 health

**D** TRACK 11 TB p. 214 **Now listen to Skyla and Rishi. Why do these libraries travel to different places?**

- Tell students they are going to listen to Skyla from the Netherlands and Rishi from India talking about libraries. Ask *Where are these countries?* Use a map to find them.
- Ask students to look at the pictures of the children and speculate about what each child is reading. Ask *Are the books fiction or nonfiction? Are they reading for fun? Do you think they like the book? Is it their book, or is it from the library?*
- Ask the gist question *Why do these libraries travel to different places?* Play the audio and elicit answers.

**Answers**

These libraries travel so that people who don't live near libraries can borrow books.

**E Listen again. Check (✔) the correct country.**

- Listening for details: have students look at the questions before they listen again to see how many things they remember. Then play the audio and have students check the correct country.
- To check answers, read each question and have students raise their right hand for *India* and their left hand for *The Netherlands.*

**Answers**

1 *The Netherlands* 2 India 3 The Netherlands 4 India 5 India

### Discussion Questions

- Draw students' attention to the discussion questions: *What things can you do at your library? How can we share books in our communities?* Have a Group Time discussion (see TB p. 21).
- Return to the opening question to ask again *How do libraries bring people together?* Focus on the concept of how important books are and different ways of sharing books. Encourage students to think about libraries as social places where people can meet and share ideas about what they read. See **ETB** for extension activities and projects.

### Cool Down

Have students talk about their favorite books in pairs. Write questions on the board to help scaffold the discussion: *What's the title? What kind of book is it? What's it about?*

**Practice** **Student's App:** Vocabulary Practice; Listening Practice

# Lesson 4 Walkthrough: Explore Language

This lesson presents and practices the second grammar structure(s) and has the same structure and purpose as Lesson 2.

### Activity A Contextualized Presentation

See **TB p. 36**.

### Activity B Grammar Analysis Table

See **TB p. 36**

### Activity C Inductive Analysis

See **TB p. 36**

### Activity D Drill: Sentence Level

**Activity D** is a drill of four to five sentences/questions to allow students to familiarize themselves with the new language. Drills give students intensive practice in hearing and saying new phrases.

The first time you play the audio, focus on pronunciation. Then play it again, this time encouraging students to concentrate on intonation. Using different activities will help you to keep drills fun and stop them from becoming repetitive. For ideas on how to vary the drill, see **TB p. 23**.

### Activity E Controlled Practice: Written

**Activity E** is a controlled practice activity and gives students some heads-down time to use the new grammar structure. Encourage students to do this as independently as possible, using the table in Activity B, so that they can process what they have learned and you can assess their level of understanding.

### Activity F Freer Practice: Communication

**Activity F** allows students to practice the target language through a freer, more communicative activity or game. Where there is text inside speech bubbles, this provides a model, but make sure students understand that they can choose what to say. This is a chance for students to communicate and collaborate while using and practicing the target language. Students learn more by working with different people, rather than the same friend each time. One way to achieve this is by giving students a word or picture card and asking them to find another student with the same card. Students with matching cards will work together in the activity.

Throughout the digital **ETB** there are ideas to differentiate lesson content in a mixed ability class. *Support* ideas suggest a simpler pathway for completing an activity or provide scaffolding to enable less-confident students to complete the activity. *Challenge* ideas encourage more-confident students to use additional language to take activities further. For more activity-specific differentiation ideas see **TB p. 24**.

# Explore Language

## Lesson Objectives

- to learn adverbs of manner
- to review adjectives
- to practice school subjects vocabulary

**Materials**

Audio Tracks 12 and 13

## Warm Up

Play *Word Tennis* by saying different adjectives of manner (see TB p. 27). In this version students can think of animals or activities that they associate with each adjective.

**A** TRACK 12 TB p. 214 **Listen and read. What did Lena learn about penguins?**

- Tell students that they are going to listen to Millie talking to her friend Lena about books they're reading. Ask *Can you remember which book Millie had in Lesson 1?* Elicit the answer (*Robot Tales*) or have students look back and find the answer. Play the audio and have students follow the dialogue in their books.
- Ask the comprehension question *What did Lena learn about penguins?* and elicit the answer. Play the audio again for students to check. Ask *Does Lena read quickly?* (no) Play the audio again to check if necessary.

**Answer**

Lena learned that penguins are birds but they can't fly.

**B Look at A. Complete.**

- Write or project the table onto the board. Tell students that the sentences are all in the dialogue.
- Point to the three words in orange on the left-hand side of the table. Have students look back at A to find out who is a quick/slow/careful reader. (Millie, Lena, Lena) Elicit actions for each adjective. Ask *What kinds of words are these?* (adjectives) *What do we use adjectives for?* (to describe things, animals, or people)
- Have students work in pairs to complete the rest of the table. Check answers as a class. Have students notice the adjective and adverb forms.
- Draw students' attention to the Look box. Point out that most adjectives can be turned into adverbs by adding *ly*. Remind students of the spelling rule to drop the *y* and change it to an *i* before adding the *ly*. Note: spelling rules are practiced in the Write About It lesson.

**Answers**

quickly; slowly; carefully

**Practice** Resource Bank: Grammar Printout
Student's App: Grammar Practice

**C Think and discuss. Then choose.**

- Review nouns and verbs with students: a noun is an object or a person and a verb is an action. Elicit some examples of both.
- Have students work in pairs to discuss the sentences. Refer them to the table in B for examples of adjectives and adverbs. Then check answers.
- Have students demonstrate walking *quickly*, *slowly*, and *carefully*. Point out that these words answer the question *How …?* Elicit an example, e.g. *How do you read?*

**Answers**

1 adjective 2 adverb 3 how

**D** TRACK 13 TB p. 214 **Listen and say.**

- Tell students they're going to practice saying the new structures. Play the audio, having students repeat each sentence chorally.
- Play it again and have students do actions to demonstrate each sentence after they say it.
- For ideas on how to vary the drill, see TB p. 23.

**E Read and choose.**

- Read the example, including both options. Point out the verb *talk* and ask *Do we need an adjective or an adverb?* (adverb) Elicit which option is the adverb (quietly).
- Have students circle the correct words in their books.
- Check answers as a class by acting out each sentence in a random order and having students call out the correct word.

**Answers**

1 *quietly* 2 slowly 3 easy 4 carefully 5 quickly 6 happy

**F Choose and say. Make sentences about you, your family, and friends.**

- Focus on the two boxes. Elicit what kinds of words are in each box (verbs and adverbs). Ask *Do we usually put the adverb before the verb or after?* (after)
- Students will play in groups. Set a time limit. Each group should try to make up as many sentences as they can in the time allotted. Tell students that the sentences need to be grammatically correct and make sense. When you call *Time!*, someone from each group reads their sentences aloud. Correct sentences receive one point each. Continue for as long as time and interest allow, reusing verbs and adverbs if necessary. The group with the most points is the winner.

## Cool Down

Write a sentence on the board. Then call out adverbs and have students read the sentence in that way to their partner.

Suggested adverbs: *quickly, slowly, quietly, loudly, happily, excitedly, angrily, beautifully*

**Next Lesson:** Tell students to find two books they like and bring them to class for the next lesson.

# Lesson 5 Walkthrough: Take the Stage / Talk About It

The first productive skills lesson is dedicated to speaking and functional language. Take the Stage lessons present and practice a presentation. Talk About It lessons present and practice a conversation. The productive task is modeled by a child or children in a video, which shows the students what they are going to do themselves and helps to bring the language alive. Ideally the video should be watched in class. However, if this isn't possible, use the Flipped Classroom Approach (see **TB p. 15**) and have students watch the video before the lesson.

Building students' confidence in speaking is a key part of the language-learning classroom and the activities are carefully staged to help them analyze the language, brainstorm their own ideas, and plan what they will say. Performing successfully, in a conversation or a presentation, helps ensure learners are receptive to future learning.

### Activity A Video Showcase

**Activity A** asks students to watch the video and answer a gist or comprehension question. Ask some additional comprehension questions to make sure students understand the video. This is important because the video models the spoken practice students will do later on in the lesson. Comprehension questions have been provided in the digital **ETB**. The digital **ETB** also provides a Video Focus idea in every speaking lesson. There is a *Watch* callout question which encourages students to notice something about the model presentation/conversation in the video (e.g. body language). This feature is often picked up in the *Reflect* callout. Notes for the Watch callout are provided in the **ETB**.

### Activity B Functional Language

**Activity B** asks students to watch the video again, this time with their books open; the functional language is highlighted for students to notice. Students can try to do the activity from memory first and then check their answers when you re-play the video. Giving students a critical thinking task, such as analyzing and categorizing the key phrases, will help them to prepare for structuring their presentation or conversation later in the lesson.

### Pronunciation

**Pronunciation** activities in the **Language Book** are about communicating clearly and intelligibly. Students will practice saying sounds and words accurately, first by watching and copying your mouth movements and then by listening to and repeating the audio. The sounds featured here have been chosen because they are difficult for many non-native speakers and may require additional practice. Students are then encouraged to identify other words with the same sounds and practice saying them.

### Activity C Planning

**Activity C** is the planning stage of the presentation or conversation; it allows students to personalize their ideas using the functional language from the video. It is important to teach students to brainstorm ideas and plan before giving a presentation. C helps them prepare their ideas before organizing them in D. You could use a cooperative learning routine to encourage students to generate ideas (see **TB p. 42**).

### Activity D Preparation

**Activity D** is where students use their ideas from C to prepare a presentation/conversation, guided by the template provided in the book. Students will prepare presentations individually and conversations in pairs. Often students are asked to choose one or two ideas to take forward from C. Encouraging students to make choices is an important part of this course, because it promotes engagement and critical thinking.

In this level, students are encouraged to write notes to prepare for a presentation, rather than writing it out in full.

### Activity E Practice and Production

**Activity E** is an opportunity for students to practice with a partner and perform or present. For the presentation lessons, a few students each lesson to perform to the class—keep a record so each student gets a chance to perform over the course of the year. If students don't perform to the whole class, have them perform to each other in small groups. At this age, it may not be appropriate to ask students to reflect on how their peers did, in order to avoid any negative comments; instead suggest ways of appreciating each other's efforts, e.g. by clapping or saying *Good job!* For the conversation lessons, it is enough that they have the conversation with a friend; they don't need to perform it. You can go round to monitor and offer praise and support.

The activity ends with a *Reflect* callout feature for students to think about how they did. Encourage them to be honest here and tell them that it is easy to forget to do things when we are nervous, but that speaking gets easier with practice! Notes for the *Reflect* callout are provided in the digital **ETB**.

# Talk About It

## Lesson Objectives

- to prepare and practice a conversation about recommending a book
- to recognize and reproduce /sk/ and /gr/

**Materials**

Video; Audio Track 14; books students have brought in from home (Activity C)

## Warm Up

Have students think about when they go to the library or a bookstore. Write on the board *cover, title, author,* and *type of book* and have students discuss which is the first thing they think about when choosing a book; for example, *I look for a nice picture on the cover / I like an interesting title / I look for authors that I know.*

**A** TB p. 238 **Watch and listen. Which book does Rania choose?**

- Tell students they are going to watch a video of a conversation between a girl named Rania and her friend Natalia choosing a book to read. Write the titles on the board: *Lily B on the Brink of Cool*; *Little Queen*; and *Sarah, Plain and Tall.*
- Ask the comprehension question *Which book does Rania choose?* Ask students to look at the titles and guess which book she chooses. Play the video and then check the answer. Ask more comprehension questions; for example, *What kinds of books does Rania like?* (novels and history) Play the video again and encourage students to notice the girls' body language while they watch.

**Answer**

*Sarah, Plain and Tall*

**B Watch again. Check (✔) the phrases you hear.**

- Have students read the phrases.
- Play the video again and have students check the phrases they hear. Check answers as a class.
- Look at the example together. Explain that *Why don't you ...?* is a way of making a suggestion. Can students find a similar phrase? (*How about ...?*) Ask *How does Rania decide?* (She says, "OK, let's get it.") *How does she show she's interested?* (She says, "It sounds great.") Have students find two questions we use to find out more about a book (What's it about?; What happens?).
- Summarize the functions of the phrases by reiterating that in the dialogue students hear the speakers give suggestions, ask for information, give opinions, and make decisions.

**Answers**

1; 2; 3; 4; 6; 7; 9

## Pronunciation /sk/ and /gr/

TRACK 14 TB p. 214 **Listen and say.**

Demonstrate the two sounds first. Isolate each phoneme in the cluster and elicit how to pronounce it (/s/; /k/). Then put the two sounds together slowly /sk/ and have students repeat it. Do the same for /gr/.

Play the audio and have students repeat the words.

Say *These words are used in the video. What other words do you know with these sounds?* Elicit ideas (e.g. sculpture/grandma) and write them on the board in two columns. Drill the pronunciation of each word.

**Suggested Answers**

/sk/ scooter, skirt, skate, skating, sky; /gr/ grandpa, grandparents, grass, gray, grocery, grab, grumpy

**C Plan. Think about two books to recommend. Complete.**

- Tell students they are going to prepare a conversation about recommending books. Project the infographic using the TTL or write the headings on the board. Do an example with a book most students will know. Elicit the information and complete the infographic. Encourage students to think about the benefits of reading the book.
- Students are now going to plan recommendations about the two books they have brought in. Have them complete the notes about their books individually.

**D Prepare your conversation. Use your ideas from C and the phrases from B.**

- Play the video again as a model.
- Project and fill in the template with the class using your example plan from C. Ask questions to elicit ideas, e.g. *How can you suggest a book? What do you want to know about the book? Does it sound good?* Then ask two volunteers to demonstrate the conversation.
- Have students choose one of their books. Then tell them to work in pairs to prepare conversations, using their notes in C and phrases from B. Students will need to prepare two conversations: one where they recommend a book and one where their partner recommends a book. Remind them to include questions and be ready to answer questions about their book.

**E Practice with a friend.**

- Have students practice their conversations as many times as they like. Remind them to take turns, look at their partner, and listen when their partner is speaking.

## Cool Down

Ask students if they heard about a book they would like to read during the lesson. Give them the opportunity to look at each other's books and make a note of any they would like to read. You will find ideas for a book-swapping scheme in the Writing lesson.

**Practice** **Student's App:** Speaking Skills Practice; Speaking Video

# Lesson 6 Walkthrough: Write About It

The second productive skills lesson focuses on the mechanics of writing, e.g. punctuation, word-building, and sentence-building. There is always a model text, as well as a brainstorm/planning stage, for the final production task. The structure of the lesson is similar to Lesson 5.

## Activity A Contextualized Writing Mechanics

**Activity A** presents the lesson's writing focus through a model text. It is important to ask students comprehension questions to ensure they have understood the text, since they will be expected to produce their own writing based on this model by the end of the lesson. Some additional comprehension questions are provided in the digital **ETB**. The teaching notes take an inductive approach, by encouraging students to look at the model and notice the mechanic.

## Activity B Controlled Practice

**Activity B** builds on A by having students practice using the target writing mechanic. Encourage them to use the model in A as a guide.

## Activity C Planning

**Activity C** teaches students to brainstorm and plan before writing by providing a graphic organizer to help students collate their ideas. Stronger students can be given the Challenge printout from the Resource Bank, which has another column/section to complete.

## Activity D Production: Writing Task

**Activity D** is the productive writing task. Encourage students to do a draft version, then either peer or self-correct, before writing their final version, since research shows that feedback is more useful between drafts and it gets students into the habit of self-correcting. As well as the Challenge printouts, mentioned for C, there are two other writing printouts, which can be downloaded and printed from the Resource Bank: the Standard template can be used by most students for their final written piece. Less-confident students can have the Support printout which gives them more scaffolding to complete the same task as the rest of the class. Stronger students should be encouraged to expand on the model given in A by recycling language from previous lessons and giving more examples where relevant.

As with the Speaking lesson, there is a *Reflect* callout, which relates to the mechanic explored in A and B. Focus on this callout before students write their final draft and give students time to self-correct their work where necessary. Notes are provided in the digital **ETB**.

## Cool Down

Cool Down activities give closure to the lesson. They are designed to get students thinking about what they learned and might include a game to review new language and concepts, or provide an opportunity to share classwork completed during the lesson.

# Write About It

## Lesson Objectives

- to learn the spelling of adverbs ending in *–ly*
- to plan and write a book report

**Materials**

(Optional) Support, Standard, and Challenge writing printouts from the Resource Bank, one per student (Activities C and D)

## Warm Up

Write some of the following adjectives on the board and give students two minutes to find as many as they can in their books. Students can work in pairs and should call out when they have found all the adjectives. Adjectives: *exciting, complicated, boring, interesting, popular, famous, quick, slow, easy, difficult, noisy, quiet, new, clean, surprised, angry, tired.*

**A Read the book report. Underline the adverbs of manner.**

- Introduce students to the concept of a book report. Say *After you read a book, you can write about it to show other people what it is about.* Ask *What does the writer of the book report think about the book?* Give students one or two minutes to read the book report and answer the question. (She really likes it.) Then ask *What information do we find out from the book report?* (title, author, main characters, what happens, the writer's opinion) Have students notice the drawing and elicit that it is the writer's favorite part of the story. Ask *Why is a book report useful to read?* (it tells you about the book and gives and opinion and recommendation to help you decide if you want to read it).
- Have students look quickly at the report and find an adverb. Then have them work individually to read the report again and underline the adverbs.
- Check answers as a class. Ask *Does the book report make you want to read the book? Why or why not?* Encourage students to share their ideas with the class.

**Answers**

angrily; easily; quickly

**B Change the adjectives into adverbs. Complete.**

- Have students look at the adjectives in the box. Check meaning by having students act out each one (e.g. *angry*—make an angry face).
- Ask students how we can make *angry* into an adverb (angrily). Write both adjective and adverb forms onto the board. Ask *How does it change? What is different?* Elicit that adverbs end in *–ly*. Ask *Is anything else different?* Help students notice the spelling change. If necessary, underline the *y* in *angry* and the *i* in *angrily*. Repeat with the next adjective, *careful*. Elicit that this time there are no spelling changes. Ask *When do we make a spelling change?* (when the adjective ends in *y*)
- Have students write the adverbs in the table using A to help them. Then project the answers using the TTL and check them as a class.

**Answers**

angrily; easily; happily
*carefully*; cleverly; loudly; quietly; quickly; sadly; slowly

**C Think about a book you read. Complete the story map.**

- Tell students they are going to plan their own book reports. They can use the book that they used in the Lesson 5 or a different one. Tell students that, if they prefer, they can write a book report on a book they don't like.
- Project the story map using the TTL and do an example using the book report in A. Elicit which information should go in each box of the Story Map. Then tell students to make a story map for the book they have chosen. Remind students that they don't need to write full sentences. Challenge printouts can be handed out now.

**D Write your book report.**

- Have students write their book reports in their notebooks or on paper using their ideas from C. Support printouts can be handed out now.
- Have students self-correct or exchange their work with a friend and peer-correct. You can put a checklist of things for students to look out for on the board (e.g. spelling, use of adjectives and adverbs, verb forms, punctuation).
- Have students write their final versions neatly on paper or on the Standard printouts from the Resource Bank. They can draw a picture of their favorite part of the story/book.

## Cool Down

Play *Twenty Questions* (see TB p. 27) with a book your students will know. This could be one of the books you have discussed during the unit. Alternatively, display three different book covers using the projector or at the front of the classroom.

Example questions: *Is it fiction? Is it a novel? Is the main character a (boy)? Is it about (animals)? Can you read it quickly?*

**Practice** **Student's App:** Writing Practice

# Lesson 7 Walkthrough: Think It Over

The final lesson in the **Language Book** encourages students to reflect on what they have learned and what they want to explore further. Students are not expected to articulate all their ideas in English. It is important that the students reflect for themselves rather than being told what they studied as this gives them another opportunity to develop as independent thinkers while also beginning to take responsibility for their learning and learning styles. This lays the groundwork for Assessment for Learning and Learning to Learn approaches. At this level, their responses will help you to adapt future lessons to suit your students' needs and to make targeted suggestions for further practice. It also serves as a home-school connection tool, allowing parents to see and engage with their children's learning.

### What did I do?

This question focuses students on the activities they did during the unit, both in and outside of the **Language Book**. Help them to recognize that they are able to do a lot of different things, and bring in props to trigger memories.

Encourage students to make a personal and creative response to the question by choosing activities to draw or write about. This allows you to see what students found interesting and challenging, and what they feel they've achieved. Ask students to think about why they enjoyed certain activities and didn't enjoy others. Ask them how they felt when they were doing something they found difficult and how they felt when they had finished the task.

### What did I learn?

The purpose of this question is to find out what students think they have learned, rather than what *you* think they have learned. Explain that ideas can be content-related, as well as to do with language. In early units, brainstorm ideas on the board for students to choose from or to help them think of others. In later units, have students discuss their ideas in pairs, but be careful not to pair quieter students with dominant ones, as it is important for each student to have the opportunity to make a personal response. The digital **ETB** provides differentiation activities to support this question.

### How did I learn? / What was my favorite part?

These two questions alternate across the units. Their purpose is to help students begin to identify personalized learning strategies.

For *How did I learn?* encourage students to think about what helped them to remember something, e.g. repeating something a lot of times in a drill or through a cooperative learning routine, using the **Student's App** on **Navio** at home, or creating a mental picture of the vocabulary.

*What was my favorite part?* gets students to personalize their learning. Encourage them to notice that our favorite part is often the way we learn best. Have students think about how they can make the learning more enjoyable for themselves. This helps them to start taking responsibility for their personal learning journey.

### How well did I do?

This question asks students to evaluate their own progress. However, answers will only be valuable if students feel they can be honest. You may find it helpful to explain what it means to analyze ourselves and to provide some concrete examples to help them understand, e.g. *if you can remember 20 words, color in five books. If you can remember one or two, color in one book.* Let them know that it's OK to color in one book; it just means they need to do more practice. You can suggest targeted practice to suit different students' needs, such as the grammar printouts from the Resource Bank or the **Student's App** on **Navio**.

### What can I do next?

Encourage students to think of all the different ways they can continue their English learning journey outside of the classroom, including use of new media, e.g. apps, video games, vlogs. Brainstorm ideas as a class. In Units 1 and 2, you can use the suggested words as prompts. Encourage students to be creative with their ideas and to make suggestions based on the things they identified as enjoyable. Follow up in the next lesson by asking questions, e.g. *What did your mom say when you sang the song? Tell me about the English movie you watched.*

### Looking Forward

This features a teaser question about the next unit creating excitement and interest, and linking the characters from one setting to the next. This raises awareness of people in a global world having different roles in different situations. Brainstorm possible answers and review these predictions in the first lesson of the next unit to see who was correct.

### Further Review and Recycling

Regular recycling of new language helps increase exposure and build confidence and understanding.

**Put It Together** communicative games come after every two units, providing an opportunity to review and recycle the language learned in the previous lessons. These fun activities are designed to encourage students to use the language in context and to want to play again and again.

**Plays** review and recycle language from Units 1–5 and Units 6–10 in amusing contexts which could be used as performance pieces mid-year or end-of-year.

# Think It Over

## Lesson Objectives

- to review what has been learned in the unit
- to reflect on the unit and their own progress
- to think about learning strategies and how to continue learning at home

## Warm Up

Ask students what the unit theme was (reading/libraries) and write it in the middle of the board. Brainstorm any words or phrases students can think of that relate to the topic. This is a chance to review language and themes from the unit and to bring the topic back into focus. Encourage students to think about the things we read and why, and the importance of books.

**Read the questions and draw or write your answers.**

- Give students time to think about and discuss activities in the unit before they complete each question. Explain that they can choose either to write a few words or sentences or to draw a picture. Allowing students to make a personal response will help them retain knowledge and engage with the learning points.

**What did I do?**

- Give students a few minutes to look back through the unit at the different activities they did. Ask questions about the unit or write questions on the board for students to discuss in pairs or small groups; for example, *What types of books can you read at a library? What types of texts did you look at?*
- Encourage students to identify something in the unit that they found challenging or something that was particularly memorable for them. Students can draw or write about their chosen activity.

**What did I learn?**

- Ask questions about the unit to help students think about what they learned; for example, *What new words do you know? What sentences can you say about the past? What did you learn about libraries? What did you learn about reading? What did you learn about other countries?* Elicit ideas from the class and discuss them together.
- Encourage students to draw a picture or write sentences about their learning outcomes.

**How did I learn?**

- Ask students how they learned the book genre and adjectives in Lesson 1. Elicit ideas (e.g. by listening to the song, by classifying the words, by doing the visualization). Encourage students to think about the spelling and pronunciation of the new words. Ask *What helps you remember how to say and write the new words?*
- Encourage students to think about how they learned throughout the unit (e.g. how they learned the grammar structures and understood their function).
- Have students draw or write about the activities that helped them learn.

**How well did I do?**

- Tell students to color in the number of books that best expresses how well they have learned the unit content (i.e., the more books they color, the more they feel they have learned). Ask *What do you understand? What do you need to practice more?* Encourage students to look back through the unit to see how much they remember, what they did well, and what they found difficult.

**What can I do next?**

- Brainstorm ideas with the class about what they can do to continue to learn (e.g. watch the video again, play the chain game on p. 13 of the **Language Book** again, talk about favorite and least favorite book genres, write another book report). Encourage them to suggest their own ideas for different activities they can do.
- Draw students' attention to the options in the box. Encourage students to think about what they can do at home to improve their English using the verbs in the box as prompts. Some suggestions are: sing the song to a family member, find out more about different types of libraries, find out more about the Netherlands and India, share your completed Think It Over page with your family, and talk to your friends about different books and what they recommend.
- Ask students to choose one or more activities from the list (sing, find out more, share, talk) that they will do to practice their English and share their ideas with a friend.

## Looking Forward

Draw students' attention to the character at the bottom of the page. Ask *Who's this?* and elicit what they remember about her (Millie appears in Vocabulary, p. 10, and in Explore Language 2, p. 16; she did a project about robots; she read a book about penguins; she reads quickly).

Draw students' attention to Millie's question: *Where do I go next?* Encourage students to make predictions about where she goes next and what Unit 2 is about. Tell students they will find out the answer in Lesson 1 of the next unit.

**Practice** **Resource Bank:** Unit Test
**Student's App:** Vocabulary and Grammar Review

# Lesson 1 Walkthrough: Get Ready to Read

There are two sections to this lesson: Section 1 is always a Visible Thinking Routine (VTR). See **TB p. 19** for more on VTRs. Section 2 contains pre-reading activities and previews a reading skill which will be explored in more detail in later lessons. The teaching notes on this page are flexible, so you can tailor lessons to suit your learners. You can either choose to do the VTR and pre-reading activities in one lesson, or alternatively spend longer developing the VTR discussion and start the next lesson with the pre-reading activities, then go straight into the reading. There is no Cool Down activity in the main teaching notes, but an extension activity may be used as a Cool Down.

## Warm Up

**Warm Up** activities are designed to generate interest in the topic and activate schema to help students make connections between their own experiences and the readings. Activities are purposely not vocabulary-focused to give the **Literacy Book** a distinct first language (L1) feel.

The **ETB** provides a quick Two-Minute Review activity for each Lesson 1, which provides a link between the previous unit and the existing unit. You can choose to do both the Two-Minute Review and the Warm Up or just one or the other, to suit the needs of your class.

## Activities A, B, C Visible Thinking Routine: Question Starts / See, Think, Wonder / Think, Pair, Share

**Activities A, B, and C** relate to a Visible Thinking Routine (VTR). Each routine uses a striking image connected to the unit's topic to foster thoughtful and constructive classroom discussions.

For Question Starts and Think, Pair, Share, give students a minute to look at the picture and encourage them to think about what they can see. Have them share their ideas and write useful words on the board. This provides students with a bank of vocabulary to draw on during the discussion part of the routine. Make sure students have enough time to think about their own ideas before they discuss in pairs or groups, as this will lead to a richer discussion.

For See, Think, Wonder, allow students to think silently for one minute at each step of the routine. Then take ideas from the class. After the first flurry of ideas, encourage students to keep looking and to see more things. Explore the difference between students seeing on their own and seeing things together (group discovery). You can allow some discussion in L1 here, but try to re-formulate the students' ideas into simple English. Avoid leading students to an answer by keeping supporting questions open, e.g. *What (else) do you see/think/wonder about the picture? What colors / shapes do you see? Why do you think that?*

Model class discussions for each of the VTRs are provided in the teaching notes. When students are sharing their ideas, encourage other students to say if they agree or not, using language like: *Us too. / We agree. / We have a different idea. / Really?* Make sure you write down students' questions and ideas on construction paper or post-it notes, so you can revisit them later on in the unit.

## Transition

The **Transition** is a discussion question or questions designed to move you smoothly between the two sections of this lesson (VTR and pre-reading activities). This helps students make connections between the ideas they explored in the VTR and the reading. Alternatively, you can use this question as a Warm Up, if you decide to start the pre-reading activities in the next lesson.

## Activity D Activate Schema

**Activity D** poses a discussion question for students to apply the work they did in the VTR even more closely to the unit's topic. Have students discuss the question in pairs before sharing their ideas as a class. You can write up their ideas and suggestions in graphic organizers on the board, to develop critical thinking skills.

## Activity E Skill Preview

**Activity E** previews the unit's reading skill. This will be addressed fully in the second Get Ready to Read lesson. You are not expected to actively teach the skill in Lesson 1. The goal is to introduce the concept gently and attune students to look for and/or use it as they read.

# Literacy

## Get Ready to Read

### Lesson Objectives

- to activate prior knowledge about books and reading
- to guide enquiry and deepen understanding through a Question Starts Visible Thinking Routine (VTR)
- to preview the reading skill of skimming a text

**Materials**

(Optional) VTR printout from the Resource Bank (Activities A, B, C)

### Warm Up

Do a *Gradient Line* to engage students in the topic of reading (see TB p. 26). Ask questions about different reading materials; for example, *I (love) reading comics. How much do you like reading comics?*

### Question Starts

**A Think about the picture. Then brainstorm questions. Write a list.**

Students are going to do a Question Starts VTR to explore the image of the girl who is reading.

- Have students look at the picture for a minute and then say what they can see. If students don't know a word in English, ask them to describe what they see so you can provide the word.
- Draw students' attention to the question words. Ask *What questions do you have about the picture?*
- Give students a few minutes to write questions in their notebooks, based on the prompts.
- Encourage students to raise their hands to suggest questions. Write all suggestions on the board, helping students correct their questions when needed.

**B Look at your list from A. Which questions seem the most interesting? Discuss them with the class.**

- Ask students to look at their list of questions individually and identify the questions they would most like to know the answers to.
- Tell students that they are going to practice negotiation skills by working as a group to decide which three questions they want to ask. Have students work in groups of three to review the questions and discuss possible answers. This will help them decide which questions they think are the most interesting. Have students write the questions in their books. Then discuss them as a class and decide on the most interesting questions.

Here's an example of this part of the routine.

**Teacher:** Which questions seem the most interesting? What do you really want to know?
**Student A:** What book is she reading?
**Teacher:** What do you think?
**Student A:** A school book.
**Teacher:** Does everyone agree?
**Student B:** No, I don't think she's studying.
**Teacher:** Why do you say that?
**Student B:** She's sitting in a big chair. There's no desk.
**Student C:** I think it's a novel. It looks long!
**Teacher:** Great, what else do you want to know?
**Student B:** Who drew the light bulb?

**C What new ideas or questions do you have now? Talk about your ideas with your partner.**

- Encourage students to think about ideas and questions about books and reading globally. They shouldn't limit their ideas to what they see in the picture. Refer students to the example questions and give them a couple of minutes to think of their own questions. Then have students share their questions in pairs and discuss any possible answers.

### Transition

Have students tell a partner about a fictional book they have read recently, giving information about the characters and the setting.

**D Think and discuss. How does reading take us to other times and places?**

- Use one of the examples from the transition activity to focus on where and when a book may be set. Ask *Have you read a book set in the past or the future? Have you read a book set in a different country? What did you learn?*
- Have students work in pairs to discuss books they have read set in a different time or place. Then have them share their ideas with the class. Encourage them to say what they learned or experienced from reading the book.

**E Look quickly at the story on the next page, but don't read all the words. Answer the questions.**

In this activity students will preview the skill of skimming a text to get the gist of the story.

- Have students look at the first page of the story. Encourage them to look at the pictures and focus on "big" content words rather than "small" grammar words. This will help them look through the text more quickly.
- Give them one or two minutes to answer the questions individually. Then have students discuss their ideas in pairs.

**Answers**

1 Alice feels bored. 2 She sees a rabbit.

Now read **The Beginning of Alice's Adventures**

# Lesson 2 Walkthrough: Reading 1, Fiction

The reading lessons aim to support the development of literacy and to foster a love of reading, to encourage students to become lifelong readers. In every unit, there is one fiction and one nonfiction text to engage and appeal to different interests and learners.

In addition, one reading in each unit is supported by a video. Digital storytelling is helpful because it transcends language and culture by engaging students in a way that is both visual and auditory, as well as textual. Learners can make connections to previous experiences more easily, think critically about new information, and use their own knowledge to fill in any gaps in understanding.

Videos can be used as part of the overall reading strategy: as a way of engaging students with the text; as part of the process of analysis; and as a tool to help them interact with the text on a more personal level. The digital **ETB** provides extension activities for each video lesson. If you aren't able to play the video in class, use the Flipped Classroom approach and have students watch it at home prior to the lesson (see **TB p. 15**).

## Warm Up

This **Warm Up** allows you to review the ideas generated at the end of the previous lesson in preparation for the reading. Alternatively, if you are carrying the lesson straight on from the previous page, use this activity to transition between the pre-reading and reading part of the lesson.

## Reading Approach

### First Reading: Engage with the Text

The purpose of the first reading stage is to engage students and help them become familiar with the text. This sets the scene for the comprehension and analysis work that will come next. Before they read, encourage students to identify things in the pictures that they find interesting, surprising, or unusual. Engagement is more important than vocabulary at this stage, so it's fine for students to point if they are unable to name what they see.

For this first exposure to the text read it out loud, play the video, or have students listen to the audio and follow along in their books. To help students feel comfortable and enjoy watching/listening to the story, have everyone seated in a circle at the front of the class. This is a great opportunity for students to see and hear how to read fluently and with expression, so if you are reading, do character voices and use facial expressions where appropriate. Pause only to ask prediction questions, which can help to motivate students and encourage them to want to find out what happens next. Do not spend time analyzing the language at this point, as full comprehension is not necessary for students to enjoy a text.

### Second Reading: Analyze the Text and Features

Ensure students get to explore the text in a variety of ways to keep them motivated and active participants in the learning process. If you read the text out loud in the first reading stage, have students read chorally in the second stage, or have them read silently with or without the audio.

The purpose of the second reading stage is to analyze the text and features using basic comprehension questions provided in the teaching notes and the callout questions from the colored boxes in the **Literacy Book**. The teaching notes tell you the purpose of the questions, e.g. gist, detail, making connections, personalization, fact, language focus and give ideas about how to exploit them.

The digital **ETB** provides extension activities for checking comprehension further, using the video, and highlighting and exploiting each reading genre.

### Third Reading: Interact with the Text

The third reading stage gives students the chance to interact with the text on a more personal level. With fiction texts students are encouraged to role-play or act out the text. This activity allows students to explore what characters are thinking and how they are feeling. They can also experiment with different voices and patterns of intonation. For more ideas on using role-play, see **TB p. 23**.

The video or Story Player is available on the Student's App for students to watch again at home.

## International English

This feature exposes students to differences in vocabulary, language, and spelling between American (US) English and British (UK) English. Elicit that the flag with stars and stripes is for the USA (United States of America), and the flag with crosses is for the UK (United Kingdom). Then elicit that in both countries people speak English but that some words are spelled differently, pronounced differently, or are just different! Tell students that they will see mostly American English words used in this course, but that British English is also correct. It is important that while they are aware of the differences, you and they choose one variety of English to use consistently, especially in exams.

To make the most of this feature, set up a class ebook where students can add the international English words and phrases as they appear in the book. This could be a wiki or shared document that students can access and edit at home.

International English words appear in both the **Language** and **Literacy Books**.

# Fiction: *The Beginning of Alice's Adventures*—Fantasy

## Lesson Objectives

- to read fantasy fiction about the characters Alice and the rabbit
- to explore the SEL competency of self-awareness by labeling and recognizing own and others' emotions
- to make a personal connection to the reading

**Materials**
Audio Tracks 5 and 6; Video

## Warm Up

Ask students what they know about rabbits. Ask questions: *What do rabbits look like? What do they eat? How do they move?* Then have students look at the pictures on pp. 10–11 and identify what is unusual about the rabbit.

## TRACK 5 TB p. 229 Reading Approach

**First Reading: Engage with the Text**

- Ask students to notice the title, text, and characters on the page and use this information to predict ideas about the story.
- Have students sit in a circle to listen to the story the first time you read it. Read the story to students using facial expressions, gesture, and sound effects (e.g. yawning) or play the audio. Students can interact with the story by copying the gestures.
- Ask prediction questions before turning the page; for example, *Where is the rabbit going? What is at the bottom of the hole?*
- Read the whole story before looking at the Words in Context.

## TRACK 6 TB p. 229 Words in Context

- Play the audio and have students repeat the words.
- Have students race to find the words in the reading.
- Encourage students **to use the pictures to help establish the meaning of the new words.** Have them discuss their ideas in pairs.
- Then bring the class together and use these questions to confirm the meanings.

**sleepy** (p. 10) Say *How do you feel when it's hot and you aren't doing anything?* Have students look at Alice in the first scene. How does she feel? Elicit the synonym *tired*.

**chased** (p. 12) Say *The rabbit runs away. What does Alice do?* Elicit that *run after* and *chase* are synonyms.

**fell** (p. 13) Encourage students to look at the pictures. Ask *What is happening to Alice?* (She's falling.) Elicit that *fell* is the simple past of *fall*.

**shelves** (p. 13) Ask *Where are the books?* (on the shelves) If there are shelves in the classroom, have students point them out.

**corner** (p. 14) Ask *Where did the rabbit run?* (around the corner) *Can Alice see him?* (no) *Why not?* (because there is a wall) You could draw a corner on the board to help comprehension.

**Second Reading: Analyze the Text and Features**

- Play the video to consolidate students' understanding of the story.
- Ask some questions to check comprehension: *Who's the main character in the story?* (Alice) *What does she do?* (She follows the rabbit.) The **ETB** provides more questions.
- Discuss the questions in the green boxes.
    - **Language in Context** (p. 10): *What do you think* Goodness me! *means?* Make a connection to the SEL competency of labeling and recognizing emotions by asking students how Alice feels when she sees the rabbit (surprised) and why (because it's wearing a waistcoat). Elicit that we say "Goodness me!" when we are surprised.
    - **Fun Fact** (p. 11): *Lewis Carroll wrote* Alice's Adventures in Wonderland *in 1865. Today, it's in over 170 languages!* Have students suggest some of the languages the book might be in. How many can they think of? You could suggest students visit the local library to see if they have a copy.
    - **Personalization** (p. 13): *Imagine you fell through the Earth. Where would you land?* Accept any suggestions. You could show students a globe and have them see which country is on the opposite side to theirs.
    - **Critical Thinking** (p. 15): *Did the adventure really happen, or did Alice imagine it?* Remind students that in fictional stories anything can happen, even if it is impossible in real life. Take a class vote on this question.

**Third Reading: Interact with the Text**

- Have students read and act out the story in groups of three: a narrator, Alice, and the rabbit. Encourage students to use actions and gesture as they read together. For more ideas on using role-play, see TB p. 23.

**International English**

Point to the flags and elicit which words are American English and which words are British English. Ask *Why do you think the story uses the British English word?* (Lewis Carroll was a British writer.)

## Cool Down

Have students choose their favorite image, scene, and/or phrase from the story; for example, *I like the colors; I like the repetition of "down, down, down."* Allow students to use L1 to justify their choices where necessary.

**Practice** **Student's App:** Fiction Video

# Lesson 3 Walkthrough: Explore the Reading

This lesson allows students to explore the previous text further with comprehension, analysis and discussion activities.

## Activity A Reading Comprehension

Start this lesson with oral comprehension questions to remind students about the text. Have a Group Time discussion about the story (see **TB p. 21**). The teaching notes suggest *Wh- questions* you can ask to help students to remember the gist and details of the reading (who, where, what, when, why). Play the video to review the story if you don't want to read the text as a class again.

The lesson then moves on to a heads-down activity which allows you to check students' understanding of the reading. If there are areas that you find students don't understand, you can return to the text and address these before moving on to the analysis part of the lesson.

## Activity B Text Analysis

**Activity B** is an age-appropriate analysis task, which asks students to think critically about what they have read and to consider the causes, problems, solutions, or consequences. They will need to look back at the reading to answer questions. Help students find a strategy for doing this by encouraging them to look at the pictures and scan the text for key words, rather than re-reading the whole text again.

## Activity B/C/D Post Reading Discussion, Writing, & SEL

One activity in each fiction Explore the Reading lesson has a SEL focus. Productive think and write or discuss questions are designed to help students make connections between the text and their own knowledge and understanding of the world through a SEL competency. There are often opportunities here for critical literacy, as students can be encouraged to consider the point of view of different characters.

# Explore the Reading

## Lesson Objectives

- to understand and analyze *The Beginning of Alice's Adventures* through reading comprehension activities
- to explore the SEL competency of self-awareness by labeling and recognizing one's own and others' emotions

**Materials**
(Optional) Video or Audio Track 5

## Warm Up

Have students secretly choose a scene from *The Beginning of Alice's Adventures* and act it out silently using gestures and facial expressions. The other students try to find the scene in their books. Do an example with the class and then have students do the activity in pairs. Finally, have students act out the scene with the words. Because they have already focused on the gestures and facial expressions only, they should incorporate them more easily when they act out the scene.

### A Read and number. Put the events in order.

- If more than one day has passed since students read *The Beginning of Alice's Adventures*, play the video or audio again.
- With books closed, have a Group Time discussion (see TB p. 21) to check students' comprehension of the text. Ask *How does Alice feel at the beginning of the story?* (bored and sleepy) *What did she see?* (a white rabbit) *Why did the rabbit run off?* (He was late.) *Where did Alice fall?* (down a hole) *What did Alice find on the table?* (a key) *Do you think that Alice had more adventures?* (Yes—but this is implied, and students may find it tricky to answer.)
- Have students open their books and look at the first sentence in A. Have students look back at the story and find the event. (It is in the opening sentence and picture.) Say *Which event comes next?* and elicit answers.
- Have students do the rest of the activity individually. Check answers as a class.

**Answers**
6, 4, 1, 3, 5, 2

### B Look and write. How do they feel?

This activity explores the SEL competency of labeling and recognizing one's own and others' emotions.

- Review the meanings of the words in the box by having students use gestures and facial expressions to represent them. Do an example first. Then have students call out examples of things that make them feel this way: *Tests make me worried; When it's raining, I'm bored.*
- Look at the example together, then have students complete the activity. Check answers as a class.
- Ask students how Alice felt at different points in the story. Encourage them to give reasons; for example, *Alice was bored because she had nothing to do.* Then have them say how they would feel and what they would do in the same situation; for example, *I (would) feel bored, too. I would climb a tree.* Use students' suggestions to have them think about how the story could change; for example, *If Alice climbed a tree, would she see the white rabbit? How would the story be different?*

**Answers**
1 *surprised* 2 interested 3 bored 4 worried

### C Think and discuss. Do you have a big imagination like Alice? What do you imagine?

- Elicit how Alice uses her imagination when she feels bored. Draw a big thought cloud on the board and write students' suggestions inside. Ask *Does Alice have a big imagination?* (yes)
- Draw students' attention to the questions: *Do you have a big imagination like Alice? What do you imagine?* Have two students model asking and answering the questions. Then have students do a Think, Pair, Share routine (see TB p. 20) to explore the questions.
- During the Share part of the routine, encourage students to say *Me, too!* if they imagine similar things to other students. Then ask questions about what some of the students said; for example, *What does (Lara) imagine when she's happy? What does (Juan) imagine when he's bored?*

## Cool Down

Play *Correct the Teacher* (see TB p. 25). Have students make rabbit ears with their hands on their heads for true sentences. Example sentences: *Alice was hot; Alice didn't have anything to do; the rabbit wore a pink waistcoat; the rabbit stopped and looked at his cell phone; Alice fell down a big hole; Alice knew about geography.*

**Practice** Student's App: Reading Practice

# Lesson 4 Walkthrough: Get Ready to Read

This lesson provides pre-reading activities, including a reading skill focus, to prepare students for the second text.

### Activity A Reading Skill Focus

**Activity A** practices the reading skill that was previewed in Lesson 1. It takes an inductive approach to learning, with students being encouraged to practice the reading skill and notice how it can help them understand the reading before the skill is named in the skills box.

Callouts in colored boxes highlight facts or questions for students to focus on and can be used as a starting point for discussion.

### Activity B Reading Skill Practice

**Activity B** allows students to practice the reading skill from Activity A and apply it to the forthcoming reading. When they have finished, discuss what students think and encourage them to say why they think it.

### Activity C Pre-Reading Discussion

**Activity C** is a discussion question relating to the reading on the next pages. The discussion question personalizes the learning and encourages students to become active participants, by asking them either to connect the reading to their own lives or to think and express opinions. You can vary the activity by using a Cooperative Learning Routine such as a Rally Robin or a Think, Pair, Share (see **TB p. 20**).

### Cool Down

Cool Down activities give closure to the lesson. They are designed to get students thinking about what they learned and might include a game to review reading skills or an activity to encourage students to make a personal response to what they have read.

## Get Ready to Read

### Lesson Objectives

- to practice the reading skill of skimming a text
- to activate prior knowledge about learning and the brain
- to make a personal connection to the reading

**Materials**

(Optional) Rulers or measuring tapes (Activity A)

### Warm Up

Have students work in pairs to remember three important things from *The Beginning of Alice's Adventures*. Then have students get together with another pair and compare their ideas. Do they think the same things are important? This helps students practice identifying key ideas that they will develop further in A.

**A Read quickly. Don't read all the words. Write three important pieces of information. Then discuss.**

Students are going to practice the reading skill of skimming a text.

- Before students attempt the activity, demonstrate the reading skill with books closed. Display a nonfiction text (ideally an infographic about the importance of reading) on the whiteboard and model skimming for the class. Skimming is a quick reading strategy to get the main idea. When we skim, we look for main ideas. Headings, titles, words in bold, the introductory paragraph, and the topic or first and last sentences of paragraphs can give us useful information about a text. Show how you go through the text looking for main ideas, picking out headings and words in bold and looking at the very beginning and end of the text.
- Draw students' attention to the instructions and check they know what to do. You may wish to set a time limit of one minute to make sure students don't read all the words. Encourage students to write down any words or phrases that jump out at them and that they feel are important.
- When students have finished writing their ideas, discuss as a class. During the class discussion, tally how many students gave the same answers. Then read the skills box. Ask students which words helped them know what the reading was about.

**Answers**

Students' own answers

- Point out the fact in the green box, *38 centimeters = 15 inches*. Ask *How big is the door?* See if students can use their hands to show how big they think it is. Ask students which measurements they usually use in L1. You could have students use a ruler or measuring tape to check.

**B Skim *Learning and Your Brain* on the next page. What is it about? Check (✔).**

- Draw students' attention to the instructions. Ask *How to do we skim?* (We look at the title, headings, captions, and first and last sentences to get the main idea.) Ask *Do we read all the words?* (no) *Which words don't we need to pay attention to?* (the small grammar words, e.g. *a*, *the*, *is*, *are*, etc.) Give students one to two minutes to skim the reading on pp. 18–19.
- Explain that a reading can have more than one main idea. Have students read the options and decide if each one is a main idea in the reading. Check answers as a class.

**Answer**

2; 3

**C Think and discuss. What do you know about the brain? What does the brain do?**

- Brainstorm with the class what students know about the brain. One way is to make a class KWL (know, want to know, learned) poster. Start by asking students what they know about the brain and record their ideas in the *Know* section.
- Have students discuss their ideas in pairs or small groups.
- Then ask students if they have any questions about the brain. Encourage them to think of *Wh-* questions rather than yes/no questions. Write the questions in the *Want to Know* section of the poster. Discuss with students how they can find out more. Could they research at home? Do they know someone (such as a doctor) who could help explain how the brain works? Can they find any books at school or in a library that have the information? Come back to this poster during the unit and have students add anything they have learned.

### Cool Down

Have students work in groups of four and compare their ideas from C. They can work together to make a spidergram of all the things they use their brains for. Display the spidergrams around the classroom and have students look at the other groups' work. Tell them to find at least one new idea each and to add it to their own spidergram.

Now read **Learning and Your Brain**

# Lesson 5 Walkthrough: Reading 2, Nonfiction

The structure of the reading lessons whether fiction or nonfiction, allows students to be exposed to the text multiple times. This helps them to connect oral and written forms, which is important for the development of reading skills. There is a focus on reading for analysis and pleasure, rather than simple mechanics. Students will gain independence with each reading as you progress through the course.

Fiction texts are laid out to emulate storybooks inspired by ESL/L1 materials and expose students to language in context which may be slightly above level. This is because research shows that with the right support, reading slightly above level can significantly improve overall reading skills.

Nonfiction texts give students a chance to learn new concepts and vocabulary, as well as broaden their view of the world. They also often appeal to reluctant readers. Nonfiction texts are laid out to look like nonfiction books, websites, and articles to give a realistic and aspirational feel to the book.

## Warm Up

See **TB p. 50**.

## Reading Approach

The three-step reading approach is the same for fiction and nonfiction texts (see **TB p. 50**). The teaching notes give a lot of different ideas to use within these steps throughout the course.

One reading in each unit includes a Text Focus point written in blue with arrows pointing to the area of the text being highlighted. The teaching notes provide support to help you address these Text Focus points as part of the second reading stage. There is always an additional extension activity in the **ETB** to give students additional practice.

## Words in Context

Each reading lesson has a **Words in Context** box which pulls out certain key words from the text for students to explore in greater detail. It is recommended you look at these Words in Context after the students have read the text at least once through. This is so that the first reading can be about enjoyment and engagement, rather than vocabulary learning. Don't pre-teach these words; it is more valuable to offer students strategies to help them decode the meaning for themselves. Different strategies are suggested in the notes, with more detail on **TB p. 22**.

Introduce a different strategy in each lesson and encourage pairs to use a combination of strategies to help them figure out the meaning of the words. It is fine for students to use L1 for this, to enable them to express their thoughts and ideas clearly. Ask students which strategies they used to help them understand the new words.

Then ask questions (provided in the notes) to check understanding and clarify meaning. Effectively you are providing students with tools which will help them to figure out the meaning of other unfamiliar words they encounter in the future.

It should be noted that these words have been highlighted to help students' comprehension of the texts; they are not part of the course's key language and will not appear in any assessment material.

# Nonfiction: *Learning and Your Brain*—Infographic

## Lesson Objectives

- to read an infographic / informational text about the benefits of reading on the brain
- to make a personal connection to the reading

**Materials**
Audio Tracks 7 and 8

## Warm Up

Play *Stand Up, Sit Down* (see TB p. 27) with these statements based on the reading. Have students guess whether they're true or false. *You use one part of your brain when you read* (False); *When you practice something, you get better at it* (True); *Reading is bad for your brain* (False). Don't check answers at this stage.

## TRACK 7 TB p. 230 Reading Approach

**First Reading: Engage with the Text**

- Ask students to notice the title, text, and pictures on the page. Ask *What interesting information about the brain do you think we will learn in the reading?*
- Have students read silently. Remind them that they don't need to know every word. Once they have finished, check the answers from the Warm Up. Have students say which true statement is the most interesting or surprising for them.
- Then, look at the Words in Context.

## TRACK 8 TB p. 230 Words in Context

- Play the audio and have students repeat the words.
- Have students race to find the words in the reading.
- **Use the words around the new words to guess their meaning.** Encourage students to identify other words that mean the same, or that have a connection to the new words (see TB p. 23). Students may come up with the following: lobes/parts; workout/exercise; cells/neurons; fibers/branches; messages/information; connecting/join together; creative/imagination.
- Then bring the class together and use these discussion points to confirm the meanings.

**lobes** (p. 18) Ask *How many lobes, or parts, does the human brain have?* (four). Have students point to them in the picture.

**workout** (p. 18) Say *If you do a lot of sports and exercise, your body is in good shape. If you read and learn, your brain is in good shape. Learning is like going to the gym for your brain. How do you give your body and brain a workout?*

**cells** (p. 20) Encourage students to look at the picture. Explain that all living things (people, animals, and plants) are made of *cells* and that these work together to make each part of the body.

**fibers** (p. 20) Have students look at the first part of the sentence on p. 20 *Each neuron has a body with fibers.* Ask *Can you see the neuron's body?* Then have them read the second part *like the branches of a tree.* Have students point to the fibers in the picture.

**messages** (p. 20) Say *Neurons send messages* and draw an envelope between two neurons. Elicit or provide synonyms (*information, signals*). Ask what messages students think their brains are sending right now.

**connecting** (p. 20) Have students look at the picture and point out how the neurons are *connecting* to each other.

**creative** (p. 20) Ask *If you have a lot of ideas and you use your imagination, are you creative?* Ask students to give examples of how they are creative.

## International English

Have students notice the spelling differences. Say the words and point out that the pronunciation is the same.

**Second Reading: Analyze the Text and Features**

- Play the audio and have students follow along in their books. Check comprehension after each page by asking questions such as *Which part of the brain do you use when you speak?* (the front part)
- Play the audio again and pause to discuss the questions in the green boxes as they appear on the pages.
  - **Critical Thinking** (p. 18): *What parts of your brain do you use when you read?* Have students discuss in pairs which parts of the brain they think they use when reading. Encourage them to look at the images and text to justify their answer (seeing, hearing, speaking).
  - **Fun Fact** (p. 20): *Your brain uses about 20 percent of all your energy!* Ask *Do you think that's a lot?* Tell students that a brain only weighs about two percent of person's body weight. So even if you don't move, you are still using a lot of energy.
  - **Gist** (p. 21): *Why is learning good for your brain?* (It keeps the brain in good shape.)
- Point out the text focus (in blue): *Labels help you understand different parts of the picture.* Have students identify all the labels.

**Third Reading: Interact with the Text**

- Now play *Correct the Teacher* (see TB p. 25) with the text.
  Example sentence: *When you read, different parts of your brain work together like a giraffe!*

## Cool Down

Have students choose one thing they are going to do to try to keep their brain in shape. Offer some suggestions (e.g. read a book, play a musical instrument, do word/jigsaw puzzles, play memory games, learn a foreign language).

# Lesson 6 Walkthrough: Explore the Reading

This lesson follows the same structure as the first Explore the Reading lesson with comprehension, analysis, and discussion activities to explore the second reading text. It also provides further practice of the reading skill.

### Activity A Reading Comprehension

Before doing **Activity A**, have a Group Time discussion (see **TB p. 21**) with books closed to check students' comprehension of the text. This can be a nice routine to have at the beginning of each Explore the Reading lesson.

### Activity B Text Analysis and Practice

**Activity B** usually involves practicing the unit reading skill. Have students answer the questions individually first. Then they can look back at the reading in pairs to check their answers.

### Activity C/D Post-Reading Discussion, Writing & CLIL Focus

One activity in each nonfiction Explore the Reading lesson has a CLIL focus. Productive think and write or discuss questions enable students to learn about a subject area through the reading and to see language used in a real-world context.

Questions can be discussed in pairs or small groups. Then have a class discussion and write students' keys ideas on the board in the style of a survey. Display results in a bar graph or tally chart to lay the foundations for reasoning skills and teaching students to analyze data.

### Spelling Patterns

A spelling pattern box is always attached to one of the Explore the Reading lessons in each unit. This highlights a high-frequency letter combination with examples taken from the previous reading.

The spelling activity is supported by audio, but the focus of the activity should be on reading and spelling (there is targeted pronunciation work in the **Language Book**).

Students listen to a set of words with a letter pattern, notice where those letters appear, and complete the words to reinforce understanding. What matters most at this stage is that students are actively thinking about how written words are constructed.

The second part of the audio spells out each word, allowing students to check and correct their spelling. Students should be encouraged to read the words aloud to establish a connection between the sound of the word and the way it is written.

Finally, students find other words within the reading with the same spelling patterns. Making connections with other words reinforces pattern recognition and helps students learn to decode more effectively when reading.

The digital **ETB** provides additional activities to encourage students to spot letter patterns and sort words into groups based on these patterns. See Spelling Patterns, **TB p. 13**.

## Explore the Reading

### Lesson Objectives

- to understand and analyze *Learning and Your Brain* through reading comprehension activities
- to make a personal connection to the reading
- to learn about neuroscience through CLIL (science): exploring how we can keep our brains in shape
- to reproduce and write words with the *–er* ending

**Materials**
Audio Tracks 7 and 9

### Warm Up

Play *Mime It!* (see TB p. 26). Use the following words from the reading: *neuron, strong, speech, connecting, imagination, goal.* Students will have to use their imagination!

**A Write *True* or *False*. Say the page where you found the answer.**

- If more than a day has passed since students read *Learning and Your Brain*, play the audio again. Students can follow in their books if they wish.
- With books closed, have a Group Time discussion (see TB p. 21) to check students' comprehension of the text. Ask *Does your brain work hard when you read and learn?* (yes) *What is your brain made up of?* (cells/neurons; water) *How can reading make us more creative?* (It makes connections in the brain stronger.) *What different actions are mentioned in the reading?* (solving math problems, kicking a ball, listening to music, reading)
- Have students open their books and look at the activity. Have a student read the first sentence. Ask *True or false?* (False) Have students look back at the reading and find the sentence with the correct information.
- Have students do the rest of the activity individually. Check answers as a class, making sure students say on which page they found their answer.

**Answers**
1 False; 20 2 True; 20 3 True; 18 4 True; 20
5 False; 20

**B Read and color the parts of the brain.**

- Place four flashcards for the following colors, each in a different part of the classroom: red, purple, green, and yellow. Refer students to the key on the page. Have students stand in the middle of the classroom. Call out activities that use different parts of the brain; for example, *You taste a cake; You see a cat; You say your name; You listen to the ocean; You touch the table.* Students should go and stand next to the relevant color.
- Have students color a circle inside the different parts of the brain by looking back at the diagrams in the reading. Check answers as a class.

**Answers**
1 red 2 green 3 yellow 4 purple

**C Think and discuss. Do you give your brain a good workout?**

Students are going to do a Think, Pair, Share routine (see TB p. 20) to discuss the question and connect the reading with their own habits. This draws on the CLIL science focus of exploring how we can keep our brains in shape.

- Encourage students to think about the different types of activities that are good for the brain. As an example, ask *Do you read at different times of the day?* Ask students to think about when they could read more. You could suggest that students set themselves a reading target (e.g. read five pages every day). If students are interested, expand the discussion to ask *What do you do well? What do you need to work on? How can you get better?*

### TRACK 9 TB p. 230 Spelling Pattern *–er*

**Listen and write. Then check your answers.**

- With books closed, write the suffix *–er* on the board and elicit how to pronounce it, making sure students pronounce the *schwa* correctly.
- Play the first part of the audio and have students repeat each word. Then have them open their books. Play the first part of the audio again and have them complete as many words as they can.
- Then play the second part of the audio for students to check their spelling and complete the words correctly. Have them underline *er* in each word and read them aloud.
- Have students look back at the reading to find more words with the *–er* ending and write them down in a word list. Give them one or two minutes, then invite students to read a word from their list.

**Answers**
1 computer 2 water 3 answer 4 flower 5 river
In the reading: together, another, teacher, fiber(s), stronger, other

### Cool Down

Have students work in pairs to write a silly sentence containing as many *–er* words as they can, e.g. *flowers and towers get bigger in a river.* They can then perform their sentence to the class or write it on the board and have the other students practice it.

**Practice** **Resource Bank:** Spelling Printout
**Student's App:** Reading Practice; Spelling Pattern Practice

# Lesson 7 Walkthrough: Think Together

This lesson brings the unit full circle to consider the key concept question. This acts as the thread for all the lessons related to the readings. The teaching notes support you to address this question.

## Warm Up

Students are encouraged to revisit the Lesson 1 VTR image to see if their perceptions have changed or shifted now that they know more about the topic. Review their initial ideas and see if students can offer more information or link the image more explicitly to the unit's topic.

In the digital **ETB** there is a Two-Minute Review idea. This is a quick, fun activity which reviews both of the readings in the unit to help students make connections between the two. You can choose to do this instead of, or as well as, the Warm Up.

## Activity A Text Comparison

**Activity A** is a text-to-text comparison task which lays the foundations for more communicative comparison analysis in higher levels. Learning how to compare and contrast is an important skill which has been shown to: improve students' ability to memorize content; develop higher-order thinking skills; strengthen comprehension skills; and improve writing skills.

If you have not done the Two-Minute Review, it may be beneficial to have students brainstorm what they remember about both texts before you start.

## Activities B/C Speaking Routine

**Activities B** and **C** have a text-to-world base. Students are first given time to think and make connections to prior knowledge. They then explore ideas through a cooperative learning routine, such as Rally Robin, Three-step Interview, or Numbered Heads Together (see **TB p. 20**). Cooperative learning routines create opportunities for purposeful communication and collaboration which encourages students to become actively engaged in their learning.

## My Reading Journal

**My Reading Journal** allows students to give a personalized response to the readings and reflect on the unit as a whole. The goal is to foster self-reflection as a learning tool, to help students to see the importance of the learning process, to encourage them to think critically about texts and to express preferences, and motivate and empower them to want to learn more.

## Think Together

### Lesson Objectives

- to make connections between the readings
- to explore the key concept: Why is reading important?
- to reflect on the unit and provide personal thoughts and opinions

### Warm Up

Have students look back at the VTR picture on pp. 8–9. Ask them how they think the picture connects to the two readings in the unit. Encourage students to be creative in their answers; e.g. *Maybe the girl's name is Alice; I think the girl is having a dream that she's in a library; The light(bulb) shows she is learning; The book she's reading is about the brain.*

Introduce the key concept question *Why is reading important?* and ask students for their initial thoughts. Write their ideas on the board in a spidergram, to return to later in the lesson.

**A What different types of things do we read? Why do we read them? Complete the table.**

- Brainstorm with the class a list of different types of reading materials. These may include stories, poems, plays, comics, newspapers, maps, instructions, letters, invitations, signs, emails, and advertisements. Elicit other reasons to read besides for fun and information. Have students think about why we read each type of text (e.g. we read a map to know where we are / where to go; we read a sign for information).
- Draw students' attention to the table on p. 23 and look at the two examples.
- Have students complete the table individually. Students can include names of books or other reading materials they have read. Then have students compare their ideas with a friend.

**Answers**
Students' own answers

**B Think and write. Why is it important to read different things?**

- Have students think about the things they read every day and brainstorm some ideas with the class. Ask *Why is it important to read different things?* Encourage students to think about all the text types mentioned in A.
- Give students a few minutes to do the activity individually. Monitor and help by writing any problematic words on the board. Don't check answers yet.

**Suggested Answer**
You can find out different information and opinions; learn about the world; use your imagination; have fun; learn about other people; keep in touch with your friends; and find out about events.

**C Discuss your ideas. Then share with your class. Do a Numbered Heads Together routine.**

- Students are going to discuss their ideas in groups and then share with the class. Set the class up for the Numbered Heads Together routine (see TB p. 20). Students have already written their ideas in B.
- Recap the ideas students shared by referring back to the key concept question. Ask students what else they can add to the spidergram.
- Ask students to decide which idea is the most important for them and why.

### My Reading Journal

**Did you like the fiction or the nonfiction reading better? Why? Write.**

This question focuses on personalization. Ask a volunteer which reading he/she liked best. Elicit ideas about why people might like each one; for example, *The story is funny. I want to know what happens next. / I want to know more about the brain.* Ask *Why are both reading genres important?*

Have students complete the sentence about the reading they liked best. Then they can compare with a partner.

**Example Answer**
I liked the (fiction) reading better, because (the story was interesting and the pictures were beautiful).

**Color the rabbits to rate the unit. Then write a short review.**

This task focuses on evaluation. Remind students that in a review we write our opinion about something. Elicit what someone might say if they gave a 5 (rabbits) rating. (*I thought this unit was excellent. I really loved the story.*)

Give students a few minutes to look back through the unit. Have them complete their reading journals individually, monitoring and providing language help when needed. Then ask students what their favorite part of the unit was.

**Example Answer**
I thought this unit was very good. The story was fun, and I want to know what happens to Alice. I learned a lot about the brain.

### Cool Down

Have students work in groups of three to write three quiz questions about the unit. The questions can be about the two readings, the VTR picture, or the Spelling Pattern section. Students can choose to write true or false questions, multiple-choice questions, or challenge questions (e.g. name five words ending in *–er*). Then they pass the questions to another group to answer.

**Practice** **Resource Bank:** Unit Test
**Student's App:** Key Concept Practice

UNIT 2

# What Lives Here?

## Unit Overview

### Themes

Plants, animals, and the environments they live in

Ecology and the importance of trees and plants

### Synopsis

In this unit, students will explore how plants, animals, and humans are connected in our world. They will learn about different biomes and their characteristics, and explore the importance of respecting and looking after living things and places in nature. Students will plan and prepare a presentation describing a biome and write instructions on how to grow a plant.

### Language Book

**Vocabulary**

*biome, camel, cheetah, desert, dry, forest, grassland, plants, polar bear, tundra, wet, wolf,*

p. 64

**Explore Language**

Comparatives and Superlatives: Short and Long Adjectives

p. 65

**Global Citizenship**

How do plants grow in difficult climates?

*bud, flower, ground, leaves, petal, pollen, roots, seeds, shoot, stem*

p. 66

**Explore Language**

Comparatives and Superlatives: Short and Long Adverbs

p. 67

**Take the Stage**

Presentation: describing biomes

p. 68

**Write About It**

Writing Instructions

Sentence Building: sequencers

p. 69

**Think It Over**

Review and Reflection

p. 70

## Literacy Book

### Think Together
How are plants, animals, and humans connected?
p. 77

### Visible Thinking
See, Think, Wonder
p. 71

### Fiction
Folk Tale: *A New Friend*
Words in Context: *swallow, roof, hit, slingshot, paid*
p. 75

### Nonfiction
Informational Text: *Two Different Forests*
Words in Context: *deciduous, hibernate, coniferous, survive, adapt*
p. 72

### Reading Skill
Understanding the author's purpose
p. 74

### Spelling Pattern
*ai*
p. 76

### Language and Literacy Connections
The connecting theme in Unit 2 is biomes and their features.

| | Language | Literacy |
|---|---|---|
| **Vocabulary** | **Set 1:** the world around us<br>**Set 2:** plants | **Nonfiction:** biome, forest, flower(s), ground, leaves, plants<br>**Fiction:** stem |
| **Grammar** | **Comparatives and Superlatives: Short and Long Adjectives**<br>This lion's bigger than the cheetah.<br>Elephants are more dangerous than lions.<br>Is the lion the biggest animal?<br>Elephants are the most dangerous animals.<br>**Comparatives and Superlatives: Short and Long Adverbs**<br>It grows more quickly than the plant next to it.<br>Desert plants grow the most slowly of all. | **Nonfiction**<br>Many of them grow in places that have longer and colder winters. This means that the summers are shorter and cooler, too.<br>**Fiction**<br>Spring is the best season.<br>The plant grew bigger. It had a dark green stem and the most beautiful leaves. |
| **Skills** | **Pronunciation:** /**pl**/ and /**kl**/ | **Reading:** understanding the author's purpose<br>**Spelling Pattern:** *ai* |
| **International English** | plastic wrap / cling film | slingshot/catapult |

## Vocabulary

### Lesson Objectives

- to learn vocabulary to describe the world around us: *camel, cheetah, polar bear, wolf; biome, desert, dry, forest, grassland, plants, tundra, wet*
- to sing a song that explores different homes and habitats

**Materials**
Audio Tracks 15 to 18; Video

### Warm Up

Play the *Alphabet Game* with the topic of animals (see TB p. 25).

**A** TRACK 15 TB p. 214 **Listen and find. Which four biomes do the girls see?**

- Have students look at the pictures and say what they see. Ask if students can see any animals from their list in the Warm Up. Draw students' attention to the gist question *Which four biomes do the girls see?* and ask a volunteer to try to explain what a biome is by looking at the examples in the picture. (It is an area with its own plants, animals, and weather.) Ask *What can you see in each one?* Encourage students to use both adjectives and nouns to describe what they can see.
- Tell students they are going to listen to Millie and Tess talking about the biomes. Ask *Can you find them?* (They are in the cable car.) Remind students of the challenge from the end of Unit 1. Ask *Where did Millie go next?* (the biome park) Explain that a biome park is a place where you can see examples of different natural spaces from around the world.
- Play the audio and have students point to the words or pictures as they listen.
- Ask the gist question *Which four biomes do the girls see?* and elicit the answer. Play the audio again for students to check.

**Answer**
forest, tundra, desert, grassland

**B** TRACK 16 TB p. 214 **Listen, say, and number the pictures in A.**

- Play the audio and have students point to the pictures and say the words.
- Tell students to listen again and write numbers next to the words in the picture. Do the example together (desert). If students need more time to write their answers, pause the audio.
- Check answers by calling out a number and having students call out the word. Alternatively, project the answers using the TTL.

**Answers**
1 *desert* 2 forest 3 tundra 4 grassland 5 camel
6 cheetah 7 wolf 8 polar bear 9 wet 10 dry
11 biome 12 plants

**C** TRACK 17 TB p. 214 **Close your eyes. Listen, visualize, and say.**

- Prepare students for the visualization (see TB p. 21).
- Play the audio, allowing students to visualize and act out the ideas as they listen. Make sure students know not to speak until they hear the word *say*. Put your finger to your lips if necessary.
- Have students choose one of the biomes from the visualization and draw a picture. They can add animals and climate features (e.g. rain) to their pictures. Then have students show each other their pictures, describing what they drew.

**D Look and write.**

- Students are going to categorize the vocabulary. This encourages critical thinking, because students must group words in a logical or meaningful way. Point to the table and elicit that some of the words in A are biomes, some are animals, and others are climates (weather). Look at the examples together.
- Tell students to write the words from A in the table. Then check answers as a class. You could project the answers using the TTL.

**Answers**
Biomes: *forest*; tundra; desert; grassland
Animals: cheetah; camel; polar bear; wolf
Climate: wet; dry

**E** TRACK 18 TB p. 214 **Listen and complete. Then watch and sing.**

- Point to the song title *Different Homes* and elicit the homes that appear in A. Ask *What plants and animals live there?* Explain that these are the four main land biomes but that there are also aquatic biomes for oceans and rivers. Then play the song once, allowing students to listen and enjoy it.
- Explain to students that some of the words are missing and they have to complete them. Ask *Can you guess what words they are?* Play the song again, this time pausing where necessary for students to write their answers.
- Check answers as a class.
- Play the song video and encourage students to sing and move to the music as they watch.

**Answers**
1 *desert* 2 camel 3 tundra 4 polar bear
5 grassland 6 cheetah 7 forest 8 wolf

### Cool Down

Give students a critical-thinking question to discuss in pairs or small groups; for example, *Would you rather live in the desert or the tundra?* Tell students to think of the different aspects of each biome (animals, plants) and to think about how easy or difficult it would be to live there (e.g. food and climate).

**Practice** Student's App: Vocabulary Practice; Song Video

# Explore Language

## Lesson Objectives

- to review comparative and superlative adjectives
- to practice vocabulary to describe the world around us

**Materials**
Audio Tracks 19 and 20

## Warm Up

Write *grassland* on the board. Elicit words students associate with this biome. Write the words on the board. Encourage students to name plants and animals that live in the grassland (grass, trees, zebras, lions, cheetahs, elephants, etc.).

**A** TRACK 19 TB p. 214 **Listen and read. Which animals do the girls talk about?**

- Remind students of the scene on pp. 22–23. Ask *What were the names of the two girls visiting the biomes?* (Millie and Tess) Tell students that Millie and Tess are in the grassland biome with their friend Ava. Ask *What animals live in the grassland biome?* Play the audio and have students follow the dialogue in their books.
- Ask the gist question *Which animals do the girls talk about?* and elicit the answer. Play the audio again for students to check.

**Answer**
cheetahs; lions; elephants

**B Look at A. Complete.**

- Write or project the table onto the board. Tell students that the words they need are all in the dialogue.
- Look at the first sentence in the table. Ask *Which adjective is in the sentence?* (bigger) Have them find the sentence in the dialogue to find the missing word (than). Explain or remind students that we use comparative adjectives, like *bigger,* + *than* to compare things. Then look at the superlative question. Have students look at the dialogue in A to find the missing words (the biggest). Highlight the definite article, saying that superlatives have *the* in front.
- Have students work in pairs to complete the rest of table. Check answers as a class.
- Ask students to notice the differences between the short and long adjective forms. Ask *Which adjective is short?* (big) *How do we make the comparative form?* (add another g + er) *How do we make the superlative form?* (add another g + est and put *the* before the adjective) Repeat the questions for long adjectives.
- Draw students' attention to the Grammar tip *Remember.* Focus on the comparative and superlative forms of *good* and *bad.* Ask *Are they short or long adjectives?* (short) Ask *Do we add –er and –est?* Explain that *good* and *bad* are irregular.

**Answers**
than; more; dangerous; the; biggest; the; most; dangerous

**C Think and discuss. Then choose.**

- Have students work in pairs to discuss the sentences. Refer them to the table in B for examples. Then check answers. Ask *When we compare the lion with the cheetah, how many animals are there?* (two) *When we say* Elephants are the most dangerous animals of all, *what are we comparing them with?* (all the other animals in the grassland).

**Answers**
1 comparative 2 superlative

**D** TRACK 20 TB p. 214 **Listen and say.**

- Tell students they're going to practice saying the structures. Play the audio, having students repeat each sentence chorally.
- For ideas on how to vary the drill, see TB p. 23.

**E Read and complete.**

- Look at the example together. Check students' understanding of *soft* by eliciting what animals they can describe as *soft.* Elicit the comparative and superlative forms of *soft.* Ask students why the superlative is used in the first sentence. (*In the world* is comparing sand in the desert with all the other types of sand—i.e. more than two.)
- Have students complete the other sentences individually, by writing either a comparative or superlative adjective. Remind them to write *than* in comparative sentences and *the* in superlative sentences. Check answers as a class.

**Answers**
1 *the softest* 2 colder than 3 better than
4 more beautiful 5 the best 6 most interesting

**F Make sentences about biomes. Choose and say.**

- Quickly review the four biomes from the previous lesson and write them on the board. Elicit what students know about each one.
- Demonstrate the activity with a student. Read the example superlative sentence. Then say *Can you compare two biomes using "cold"?* and ask a volunteer to read the second example. Ask that student to choose an adjective. Elicit either a superlative or comparative sentence from the class.
- Tell students to take turns choosing an adjective in pairs. The other student has to make either a superlative or a comparative sentence about two biomes.

## Cool Down

Play *Basketball* (see TB p. 25) using the four biomes as the categories: forest, grassland, tundra, and desert. Call out statements about the biomes; for example, *It is hot and dry here.*

**Practice** **Resource Bank:** Grammar Printout
**Student's App:** Grammar Practice

# Global Citizenship

## Lesson Objectives

- to learn parts of plants/trees vocabulary: *bud, flower, ground, leaves, roots, seed, shoot, stem, petal, pollen*
- to explore how plants grow in difficult climates
- to explore how we can help plants grow in our local area
- to practice listening for gist and details

**Materials**

Audio Tracks 21 to 23; Audio Track B; a globe or map (A, D); pictures of flowers (CD)

### Opening Question

Ask the opening question: *How do plants grow in difficult climates?* Elicit ideas and encourage students to think about what plants need to grow (water, sunlight, air, a suitable temperature) and the best climate for this. Ask *Which climates might make it hard for plants to grow?* (very hot or cold places, dry places). Then have students think about how a plant may grow in an extreme climate like the tundra or the desert.

**A** TRACK 21 TB p. 214 **Listen to Iqaluk talk about a flower on the tundra. What color is it?**

- Tell students they are going to listen to a girl named Iqaluk talking about where she lives. Before they listen, have students predict where in the world Iqaluk lives. You could show students a globe or map of the world and have them suggest places.
- Play the audio and have students point to the words or pictures as they listen.
- Ask the comprehension question *What color is it?* Play the audio again for students to check.

**Answer**

It's purple.

**B** TRACK 22 TB p. 214 **Listen, say, and number the pictures in A.**

- Play the audio and have students point to the pictures and say the words.
- Tell students to listen again and this time number the pictures. Do the example together (ground).
- Check answers and make sure students know what each word means.

**Answers**

1 *ground* 2 bud 3 seeds 4 flower 5 roots
6 petal 7 shoot 8 leaves 9 stem 10 pollen

TRACK B TB p. 214 **Visualization**

The TTL has a visualization audio track for this vocabulary set. (See TB p. 21.)

**C Look and complete.**

- Students are going to label the picture with the vocabulary from A. Look at the example together.
- Have students complete the labels individually and draw a line to the correct place on the flower. Then check answers as a class.

**Answers**

1 *flower* 2 petal 3 pollen 4 leaves 5 stem
6 roots

**D** TRACK 23 TB p. 215 **Now listen to Amadou and Seba. Which plant grows in the water?**

- Have students look at the two pictures and say what they see. Ask *What do both plants have?* (leaves) Encourage them to say what is the same and what is different about them.
- Tell students they are going to listen to two children from different countries talking about plants. Ask *Where are the children from?* (Senegal and Egypt) You could identify the countries on a globe or map. Encourage students to share any knowledge they have about either country, in particular any information about its flora and fauna.
- Listening for gist: Ask the gist question *Which plant grows in the water?* and elicit the answer. Play the audio for students to check.

**Answer**

the blue water lily

**E Listen again. Write *True* or *False*.**

- Listening for details: have students look at the statements before they listen again to see how many answers they remember. Then play the audio and have students write *true* or *false*.
- To check answers, play *Stand Up, Sit Down* (see TB p. 27)

**Answers**

1 *False* 2 False 3 True 4 False 5 True

### Discussion Questions

- Draw students' attention to the discussion questions: *What plants or flowers grow in your country? How can people help plants or flowers grow?* Have students discuss the questions in small groups. See **ETB**.
- Return to the opening question to ask again: *How do plants grow in difficult climates?* Recap the ideas shared at the beginning of the class, and then encourage students to share any new ideas they learned from the lesson. Focus on what plants need, and how we can help them.

### Cool Down

Do a quick survey to find out students' favorite flowers. Show students pictures of different flowers and take a class vote. Remind them they can only have one favorite, so they should raise their hands only once! Tally the votes on the board and then ask *What is the most popular flower?*



**Practice** **Student's App:** Vocabulary Practice; Listening Practice

## Explore Language

### Lesson Objectives

- to learn to use comparative and superlative adverbs
- to practice parts of plants/trees vocabulary

**Materials**
Audio Tracks 24 and 25

### Warm Up

Review comparative and superlative adjectives with students. In pairs, ask students to look through their books and make one comparative and one superlative sentence about any pictures of animals or plants they find. Have pairs share their sentences with the class, pointing to the pictures they are talking about. Ask the rest of the class if they agree with the sentences.

**A** TRACK 24 TB p. 215 **Listen and read. What happened to Ava?**

- Tell students that they are going to listen to Ava talk to her friend Owen about plants. Play the audio and have students follow the story in their books.
- Ask the gist question *What happened to Ava?* and elicit the answer. Play the audio again for students to check. Ask *How many plants does Owen have?* (three, plus a bamboo plant).

**Answer**
Ava didn't listen to Owen. The plant was sharp, and it hurt her finger.

**B** **Look at A. Complete.**

- Write or project the table onto the board. Tell students that the sentences they need are all in the story.
- Have students look at the first sentence and look back at the story in A to find the missing words. Point out the adverb and quickly review its meaning. Ask *What kind of word is it?* (adverb) *What do we use adverbs for?* (to describe actions)
- Have students work in pairs to complete the rest of table. Check answers as a class. Have students notice that all the adverbs in the story end in *-ly*. Point out that we alway use *more* with comparative adverbs ending in *-ly* and *most* with superlative adverbs ending in *-ly*.
- Draw students' attention to the Grammar tip *Remember.* Remind students of the two things to remember and have them circle these words in the table.

**Answers**
more; quickly; than; the; most; slowly

**C** **Think and discuss. Then choose.**

- Have students work in pairs to discuss the sentences. Refer them to the table in B for examples. Then check answers.
- Have students compare the sentences here with those in Lesson 2. Ask *What is different?* (Comparative and superlative adjectives are used to compare things; adverbs are used to compare actions.) Elicit that the sentence structure is the same.

**Answers**
1 comparative 2 superlative

**D** TRACK 25 TB p. 215 **Listen and say.**

- Tell students they're going to practice saying the new structures. Play the audio, having students repeat each sentence chorally.
- For ideas on how to vary the drill, see TB p. 23.

**E** **Read and complete.**

- Look at the example together. Elicit the comparative and superlative forms of *easily.* Ask students why the comparative is used in this sentence. (It is comparing *growing here* with *in the desert*—two actions.)
- Have students complete the activity individually. Elicit that they have to use *than* in comparative sentences and *the* in superlative sentences. Check answers as a class.

**Answers**
1 *more easily than* 2 more slowly than
3 the most quickly 4 more carefully than
5 the most easily 6 more quickly than

**F** **Make sentences comparing how your classmates do things. Do you agree or disagree?**

- Tell students to write four or five comparative or superlative adverb sentences about students in the class.
- Divide the class into two teams, A and B, who stand in line. The first person in Team A says one of his/her sentences about someone in the class. The first person in Team B confers with rest of his/her team and then responds with *Agree* or *Disagree.*
- If they agree, the first person in Team B repeats the sentence. If they disagree, the student says what his/her team believes is true. Then it is Team B's turn.
- You are the judge. Give two points for a grammatically correct sentence and one point for a grammatically correct response. (Remember that opinions are subjective!)
- Then the first person in Team B says a sentence. Continue until everyone has said a sentence. The team with the most points wins.

### Cool Down

Write a sentence on the board. It can be as simple or complicated as you see fit for the class. Then call out an adverb and have two students read the sentence in that way. The class decides who said the sentence better; for example, *Sara said it more loudly!*

Suggested adverbs: quickly, slowly, quietly, loudly/noisily, happily, excitedly, angrily, beautifully, calmly, carefully

**Practice** **Resource Bank:** Grammar Printout
**Student's App:** Grammar Practice

# Take the Stage

## Lesson Objectives

- to prepare and give a presentation describing biomes
- to recognize and reproduce /pl/ and /kl/

**Materials**
Video; Audio Track 26

## Warm Up

Do a multisensory visualization. Take students on an imaginary trip to one or more biomes, asking them what they can see, hear, smell, and touch at different points. See TB p. 21.

**A** TB p. 238 **Watch and listen. Would you like to live in Rania's biome?**

- Tell students they are going to watch a video of a girl named Rania giving a presentation about her favorite biome. Show a still of Rania's poster from the video. Ask the prediction question *Why does she like it?* Elicit ideas and write them on the board. Then play the video and encourage students to notice what Rania does when she talks about something on her poster. Review the predictions to see if any were correct.
- Ask the gist question *Would you like to live in Rania's biome?* Play the video again and then elicit answers. Encourage students to give reasons for their answers. Ask further comprehension questions; for example, *What animals are there?* (sunkeys) Ask *Are sunkeys real animals?* Elicit that Rania has made up or invented a new biome.

**Answer**
Students' own answers

**B Watch again. Check (✔) the phrases you hear.**

- Have students read the phrases.
- Play the video again and have students check the phrases they hear. Check answers as a class.
- Explain that *I'm going to talk about …* is a way of introducing your topic. Ask students *Does Rania say it at the beginning, in the middle, or at the end?* Can students find a similar phrase that could go at the beginning of a presentation? (*Let me tell you about …*) Then have students categorize the other phrases into those we say in the *middle* and at the *end* of a presentation. (All the other phrases can go in the middle except *I like my biome best because …*)

**Answers**
*1*; 3; 6; 7; 8

### Pronunciation /pl/ and /kl/

TRACK 26 TB p. 215 **Listen and say.**

Demonstrate the two sounds first. Isolate each phoneme in the cluster and elicit how to pronounce it (/p/; /l/). Then put the two sounds together slowly /pl/ and have students repeat it. Do the same for /kl/.

Play the audio and have students repeat the words. Repeat if students need more practice.

Say *These words are used in the video. What other words do you know with these sounds?* Elicit ideas and write them on the board in two columns (e.g. *plan, classroom*). Drill the pronunciation of each word.

**Suggested Answers**
/pl/ plate, playground, please; /kl/ claws, clean, clever, climb, clock, closet, cloth, club

**C Plan. Think about your dream biome. Write.**

- Tell students they are going to plan a presentation about a dream biome. Elicit the information Rania includes in her presentation (type of biome, its climate, the plants and animals that live there, a summary sentence about why it's the best biome). Do an example with a biome students are familiar with.
- Say *Now plan what you can say about your dream biome.* Encourage students to be creative in imagining their dream biomes. Monitor and provide language help when needed.

**D Prepare your presentation. Use your ideas from C and phrases from B.**

- Play the video again as a model.
- Tell students they are now going to prepare their presentation in more detail using their plan from C and the phrases from B.
- Elicit which phrases to use at the beginning, middle, and end of their presentation. Then have students plan their presentation individually.
- Once they have decided on the details they want to describe, have students make a poster like Rania's that will help the audience visualize what they are describing.

**E Practice with a friend. Then share with your class.**

- Have students practice their presentation with their partner as many times as they need to. Remind them to look at the audience, smile, and speak slowly and clearly.
- Encourage students to refer to the poster as they talk. The poster will help them keep their presentations organized and will remind them about what information they want to share.
- Invite volunteers to come to the front of the classroom to give their presentation. Have the audience give a round of applause after each presentation.

## Cool Down

Create a gallery of students' posters by placing them on the walls around the classroom. Have students walk around the gallery. When they see something they like, they should find the student who made the poster and tell the student what they liked about it. This will help foster a positive relationship among students.



**Practice** Student's App: Speaking Skills Practice; Speaking Video

## Write About It

### Lesson Objectives

- to learn to use sequencers
- to plan and write instructions

**Materials**

(Optional) Support, Standard, and Challenge writing printouts from the Resource Bank, one per student (C and D); *Spinner and Counters* printout from the Resource Bank, one spinner per student (CD)

### Warm Up

Do a lively TPR game that introduces the topic of beans. Call out different types of beans and have students do an action. Demonstrate the actions as follows, encouraging students to join in.

Runner bean: Run on the spot. / Jumping bean: Jump up and down. / String bean: Join hands with a partner. / Kidney bean: Make a C-shape with your body.

**A Read the instructions. Circle the sequencers and underline the imperatives.**

- Introduce students to the concept of a *How To …* set of instructions. Say *Sometimes you don't know how to do something and you need help. You can follow some instructions.* Have students look at the title. Elicit what these instructions are going to tell us (how to grow a bean plant).
- Give students two or three minutes to read the instructions. Ask *What information can we find out?* (what we need and what to do) Draw students' attention to the picture and the list at the top of the text. Ask *What things do you need?* (a jar, a bean, water, two paper towels, plastic wrap)
- Elicit that sequencers are words that tell us in what order we should do things (e.g. *First*). Have students read the instructions again and circle the sequencers. Students should notice that they are followed by a comma.
- Elicit or explain that imperatives are instruction verbs that tell us what to do (e.g. *make*). Have students read the instructions again and underline the imperatives. Make sure students notice that the imperative verb forms don't need a subject. Consolidate this by asking volunteers to call out a few commands; for example, *Close the window. Sit down!* Then check answers as a class.

**Answers**

Sequencers: *Before*; Then; First; Next; Then; After that; Finally

Imperatives: *make*; find; take; put; cover; cut; Don't make; Watch

### International English

Ask *Can you find the flags?* Look at the words. Elicit *plastic wrap* is American English and *cling film* is British English. Ask *Which do we use?*

**B Add sequencers and change the sentences into imperatives. Write.**

- Have students look at the example. Elicit the differences between the original sentence and the new sentence (there is no *you*, and *First* has been added).
- Have students write imperative sentences in their books. To check answers, have students call out the instructions one by one and pretend to do as they say. If a sentence is incorrect, don't do anything until the class corrects the sentence.

**Answers**

1 *First, make a list.* 2 Then, look for everything you need.
3 Next, put one wet paper towel in the jar.
4 After that, put the seed in the jar.
5 Finally, find a sunny place for the jar.

**C Plan. Complete the steps to grow a pumpkin.**

- Brainstorm different types of plants and the different things they need to grow. Write them on the board.
- Tell students they are going to make a poster about how to grow a pumpkin plant. Elicit what a pumpkin looks like.
- Enlarge the images on p. 32 using the TTL and elicit what is happening in each one. Encourage students to use imperatives by asking *What do I need? What do I do first?* and so on.
- Then have students complete the table in their books. Challenge printouts can be handed out now.

**Suggested Answers**

What I need: a pot, soil, a pumpkin seed, water, a sunny place
Steps: 1 Put the pumpkin seed into a hole in the soil. 2 Give the seed some water. 3 Put the jar in a sunny place near a window. 4 Watch your pumpkin grow.

**D Write your instructions. Make a poster and add pictures.**

- Students should write the full instructions for how to grow the plant, including *What you need*, and other sequencers to show the order of instructions.
- Have students write a draft and then self-correct or exchange their work with a friend and peer-correct.
- Have students make their posters on large sheets of paper and draw pictures to illustrate the steps. Alternatively, hand out the Standard and Support printouts from the Resource Bank for students to look at and complete.

### Cool Down

Play *Spinner Drawing Game* (see TB p. 27). Students can play in groups to use their spinners to draw a plant.

**Practice Student's App:** Writing Practice

# Think It Over

## Lesson Objectives

- to review what has been learned in the unit
- to reflect on the unit and their own progress
- to think about learning strategies and how to continue learning at home

## Warm Up

Ask students what the unit theme was (the world around us) and write it in the middle of the board. Brainstorm any words or phrases students can think of that relate to the topic and write them on the board. This is a chance to review language and themes from the unit and to bring the topic back into focus. Ask students to identify which biomes the four plants illustrated on p. 33 are from. Review the climate of each biome and examples of animals that live there. Encourage students to think about how people, animals, and plants are connected.

**Read the questions and draw or write your answers.**

- Give students time to think about and discuss activities in the unit before they complete each question. Explain that they can choose to either write a few words or sentences or to draw a picture. Allowing students to make a personal response will help them retain knowledge and engage with the learning points.

**What did I do?**

- Give students a few minutes to look back through the unit at the different activities they did. Ask questions about the unit or write questions on the board for students to discuss in pairs or small groups; for example, *What was the song about? Which plants and animals did you read about?*
- Encourage students to identify something in the unit that they found challenging or something that was particularly memorable for them, but tell them not to choose their favorite activity yet. Students can draw or write about their chosen activity.

**What did I learn?**

- Ask questions about the unit to help students think about what they learned; for example, *What new words do you know? What did you learn about special flowers? What did you learn about other countries?* Elicit ideas from the class and discuss them together.
- Encourage students to draw a picture or write sentences about their learning outcomes.

**What was my favorite part?**

- Have students look back through the unit and decide what they enjoyed the most. Tell them it can be an activity they found fun, a text they enjoyed reading, a favorite character, or a favorite action. They should try to choose just one and draw a picture or write about it. Explain that when we like something, it is often easier to learn.

**How well did I do?**

- Tell students to color in the clump of grass that best expresses how well they have learned the unit content (i.e. the bigger the clump of grass they color, the more they feel they have learned). Ask *What do you understand? What do you need to practice more?* Encourage students to look back through the unit to see how much they remember, what they did well, and what they found difficult.

**What can I do next?**

- Brainstorm ideas with the class about what they can do to continue to learn (e.g. watch the videos again, think about the biomes again and the plants and animals that live there, find and pronounce words with the /pl/ and /kl/ sounds, compare classmates).
- Draw students' attention to the options in the box. Encourage students to think about what they can do at home to improve their English using the verbs in the box as a prompt. Some suggestions are: read different instructions and identify imperatives and sequencers, practice the presentation and present in front of your family, write about your dream biome, listen to the song again.
- Ask students to choose one or more activities from the list and share their ideas with a friend.

## Looking Forward

- Draw students' attention to the character at the bottom of the page. Ask *Who's this?* and elicit what they remember about him. (Owen appears in Explore Language 2, p. 28; he has a tall bamboo plant; he has three desert plants; he knows a lot about plants.)
- Draw students' attention to Owen's question: *What store do I go to?* Encourage students to make predictions about where he goes and what Unit 3 is about. Tell students they will find out the answer in Lesson 1 of the next unit.

# Put It Together

To further review and recycle the language in Units 1 and 2, play the game, *Where in the World?*, on pp. 34–35. See TB p. 206 for teaching notes.

**Practice** Resource Bank: Unit Test
Student's App: Vocabulary and Grammar Review

## Get Ready to Read

### Lesson Objectives

- to activate prior knowledge about biomes, trees, and forests
- to guide enquiry and deepen understanding through a See, Think, Wonder VTR
- to preview the reading skill of understanding the author's purpose

**Materials**

Sound effects from a nature app including animal/bird sounds (WU); (Optional) VTR printout from the Resource Bank (A, B, C); (optional) pictures of trees and plants that grow nearby; books on local wildlife (D)

### Warm Up

Play different sound effects from nature and have students listen. These could include forest or jungle sounds, birdsong, running water or waves, wind in the trees, and other types of weather. Students can close their eyes and try to imagine the place. Then ask *What do you think lives here?* and elicit suggestions.

### See, Think, Wonder

**A Look at the picture. What do you see?**

Students are going to do a See, Think, Wonder VTR to explore the image of the river.

- Have students look at the image. Ask them to work individually to brainstorm words connected to nature. Write ideas on the board.
- Ask students *What do you see?* Then give students one minute to look at the picture before sharing answers in small groups and then as a class.

Here's an example of this part of the routine.
**Teacher:** What do you see?
**Student A:** I see a river.
**Teacher:** What colors do you see?
**Student B:** (The water is) gray, and (the trees are) green.

**B What do you think?**

- Say *I think it's cold in the picture. What do you think about the picture?* Elicit a response from a student. Then ask *What makes you say that?* and encourage the student to give a reason.
- Give students one to three minutes to think about the picture silently. Then have students work in small groups to share their ideas before sharing as a class. Encourage them to give reasons for their answers and provide language help when needed.

Here's an example of this part of the routine.
**Teacher:** What do you think about the picture?
**Student A:** (I think) the people are tourists.
**Teacher:** What makes you say that?
**Student A:** They have cameras. And they're in a group.
**Teacher:** What else do you think?
**Student B:** (I think) they're wet, but they're happy—they can see a bear!

**C What do you wonder?**

- Say *I wonder if the bear is looking for food. What do you wonder about the picture? What questions do you have?* Give students one to three minutes to think about the picture silently.
- Have students share their ideas in groups or as a class. Allow students to be creative and accept all their ideas.

Here's an example of this part of the routine.
**Teacher:** What do you wonder?
**Student A:** Is the bear taking a bath?
**Teacher:** Good question! What do you think?
**Student A:** I think he is!
**Teacher:** Does everyone agree?
**Student B:** No, I think he's looking for food!
**Teacher:** OK. What else do you wonder?
**Student B:** Is it spring or fall?

### Transition

Ask students *Where in the world do you think this river is? What other animals do you think live here?* Ask students if they know a place in their country that is similar to the place in the picture.

**D Think and discuss. What kinds of plants and animals do you have in your area? What do they look like?**

- Focus students on the first part of the question. You could display some pictures and books on plants and animals in your country for students to look at.
- Have students draw pictures of local wildlife and then discuss their ideas in pairs.

**E Read and check. These two headings are from the article. Why do you think the author used them?**

Students will preview the reading skill of understanding the author's purpose.

- Have students read the headings from the article. Tell students not to worry about the tricky words (*deciduous, coniferous*). Ask *What do you think the article is about?* (forests) *Is the article about one kind of forest or more?* (two)
- Ask *Why did the author use these headings?* Have students read the three options, then take a class vote on the answer.

**Suggested Answer**
2

Now read **Two Different Forests**

# Nonfiction: *Two Different Forests*—Informational Text

## Lesson Objectives

- to read an informational text about different types of trees
- to make a personal connection to the reading

**Materials**

Audio Tracks 10 and 11; Video

## Warm Up

Ask students to visualize walking in a forest. Ask *What country are you in? Is it summer or winter? What do the trees look like?* Say *Now imagine taking a walk in the forest at a different time of year. Is it hot or cold? Do the trees look different?*

## TRACK 10 TB p. 230 Reading Approach

**First Reading: Engage with the Text**

- If you are using the TTL, project each spread of the reading to activate schema. Ask students to look at the pictures and decide which forest they like the most and why.
- Ask a gist question, e.g. *Which forest has trees with leaves all year round?* Play the video and then check answers. Remind students about their answer to E on p. 25. Do they still agree with their choice?

## TRACK 11 TB p. 230 Words in Context

- Play the audio and have students repeat the words.
- Have students race to find the words in the reading.
- Tell students that sometimes **the next sentence gives clues to explain the meaning of a word** (see TB p. 23). Tell students to continuing to read *after* they find a new word. Have them discuss their ideas in pairs.
- Then bring the class together and use these questions to confirm the meanings.

**deciduous** (p. 26) Have students find the word in the first paragraph. Elicit what information students can find about this type of tree. Ask *Do you think "deciduous" means "all over the world" or "their leaves fall"?*

**hibernate** (p. 27) Have students point to the word in the reading. Say *The next sentence explains the meaning of "hibernate."* Have students read the sentence. Ask *What does it mean?* (to sleep all winter)

**coniferous** (p. 28) Have students find the word in the second section of the reading. Ask *Why are these trees called "coniferous"?* (because they have cones) Can students spot how the two words start with the same letters? Ask *How are they different from deciduous trees?* (They have leaves all year round.)

**survive** (p. 29) Ask *Can animals live outside when it's very cold?* Students may suggest that some animals live in cold places (e.g. penguins or polar bears). Point out the first two sentences of p. 29. Elicit why many animals hibernate (to survive the cold during the winter).

**adapt** (p. 29) Say *Animals adapt to the climate. If it's cold, what do they do?* (change color or hibernate) Elicit that *adapt* means "change."

**Second Reading: Analyze the Text and Features**

- Have students open their books. Play the audio as students read the text.
- Ask some questions to check comprehension; for example, *What two types of forests do we learn about?* (deciduous, coniferous) *What are the differences between the two?* (the trees, the climate/weather, animals)
- Discuss the questions in the blue boxes.
  - **Personalization** (p. 26): *Do you have a favorite kind of tree?* Ask *Do you prefer deciduous or coniferous trees?* Encourage students to give reasons for their choices.
  - **Critical Thinking** (p. 27): *Why are the animals that live in deciduous forests usually brown?* Ask *What brown animals live in forests?* Point out that everything around the animals is brown, too (i.e. the ground, the tree trunks). Elicit the concept of camouflage and encourage students to give other examples of animals that use camouflage.
  - **Fact** (p. 28): *In some coniferous forests, the winter temperature can drop to –50°C!* Draw students' attention to the temperature on the thermometer. To compare, ask what their body temperature should be (37°C).
  - **Detail** (p. 29): *Why do animals in coniferous forests often have thick white fur or feathers in the winter?* Recap why animals in deciduous forest are often brown before eliciting the answer to this question (for camouflage in snow and to keep warm in cold weather).
- Discuss the text focus: *Headings tell us what the reading is going to be about.* Ask *How many headings are in this reading?* (two) Ask students *Why are headings useful?* (They help us find information quickly because they are short and they signpost where the information is.)

**Third Reading: Interact with the Text**

- Play the video on mute and have students take turns narrating it in pairs or small groups.

## Cool Down

Have students choose which of the two forests they would like to visit. Encourage students to close their eyes and visualize the forest. They should think about what they can see, hear, smell, and feel. Then have students share their ideas with a friend.

**Next lesson:** Have students find examples of different leaves, seeds and cones in the area.

**Practice** **Student's App:** Nonfiction Video

## Explore the Reading

### Lesson Objectives

- to understand and analyze *Two Different Forests* through reading comprehension activities
- to learn about ecology through CLIL (science): exploring how trees, people, and animals adapt to their environment
- to make a personal connection to the reading

**Materials**
(Optional) Video or Audio Track 10; leaves, seeds, and cones from various trees (WU)

### Warm Up

Have students sit in a circle, or several smaller circles with large classes. Have them pass around the leaves, seeds, and cones they have brought in and examine the similarities and differences. Ask (or write on the board) questions, pre-teaching language where necessary: *What color is it? Is it big or small? Is it hard or soft? Is it smooth or rough? Is it thick or thin? Is it from a deciduous or coniferous tree?*

**A Read and check (✔).**

- If more than one day has passed since students read *Two Different Forests*, play the video or audio again.
- With books closed, have a Group Time discussion to check students' comprehension of the reading (see TB p. 21). Ask *What falls from deciduous trees?* (leaves) *When do leaves fall from deciduous trees?* (in autumn) *Which forest has long, cold winters?* (coniferous) *Which trees have new leaves every year?* (deciduous) *How do coniferous trees protect their fruit?* (The cones are hard.) *Why do some animals hibernate?* (to survive the cold winter)
- Have students open their books and read the example sentence. Say *Can you find this information in the reading?* Have students look back and find the sentence (Coniferous Forests, paragraph 2). Remind students not to read every word.
- Have students do the rest of the activity individually, then look back at the reading to check answers. Check answers as a class.

**Answers**
1 *Coniferous Forests* 2 Deciduous Forests
3 Deciduous Forests 4 Coniferous Forests
5 Coniferous Forests 6 Deciduous Forests

**B Read and match. How do trees and animals adapt to the cold?**

This activity connects to the CLIL science focus of exploring how trees and animals adapt to their environment.

- Review the meanings of some of the words such as *thin*, *lose*, *fur*, and *hibernate*.
- Do the first question together, then have students complete the matching activity individually. Check answers as a class, discussing how and why the trees and animals need to do this. (Deciduous trees drop their leaves to save water and energy in cold weather and to protect their branches. If the leaves didn't fall, they would collect snow, which would make the branches heavy and cause them to break. / Coniferous leaves are pointed so that they don't lose heat or water during winter. / Some animals hibernate because it is too cold and there is not enough food for them to be active and survive during the long winter. / The fur of some animals changes color as a form of camouflage and to protect themselves from predators in snowy weather.)

**Answers**
1 b 2 a 3 d 4 c

**C Think and write. How do you adapt to your environment?**

Students are going to connect the reading with their own lives. This draws on the CLIL science focus of exploring how people adapt to their environment.

- Write the following prompts on the board: *clothes*, *daily routine*, *activities*, *food and drink*, *sleep*. Brainstorm as a class some ways in which students adapt to the seasons and climate throughout the year (e.g. they put on sunscreen so that they don't get sunburned in the summer; they get up earlier; they play outside more).
- Draw students' attention to the table. Then have students do the activity individually.
- Have students work in pairs or small groups to discuss and compare their ideas.

### Cool Down

Play *Versus* (see TB p. 27) using the following statements: *Cold climate or warm climate? Deciduous tree or coniferous tree? Spring or fall? Desert or forest? Bear or rabbit? Boat or plane?* Do a class poll to see which choices are the most popular.

**Practice** **Student's App:** Reading Practice

## Get Ready to Read

### Lesson Objectives

- to practice the reading skill of understanding the author's purpose
- to activate prior knowledge about respecting living things

**Materials**
Slips of paper, one per student (CD)

### Warm Up

To introduce the idea of purpose, focus on actions students are doing in the classroom right now. Ask students why they did certain actions; for example, a student puts her eraser in her pencil case. Ask *Why did you put your eraser in your pencil case?* and elicit suggestions from the class (e.g. *so I know where it is; so it doesn't fall on the floor; because I don't need it right now*).

**A Think and check (✔). Why did the author write *The Beginning of Alice's Adventures?***

Students are going to practice the reading skill of understanding the author's purpose.

- Tell students they are going to retell the story of *The Beginning of Alice's Adventures*. Give students one or two minutes to look back in their books to review key points. Then have them retell the story in pairs. Ask *Did you give the same details as your partner?*
- Draw students' attention to the instructions. Ask *Who is the author?* to check comprehension. (Lewis Carroll) Ask students to think about why Lewis Carroll wrote the story. *What did he want to do?* Go through the three options with the class. Ask *Did the author want to teach you about rabbits? Is the rabbit in the story a real rabbit?* (No, he talks and wears clothes, so we aren't learning factual information about rabbits.) *Does he want you to understand Alice? Do you understand Alice? Do you know how Alice feels? Does he want to help you have fun? When you read an interesting story, are you having fun?* Have students choose the best answer.
- Then draw students' attention to the skills box. Recap the author's purpose in *The Beginning of Alice's Adventures* (to entertain).

**Answer**
help me have fun

**B Read and write *Yes* or *No*. Then write the author's purpose.**

- Ask students if they know of any stories about birds. If they do, have them describe the story. Then ask *Does the story have a specific message? If so, what?*
- Tell students they are going to read a story about a *swallow* (a kind of bird). Have students read the story excerpt and complete the activity in pairs.
- Elicit some answers, then ask *Do you think the author likes swallows?* (yes) Point out that the author wants the reader to feel a certain way (e.g. to like the birds, to worry about the baby bird, to admire Go Ne and his father). Then explain that the way we feel about the characters might change as we read the story. We might start out not liking a character but later decide that we do like them. Ask students if they can think of examples of this in any stories they have read. Come back to the questions in B after reading the story.

**Answer**
1 Yes 2 No 3 No 4 Students' own answers

**C Think and discuss. Think about something you wrote. Why did you write it? What was your purpose?**

- Brainstorm with the class things they write, adding their suggestions to the board. Some examples may be a card or letter, a message to a friend or family member, a poem or story, a piece of writing for school.
- Choose an example from the board (e.g. an invitation) and ask the student who wrote it why they wrote it (e.g. to give friends information about a party).
- Give students a few minutes to think about things they wrote and why they wrote them. Have students share their ideas in groups using a Roundtable routine (see p. 20).

### Cool Down

Give each student a slip of paper as an exit pass. Have them write one question they have about the story they are going to read. They should give you the paper as they leave the classroom.

Now read **A New Friend**

# Fiction: *A New Friend*—Folk Tale

## Lesson Objectives

- to read a folk tale about a boy who finds a baby bird
- to make a personal connection to the reading

**Materials**

Audio Tracks 12 and 13; sticky notes (CD)

## Warm Up

Elicit the characters in the summary of *A New Friend* (Go Ne, his father, the swallows, Wen Shu). Remind students that the summary talks about something Wen Shu does. Have students work in pairs to decide who Wen Shu is, his relationship with the other characters, and what he might do. Give students a time limit and then have them share their ideas with the class.

## TRACK 12 TB p. 230 Reading Approach

### First Reading: Engage with the Text

- If you are using the TTL, project the opening spread of the story to activate schema. Ask students to notice the title, text, speech bubbles, and pictures on the page and use this information to predict ideas about the reading. Ask *Does Go Ne like the swallows?*
- Have students sit in a circle to listen to the story the first time you read it. Read the story to students using facial expression and gesture, or play the audio. Students can interact with the story by copying the gestures.
- Ask prediction questions as you read: *What will happen to the plant? Will the bird be OK?*

## TRACK 13 TB p. 230 Words in Context

- Play the audio and have students repeat the words.
- Have students race to find the words in the reading.
- Have students **use the pictures to help establish the meaning of the new words.** Have them discuss their ideas in pairs.
- Then bring the class together and use these suggestions to confirm the meanings.

**swallow** (p. 32) Have students point to a picture of a swallow and elicit that it is a type of bird.

**roof** (p. 32) Have students point to the roof of the house in the picture and point out what is under the roof (the nest).

**slingshot** (p. 35) Have students find the slingshot in the picture. Ask *What does he put in his slingshot?* (a stone)

**hit** (p. 35) Encourage students to look at the pictures of the bird falling. Ask *What has happened?* Have students use gesture to demonstrate the meaning of *hit*.

**paid** (p. 37) Have students look at the pictures of the vet. Ask *How do the boys pay the vet?* Point out that *paid* is the simple past form of the verb *pay*.

## International English

Elicit that *slingshot* is American English and *catapult* is British English. Ask *Which word do we use?*

### Second Reading: Analyze the Text and Features

- Play the audio and have students follow along in their books.
- Ask some questions to check comprehension; for example, *What did Go Ne love?* (animals) *What happened to the baby swallow?* (It fell out of its nest.) *What bad thing did Wen Shu do?* (He hurt the bird.) *Why can't Go Ne's father fix the roof?* (Go Ne spent the money at the vet.)
- Then discuss the questions in the blue boxes.
  - **Personalization** (p. 32): *Do you like spring? Why?* Have students think about what they like and don't like about spring. Then elicit some answers from the class.
  - **Making Connections** (p. 34): *What else can they do with the coins?* Say *The family is going to fix the roof. What other things need fixing?* Have students look at the picture of the house and garden and suggest what the family might spend the money on. (the ceiling, a new table)
  - **Gist** (p. 35): *Why did Wen Shu do that?* Point out the sentence "*I want a seed, too!*" Ask *Why does Wen Shu want a seed?* (to get a money plant) Ask *How did Wen Shu feel when he saw Go Ne's coins?* (jealous)
  - **Personalization** (p. 37): *What do you do when you're sorry?* Ask students what they can do for someone if they have done something that they are sorry about (buy the person a present, do something kind to help that person). Ask *What does Wen Shu do for Go Ne's family to say sorry?* (He gives them equipment to fix their roof.)

### Third Reading: Interact with the Text

- Have students read and act out the story in groups of four or five. Encourage students to use actions and gesture as they read together. For more ideas on using role-play, see TB p. 23.

## Cool Down

Have students recall the questions they wrote down in the Cool Down of the previous lesson. Ask *Can you answer your question now?* Have students discuss this in pairs. Then have them think of one thing they have learned during the lesson, write it on a sticky note, and stick it on the door. As students leave the classroom, have them choose a sticky note (not their own) to take home and read.

# Explore the Reading

## Lesson Objectives

- to understand and analyze *A New Friend* through reading comprehension activities
- to explore the SEL competency of responsible decision-making by making decisions based on moral, personal, and ethical standards
- to make a personal connection to the reading
- to reproduce and write words with *ai*

**Materials**

Audio Tracks 12 and 14; slips of paper with situations in which people need help (CD)

## Warm Up

Check students know the names of the two main characters from *A New Friend* (Go Ne and Wen Shu). Then play *Who Said It?* (see TB p. 27). Suggested quotations: *They're so tiny!* (Go Ne); *Let's cut it open!* (Go Ne's mom); *Now we can fix the roof!* (Go Ne's dad); *I want a seed, too!* (Wen Shu); *Please make the baby bird better!* (Go Ne); *Go Ne, why did you spend that money?* (Go Ne's dad)

**A Read and answer.**

- If more than one day has passed since students read *A New Friend*, play the audio again. Students can follow along in their books if they wish.
- With books closed, have students say what they remember about the story. Write the following question prompts on the board: *Who? What? Where? When? Why? How?* Encourage students to use simple structures in English, but allow some use of L1 if necessary.
- Have students open their books and look at the first question and example answer. (Go Ne's favorite season is spring.) Point out that the answer is a complete sentence.
- Have students do the rest of the activity individually, looking back at the reading to find the answers. Check answers as a class and have students say on which page they found their answer.

**Suggested Answers**

1 *Go Ne's favorite season is spring.*
2 He climbed the ladder. 3 He planted it in a pot.
4 He wanted a gold seed, too. 5 He felt (really) sorry.

**B Look and read. Then match the sentences to the characters.**

- Write the two characters' names in large letters each on a piece of paper. Stick these on the walls on either side of the classroom. Have students stand in the middle of the classroom. Call out the sentences in any order. Students should go and stand next to the relevant character.
- Have students open their books and complete the activity. Check answers as a class.

**Answers**

Go Ne: 2; 3; 5
Wen Shu: *1*; 4; 6

**C Think and check (✔). What else did you learn from the story?**

Students are going to reflect on the moral of the story. This draws on the SEL competency of making decisions based on moral, personal, and ethical standards.

- Draw students' attention to the activity and the question *What else did you learn from the story?* Have three students read an option each. Check comprehension of *be nice* and *be kind*. Ask questions to help students think about each option; for example, *Does the story tell us to be nice to other people? Only to some people or all people? Does it tell us to be kind to animals? And people, too? Does it say that friends are important or not important?*
- Make sure students understand that although Go Ne is rewarded for his kindness, he is kind because he respects living things, not because he wants a reward. Wen Shu is jealous of Go Ne, but at the end of the story he realizes that helping people is more important than being rich.

**Answer**

2

## Spelling Pattern *ai*

TRACK 14 TB p. 230 **Listen and write. Then check your answers.**

- With books closed, write *ai* on the board.
- Play the first part of the audio and have students repeat each word. Then have them open their books. Play the first part of the audio again and have them complete as many words as they can.
- Then play the second part of the audio for students to check their spelling and complete the words correctly. Have students read the words aloud. Ask *Which words have the same sound?* (rain, paint, train) *Which are different?* (mountain and chair) Have students underline *ai* in each word and notice that there is a consonant before and after.
- Have students look back at the reading to find more words with *ai* and write them in a word list. Invite students to read a word from their list.

**Answers**

1 rain 2 mountain 3 paint 4 train 5 chair
In the reading: said; sailed; air; waited; paid

## Cool Down

Prepare some situations in which people or animals need help (an older person with shopping bags; a lost dog; a cat stuck in a tree; a friend who has problems with homework; etc.) and write them on slips of paper. Have two students come to the front and act out a situation, one helping the other. The other students guess the situation.

**Practice** **Resource Bank:** Spelling Printout
**Student's App:** Reading Practice; Spelling Pattern Practice

## Think Together

### Lesson Objectives

- to make connections between the readings
- to explore the key concept: How are plants, animals, and humans connected?
- to reflect on the unit and provide personal thoughts and opinions

### Warm Up

Have students look back at the VTR picture on pp. 24–25. Ask them how they think the picture connects to the two readings in the unit. If necessary, write prompts on the board: *place, people, animals, weather, actions*. Encourage students to be creative in their answers; for example, *I think the story is set near the same forest; I think the forest is coniferous; The bear's home is in the forest and the swallow's home is under the roof; One of the people on the boat is a vet.*

**A Think and write. What do trees and plants give to people and animals?**

- With books closed, write the question on the board. Have students recap what they learned about trees and animals in *Two Different Forests*. Then have students recap what they learned about animals and people in *A New Friend*. Brainstorm ideas as a class and write suggestions on the board. Students can also use their own experience of the world to think of possible benefits of trees and plants.
- Draw students' attention to the leaves on p. 39. Discuss the example. Ask *Do you eat fruit from trees or plants? Do animals eat fruit or seeds?* Have students give examples (e.g. squirrels eat nuts).
- Have students work in pairs to discuss their ideas and write them in the leaf outlines. Then check answers as a class.

**Suggested Answers**
*fruit to eat*; wood to build houses/furniture; a place to build nests; homes for animals; shade in summer; clean air; a place to play; oxygen to breathe

**B Imagine a world without trees or plants. What happens? Make a list together. Do a Roundtable.**

- Students are going to do a Roundtable routine (see TB p. 20) to come up with a collaborative list. Each group needs a piece of paper and a pen.
- Write the statement and question on the board. Give students one or two minutes to think about the statement and possible answers to the question. They could create a spidergram with their ideas.
- If students are generating a lot of ideas, give them some more thinking time.

**C Think and discuss. What's on your list?**

- Students are going to look at all their ideas from B and then share with the class. In both B and C, students are working toward answering the key concept question *How are plants, animals, and humans connected?*
- Have students look at their ideas together in their groups. Then ask each group to call out their ideas. Did different groups have similar ideas? Did anyone hear a new idea? Write students' ideas on the board. Point out that these reiterate the concept that plants, animals, and humans are all connected and that we need plants and animals to survive.
- If students have any questions after this activity, have them write them on sticky notes and research the answers for homework.

### My Reading Journal

**Which places in this unit do you want to visit? What do you want to see?**

This question focuses on personalization. Briefly brainstorm the places that appeared in the unit (the river and forest in the VTR picture, the deciduous and coniferous forests, Go Ne's home). Elicit why they might be good places to visit. Ask *What can you see in each place?*

Have students write their ideas in their reading journals. Monitor and provide language help when needed. Then encourage students to compare with a friend.

**Example Answer**
I want to visit the coniferous forest. I want to see the animals that change color in winter.

**Tell the class one thing you learned about plants or animals.**

This task encourages students to review and remember what they learned. Tell the class one interesting thing that you learned from this unit; for example, *I learned that some animals change color in the winter.* Give students a few minutes to look back through the unit and find one thing they learned.

**Example Answer**
I learned that plants are very important for people and animals. They give us food and clean air to live.

### Cool Down

Play *Snowballs* (see TB p. 27). Have students think of one thing they learned during the unit (it can be what they wrote in their Reading Journal or something different) and write it on their piece of paper.

**Practice** **Resource Bank:** Unit Test
**Student's App:** Key Concept Practice

UNIT 3

# How Much Is It?

## Unit Overview

### Themes

What we use money for

The history of money and why we need it

### Synopsis

In this unit, students will explore the uses and value of money. They will learn about different types of money and how it has changed. They will discuss the different ways of spending and saving money and explore the theme of shopping. Students will plan and prepare a conversation about buying a present and write an anecdotal paragraph.

**Language Book**

**Vocabulary**
*allowance, buy, cashier, customer, change, cheap, expensive, pay, save, sell, spend, wallet*
p. 80

**Explore Language**
Modal Verbs: *Have to* and *Don't have to*
p. 81

**Global Citizenship**
What can people do with money?
*add, bills, dime, cents, coins, dollar, equals, nickel, penny, quarter, subtract*
p. 82

**Explore Language**
Modal Verbs: *Should, Shouldn't,* and *Could*
p. 83

**Talk About It**
Conversation: buying a birthday present
p. 84

**Write About It**
Anecdotal Paragraph
Sentence Building: conjunctions (*and, but, so*)
p. 85

**Think It Over**
Review and Reflection
p. 86

# Literacy Book

### Think Together
Why do we need money?
p. 93

### Visible Thinking
Think, Pair, Share
p. 87

### Fiction
Story: *The $100 Bill*

Words in Context: *belong to, return, pocket, restaurant, money is tight*
p. 91

### Nonfiction
Informational Text: *The History of Money*

Words in Context: *bartered, metal, valuable, credit card, plastic*
p. 88

### Reading Skill
Identifying problems and solutions
p. 90

### Spelling Pattern
*ar*
p. 92

## Language and Literacy Connections

The connecting theme in Unit 3 is finding out what money is and why we need it.

| | Language | Literacy |
|---|---|---|
| **Vocabulary** | **Sets 1 and 2:** money | **Nonfiction:** buy, sell(ing), coins<br>**Fiction:** cashier, expensive, pay, save, dollar(s) |
| **Grammar** | **Modal Verbs:** ***Have To* and *Don't Have To***<br>What do you have to do?<br>I have to clean my room.<br>I don't have to wash the dishes.<br>**Modal Verbs:** ***Should, Shouldn't,* and *Could***<br>You should buy the lamp.<br>You shouldn't spend it all.<br>You could buy these lights. | **Nonfiction**<br>People didn't have to use paper money or coins.<br>**Fiction**<br>You really should get one.<br>I should save the money.<br>You don't have to pay. |
| **Skills** | **Pronunciation:** /pr/ and /dr/ | **Reading:** identifying problems and solutions<br>**Spelling Pattern:** *ar* |
| **International English** | allowance / pocket money; bill/note; college/university | bill/note |

## Vocabulary

### Lesson Objectives

- to learn money vocabulary: *allowance, buy, cashier, change, cheap, customer, expensive, pay, save, sell, spend, wallet*
- to sing a song that explores money

**Materials**
Audio Tracks 27 to 30; Video

### Warm Up

Ask students about shopping. Ask *What kinds of things do you buy? What do your parents buy? Who do you go shopping with? What shops do you go to? Do you buy clothes/toys/candy? Do your parents shop online? Do you like shopping?*

**A** TRACK 27 TB p. 216 **Listen and find. How much does the shirt cost?**

- Have students look at the picture and say what they see. Ask *Who can you see?* (Owen from Unit 2) *What's he doing?* (shopping / looking at a phone case)
- Tell students they are going to listen to Owen and his friends while they are shopping. Play the audio and have students point to the words or pictures as they listen. Remind students of the challenge from the end of Unit 2: *What store do I go to?* and elicit the answer (a gift store) in L1 if necessary.
- Ask the comprehension question *How much does the shirt cost?* and elicit the answer. Play the audio again for students to check.

**Answer**
$9.25

**B** TRACK 28 TB p. 216 **Listen, say, and number the pictures in A.**

- Play the audio and have students point to the pictures and say the words.
- Tell students to listen again and write numbers next to the words in the picture. Do the example together (save).
- Check answers by pointing to different people and actions in the picture and having students say the number and word. Alternatively, project the answers using the TTL.

**Answers**
1 *save* 2 spend 3 sell 4 customer 5 buy
6 expensive 7 cheap 8 cashier 9 pay 10 change
11 wallet 12 allowance

**International English**

Elicit that *allowance* is American English and *pocket money* is British English. Ask *Why do you think it's called* pocket money?

**C** TRACK 29 TB p. 216 **Close your eyes. Listen, visualize, and say.**

- Prepare students for the visualization (see TB p. 21).
- Play the audio, allowing students to visualize the ideas as they listen. Make sure students know not to speak until they hear the word *say*. Put your finger to your lips if necessary.
- Have students work in pairs to mime two or three ideas for their partner to guess. If necessary, give an example first: mime picking up a jacket, smiling to show you love it (even trying it on), looking at the price tag, and then whistling and putting it back.

**D** **Look at A. Complete.**

- Students are going to categorize the vocabulary in a spidergram. This encourages critical thinking and makes the vocabulary more visual and therefore more memorable. Tell students that we use different words to talk about money and shopping. See if they can they can think of any.
- Draw students' attention to the spidergram. Point out that some of the words in A are things, some are people, some are verbs, and others are adjectives to describe things.
- Tell students to write the words from A in the spidergram. Then check answers as a class. You could project the answers using the TTL.

**Answers**
Things: *change*, wallet, allowance
People: customer, cashier
Verbs: save, spend, sell, buy, pay
Adjectives: expensive, cheap

**E** TRACK 30 TB p. 216 **Listen and complete. Then watch and sing.**

- Point to the song title *Money, Money, Money!* Ask *What do children spend money on?* and elicit suggestions. Then play the song once, allowing students to listen and enjoy it. Are students' ideas in the song?
- Look at the incomplete song lyrics and ask students which words they can unscramble to complete the lyrics (do this orally). Play the song again, this time pausing where necessary for students to write their answers.
- Check answers as a class.
- Play the song video and encourage students to sing as they watch. They can move to the music.

**Answers**
1 *spend* 2 wallets 3 buy 4 customers 5 sell
6 save

### Cool Down

Have students do a shop role-play in groups. For more ideas on using role-play (see TB p. 23). One student in each group is the sales clerk, and the others are customers. Write key phrases on the board as prompts; for example, *Excuse me; Can I help you?; I'd like a …, please; How much is it?* Ask volunteer groups to perform the role-play in front of the class.

**Practice** **Student's App:** Vocabulary Practice; Song Video

# Explore Language

## Lesson Objectives

- to learn to use the modal verbs *have to* and *don't have to*
- to practice money vocabulary

**Materials**

Audio Tracks 30 to 32

## Warm Up

Ask students if they help at home to get money from their parents. If they do, ask volunteers to say what kinds of things they do. If they don't, ask students if they receive some money from their parents every week/month. Explain that this money is sometimes referred to as spending money, pocket money, or an allowance. Ask *Do you save it, spend it, or both?*

**A** TRACK 31 TB p. 216 **Listen and read. How does Owen get his money?**

- Remind students of the scene on pp. 36–37. Ask *What did Owen want to buy?* (a phone case) Ask *Who was Owen with?* (his friend Charlie). Tell students that they are going to listen to Owen talking to Charlie after they finish shopping. Play the audio and have students follow the dialogue.
- Ask the gist question *How does Owen get his money?* and elicit the answer. Ask *What does he do to get the money?*

**Answer**

He gets his money from his parents when he helps at home, by making the bed and washing the dishes.

**B Look at A. Complete.**

- Write or project the table onto the board.
- Look at the first question in the table. Ask *How can we answer the question?* Elicit that the sentences below the question are ways of answering it. Have students find the first missing words (have to) in the dialogue in A. Ask *Do you think Charlie likes cleaning his room? Why does he do it?* Elicit that Charlie's parents tell him to clean his room. Repeat for the next blank and ask *Does Charlie have to wash the dishes?* (no)
- Have students work in pairs to complete the rest of table. Check answers as a class. Encourage students to notice the difference between the first-person and third-person forms of the verb.
- Review the short answer forms. Write the question *Do you have to make your bed?* on the board. Elicit answers. Then have students read the Grammar tip *Watch Out*. Make sure students notice that questions that start with *Do/does* are also answered with *Do/does* (not *have*).

**Answers**

have to; don't have to; Do; have to; do

**C Think and discuss. Then choose.**

- Check students understand the meaning of *need to*. Say *I'm very hungry. I need to* … and encourage students to complete the sentence.
- Have students work in pairs to discuss the two statements and circle the answers. Refer them to the table in B for examples. Then check answers.

**Answers**

1 need to 2 don't need to

**D** TRACK 32 TB p. 216 **Listen and say.**

- Tell students they're going to practice saying the structures. Play the audio, having students repeat each sentence chorally.
- For ideas on how to vary the drill, see TB p. 23.

**E Look, read, and complete.**

- Have students look at the picture and describe what they see. Ask *What do they have to do?* and elicit suggestions orally, pointing to the verbs in the box.
- Say *Complete the sentences using "have to" and one of the verbs.* Have students do the activity individually. Remind them to use the correct form of *have to* and to look at the table in B to help them. Check answers as a class.

**Answers**

1 *has to clean; doesn't* 2 have to finish 3 has to wash
4 don't have to clean 5 Does; have to help

**F Play *Find Someone Who*. Write three sentences about jobs you have to do at home.**

- Have students draw a table with three columns: *Jobs*, *Me*, and *My Friends*. First, have them make a list of jobs in the *Jobs* column. Then have them complete the *Me* column by checking the jobs they do. Have them write three sentences under the table about the jobs they do at home.
- Then have students work in pairs to ask each other about the jobs they do. Students should write their partner's name in the *My Friends* column next to the jobs they do. Have two students demonstrate using the examples on the page.
- Have students play *Find Someone Who* (see TB p. 24) to find people who do the remaining chores on their lists.

## Cool Down

Play the *Yes/No Game* (see TB p. 27) to review the grammar. Call out statements using *have to* and *don't have to*; for example, *I have to do homework every day*; *I don't have to go to school on Sundays*.

**Practice** **Resource Bank:** Grammar Printout
**Student's App:** Grammar Practice

# Global Citizenship

## Lesson Objectives

- to learn math and money vocabulary: *add, equals, subtract; bills, cents, coins, dime, dollar, nickel, penny, quarter*
- to explore how money can be used to help our communities
- to practice listening for gist and details

**Materials**

Audio Tracks 33 to 35; Audio Track C; a world map (D)

### Opening Question

Ask the opening question: *What can people do with money?* Elicit ideas and encourage students to think about the different things you can buy or spend money on. Write students' ideas on the board.

**A** TRACK 33 TB p. 217 **Listen to Annette talk about her American coins. Why does Sumiko like coins?**

- Tell students they are going to listen to two girls named Annette and Sumiko talking about money. Play the audio and have students point to the words or pictures as they listen.
- Ask the gist question *Why does Sumiko like coins?* Play the audio again for students to check. Then hold a few coins in your hand and shake them to show students the sound they make together. Ask *Do you like the sound? Do you prefer coins or bills? Why?*

**Answers**

She thinks it's fun to collect them.

**B** TRACK 34 TB p. 217 **Listen, say, and number the pictures in A.**

- Play the audio and have students point to the pictures and say the words.
- Tell students to listen again and write numbers next to the words in the picture. Do the example together (penny).
- Project the answers using the TTL.

**Answers**

1 penny 2 cents 3 quarter 4 bills 5 dollar
6 nickel 7 coins 8 equals 9 subtract 10 add
11 dime

TRACK C TB p. 217 **Visualization**

The TTL has a visualization audio track for this vocabulary set. (See TB p. 21.)

**C Read and complete.**

- Students are going to complete the sentences with the vocabulary from A. Look at the example together. Ask *How much is a penny?* (one cent) Then ask *What word comes after "five"?* (five cents) *Which coin is worth five cents?* (a nickel)
- Have students complete the sentences individually. Then check answers as a class.

**Answers**

1 *penny*; nickel; cents; dime 2 quarters; dollar
3 coins; bills 4 Add; 30 5 Subtract; 90 6 equals

**D** TRACK 35 TB p. 217 **Now listen to Leena and Davi. Why does Leena save her coins?**

- Quickly review the money vocabulary from Lesson 1.
- Tell students they are going to listen to two children talking about money. Have students look at the two pictures and notice where each child is from. Point out Jordan and Brazil on a map and elicit anything students know about these countries.
- Listening for gist: Ask the gist question *Why does Leena save her coins?* Play the audio and then check answers.

**Answer**

She's saving her coins to pay for college.

**E Listen again. Check (✔) the correct person.**

- Listening for details: have students look at the questions before they listen again to see how many things they remember. Then play the audio and have students check the correct person.
- To check answers, read each question and have students raise their left hand for *Leena* and their right hand for *Davi.*

**Answers**

1 *Davi* 2 Davi 3 Leena 4 Davi 5 Leena

**International English**

Elicit that *bill* and *college* are American English and *note* and *university* are British English words. Write examples on the board to show how *bill* and *note* can be used, e.g. *a 100 dollar bill; a 20 pound note.*

### Discussion Questions

- Draw students' attention to the discussion questions: *What do you do with coins? How can we use coins to help our communities?* Have students discuss the questions in pairs. See **ETB**.
- Return to the opening question to ask again: *What can people do with money?* Encourage students to share any new ideas they have learned during the lesson.

### Cool Down

Give students some math problems to answer in pairs. Example problems: *How many cents are in a dime? If you add a dollar and a quarter, then subtract a nickel, how much do you have?*



**Practice** **Student's App:** Vocabulary Practice; Listening Practice

# Explore Language

## Lesson Objectives

- to learn to use *should*, *shouldn't*, and *could*
- to practice math and money vocabulary

**Materials**
Audio Tracks 36 and 37

## Warm Up

Tell students to imagine they can buy something new for their bedrooms. What do they buy? Have students discuss their ideas in pairs and then share with the class.

**A** TRACK 36 TB p. 217 **Listen and read. How much money does Andie spend?**

- Tell students that they are going to listen to Ting talking to her friend Andie in a shop. Have students look back at p. 37 and find Ting. Play the audio and have students follow the dialogue in their books.
- Ask the gist question *How much money does Andie spend?* and elicit the answer. Ask *What does she buy?* (a set of lights)

**Answers**
Andie spends $10.

**B** **Look at A. Complete.**

- Write or project the table onto the board.
- Have students look at A to find the first sentence. Ask who says the sentence. (Andie) Have them notice the two verbs together, *should buy*.
- Have students work in pairs to find the other missing words in the table. Check answers as a class.
- Point out the word order in the question and the short answer forms.
- Draw students' attention to the Grammar tip *Remember*. Write *good* on the board and elicit its pronunciation. Write *should* and *could* and point out that they rhyme with *good*. Drill the pronunciation of the three words one after the other. For more ideas on how to do drills, see TB p. 22.

**Answers**
shouldn't; could; should; Should; should; shouldn't

**C** **Think and discuss. Then choose.**

- Check students understand the meaning of *advice* and *choices*.
- Have students work in pairs to discuss the statements. Refer them to the table in B for examples of the two verbs.
- Check answers as a class. Ask *What is Andie's advice?* (At first she says Ting should save her money. At the end she says she should buy the lamp.) *What are Ting's choices?* (She could buy the lamp or she could buy the lights.)

**Answers**
1 should 2 could

**D** TRACK 37 TB p. 217 **Listen and say.**

- Tell students they're going to practice saying the new structures. Play the audio, having students repeat each sentence chorally.
- For ideas on how to vary the drill, see TB p. 23.

**E** **Complete the sentences with *could* or *should*.**

- Look at the example. Say *Is it a choice or advice?* (a choice)
- Have students complete the sentences with *could* or *should*. Then check answers as a class.

**Answers**
1 *could* 2 should 3 Should 4 could 5 could; could
6 should

**F** **Play *What to do?* Read, think, and discuss.**

- Have students look at the pictures of the snacks. Elicit what students see. Ask a few questions to practice prices; for example, *How much are the pizza slices?*
- Have students read the situation. Ask questions to check comprehension; for example, *How much money do you and your partner have?* ($6) Ask students to suggest snacks they could buy with this money. Look at the examples and have two students demonstrate.
- Then have students work in pairs to discuss what they could buy and how to spend their money together. Encourage them to think of different ways of spending the money.
- To turn this into a game, have students try to come up with as many different ways of spending the money as they can. The pair who comes up with the most ways to spend the money wins.
- Have students share their ideas with the class.

## Cool Down

Play *Versus* (see TB p. 27). Example statements: *You should study a little every day / You should study a lot on weekends.*

**Practice** **Resource Bank:** Grammar Printout
**Student's App:** Grammar Practice

# Talk About It

## Lesson Objectives

- to prepare and practice a conversation about buying a birthday present
- to recognize and reproduce /pr/ and /dr/

**Materials**
Video; Audio Track 38

## Warm Up

Tell students to remember the last time they bought a present for someone. Ask *What was the present? Who was it for? Did they like it?* Have students talk in pairs and then share with the class. Take a vote on the most interesting present.

**A** TB p. 238 **Watch and listen. What present does Anya buy?**

- Tell students they are going to watch a video of a conversation between a girl named Anya and a boy named Stephen who is pretending to work in a shop.
- Play the first two lines of the video. Ask *Who is the present for?* (Anya's little sister) Ask the gist question *What present does Anya buy?* With books closed, play the video and then check the answer. Ask further comprehension questions; for example, *How much is the present?* ($30) Play the video again and ask students what they notice about Anya's body language.

**Answer**
Anya buys a video game.

**B Watch again. Check (✔) the phrases you hear.**

- Have students read the phrases.
- Play the video again and have them check the phrases they hear. Check answers as a class. Play the video again and have students raise their hands when they hear a similar sentence to those they didn't check. Choose one student to call out the new sentence; for example, *I'm looking for a present for my sister.*
- Ask *Who speaks first?* (the cashier) *What does he say?* ("Can I help you?") *How does Anya respond?* ("Yes. I'm looking for a birthday present for my sister.") Ask *How does he make a suggestion?* ("You could get her …") *Which sentence gives advice?* ("I think you should buy …") *How does the conversation end?* ("Have a nice day!" / "You, too!")

**Answers**
*1*; 3; 5; 7; 8

### Pronunciation /pr/ and /dr/

TRACK 38 TB p. 217 **Listen and say.**

Demonstrate the two sounds first. Isolate each phoneme in the consonant cluster and elicit how to pronounce it (/p/; /r/). Then put the two sounds together slowly **/pr/** and have students repeat it. Do the same for **/dr/**.

Play the audio and have students repeat the words. Repeat if students need more practice.

Say *These words are used in the video. What other words do you know with these sounds?* Elicit ideas and write them on the board in two columns (e.g. *princess, dragon*). Drill the pronunciation of each word.

**Suggested Answers**
**/pr/** problem, protect, proud; **/dr/** drawbridge, dream, drop, dry

**C Plan. Choose two people. Think about buying them a present. Check (✔) and write.**

- Tell students they are going to plan a conversation about buying a present. Say *In the video, who is Anya buying a present for?* (her six-year-old sister) Ask *What kinds of toys does she like?* (games and puzzles) Tell students that we need to think about what people like when we are buying them a present.
- Say *Now think about the presents you could buy for different people.* Project the plan onto the board. Ask questions to show students how to complete it; for example, *Does your mom like flowers?*
- Encourage students to add the name of one more person they could buy a present for and two more possible present ideas to the plan. Then have students choose and check two people they would like to buy presents for and circle what they would buy them. Have them write the names and the presents in the box.

**D Prepare your conversation. Use your ideas from C and phrases from B.**

- Play the video again as a model.
- Have students work in pairs to prepare their conversation using one of their ideas from C and phrases from B.
- Together students should plan two conversations, as they will take turns being the sales clerk and the customer. Before they begin, the sales clerk needs to plan what he/she will suggest and what to say about it.

**E Practice with a friend.**

- Have students practice their conversation with their partner as many times as they like. Remind them to take turns, look at their partner, listen when their partner is speaking, and smile. Monitor and offer help and praise.

## Cool Down

Ask students to work in pairs to choose the perfect present for different people (e.g. their teacher, the president/monarch of your country, a famous actor/sports person from your country). They should justify their choices.

**Practice** **Student's App:** Speaking Skills Practice; Speaking Video

## Write About It

### Lesson Objectives

- to learn to use conjunctions *and*, *but*, and *so*
- to review punctuation
- to plan and write an anecdotal paragraph

**Materials**

(Optional) Support, Standard, or Challenge writing printouts from the Resource Bank, one per student (C and D)

### Warm Up

Ask *Did you ever want something that was very expensive and you didn't have enough money to buy it? What happened? Did your parents buy it for you? Did you save money for it? How did you feel when you got it?*

**A Read the paragraph. Underline *and*, *but*, and *so*. Circle the punctuation that comes before these words.**

- Introduce students to the concept of an anecdote. Tell them that an anecdote is a short, interesting story about something that happened, often in normal, everyday life. Anecdotes are generally based on fact. Give students one or two minutes to read the anecdotal paragraph. Ask *What did the writer do to get his paddle board?* (saved his birthday money, helped at home) Have students notice the picture and elicit that it shows the outcome of the story.
- Have students read the instructions. Ask *What three words do you have to look for?* (*and*, *but*, and *so*). *What do you have to circle?* (punctuation—commas) Have students look at the example and elicit what comes before the *and* (a comma).
- Check answers as a class. Highlight how the conjunctions help connect the words to create longer sentences. Without the conjunctions, the sentences would be very short and would make the anecdote more difficult to read. Elicit that a comma precedes most of the conjunctions in the anecdote and have students identify where there is no comma (mom and dad). Can they suggest why we don't need a comma here? (This conjunction connects two words, not two ideas: if we took away the *and* we wouldn't have two sentences!)

**Answers**

Last summer, I wanted a paddle board. I tried one at the lake, and it was fun! At first, I fell in the water, but I quickly learned to stand. I wanted one, so I saved my money all year. People gave me money for my birthday, and I saved it in a box. I also saved my allowance from my mom and dad. I have to help at home to get it. Every week, I have to clean my room, and every day I have to wash the dishes. After a year, I counted my money. My dad took me to the store, and I finally bought my paddle board. It's beautiful!

**B Look at A. Match.**

- Review how to use *and* and *but*. Give a couple of example sentences: *I wanted to buy a new jacket, and I had some birthday money to spend. I found a great jacket, but I didn't like the color.* Elicit example sentences for each one from the class and write these on the board. Ask *Which word do we use before we say something different?* (but) *Which word do we use to add more information?* (and)
- Look at the example together. Say *We use* so *when we explain why. What did the boy do because he wanted a paddle board?* Elicit that he saved his money for a year. Then have students do the rest of the activity. Check answers as a class.

**Answers**

1 c 2 e 3 a 4 b 5 d

**C Plan. Think about something you saved money for. Answer the questions.**

- Encourage students to think of a time when they saved money to buy something. If they have no experience of doing this, brainstorm ideas with the class instead, having students pretend they saved up for something.
- Go through the questions one by one using an example from a student or the story you brainstormed with the class.
- Then have students answer the questions individually to plan their anecdotal paragraph. Challenge printouts can be handed out now.

**D Write your paragraph. Find or draw a picture to go with it.**

- Have students write a draft of their anecdotal paragraphs in their notebooks or on paper using their ideas from C. Students should include an introductory sentence and an ending sentence that expresses their feelings about what they bought. Support printouts can be handed out now.
- Students should self-correct or exchange their work with a friend and peer-correct. You can put a checklist of things for students to look for on the board (e.g. spelling, use of adjectives and adverbs, verb forms, punctuation, sequencers, conjunctions).
- Have students neatly write their final versions on paper or on the Standard printouts. Give them time to find or draw a picture of what they saved up for.

### Cool Down

Play *Never-Ending Sentence* (see TB p. 26). For this version, use the story starter *Last summer I wanted a skateboard.* Encourage students to use *and*, *but*, and *so*.

**Practice** **Student's App:** Writing Practice

# Think It Over

## Lesson Objectives

- to review what has been learned in the unit
- to reflect on the unit and their own progress
- to think about learning strategies and how to continue learning at home

## Warm Up

Ask students what the unit theme was (money) and write it in the middle of the board. Brainstorm any words or phrases students can think of that relate to the topic and write them on the board. Encourage students to think about the things we spend money on and the different things we do with money.

**Read the questions and draw or write your answers.**

Give students time to think about and discuss activities in the unit before they complete each question. Explain that they can choose to either write a few words or sentences or to draw a picture. Allowing students to make a personal response will help them retain knowledge and engage with the learning points.

**What did I do?**

- Give students a few minutes to look back through the unit at the different activities they did. Ask questions about the unit or write questions on the board for students to discuss in pairs or small groups; for example, *What different things did the children in the unit spend money on? What else can you do with money?*
- Encourage students to identify something in the unit that they found challenging or something that was particularly memorable for them. Students can draw or write about their chosen activity.

**How did I learn?**

- Ask students how they learned the money vocabulary in Lessons 1 and 3. Elicit ideas (e.g. by listening to a dialogue, by classifying words, by solving mathematical problems). Encourage students to think about the spelling and pronunciation of the words. Ask *What helps you remember how to say and write the new words?*
- Then encourage students to think about how they learned throughout the unit; for example, how did they develop their listening skills?
- Have students draw or write about the activities that helped them learn.

**What did I learn?**

- Ask questions about the unit to help students think about what they learned; for example, *What new words do you know? What advice can you give? What did you learn about saving money? What else did you learn?* Have students discuss their ideas in pairs.
- Encourage students to draw a picture or write sentences about their learning outcomes.

**How well did I do?**

- Tell students to color the savings bank that best expresses how well they have learned the unit content (i.e., the bigger amount they color, the more they feel they have learned). Ask *What do you understand? What do you need to practice more?* Encourage students to look back through the unit to see how much they remember what they did well, and what they found difficult.

**What can I do next?**

- Brainstorm ideas with the class about what they can do to continue to learn (e.g. think about the different ways to spend and save money, notice the price of things on TV advertisements, find and pronounce words with /pr/ and /dr/, do another role-play in a store, find and play a math app about money).
- Draw students' attention to the *What can I do next?* box. Encourage students to think about what they can do at home to improve their English. Have them suggest some verbs that they can use (e.g. *read, write, talk about, ask, research*) and write the verbs in their books. Students can look back at the previous units to get more ideas. Encourage students to suggest their own ideas for different activities they can do.
- Have students choose several activities that they would like to do and write them in their notebooks. They can then share their ideas with a partner.

## Looking Forward

Draw students' attention to the character at the bottom of the page. Ask *Who's this?* and elicit what they remember about her (Ting appears in Explore Language 2, p. 42; she bought a lamp for her bedroom).

Say *Ting thinks carefully about buying something expensive. Do you?* Have students raise their hand and give an example.

Draw students' attention to Ting's question: *What will I perform?* Encourage students to make predictions about what she will perform and what Unit 4 is about. Tell students they will find out the answer in Lesson 1 of the next unit.

**Practice** **Resource Bank:** Unit Test
**Student's App:** Vocabulary and Grammar Review

## Get Ready to Read

### Lesson Objectives

- to activate prior knowledge about different kinds of money and its uses to guide enquiry and deepen understanding through a Think, Pair, Share VTR
- to preview the reading skill of identifying problems and solutions

**Materials**
(Optional) VTR printout from the Resource Bank (Activities A, B, C)

### Warm Up

Say *Imagine you have all the money you want but you can only buy three things. What do you buy?* Give students a few seconds to think. Have them discuss their ideas with a partner. Then say *Now you can only buy one thing, and you have to agree!* Students talk with their partner to decide which single thing they want to buy. Have students share their ideas with the class.

### Think, Pair, Share

**A Look at the picture. What labels do you want on your jars? Think about it.**

Students are going to do a Think, Pair, Share VTR to explore an image of jars used for saving money.

- Have students say what they can see in the picture. Encourage them to use adjectives such as colors and shapes. If students don't know a word in English, ask them to describe what they see for you to provide it in English.
- Ask *What are the jars for?* Elicit that they are for saving money for different things. Ask *What is this person saving money for?* Elicit the meaning of *donating* by asking *What does the person want to help? How is the person helping? What's a synonym for "donating"?* (giving)
- Ask *Is it a good idea to save? What do you want to save for? What do you want to write on your jars?*
- Give students a couple of minutes to think about their ideas silently. Tell them to cross their arms when they have thought of some ideas.

**B Discuss with your partner.**

- Ask two volunteers to read the example dialogue in B.
- Divide the class into pairs and have students share their ideas. Encourage them to discuss any questions they might have and to think of possible answers together.
- Remind students to use phrases such as *Me, too* and *Really? I don't think so* and *Yes, I agree.*
- Monitor and provide language help when needed as students discuss their ideas.

**C Share your ideas with the class.**

- Ask pairs to share their ideas about the picture with the class. Encourage students to use *we*, as they are talking about their partner's opinion, too.

Here's an example of this part of the routine.

**Teacher:** What do you both think?
**Student A:** We think it's a good idea to save money.
**Teacher:** Why do you think that?
**Student A:** So we can buy the things we need.
**Teacher:** Good. What do you want to write on your jars?
**Student B:** Toys and vacation.
**Teacher:** Great ideas! What do you want to do with the vacation money?
**Student A:** We want to go horseback riding.
**Teacher:** OK, (Student C), what do you and your friend want to write on your jars?
**Student C:** We have a label for presents—we can buy birthday presents for our families.

### Transition

Have students begin to think about why we need money and what we did before money existed. Say *Imagine you don't have any money but you need to buy something. What can you do?* Encourage students to think about the concept of exchanging things or helping out.

**D Where do people use money? Make a class list of places.**

- Brainstorm with the class places where we use money, writing students' suggestions in a list on the board. Explore the various uses of money, thinking about the kinds of things people buy with money and services people pay for. Encourage students to think about travel, medical treatment, building work, and so on, as well as services they might use themselves like a hairdresser's or a sports class.

**E Think and discuss. What's wrong? How can they fix it?**

In this activity students will preview the skill of identifying and solving problems.

- Have students look at the picture. Ask *What does the first man have?* (grain) *What does he want?* (a goat) *What does the second man have?* (a goat) *What does he want?* (grain)
- Ask *What's the problem? How can they fix it?* Have students work in pairs to identify the problem and think of possible solutions. Encourage students to think of more than one solution to the problem.
- Then have students share their ideas with the class.

**Suggested Answers**
They each need what the other one has.
They could swap the goods. They could sell the goods to each other. The man with the grain could help the other man to grow grain in exchange for a goat. The man with the goat could give the other man some milk in exchange for grain.

Now read **The History of Money**

# Nonfiction: *The History of Money*—Informational Text

## Lesson Objectives

- to read an informational text about the history of money
- to make a personal connection to the reading

**Materials**

Audio Tracks 15 and 16; Video; money (WU)

## Warm Up

Bring in some money for students to look at. This could be current currency in your country, foreign currency, old currency, or replica/toy money. Have students examine the money and discuss how much it is worth. If you have different currencies, students can compare and contrast them, thinking about the number value, size, weight, color, and so on.

### TRACK 15 TB p. 231 Reading Approach

**First Reading: Engage with the Text**

- Before students open their books, have them predict when money was invented. Find out if they have ever seen old coins in a museum.
- Have students open their books and look at the reading. Ask them to notice the title, text, and pictures on the page and use this information to make predictions. See if they recognize any of the money in the pictures. Ask *What did people do before money existed?* Have students look at the pictures and make suggestions.
- Play the audio and have students read along as they listen.
- Ask prediction questions before moving on to the next page; for example, *Which country do you think started using money first?* (China) *What type of money do you think came next?*
- Read the whole reading before looking at the Words in Context.

### TRACK 16 TB p. 231 Words in Context

- Play the audio and have students repeat the words.
- Have a word race to find the words in the story.
- Remind students to **use the words around the new words to guess their meaning** and to **read the next sentence to get examples to help them understand the meaning of the new words** (see TB p. 23). Have students discuss their ideas in pairs.
- Then bring the class together and use these questions to confirm the meanings.

**bartered** (p. 42) Point to the first picture and elicit what the people are doing. Remind students to find the word in the text and continue reading. The following sentence gives an example of *bartering*. Ask *When two people bartered, did they both get something?* Tell students a similar word is *exchange*.

**metal** (p. 43) Have students point to something metal in the pictures. Elicit examples of metals.

**valuable** (p. 44) Focus on the phrase *valuable metals like silver and gold*. Elicit that these metals cost a lot of money. Ask students if they own anything valuable.

**credit card** (p. 45) Read the sentence *People didn't have to use paper money or coins.* Ask *What do people use to pay?* Have students look in the picture to find the credit card.

**plastic** (p. 43) If possible, show students a credit card. Ask *What is it made from?*

**Second Reading: Analyze the Text and Features**

- Play the video to consolidate students' understanding of the reading.
- Ask some questions to check comprehension; for example, *What kinds of things did people want to buy in 6000 BCE?* (food) *What did the Chinese first use as metal money?* (knives and spades) *What metals were used in making coins?* (gold and silver) *What's electronic money?* (using your phone or online account to pay for things)
- Discuss the questions in the blue boxes.
  - **Fact** (p. 42): *BCE stands for Before Common Era. BCE dates count backwards, so something from 6000 BCE is older than something from 1200 BCE. Can you guess what CE stands for?* Elicit ideas. (Common Era) Then ask *Which came first, 1200 BCE or 1200 CE?* (BCE)
  - **Creative Thinking** (p. 43): *Why do you think they put holes in the coins?* Elicit ideas from students. Ask *Did they put something in the hole? Maybe the coins were heavy and the hole makes them lighter? Any other ideas?* If students are interested, have them investigate the answer for homework.
  - **Personalization** (p. 45): *Do you wish we used different money today?* Ask *Which money do you like? Why? Do you think it's a good idea to pay with your phone?*
- Point out the text focus: *A timeline is an infographic that shows information in time order.* Have students look at the timeline. Ask students *Is it easy to understand the information? Why or why not?*

**Third Reading: Interact with the Text**

- Play the video again on mute and have students narrate it in groups of four. Each student can read one paragraph on each two-page spread.

## Cool Down

Play *60 Seconds* (see TB p. 25).

**Practice** **Student's App:** Nonfiction Video

## Explore the Reading

### Lesson Objectives

- to understand and analyze *The History of Money* through reading comprehension activities
- to compare and contrast different types of money
- to learn through CLIL (history): exploring different types of money through time to present day and beyond

**Materials**

(optional) Video or Audio Track 15

### Warm Up

Play *Stand Up, Sit Down* (see TB p. 27) using the following statements: *Bartering was a fast way to buy things* (False); *Shells were easier to carry than goats* (True); *The Chinese were the first people to use paper money* (True); *The coins from Turkey had pictures of houses on them* (False). Review answers as a class.

**A Think and check (✔). Which of these is or was money?**

- If more than one day has passed since students read *The History of Money*, play the video or audio again.
- With books closed, have a Group Time discussion (see TB p. 21) to check students' comprehension of the text. Ask *What did people use before money?* (goats, grain, shells, etc.) *Who used metal knives and spades?* (the Chinese) *Where were the first true coins made?* (Turkey) *What materials were used to make coins?* (metal—silver, and gold) *How do people pay now without money?* (with a credit card or electronic money)
- Activities A and B help students learn about history through CLIL, by exploring the types of money used during different times and places. Have students open their books and look at the question. Say *Look at number 1. What are they?* (cowrie shells) *Is it money?* (Yes, it is an early form of money.) Tell students to look at each picture and decide if it is money or not.
- Have students do the rest of the activity individually. Check answers as a class.

**Answers**

1; 3; 5; 6

**B Compare and contrast the types of money. Complete the chart.**

- Have students find the types of money quickly in the reading on pp. 42–45. This can be a race.
- Draw students' attention to the chart and do an example together. Ask *When were knives and spades used?* and have students look back at the reading to find the answer (1000 BCE). *What were they made of?* (metal) Then have students complete the rest of the activity individually. Check answers as a class.
- Have students work in pairs or small groups to try to think of other similarities and differences between the types of money (e.g. size). Then ask *Which type of money do you like best? Which is more practical?*

**Answers**

Cowrie shells: *1200 BCE*, shells; *Knives and spades*: 1000 BCE, metal; Paper money: *800–900 CE*, paper; Credit card: 1958 CE, *plastic*

**C Think and discuss. Design the next type of money.**

- Students are going to use their knowledge of different types of money to design a new type of money. This draws on the CLIL history focus of exploring different types of money through time. Say *You are going to design a new type of money for the future.* First, have them think about the future and how it will be different from the present. Write the following prompts on the board: *products, stores, shopping habits, prices, transportation*. Have students think of ideas individually and then share their ideas with a partner.
- Then tell students to think carefully about the materials for their new money and how practical it is to carry around and use in the future they have described. You could give students a series of questions to answer to help them choose; for example, *What does it look like? How big is it? Is it heavy or light? Is it resistant to water and fire? Can people lose it easily? How does it work?*
- Have students discuss their ideas in pairs or small groups. They can then share their ideas with the class. Students could give a presentation to the class, explaining how their new money works.
- Have students compare and contrast the different designs, as they did in B. Encourage them to think about how each type of money is used and why it is better than the money we use today.
- Students could then draw/design their own timeline showing the history of money, including a section for the future, with an image and a caption about their new money.

### Cool Down

Play *Backs to the Board* (see TB p. 25) with words from the lesson. Then have students swap places and repeat.

**Practice** **Student's App:** Reading Practice

# Get Ready to Read

## Lesson Objectives

- to practice the reading skill of identifying problems and solutions
- to activate prior knowledge about different kinds of money
- to make a personal connection to the reading
- to explore the SEL competency of responsible decision-making by identifying problems when making decisions and generating alternatives

## Warm Up

Have students do a ranking activity. Write the following problems on the board: *I have too much homework; My best friend isn't talking to me; I lost $10; I want to buy my friend a birthday present, but I don't have enough money; I am sleepy at school.* Say *Here are some problems children may have. Put them in order from most important to least important. One is the most important.* Students work in pairs to rank the problems in order of seriousness.

**A Read this retelling of *A New Friend*. Then write the problem and the solution.**

Students are going to practice the reading skill of identifying problems and solutions.

- Quickly recap the story with students by asking questions: *What do you remember about Go Ne?* (He loved swallows, and his family didn't have much money.) *What did Go Ne and his dad do?* (They helped a baby bird.) *How did the mommy bird say thank you?* (She gave them a special seed.) *What did Wen Shu do?* (He hit the nest and hurt the bird.) *What did Wen Shu do in the end?* (He gave Go Ne's family the things they needed.)
- Before students read the text, ask *What problems are there in the story?* Elicit ideas from the class. Don't correct answers at this stage.
- Tell students they are going to find a problem and a solution in the story. Have students read the text and complete the activity individually.
- When students have finished writing their ideas, discuss them as a class. Then read the skills box. Ask students if they found it easy or hard to identify the problem and solution.

**Answers**

Problem: Wen Shu hit the bird with the stone / the bird is hurt.
Solution: Go Ne takes the bird to the vet / the vet makes the bird better.

**B Think and write. Look at these pictures of early money. What were the problems with them? What solutions did people use?**

- Draw students' attention to the instructions. Have students look at the pictures and name the types of "money" (bartering and small knives and spades). Discuss with the class the possible problems with each type of money.
- Then ask *What solutions did they use? How did they change the money?* Encourage students to suggest ideas. Ask them for evidence of their thinking by saying *What makes you say that? They can look back at the reading if necessary.*

**Suggested Answers**

1 Problem: It took time for the buyer and seller to agree how much something was worth. Solution: People started using cowrie shells as money.
2 Problem: Knives and spades were difficult to carry. Solution: People started to use round metal money.

**C Think and discuss. Think of a problem you had. What did you do? How did you fix it?**

This activity draws on the SEL competency of identifying problems when making decisions and generating alternatives.

- Review the problems from the Warm Up. Ask *Did you have any of these problems?* You could have students raise their hands if they have experienced each problem. Brainstorm more problems with the class and write these on the board. Then ask a few students who raised their hands how they fixed the problem.
- Give students a few minutes to think about a problem they had and how they fixed it. They could draw pictures or make notes to help with the following discussion. Then have them discuss their ideas in pairs or small groups.
- Have some students share their ideas with the class. Encourage the other students to listen to and say *Great idea!* when they hear a solution they think is good. If students have problems they weren't able to solve, have the class suggest possible solutions.

## Cool Down

Play *Me, Too!* Have students sit in groups. One student must name a problem they have/had (this could be from C); for example, *I'm worried about a test.* If another student in the group has the same problem, that student calls out *Me, too!* and then names another problem. If students find it hard to think of different problems, allow them to make any statement about themselves.

Now read **The $100 Bill**

# Fiction: *The $100 Bill—Story*

## Lesson Objectives

- to read a story about a girl who finds some money
- to explore the SEL competency of responsible decision-making by identifying problems when making decisions and generating alternatives

**Materials**

Audio Tracks 17 and 18; slips of paper, one per pair (CD)

## Warm Up

Say *You're rich. You have $100. What do you spend it on?* Then say *You're poor. You have $100. What do you spend it on?* Have students discuss their ideas in pairs or small groups.

## TRACK 17 TB p. 231 Reading Approach

**First Reading: Engage with the Text**

- Have students look at the reading and notice the title, text, and pictures on the page. What do they think the story is about?
- Have students sit in a circle to listen to the story the first time you read it. Read the story to students using facial expression and gesture.
- Ask prediction questions before turning the page; for example, *What do you think Paige sees in the leaves? Will she spend the money?*
- Read the whole story before looking at the Words in Context.

## TRACK 18 TB p. 231 Words in Context

- Play the audio and have students repeat the words.
- Have students race to find the words in the reading.
- Encourage students to **use the pictures to help establish the meaning of the new words.** Have them discuss their ideas in pairs.
- Then bring the class together and use these questions to confirm the meanings.

**belong to** (p. 50) Ask *Was the money Paige's?* (no) Say *It didn't belong to Paige. Who did it belong to?* (We don't know.) Explain that if something *belongs to* you, it is yours. Demonstrate by pointing to students' possessions and asking *Who does it belong to?*

**return** (p. 50) Ask *When Paige picks up the money, can she return it? Why?* (no—there's no way to find the owner.) Elicit that *give back* is a synonym of *return*.

**pocket** (p. 51) Ask students to point to the pocket in Paige's coat. Ask *Is it safe to put money in your pocket?* Encourage students to justify their answers.

**restaurant** (p. 53) Ask *Where does Paige want to go with he dad?* (to a restaurant) Have students find the picture of the restaurant. Ask *What type of restaurant is it?* (a pizza restaurant)

**money is tight** (p. 53) Say *Paige's dad says they can't go to a restaurant because "money is tight."* Ask students to look at the objects on the table (a calculator, a household bill) and also at her dad. Elicit the meaning of the phrase (they don't have much money).

### International English

Elicit *bill* is American English and *note* is British English. Ask *Which word do we use?*

**Second Reading: Analyze the Text and Features**

- Play the audio and have students follow along in their books.
- Ask some questions to check comprehension; for example, *Are Nina and Jodie friends with Paige?* (no)
- Play the audio again. Discuss the questions in the blue boxes as they appear on the pages.
    - **Making Connections** (p. 48): *How do you think Paige feels?* Encourage students to look at the pictures and identify Paige's feelings. *How do you feel when someone laughs at you?*
    - **Critical Thinking** (p. 50): *What does Paige want to ask?* Say *Imagine there are people in the park. What question would she ask?* ("Is this your money?")
    - **Critical Literacy** (p. 51): *How do you think Paige feels about Jodie?* Have students look at the picture and think about the situation (Paige looks surprised or even scared). This is an opportunity to talk about bullying and what we can do if we see it taking place. Brainstorm what kinds of actions can be considered bullying. Ask *How can Paige stop Jodie and Nina from bullying her?* Elicit that she should tell her teacher and her dad, and they can come up with a plan together.
    - **SEL Competency** (p. 52): *Did Paige do the right thing?* Ask students if they think that Paige made a good decision not to buy a phone. Encourage them to give reasons for their answers by asking *What makes you say that?* This question helps students explore the SEL competency of making decisions by identifying problems and generating alternatives.
    - **Gist** (p. 53): *How does Paige feel at the end of the story?* Have students look at the last picture to find out how Paige feels. Ask *Why is she happy?* (because she made the right decision and is doing something nice with her dad)

**Third Reading: Interact with the Text**

- Have students act out the story in groups of four or five (the fifth is the narrator). For more ideas on using role-play, see TB p. 23.

## Cool Down

Students are going to write a ten-word summary of the story in pairs. Give students a few minutes to write their sentences on slips of paper. Invite students to read them to the class.

## Explore the Reading

### Lesson Objectives

- to understand and analyze *The $100 Bill* through reading comprehension activities
- to make a personal connection to the reading
- to explore the SEL competency of responsible decision-making by identifying problems and generating alternatives.
- to reproduce and write words with the *–ar* ending

**Materials**

Audio Tracks 17 and 19

### Warm Up

Show students the top picture from p. 49. Ask *What is Paige thinking?* Give students one or two minutes to write in words what they think is going through Paige's head. You could have them draw a thought bubble and write inside it.

**A Write *True* or *False*. Say the page where you found the answer.**

- If more than one day has passed since students read *The $100 Bill*, play the audio again.
- With books closed, have a Group Time discussion (see TB p. 21) to check students' comprehension of the text. Ask *Why didn't Paige have a cell phone?* (because her family didn't have much money) *What did she find?* (money) *Where did she find it?* (in the park) *Could she return the money?* (No, there was no one in the park.) *How did she spend the money?* (on a pizza)
- Have students open their books and read the first sentence. Have students look back at the reading and find the sentence. Check the answer with the class. (True)
- Have students do the rest of the activity individually. Check answers as a class, making sure students say on which page they found their answer.

**Answers**

1 True; 48  2 False; 50  3 True; 51  4 False; 52
5 True; 53  6 True; 53

**B Read and complete the story map.**

- Discuss with the class the problem that Paige faces—the dilemma about what to do with the money in the face of bullying from Jodie and Nina. Ask *Is finding the money a problem? Would it be different if it were only $5?*
- Have students complete the activity in pairs. Encourage students to refer back to the story and look for the information they need to complete the chart. Check answers as a class.

**Suggested Answers**

Title: The $100 Bill
Settings: Outside a school; a park; an apartment; a pizza restaurant
Main character: Paige
Problem 1: Paige gets laughed at by girls in her school because she doesn't have a cell phone (and she can't afford one).
Solution: Paige decides she doesn't need a cell phone.
Problem 2: Paige doesn't know what to do with the money she finds.
Solution: Paige takes the money home to her dad.

**C Think and discuss. Do you think Paige did the right thing by picking up the money? What would you do?**

- Students are going to use the Think, Pair, Share routine (see TB p. 20) to discuss Paige's decision. This draws on the SEL competency of responsible decision-making by identifying problems and generating alternatives.
- Write the following checklist about doing the right thing on the board:

  *Could it hurt me? / Could it hurt anyone else? / Is it fair? / How do I feel about it? / Imagine if someone does the same thing to me?* Explain that these are questions you can ask yourself if you don't know what to do in a difficult situation.
- If students think that Paige didn't do the right thing, encourage them to say what they think she should have done instead.

### Spelling Pattern *ar*

TRACK 19 TB p. 231 **Listen and write. Then check your answers.**

- With books closed, write *ar* on the board.
- Play the first part of the audio and have students repeat each word. Then have them open their books. Play the first part of the audio again and have them complete as many words as they can.
- Then play the second part of the audio for students to check their spelling and complete the words correctly. Have students underline *ar* in each word and read them aloud. Ask *Which words have the same sound?* (barter, garden) *Which are different?* (carrot, lizard, warm)
- Have students look back at the reading to find more words with *ar* and write them in a word list. Invite students to read a word from their list.

**Answers**

1 barter  2 carrot  3 warm  4 lizard  5 garden
In the reading: hard, park, dollars, are

### Cool Down

Have students secretly choose a scene from *The $100 Bill* and act it out silently using actions and gestures. If there is more than one person in the scene, encourage them to interact with the character. The other students try to find the scene in their books. Do one or two examples with the class, then have students do the activity in pairs. If they enjoy the activity, they can also act out scenes from *A New Friend*, in Unit 2.

**Practice** **Resource Bank:** Spelling Printout
**Student's App:** Reading Practice; Spelling Pattern Practice

## Think Together

### Lesson Objectives

- to make connections between the readings
- to explore the key concept: Why do we need money?
- to reflect on the unit and provide personal thoughts and opinions

**Materials**
Large pieces of paper to cover a classroom wall (CD)

### Warm Up

Have students look back at the VTR picture on pp. 40–41. Ask them how they think the picture connects to the two readings in the unit. If necessary, write prompts on the board: *types of money, what you can do with money, problems with money.* Encourage students to be creative in their answers; for example, *Paige spends her money; she doesn't save it. Paige spends the money on her dad/family. Paige should save money in a jar because her family doesn't have much money.*

**A Look at the two readings. What are some of the different ways to use money? Think and discuss.**

- Brainstorm with the class a list of different things we spend money on. These may include food, clothes, books, bills (electricity, gas, telephone), transportation, having fun, and so on. Use these ideas to help elicit other ideas; for example, *How can you use money to have fun? You can go to the (movie theater). You can buy your favorite magazine.* Have students think about all the things they have seen people pay for; for example, *My brother pays for the bus.*
- Have students discuss their ideas in small groups. Monitor and provide language help when needed.

**B Think and discuss. Imagine you have these problems. What could you do? Do a Three-step Interview and complete the table.**

- Write the first situation (*You find $50.*) on the board. Quickly brainstorm some possible solutions with the class. Encourage students to think of a variety of different things they could do with the money.
- Give students some time to think about the other problems in the table, then set them up for a Three-step Interview to discuss their ideas (see TB p. 20) and answer the key concept question *Why do we need money?* Have them fill in the table with their partner's solutions.
- In Step 3, students share what they have learned about their friend with the class. With large classes, students can share their ideas in groups. Ask students the key concept question *Why do we need money?* and recap ideas from the whole class.

**C Think and share. Choose one problem from B. What should you do?**

- Look at the first problem with the class. Review the different solutions students came up with in B, asking the questions from the previous lesson after each one; for example, *Could it hurt me? / Could it hurt anyone else? / Is it fair? / How do I feel about it? / Imagine if someone does the same thing to me?* Make sure students are aware that *hurt* is physical and emotional (i.e. it makes somebody feel bad). Then ask *Which is the best solution? What should you do?*
- Give students a few minutes to choose a problem from table and decide what the best solution is from all the ideas they heard in B. Have students discuss their solutions in small groups and encourage them to give reasons for their choices. Then have groups share their ideas with the class.

### My Reading Journal

**The author wants new covers for the readings in this unit. Draw them.**

This task encourages students to analyze the readings. Ask *What's the genre? What are the main ideas in each reading?* Give students a few minutes to look back through the unit. (*The History of Money* tells us about how money has changed. *The $100 Bill* is about a girl who has to make a decision about how to spend money.) Then tell students to draw a suitable cover for each reading. Only give students a few minutes to draw, reminding them that their pictures don't need to be perfect.

**Do you know any other stories where money is a problem?**

This question encourages students to make connections. Ask students if they read any other stories where money is a problem. Perhaps they read stories about rich or poor people. One example is *A New Friend* from Unit 2. Have students complete their reading journals individually, monitoring and providing language help when needed.

**Example Answer**
I read a fictional story about a king who loves gold and money. One day he wished that everything he touched turned to gold, but it was a bad decision.

### Cool Down

Have students work in groups to make a *graffiti wall.* On different walls in the classroom, stick large pieces of paper. Each group will work on a different "wall." Using colored pens, have students write and draw their ideas about the unit. Encourage them to use different styles of writing (e.g. bubble letters, capitals) and different letter sizes to express how they feel.

**Practice** **Resource Bank:** Unit Test
**Student's App:** Key Concept Practice

UNIT 4

# We Can Do It

## Unit Overview

### Themes

How performances can promote community

The benefits of working as a team

### Synopsis

In this unit, students will explore how teamwork can help us. They will look at how performances can bring people together and learn about the different roles in a theater performance. Students will plan and prepare a presentation about a performance and write a diary entry on the topic.

## Language Book

### Vocabulary

*actor, audience, backstage, costume, crew, curtain, director, nervous, performance, script, set, stage*

p. 96

### Explore Language

Past Progressive: Statements

p. 97

### Global Citizenship

How do performances bring people together?

*early, lasts, late, midnight, noon, on time, rehearsal, schedule, team*

p. 98

### Explore Language

Past Progressive: Questions

p. 99

### Take the Stage

Presentation: describing a hobby

p. 100

### Write About It

A Diary Entry

Sentence Building: time phrases and commas

p. 101

### Think It Over

Review and Reflection

p. 102

Act Three

Act Four

## Think Together
How does teamwork help us?
p. 109

## Visible Thinking
Think, Pair, Share
p. 103

## Fiction
Play: *Late for the Show*
Words in Context: *show, calm, platform, sank, alive*
p. 107

## Literacy Book

## Nonfiction
Informational Text: *Teamwork Makes the Dream Work*
Words in Context: *league, court, basket, score, shooting*
p. 104

## Reading Skill
Understanding the sequence of events
p. 106

## Spelling Pattern
*or*
p. 105

## Language and Literacy Connections

The connecting theme in Unit 4 is working together.

| | Language | Literacy |
|---|---|---|
| **Vocabulary** | **Set 1:** performance<br>**Set 2:** time | **Fiction:** actor(s), audience, costume, nervous, performance, stage, late, rehearsal |
| **Grammar** | **Past Progressive: Statements**<br>Fred was standing by the curtain.<br>Tommy and Ting were practicing the script.<br>**Past Progressive: Questions**<br>What were you doing? | **Nonfiction**<br>The Los Angeles Sparks were losing by five points. |
| **Skills** | **Pronunciation:** /ð/ and /θ/ | **Reading:** understanding the sequence of events<br>**Spelling Pattern:** *or* |
| **International English** | | theater/theatre |

## Vocabulary

### Lesson Objectives

- to learn performance vocabulary: *actor, audience, backstage, costume, crew, curtain, director, nervous, performance, script, set, stage*
- to sing a song that explores performing on stage

**Materials**

Audio Tracks 39 to 42; Video

### Warm Up

Draw a picture of an empty theater stage on the board. Have students suggest things or people to add to the picture. Draw (or have students draw) their suggestions. Ask questions to prompt and encourage students to think about the scene; for example, *Are there any people on the stage? Who are they? How do you think they feel? Are there any people in the theater that we can't see? Where are they? Where is the play set?*

**A** TRACK 39 TB p. 217 **Listen and find. What time does the curtain open?**

- Have students look at the picture and say what they see. Ask questions to prompt discussion; for example, *Where is the theater? What are these* (pointing) *people doing? Can you find Ting?* (She's standing at the front of the stage.)
- Tell students they are going to listen to the children getting ready for the play. Play the audio and have students point to the words or pictures as they listen. Remind students of the challenge from the end of Unit 3: *What will I perform?* and elicit possible answers (a play). Have students look at what Ting's wearing as a clue.
- Ask the comprehension question *What time does the curtain open?* and elicit the answer. Play the audio again for students to check.

**Answer**

It opens at 7:00.

**B** TRACK 40 TB p. 217 **Listen, say, and number the pictures in A.**

- Play the audio and have students point to the pictures and say the words.
- Tell students to listen again and write numbers next to the words in the picture. Do the example together (stage).
- Check answers by calling out a number and having students call out the word. Alternatively, project the answers using the TTL.

**Answers**

1 *stage* 2 nervous 3 backstage 4 costume
5 actor 6 director 7 script 8 set 9 crew
10 curtain 11 audience 12 performance

**C** TRACK 41 TB p. 218 **Close your eyes. Listen, visualize, and say.**

- Prepare students for the visualization. (See TB p. 21.)
- Play the audio, allowing students to visualize the ideas as they listen. Make sure students know not to speak until they hear the word *say*. Put your finger to your lips if necessary.
- Have students draw a picture containing some of the words from the visualization. They can then talk about their pictures in pairs.

**D** **Look at A. Complete.**

- Students are going to categorize the vocabulary. This encourages critical thinking, and the table helps students record vocabulary neatly. Draw students' attention to the table. Point out that the words in A can be classified into four categories. If necessary, provide the complete question; for example, *Who is at the performance? What can you see? / What are you going to see? Where are people sitting/standing? How do the people feel?* Elicit what kinds of words go in each category (people, things, places, feelings).
- Tell students to write the words from A in the table. Then check answers as a class. You could project the answers using the TTL.

**Answers**

Who: audience, crew, actor, director
What: *performance*, script, set, curtain, costume
Where: stage, backstage
How: nervous

**E** TRACK 42 TB p. 218 **Listen and complete. Then watch and sing.**

- Point to the song title. Ask *Are you ready?* and elicit when we say this. (when we are going to start doing something) Then play the song once, allowing students to listen and enjoy it.
- Have students predict the missing words and write them in their books. Then play the song again for students to check their answers.
- Play the song video and encourage students to sing and move to the music as they watch.

**Answers**

1 *backstage* 2 nervous 3 stage 4 curtain
5 costumes 6 script 7 director 8 sets

### Cool Down

Tell students to imagine they are going to perform a play. Ask *What do you need?* Have students make a list, encouraging them to use the vocabulary from A and other ideas they have from their own experiences of being in a play.



**Practice** **Student's App:** Vocabulary Practice; Song Video

# Explore Language

## Lesson Objectives

- to learn to use the past progressive
- to practice performance vocabulary

**Materials**

Audio Tracks 43 and 44

## Warm Up

Ask students what the weather was like in the reading from the previous lesson (stormy—they could hear thunder and there were black clouds). Ask students if they remember a storm. What happened? How did they feel? Talk about power outages and blackouts. Have students work in pairs to discuss their experiences of storms. Then ask volunteers to share their experiences with the class.

**A** TRACK 43 TB p. 218 **Listen and read. Where was Fred?**

- Remind students of the picture scene on pp. 48–49. Ask *What were the children doing?* (performing a play). Tell students that they are going to listen to Zora and Fred a few minutes after they hear the thunder. Play the audio and have students follow the dialogue in their books.
- Ask the comprehension question *Where was Fred?* and elicit the answer. Ask *Why is it dark?* (because the storm made the lights go out)

**Answer**

He was getting a candle.

**B Look at A. Complete.**

- Write or project the table onto the board.
- Look at the first statement in the table. Have students find the sentence in the play script in A. Complete the sentence together. Elicit that *was* and *were* are past forms of the verb *be* and that we use *was* for *I*, *he*, *she*, and *it* and we use *were* for *you*, *we*, and *they*. Then point to *standing*. Ask *What kind of word is it?* (a verb)
- Have students work in pairs to complete the rest of table. Check answers as a class.
- Ask students to notice the verbs that come after *was/were*. Elicit that they all end in *-ing* and point out that this is the important verb in the sentence. Explain that it always has the same form in past progressive statements.
- Draw students' attention to the Grammar tip *Remember*. Tell students that when we talk about the time in the future or past we use *at* (e.g. *at seven o'clock*). Have students read the tip. Then have them notice the time phrase in A. Tell students they can choose where to put the time phrase: at the beginning or at the end of the sentence.

**Answers**

was; standing; weren't; performing; practicing; raining

**C Think and discuss. Then choose.**

- Have students work in pairs to discuss the statement. Refer them to the table in B for examples of verbs in past progressive. Then check the answer as a class.
- Tell students that we use the past progressive to describe actions happening at a particular time in the past.

**Answer**

1 past

**D** TRACK 44 TB p. 218 **Listen and say.**

- Tell students they're going to practice saying the structures. Play the audio, having students repeat each sentence chorally.
- For ideas on how to vary the drill, see TB p. 23.

**E Put the words in order.**

- Write the example on the board. Remind students that the subject always comes before a verb in past progressive sentences. Elicit that sometimes the time phrase goes at the beginning and sometimes at the end.
- Say *Now write the words in order to make sentences.* Have students do the activity individually. Check answers by writing them on the board or projecting them using the TTL.

**Answers**

1 *The actors were practicing the play at 4:00.*
2 The crew was finishing the set at 5:30.
3 At 6:00, we weren't waiting backstage.
4 The curtain was opening at 7:00.
5 My parents were watching the performance at 8:00.
6 At 8:30, the audience was clapping.

**F Play a chain game. Choose a time. Make sentences about yesterday.**

- Brainstorm activities that students do every day. Ask a few students what time they usually do those activities. Then tell them to think about yesterday.
- Have students play the *Chain Game* (see TB p. 25) by making sentences about yesterday. Demonstrate first with a few volunteers. Then have them play in teams.

## Cool Down

Play *Mime It!* (see TB p. 26). Ask *What was he/she doing yesterday?* and have students make guesses using the past progressive.

**Practice** **Resource Bank:** Grammar Printout
**Student's App:** Grammar Practice

## Global Citizenship

### Lesson Objectives

- to learn time vocabulary: *early, lasts, late, midnight, noon, on time, rehearsal, schedule, team*
- to explore how performances can bring people together
- to practice listening for gist and details

**Materials**

Audio Tracks 45 to 47; Audio Track D; a globe or map of the world (D)

### Opening Question

Ask the opening question: *How do performances bring people together?* Elicit ideas and encourage students to think about different kinds of performances and where they take place (e.g. in a theater; on the street; in a stadium). Don't correct students or give much feedback; they will find out more about the topic during the lesson.

**A** TRACK 45 TB p. 218 **Listen to the interview. What important thing did the performers learn?**

- Tell students they are going to listen to an interview with a man talking about a performance he was in. Have students make predictions about what kind of performance it is. Play the audio and have students point to the words or pictures as they listen.
- Ask the gist question *What important thing did the performers learn?* Play the audio again for students to check. Ask *Do you think it was difficult to be on time? Why?* (Students' own answers.)

**Answer**

to be on time

**B** TRACK 46 TB p. 218 **Listen, say, and number the pictures in A.**

- Play the audio and have students point to the pictures and say the words.
- Tell students to listen again and write numbers next to the words in the pictures. Do the example together (late).
- Check answers by having one student call out a number and nominating another student to respond. This student then calls out the next number. Alternatively, project the answers using the TTL.
- Ask students to give examples for each word; for example, If you come to school at 9:30, you're late; I have a busy schedule this week—I'm playing soccer every night!; This class starts at nine and finishes at ten—it lasts an hour.

**Answers**

1 *late* 2 early 3 on time 4 midnight 5 schedule 6 noon 7 rehearsal 8 lasts 9 team

TRACK D TB p. 218 **Visualization**

The TTL has a visualization audio track for this vocabulary set. (See TB p. 21.)

**C Read and complete.**

- Students are going to complete the sentences with the vocabulary from A. Write the example on the board. Elicit different ways of completing the sentence (e.g. *team, group, competition*). Then look at the example answer (team).
- Have students complete the sentences individually. Then check answers as a class.

**Answers**

1 *team* 2 schedule; rehearsals 3 noon; midnight; last 4 late; early; on time

**D** TRACK 47 TB p. 218 **Now listen to Li Min and Adam. How did Li Min feel?**

- Tell students they are going to listen to two children from different countries talking about performing at the Olympic Games. Have students look at the two pictures and notice where each child is from. You could point out China and England on a globe or map. Ask *What do you know about the Olympic Games? What kinds of performances do you think they will talk about?*
- Listening for gist: Ask the gist question *How did Li Min feel?* and elicit suggestions. Play the audio for students to check their ideas.

**Answer**

Li Min felt proud.

**E Listen again. Choose.**

- Listening for details: have students read the sentences before they listen again. Do they remember any answers? Then play the audio and have students choose the correct answers.
- To check answers, read each question and have students vote for the correct answer.

**Answers**

1 *flag* 2 Chinese 3 many 4 water 5 costume 6 watching

### Discussion Questions

- Draw students' attention to the discussion questions: *Would you like to be in a big performance? When are there performances in your community?* Have students discuss the questions in pairs or small groups (see TB p. 21). See **ETB**.
- Return to the opening question to ask again: *How do performances bring people together?* Recap ideas discussed and then encourage students to share any new ideas. Focus on the concept of how events (e.g. sports events, like the Olympics) can give people a sense of community—everyone has to work together to reach the same goal.

### Cool Down

Have students do an interview in pairs. One student is Li Min or Adam, the other is the interviewer. The interviewer should write three questions. Have both students write questions, as they will swap roles afterward.

**Practice Student's App:** Vocabulary Practice; Listening Practice

# Explore Language

## Lesson Objectives

- to learn to ask past progressive questions
- to practice time vocabulary

**Materials**

Audio Tracks 48 and 49; different styles of music (WU); handmade cards with verbs (CD)

## Warm Up

Ask students if they like dancing or like watching dancing. You could play different styles of music (pop, rock, Latin, reggae, classical, etc.) and allow students to dance to the music if they wish. Then ask *What music do you like to dance or move to?*

Note: if dancing is not appropriate for your context, omit this activity. Students can watch or clap their hands, if they prefer.

**A** TRACK 48 TB p. 218 **Listen and read. Why did the set fall down at the dance rehearsal?**

- Tell students that they are going to listen to Jake and his friends at a dance rehearsal. Have students look back at pp. 48–49 and find Jake (on stage taking a photograph). Play the audio and have students follow the dialogue in their books.
- Ask the gist question *Why did the set fall down at the dance rehearsal?* and elicit the answer.

**Answer**

A white cat was climbing up the set and the boxes fell down.

**B Look at A. Complete.**

- Write or project the table onto the board.
- Quickly review past progressive statements. Point to the picture in A and say *Tell me what the children were doing.* (They were practicing their dance.)
- Look at the first question in the table. Ask *Is the question about the present or the past? What makes you say that?* Elicit that the verb *to be* is in the past. Refer students to the dialogue in A. Have students find the question and notice which word is missing in the table. Complete this together.
- Have students work in pairs to complete the rest of the table.
- Check answers as a class. Have students notice that the verb *be* comes before the subject in questions and that the short answer forms take the verb *to be*.
- Draw students' attention to the Grammar tip *Watch Out*. Elicit a question in past progressive and write it on the board. Underline *was/were*. Explain that when a verb ends in *–ing*, it always needs the verb *be* before it.

**Answers**

doing; Were; dancing; were; weren't; was; watching; was; were

**Practice** **Resource Bank:** Grammar Printout
**Student's App:** Grammar Practice

**C Think and discuss. Then choose.**

- Have students work in pairs to discuss the statement. Refer them to the table in B for examples of past progressive questions. Then check the answer.
- Have students ask further questions using the past progressive in pairs.

**Answer**

1 during a period of time

**D** TRACK 49 TB p. 219 **Listen and say.**

- Tell students they're going to practice saying the new structures. Play the audio, having students repeat each structure chorally.
- For ideas on how to vary the drill, see TB p. 23.

**E Complete the questions and answers.**

- Look at the example together and have students notice the verbs in parentheses. Point out to students that they might need to write one word or more in each blank.
- Have students complete the sentences individually. Then check answers with the class by reading aloud the sentences and pausing for students to call out the answer.

**Answers**

1 *was; doing; was putting on*
2 Were; eating; wasn't
3 was; watching; was watching
4 were; thinking; were thinking
5 Was; feeling; was

**F Play *Find Someone Who*. Write three sentences about this morning. Use time phrases. Then talk to your friends.**

- Ask *What were you doing at 5:30 this morning?* Elicit one or two answers from the class.
- Tell students to write three sentences about this morning, choosing three different times.
- Explain to students that they are going to ask questions to find someone who was doing the same thing as them at the same time. Demonstrate with the two examples on the page. Then have students play *Find Someone Who* (see TB p. 26).

## Cool Down

Have students play a card game in small groups. You will need a set of cards with verbs for each group. One student picks up a card (e.g. *watch*) and makes a question in the past progressive; for example, *Were you watching TV?* He/she nominates another student to answer, who takes another card (e.g. *play*) and uses that verb in his/her answer; for example, *No, I was playing tennis.* If the question/sentence is correct, the student keeps the card. Other students can challenge if they believe the sentence to be incorrect. They have an opportunity to correct it and keep the card. Students continue in a chain until all the cards have been used.

# Take the Stage

## Lesson Objectives

- to prepare and practice a presentation describing a hobby
- to recognize and reproduce /ð/ and /θ/

**Materials**

Video; Audio Track 50; a picture of people doing a folk dance (WU)

### Warm Up

Show students a picture of people doing a folk dance. Do a See, Think, Wonder routine to have students discuss the picture (see TB p. 20).

**A** TB p. 238 **Watch and listen. What does Natalia like about performing?**

- Tell students they are going to watch a girl named Natalia give a presentation about her experience of performing. Have students look at the picture and ask *Why do you think she is wearing these clothes? What country do you think she's from?* Play the video for students to find out. Ask *Do you like her costume?*
- Ask the gist question *What does Natalia like about performing?* and elicit answers. Play the video again and have students notice Natalia's body language while she's giving her presentation and what she does to engage the audience (asks a question).

**Suggested Answers**

the music; teamwork; the audience

**B Watch again. Check (✔) the phrases you hear.**

- Have students read the phrases.
- Play the video again and have students check the phrases they hear. Check answers as a class.
- Ask *How does Natalia start her presentation?* (*I Today I'm going to talk about …*). Then have students categorize the other phrases into those we say in the middle (2–7) and at the end (8) of a presentation. Note: the middle has two parts: background and what she likes about performing. To help with categorizing the phrases, students could complete a table or flow chart in their notebooks.

**Answers**

*1*; 2; 3; 5; 6; 8

**Pronunciation /ð/ and /θ/**

TRACK 50 TB p. 219 **Listen and say.**

Demonstrate the two sounds first. Drill each sound on its own. Ask students to put their tongue between their teeth. Then ask them to try to make the sound different by making their throat vibrate. If they feel a vibration, they should be producing the /ð/ sound. Then drill the two sounds one after the other so students can physically feel the difference.

Play the audio and have students repeat the words.

Say *These words are used in the video. What other words do you know with these sounds?* Elicit ideas and write them on the board in two columns (e.g. *this, thin*). Drill the pronunciation of each word.

**Suggested Answers**

/ð/ clothes, weather, these, other
/θ/ thick, thought, thoughtful, throw, thunder, Thursday

**C Plan. Check (✔) the kinds of performances you do at or after school. Then choose one and complete.**

- Tell students they are going to plan a presentation about a performance. Make a spidergram on the board of different ways of performing, eliciting ideas from the class (e.g. singing, playing an instrument, acting, reading poetry, telling jokes, performing magic tricks, performing in competitions such as spelling bees, or performing in sports games).
- Have students look at the questions in the table. Ask a confident student a couple of the questions as an example.
- Say *Now plan what you can say about performances that you do.* Have students check the activities they do and complete the table.

**D Prepare your presentation. Choose a performance from C and use phrases from B. Complete your note cards.**

- Play the video again as a model.
- Have students choose one of the activities they wrote about in C and write about it in more detail, organizing their ideas.
- Have students look at the note cards and how the information will be divided into *Introduction, All About Your Performance*, and *Ending*. Elicit different ways of including the information on the cards; for example, *I'm Natalia* or *My name is Natalia* (introduce yourself).
- Then give students time to complete the cards, using the phrases from B. Encourage them to add more details. Remind them to ask the audience a question to establish rapport.

**E Practice with a friend. Then share with your class.**

- Students are going to practice their presentations in pairs. Allow students to practice as many times as they need to.
- Invite volunteers to come to the front to give their presentations. Remind students to look at the faces in the audience and to smile! Have the audience give a round of applause after each presentation.

### Cool Down

Tell students to imagine they can organize a variety show with a lot of different performances. Using the spidergram from C, have students work in pairs to create an act list. They should consider which kind of performance would make a good opener / a memorable ending. Have them share their act lists with another pair.



**Practice** **Student's App:** Speaking Skills Practice; Speaking Video

# Write About It

## Lesson Objectives

- to learn where to use time phrases
- to plan and write a diary entry

**Materials**

(Optional) Support, Standard, and Challenge writing printouts from the Resource Bank, one per student (C and D)

## Warm Up

Ask students if they have a diary. If any students write in a diary regularly, ask them what kinds of things they write about. Ask the class if anything interesting happened to them recently. Tell students that in a diary, we usually write about events that are important to the author or writer, including interesting or special events. Elicit some examples (e.g. a birthday party, a day when you have an exam).

**A Read the diary entry. Underline the time phrases and circle the commas.**

- Ask *What is the diary entry about?* Give students one or two minutes to read it and elicit the answer (his friend who was performing in a talent show). Ask students what Malik did in the talent show (danced). Ask a volunteer to describe what a talent show is (a stage or TV show where people compete to be the best performer).
- Do the example together. Then have students underline the other time phrases and circle the commas. Check answers. Elicit that some sentences have the time phrase at the beginning and some at the end, and that when the phrase comes first, there is a comma.
- Ask students what the time phrases help do in the diary entry. (They help order/sequence the events—this helps us understand when the different events happen.)

**Answers**

Dear Diary,
Before the talent show, …
… at 7:15, …
Then, he went on stage at 7:30!
…, but Malik wasn't …
After the show, …

**B Move the time phrases and rewrite the sentences.**

- Tell students to close their books. Write the first sentence on the board. Ask *Is the time phrase at the beginning or at the end?* (at the end) Say *If we put it at the beginning, what do we need to add?* (a comma) Elicit the new sentence starting with *At 8:00* … Then have students open their books and check.
- Have the class identify the time phrases and underline them.
- Then have students rewrite the other sentences by changing the place of the time phrases. To check answers, split the class into two groups. Have the groups take turns to read the original sentence and the transformed sentence (including the comma if there is one).

**Answers**

1 *At 8:00 last night, my sister was singing.*
2 She was feeling nervous before the performance.
3 After the show, we were waiting for her.
4 During the show, her teacher was making a video.
5 The singers were walking off the stage at 8:30.

**C Plan. Think about a time you watched a performance. Complete.**

- Tell students they are going to plan their own diary entries. Have them think about a recent performance they saw, either one they went to as a class or one they went to with their families. Guide them through a visualization of what they were doing, seeing, and feeling before the performance, during the performance, and after the performance.
- Then have students complete the table, using the questions to help them. They should describe what was happening and what they and the performers were doing and feeling in note form. Encourage them to use the past progressive and time phrases (e.g. at 8:00). Challenge printouts can be handed out now.

**D Write about the performance in your diary.**

- Have students write a draft about the performance in their notebooks or on paper using their ideas from C. Students should describe the performance, using the past progressive and time phrases at the beginning and end of sentences. Review the use of time phrases *at, before, during,* and *after.* Students should write the diary entry as if it was the night of the performance. Encourage them to add additional details. Support printouts can be handed out now.
- Have students self-correct or exchange their work with a friend and peer-correct. You can put a checklist of things for students to look for on the board (e.g. spelling, use of adjectives and adverbs, verb forms, punctuation, time phrases).
- Have students write their final versions neatly on paper. Alternatively, hand out the Standard printouts. Give them time to draw a picture of the performance.

## Cool Down

Collect students' diary entries. Read some of the diaries and have students guess who wrote them. When they find out who the author is, they can ask more questions. At the end, point out that diaries are generally top secret: you shouldn't read other people's diaries.

**Practice** **Student's App:** Writing Practice

# Think It Over

## Lesson Objectives

- to review what has been learned in the unit
- to reflect on the unit and their own progress
- to think about learning strategies and how to continue learning at home

### Warm Up

Ask students what the unit theme was (performing) and write it in the middle of the board. Brainstorm any words or phrases students can think of that relate to the topic and write them on the board. Encourage students to think about the different ways of performing and how performances bring people together.

**Read the questions and draw or write your answers.**

- Give students time to think about and discuss activities in the unit before they complete each question. Explain that they can choose to either write a few words or sentences or to draw a picture. Allowing students to make a personal response will help them retain knowledge and engage with the learning points.

**What did I do?**

- Give students a few minutes to look back through the unit at the different activities they did. Ask questions about the unit or write questions on the board for students to discuss in pairs or small groups; for example, *What kinds of performances were there at the Opening and Closing Ceremonies of the Olympics? What stopped the children's performance in the first Explore Language lesson?*
- Encourage students to identify something in the unit that they found challenging or something that was particularly memorable for them, but tell them not to choose their favorite part yet. Students can draw or write about their chosen activity.

**What did I learn?**

- Ask questions about the unit to help students think about what they learned; for example, *What sentences can you say about the past? What did you learn about performances? What else did you learn?* Have students discuss their ideas in pairs.
- Encourage students to draw a picture or write sentences about their learning outcomes.

**What was my favorite part?**

- Have students look back through the unit and decide what they enjoyed the most. Tell them it can be an activity they found interesting, a dialogue they enjoyed reading, a favorite character, or a game they played. Have students draw or write about the thing they liked the most. Remind students that when we like something, it is often easier to learn.

**How well did I do?**

- Tell students to color the child who best expresses how well they have learned they unit content (i.e., the more the child stands and applauds, the more they feel they have learned). Ask *What do you understand? What do you need to practice more?* Encourage students to look back through the unit to see how much they remember what they did well and what they found difficult.

**What can I do next?**

- Brainstorm ideas with the class about what they can do to continue to learn (e.g. think about the different ways they perform and how it makes them feel, find and pronounce words with **/ð/** and **/θ/**, start writing a diary or vlog in English, learn a song in English and the dance routine, read about different shows and performances around the world). Students can look back at the previous units to get more ideas. Encourage students to suggest their own ideas for different activities they can do
- Draw students' attention to the *What can I do next?* box. Encourage students to think about what they can do at home to improve their English. Have them suggest some verbs that they can use (e.g. read, write, talk about, ask, research) and write the verbs in their books.
- Have students choose several activities that they would like to do and write them in their notebooks. They can then share their ideas with a partner.

### Looking Forward

Draw students' attention to the character at the bottom of the page. Ask *Who's this?* and elicit what they remember about him (Jake appears in Explore Language 2, p. 54; he is a crew member / he works on the set; he saw the cat.)

Draw students' attention to Jake's question: *What animal do I want to take pictures of?* Encourage students to make predictions about what he's drinking in Unit 5. Tell students they will find out the answer in Lesson 1 of the next unit.

# Put It Together

To further review and recycle the language in Units 3 and 4, play the game, *Come to the Show!*, on pp. 60–61. See TB p. 207 for teaching notes.



**Practice** **Resource Bank:** Unit Test
**Student's App:** Vocabulary and Grammar Review

## Get Ready to Read

### Lesson Objectives

- to activate prior knowledge about working together
- to guide inquiry and deepen understanding through a Think, Pair, Share VTR
- to preview the reading skill of understanding the sequence of events

**Materials**
(Optional) VTR printout from the Resource Bank (Activities A, B, C)

### Warm Up

Play a version of the *Yes/No Game* (see TB p. 27). For this version, assign one side of the classroom as *Alone* and the other *With People*. Call out different activities and have students decide if it is better to work alone or on a team. Some activities are: *reading, playing video games, making dinner, doing a school project, playing ball, watching a movie, acting in a play, looking for treasure.*

### Think, Pair, Share

**A Look at the picture. How are they working together? Think about it.**

Students are going to do a Think, Pair, Share VTR to explore the image of a stage rehearsal for a show.

- Have students look at the picture for a minute and then say what they can see. If students don't know a word in English, ask them to describe what they see so you can provide the word. Encourage them to use adjectives such as colors and shapes to describe what they see.
- Ask students to look at the people in the picture and read the question.
- Give students a couple of minutes to think about their ideas silently.
- Tell them to cross their arms when they have thought of some ideas.

**B Discuss with your partner.**

- Ask two volunteers to read the example dialogue in B.
- Divide the class into pairs and have students share their ideas.
- Monitor and provide language help when needed, as students discuss their ideas.

**C Share your ideas with the class.**

- Ask pairs to share their ideas about the picture with the class. Encourage students to use *we*, as they are talking about their partner's opinion, too. When you ask a student a question, encourage other students to say if they agree or not.

Here's an example of this part of the routine.

**Teacher:** (Student A), what do you and your friend think?
**Student A:** We think this person (on the right) is giving instructions to the dancers.
**Teacher:** Interesting. Do you agree, (Student B)?
**Student B:** No, we think she's working with the girl (on the left) with the lights.
**Student C:** We agree!
**Teacher:** OK. What makes you say that?
**Student C:** They both have headsets.

### Transition

Point out examples of teams we see in the picture: the dancers, the musicians, and the stage team. Elicit what other kinds of teams there are (sports teams). Ask students if they have a favorite sports team (basketball, baseball, soccer, etc.). Ask *Why do you support that team? Are they a good team?* Have students talk in pairs about their favorite team.

**D Think and discuss. What is better when people work as a team?**

- To bring students' attention to the idea of teamwork versus individual work, brainstorm traditions, performances, sports, or activities students may take part in. Ask *Do you do these things on your own or with other people?* Explain that working as a team means that each person works on something to contribute to the end result.
- Have students work in pairs to discuss activities that are better when people work as a team. Have them write or draw their ideas on paper or in their notebooks while they talk.
- Have students share their ideas with the class.

**E How does the team work together to get a basket? Put the events in order.**

In this activity students will preview the skill of understanding the sequence of events.

- Have students look at the three pictures and say what is happening in each one.
- Have students complete the activity individually. Then invite three students come to the front and act out the sequence of events as the women in the pictures.

**Answers**
2; 1; 3

Now read **Teamwork Makes the Dream Work**

# Nonfiction: *Teamwork Makes the Dream Work*—Informational Text

## Lesson Objectives

- to read an article about the Women's National Basketball Association
- to make a personal connection to the reading

**Materials**

Audio Tracks 20 and 21

## Warm Up

Ask students what they know about basketball. Ask questions to prompt students; for example, *Do you play basketball? How many players are there?* (five per team) *What do they have to do?* (score points / put the ball in the basket) *What actions do they do in a game?* (run, jump, bounce, pass, throw, catch) *How do you get points?* (by putting the ball in your opponent's basket)

### TRACK 20 TB p. 231 Reading Approach

**First Reading: Engage with the Text**

- Ask students to notice the title, text, and pictures on the page and use this information to predict ideas about the reading. Ask questions to elicit ideas; for example, *What country do you think these players are from? Do you think teamwork is important in basketball? Why?*
- Have students open their books and read the text individually, in silence. Have students check their predictions about the text.
- Students should read the whole article before looking at the Words in Context.

### TRACK 21 TB p. 232 Words in Context

- Play the audio and have students repeat the words.
- Have a race to find the words in the story.
- Tell students that sometimes we can **think about whether the word is an object, a person, a place, or an action to figure out the meaning** (see p. 23). Have students look at the words and discuss their ideas in pairs.
- Then bring the class together and use these questions to confirm the meanings.

**league** (p. 58) Write *It's a professional women's basketball league* on the board and ask *What does "It's" refer to?* (the WNBA) Point out the sentence *There are twelve teams in the WNBA.* Elicit that a *league* is a group of teams that play each other. Ask *Do you know any other leagues?*

**court** (p. 58) Ask *Where are the ten players?* (on the court) Have students suggest other sports played on a court (tennis, volleyball).

**basket** (p. 58) Have students read the sentence *Each team has a basket at one end of the court* and use this description to find the basket in the picture. Ask *Why do you think the sport is called basketball?*

**score** (p. 59) Look at the sentence *A team has to get the ball into the other team's basket to score points* and ask *Is score a noun or a verb here?* (verb) Elicit that *get* is a synonym.

**shooting** (p. 59) Focus on the sentence *Chelsea Gray ... was in the air shooting the ball.* Ask *Is shooting an object or an action?* (action) Have students point to the picture which shows someone shooting the ball.

**Second Reading: Analyze the Text and Features**

- Play the audio and have students read along as they listen.
- To check comprehension, ask *Who are the two teams? Where do they play? Are they professional? How many games do they play? Which team wins the game?* (Los Angeles Sparks and Minnesota Lynx; all over the USA; yes; 34 games; Minnesota Lynx.)
- Discuss the questions in the red boxes.
  - **Detail** (p. 58): *How do you score a point in basketball?* If you didn't discuss this in the Words in Context section, do it now. Have students look back at the reading if necessary. You could discuss the points system if students are interested (one, two, or three points depending on where the player is standing or if it is after a foul).
  - **Personalization** (p. 58): *Do you prefer watching or playing sports?* Take a class vote. Then ask individual students to explain why they feel that way.
- Discuss the text focus question: *A quote is something someone said. Which is your favorite? Why?* Give students one or two minutes to read the quotes by the four players and choose their favorite.

**Third Reading: Interact with the Text**

- Have students take turns to interview each other about the WNBA in pairs, each taking on the role of one of the players from TB p. 59. Tell interviewers to think of three questions to ask and interviewees to imagine what their player might say.

## Cool Down

Focus students on the last sentence of the reading, *Their dream, of course, is to win the championship.* Ask students *What is your dream?* and have them talk about their ideas in pairs or small groups. You could then have students walk around the classroom, talking about their dreams and trying to find another student with a similar dream.

## Explore the Reading

### Lesson Objectives

- to understand and analyze *Teamwork Makes the Dream Work* through reading comprehension activities
- to learn through CLIL (social studies): exploring how teams make us feel
- to make a personal connection to the reading

**Materials**

Audio Tracks 20 and 22

### TRACK 20 TB p. 232 Warm Up

Review the reading by playing *What's the Next word?* with books closed. Play the audio, but pause before the end of a sentence and have students call out the word they think comes next; for example,

*The WNBA is short for the Women's National Basketball …* (pause audio)

Students: Association!

**A Write *True* or *False*. Say the page where you found the answer.**

- With books closed, have a Group Time discussion (see TB p. 21) to check students' comprehension of the text. Ask *What is the WNBA?* (a professional women's basketball league) *Where do they play?* (in the USA) *Which places have teams?* (Minnesota, Los Angeles, Dallas, New York) *How many people play on a team?* (five) *How can you score three points?* (by scoring from far away) *Who is Chelsea Gray?* (a basketball player) *Why is teamwork important?* (Working together is part of playing the game.)
- Have students open their books and ask a volunteer to read the first sentence. Have students look back at the reading and find the sentence. Check the answer as a class.
- Have students do the rest of the activity individually. Check answers as a class, making sure students say on which page they found their answer.

**Answers**

1 True (page 58) 2 False (page 58) 3 True (page 58)
4 True (page 58) 5 True (page 59) 6 False (page 59)

**B Think and complete. What did you already know about basketball? What did you learn?**

- Draw students' attention to the basketball hoop backboard on the page. Point out the two sections, *What I Knew* and *What I Learned*. Ask *What did you know about basketball before you read the article? Did you know how to play? Did you know how many players there were? Did you know how long a game takes? Did you know about the WNBA?*
- Give students a few minutes to complete the two sections individually.

**Answers**

Students' own answers

**C Think and discuss. What sports teams are in your area? How do people in your city feel about them?**

Students are going to use a Think, Pair, Share routine (see TB p. 20) to discuss the questions and explore the CLIL social studies concept of how teams make us feel.

- Brainstorm different team sports with the class and write them on the board. Then draw students' attention to the questions: *What sports teams are in your area? How do people in your area feel about them?* Elicit some ideas and encourage students to think about emotions. For example, *In my city the soccer team is quite famous and they play in a big stadium. The people who live by the stadium don't like the noise and all the people. / There is a basketball team and a soccer team in my town. We are excited when they win.*
- Have students discuss the questions in pairs or small groups. Monitor and provide language help when needed.

Note: if students find it hard to think of local teams, have them think of some more well-known teams from other cities or countries, or national teams.

### Spelling Pattern *or*

**TRACK 22 TB p. 232 Listen and write. Then check your answers.**

- With books closed, write *or* on the board.
- Play the first part of the audio and have students repeat each word. Then have them open their books. Play the first part of the audio again and have them complete as many words as they can.
- Then play the second part of the audio for students to check their spelling and complete the words correctly. Have them underline *or* in each word and notice whether it appears in the middle or at the end of the word. Have students read the words aloud.
- Have students look back at the reading to find more words with *or* and write them in a word cloud. Invite students to read a word from their cloud.

**Answers**

1 storm 2 history 3 airport 4 forest 5 alligator
In the reading: short, for, score, worth, working, work

### Cool Down

Play *Board Basketball*. Students are going to play in two teams. Draw a simple basketball court on the board with five symbols to mark each team. These should be placed in varying positions from the defense area to the scoring area. Use a different color for each team. Students have to answer questions correctly in order to advance from their basket to the opposing team's basket and score a point. You can ask questions about the reading or choose any other type of review question.

**Practice** **Resource Bank:** Spelling Printout
**Student's App:** Reading Practice; Spelling Pattern Practice

# Get Ready to Read

## Lesson Objectives

- to practice the reading skill of understanding the sequence of events
- to activate prior knowledge about performances
- to make a personal connection to the reading

**Materials**

Pieces of paper with a number written on them (one for each student) (WU)

## Warm Up

Give each student a piece of paper with a number on it (the numbers should be in a random order). Have students stand up and arrange themselves in a line in numerical order. This will introduce them to the concept of sequencing, which they will look at in A.

**A Look at *Teamwork Makes the Dream Work* again. Put the events in order.**

Students are going to practice the reading skill of understanding the sequence of events.

- Before students attempt the activity, demonstrate the reading skill with books closed. Write on the board the following events from *The History of Money* in Unit 3: *People use electronic money* (4); *Coins had pictures of plants and animals* (2); *People used shells as money* (1); *The credit card was invented* (3). Say *Let's put them in order. Which one was first?* Elicit and write numbers next to the sentences.
- Draw students' attention to the instructions and remind them that *sequence* means "put in order." Have students do the activity individually. Then check answers as a class, having volunteers read the sentences aloud.
- Have students read the skills box. Explain that when the events are not in sequential order, a story or reading is more difficult to understand.

**Answers**

3, 4, 2, 1

**B Put the events in order.**

- Ask students what they do every morning. Review daily routine by asking *What's the first thing you do in the morning? What do you do after that?* If necessary, write key phrases on the board: *get up, have breakfast, take a shower, get dressed, go to school, have lunch, have dinner, go to bed.* Ask *Is everyone's daily routine the same? Do we all do things in the same order?* Have students discuss their routines in pairs and make a list of similarities and differences.
- Have students look at the pictures and captions and then sequence the events.
- Check answers as a class by having one student call out the sentences and the other students do the actions. Ask students how they worked out the order. Elicit that some things have to come in a certain order (e.g. no one brushes their teeth before they wake up), and some things can be in a different order (e.g. brushing teeth and getting dressed). In this case we can use the sequencer words to help us figure out the order of Paige's daily routine.

**Answers**

1 Paige woke up early in the morning to get ready for school. 2 First, she ate a bowl of cereal for breakfast. 3 Then, she brushed her teeth and washed her face. 4 She changed into her uniform and raincoat, and then she left for school.

**C Think and write. Look at the beginning of *Late for the Show*. What's the first event? What do you think happens after that?**

- Tell students that there is a problem in the story. Ask *What do you think it is?* Have them look at the title for a clue. (Someone is late for the show.)
- Give students one or two minutes to look at the beginning of the story on pp. 62–63.
- Ask *What happens first?* Tell students that they don't need to read the story. Remind them to look at the pictures to help them identify the first event. Encourage students to read the first sentence to help them.
- Ask *What's the first event?* and check answers as a class.
- Draw students' attention to the last scene on the page. Ask *What happens next?* Brainstorm ideas as a class. Then have students complete the sentences in their book. Ask volunteers to share their answers with the class.

**Suggested Answers**

The first event is the children practicing for a play. After that, I think the car gets stuck in traffic.

## Cool Down

Check that each student has a piece of paper. Students will play in groups of four. Tell students to think of a boy's or girl's name and a place where he/she goes; for example, *A boy named Robert goes to the park.* Ask students to fold over their paper twice so that the next student can't read what they have written, and pass the paper to their left. Ask *What does he/she do next?* Each time students receive a paper, they write a new event. At the end, students open up their papers and read their collaborative stories to the class. There should be some funny ones! Have the class decide which is the best story.

Now read **Late for the Show**

# Fiction: *Late for the Show—Play*

## Lesson Objectives

- to read a play about a boy taking part in a school play
- to make a personal connection to the reading
- to explore the SEL competency of relationship skills through exhibiting cooperative learning and working toward group goals

**Materials**

Audio Tracks 23 and 24; Video; handwritten cards with quotations from the reading (CD)

## Warm Up

Ask students if they ever took part in a performance. If your school holds school performances, ask them about the most recent one. Ask *Was it a play, a musical, or another type of show? What was your role? Did you work behind the scenes (on costumes, scenery, etc.)?*

## TRACK 23 TB p. 232 Reading Approach

**First Reading: Engage with the Text**

- Have students look at the reading and notice the title, text, and characters on the page. Point out that the names in capital letters are the students' roles in the show and the other names are their real names. Ask *What do you think the play is about?* (Possible answers: a school show; trying to get to the show on time / trying not to be late)
- Play the video, pausing to ask the prediction question from the red box on p. 63: *How is Harry going to get to school now?* Elicit different possibilities (e.g. take the bus, run there).
- Play the video to the end before looking at the Words in Context.

## TRACK 24 TB p. 232 Words in Context

- Play the audio and have students repeat the words.
- Have students race to find the words in the reading.
- Play the video again. Encourage students to **use the pictures/actions/events in the video to help establish the meaning of new words** (see TB p. 13, Three-Stage Reading Approach).
- Have students work in pairs to try to figure out the meaning of each word. Then bring the class together and use these questions to confirm the meanings.

**show** (p. 62) Ask students to find another word with a similar meaning in the text (performance). Elicit examples of *shows* (e.g. plays or musicals students may have seen).

**calm** (p. 64) Say *Imagine you're late and there's a problem with the train. How do you feel?* (nervous/anxious/stressed) *What's the opposite of this?* (calm) Have students use gesture and a calm, steady voice to say *Let's stay calm.*

**platform** (p. 65) Encourage students to look at the pictures. Ask *Where are the people standing?* Have students point to the platform as they say the word.

**sank** (p. 67) Have students look at the picture of the children performing the play and read the narration by Lynn. Ask *Where were Viola and Sebastian?* (on a ship) *What happened to the ship?* (There was a storm and the ship sank.) Ask *Where is the ship now?* Elicit that it is under the water.

**alive** (p. 68) Ask *What can happen if a boat sinks in a storm?* (You can drown.) *Does Sebastian drown or is he alive?* (He's alive.)

**Second Reading: Analyze the Text and Features**

- Play the audio and have students follow along in their books.
- Ask some questions to check comprehension; for example, *Why is Harry late at first?* (There's a lot of traffic.) *What is the second problem?* (The train has a problem.)
- Then discuss the questions in the red boxes.
  - **Making Connections** (p. 64): *The subway in London is called the Underground or the Tube.* Ask *Is there a subway in your city/country? What is it called?*
  - **SEL Competency:** (p. 64) *How does Harry feel?* Have students look at the expression on Harry's face and identify his feelings. Ask *How do you feel when you are late for something important?* Link this to the SEL competency of exhibiting cooperative learning and working toward group goals and encourage students to think about how being late can affect other people.
  - **Personalization** (p. 67): *Do you like to watch plays at the theater or on TV?* Ask *What did you see at the theater? Did you enjoy it? Did you see a play on TV?*

### International English

Have students notice the different spelling of *theater* and *theatre*. Explain that the pronunciation is the same.

  - **Personalization** (p. 69): *Can you think of a time you were late for something?* Ask *Are you ever late for school? Why?* Have students discuss the question with a friend before sharing their ideas with the class.

**Third Reading: Interact with the Text**

- Have students perform part of the play in groups (starting from where Harry puts on his costume). They could work in groups of seven, or in smaller groups with some students taking two roles. Encourage students to think about how the characters are feeling and to try and show different emotions through their voice and facial expressions.

## Cool Down

Play *Who Said It?* (see TB p. 27) with quotations from the play.

**Practice** **Student's App:** Fiction Video

## Explore the Reading

### Lesson Objectives

- to understand and analyze *Late for the Show* through reading comprehension activities
- to make a personal connection to the reading
- to explore the SEL competency of relationship skills through exhibiting cooperative learning and working toward group goals

**Materials**
(Optional) Video or Audio Track 23

### Warm Up

Do a TPR activity to review some of the events from the reading. Incorporating some movement in the class will help students focus on the tasks ahead. Have students stand up and do actions or gestures as you call out the events.

*Harry is nervous. / Harry puts on his costume. / The car gets stuck in traffic. / Harry gets off the train. / Viola looks for Sebastian. / Harry plays a tree. / Mr. Williams says, "Bravo!"*

**A Complete the story map.**

- If more than one day has passed since students read *Late for the Show*, play the video again.
- With books closed, have a Group Time discussion (see TB p. 21) to check students' comprehension of the text. Ask *Who is playing a tree?* (Harry) *How did Harry try to get to school?* (by car, then by underground) *Who else was on the platform?* (his friends from school) *Why couldn't they do the play at school?* (They were too late.) *What did they decide to do?* (perform the play on the platform)
- If you are using the TTL, project the story map onto the board. Have students look back at the reading and discuss what should go in each section in pairs.
- Have students complete the story map in their books individually. Then check answers as a class. You could display the answers using the TTL.

**Answers**
Title: Late for the Show
Characters: Riya, Arush, Lynn, Harry, Mr. Williams, Harry's mom, Harry's dad
Where: school, home, car, the Underground (subway)
When: the day before the show, the day of the show, around 6 p.m.
Problem: There was a traffic jam, so they had to take the Underground (subway). There was a something wrong with the train, so it was late.
Solution: They did the show on the platform.

**B Put the events in order. Then retell the story to a partner.**

- Copy each sentence from B onto strips of paper, one sentence per student. Put students in groups of six, giving each student a different sentence. Students have to read their sentences aloud and put themselves in order, standing in a line. When they are ready, check to see if their sentences are in the right order.
- Have students complete the ordering activity. They should then tell each other the story in pairs, using the sentences to help them. Finally, check answers as a class.

**Answers**
4; 6; 2; 5; 1; 3

**C Think and discuss. How did the characters work together to put on a play? How do you work with your teammates?**

Students are going to connect the reading to the SEL relationship skills competency: exhibiting cooperative learning and working toward group goals. Have the discussion with the whole class.

- Encourage students to think about how the characters worked together. Ask *Whose idea was it to do the play?* (Lynn's) *What did each character say?* If necessary, ask more specific questions about each character; for example, *What does Lynn say?* ("Why don't we perform the show here?") *How does Harry respond?* ("Good idea!") *How does Riya help?* (She reminds them that they have their costumes, and there is an audience.) *Do you think Lynn says all that information in the real play?* (Point out that as there is no scenery, so Lynn has to explain the play's setting.) *How does Mr. Williams help?* (He claps and encourages the audience to join in.) Ask *Did working together help them achieve their goal?* (Yes, they performed the play and had their best performance.)
- Give students some time to think of a situation where they have worked as part of a team, e.g. as a member of a sports team or on a group project. Write some prompts on the board, e.g. *What was your goal? How did you work together to try to achieve it?What did you do? What did others do? Did you achieve your goal? What could you do differently next time?* Have students discuss their ideas in pairs.

### Cool Down

Have students write a two-dollar summary of the play. Each word is worth ten cents. Give students two or three minutes to write their summary. Then have them compare with a partner to see how similar or different the summaries are.



**Practice** **Student's App:** Reading Practice

## Think Together

### Lesson Objectives

- to make connections between the readings
- to explore the key concept: How does teamwork help us?
- to explore the SEL competency of relationship skills through exhibiting cooperative learning and working toward group goals
- to reflect on the unit and provide personal thoughts and opinions

### Warm Up

Have students look back at the VTR picture on pp. 56–57. Ask students how they think the picture connects to the two readings in the unit. If necessary, write prompts on the board: *group/team, working together, audience, working hard, performance/show, fun, feeling proud, different roles/positions, communication.* Encourage students to be creative in their answers; for example, *Maybe the girls will play in the WNBA when they're older; They are working hard but having fun.*

**A Compare and contrast the Los Angeles Sparks with Harry and his friends. Complete the Venn diagram.**

- Review what students know about the Los Angeles Sparks and remember about Harry and his friends. Ask *Who are their players? Did they win against the Minnesota Lynx? Who is Harry? What did he do with his friends?*
- Tell students to write information about the Los Angeles Sparks and Harry and his friends in the Venn diagram. Remind them to write things that are similar in the middle section. Do an example on the board: LA Sparks: *They play basketball*; Harry and friends: *They perform in a show*; Both: *They work together.*
- Have students complete the diagram individually in their books. Then have students share their ideas with the class.

**Suggested Answers**

**Los Angeles Sparks**
All women
They wear sports clothes.
They play a lot of games.

**Harry and his friends**
Boys and girls
They wear costumes.
They give one performance.

**Both**
They work as a team.
They are successful.
They have an audience.

**B Think and discuss. How do the people on these teams help each other? Do a Numbered Heads Together routine.**

- Students are going to discuss their ideas in groups and then share with the class. To deepen understanding of the SEL competency (exhibiting cooperative learning and working toward group goals), encourage students to think of more elements of good teamwork (e.g. team players must get along well, help each other, try to find solutions to problems together, share the success, understand their role in the team).
- Have students do a Numbered Heads Together routine (see TB p. 20) to answer the question *How do the people on these teams help each other?*

**C Think and discuss. Talk about a time teamwork helped you. What happened?**

- Students are going to discuss their ideas about the key concept question *How does teamwork help us?* using a Think, Pair, Share routine (see TB p. 20). Draw students' attention to the question and brainstorm ideas. Give a few examples to explain that there are a lot of different teams we're part of in our everyday lives. We can be part of a team related to sports, games, school, family, and so on.
- Give students two minutes to think. Then have them discuss their ideas in pairs.
- After their discussion, have students share their ideas with the class. Discuss whether students' experiences of being part of a team are positive and/or negative. Highlight the SEL competency by emphasizing the importance of making friends, good communication, and resolving conflict.

### My Reading Journal

**Find four words in this unit that are interesting or new to you. Write.**

This task encourages students to review and remember language from the unit. Give students a few minutes to look back through the unit. Encourage them to look for words they didn't know before. Monitor and ask students why they like one or more of their chosen words.

**Color the stars to rate the unit. Then write a short review.**

This task focuses on evaluation. Remind students that in a review we write our opinion about something. Elicit what someone might say if they gave a 5 (star) rating; for example, *I thought this unit was excellent. I really loved the story.*

Have students complete their reading journals individually, monitoring and providing language help when needed. Then ask students what their favorite part of the unit was.

**Example Answer**

I thought this unit was excellent. I liked the play. It was funny! I love basketball, so I enjoyed the reading about the WNBA, and I learned some things I didn't know.

### Cool Down

Play *Test the Teacher.* Have students work in groups to write questions about information from the two readings. Make sure students write the answer next to the question. Each group then takes turns to ask the teacher a question. The teacher must answer the question from memory! If the teacher answers correctly, he/she gets one point. If the answer is incorrect, the group gets one point.

**Practice** **Resource Bank:** Unit Test
**Student's App:** Key Concept Practice

# UNIT 5 Make Some Noise

## Unit Overview

### Themes

Sounds we hear around us

The importance of music

### Synopsis

In this unit, students will explore the different types of sounds and noises we can hear in our world. They will learn about the sounds different objects make and discover how music and musical instruments can affect our emotions and bring people together. Students will prepare a conversation discussing school subjects and write a description.

## Language Book

**Vocabulary**

*bang, bark, buzz, chirp, crash, crunch, splash, squeak, whisper, whistle*

p. 112

**Explore Language**

Future Plans: *Going to* Statements

p. 113

**Global Citizenship**

Why are there different kinds of music?

*cello, clarinet, conductor, drums, flute, harp, orchestra, piano, trumpet, violin, xylophone*

p. 114

**Explore Language**

Future Plans: *Going to* Questions

p. 115

**Talk About It**

Conversation: agreeing and disagreeing

p. 116

**Write About It**

A Description

Punctuation: using quotation marks and commas

p. 117

**Think It Over**

Review and Reflection

p. 118

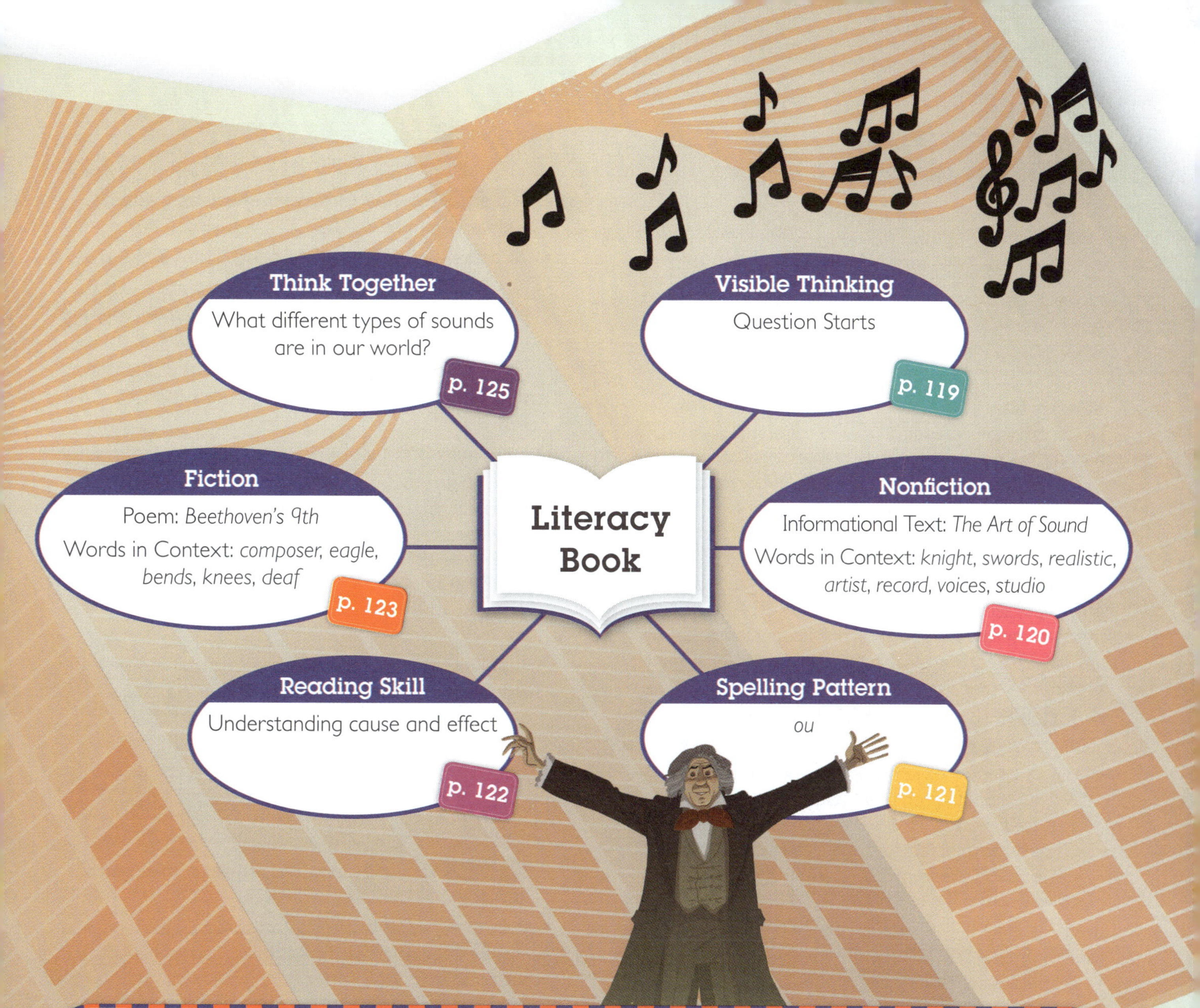


## Language and Literacy Connections

The connecting theme in Unit 5 is finding out about sounds and music.

| | Language | Literacy |
|---|---|---|
| **Vocabulary** | **Set 1:** noises<br>**Set 2:** musical instruments | **Nonfiction:** bang(ed), bark(ing), crash, crunch, squeak<br>**Fiction:** drums, flute(s), orchestra, piano, trumpet(s), violin(s) |
| **Grammar** | **Future Plans:** ***Going to* Statements**<br>I'm going to look for birds.<br>I'm not going to make any noise.<br>**Future Plans:** ***Going to* Questions**<br>What are you going to make? | Nonfiction<br>Is there going to be a storm in the movie?<br>Are the footsteps going to be soft or loud?<br>How much glass is going to break? |
| **Skills** | **Pronunciation:** /θ/ and /ʧ/ | **Reading:** understanding cause and effect<br>**Spelling Pattern:** *ou* |
| **International English** | program/programme; have a show/do a show; apartment/flat | |

## Vocabulary

### Lesson Objectives

- to learn noises vocabulary: *bang, bark, buzz, chirp, crash, crunch, splash, squeak, whisper, whistle*
- to sing a song that explores sounds at night

**Materials**
Audio Tracks 51 to 54; Video; various props for making sound effects (WU)

### Warm Up

Do an experiment to introduce the concept of sounds and hearing. Have students sit in a circle with their eyes closed. Silently choose one student and have him/her make a sound (you can give students a musical instrument / two objects, or they can clap their hands). The other students point in the direction they think the sound is coming from. Then they open their eyes and check. Repeat this with students covering one ear, to see if this distorts their sense of direction. Finally, put some headphones on another student. Can he/she hear anything? Tell students that in this unit you will be exploring the topic of noise and sound.

**A** TRACK 51 TB p. 219 **Listen and find. Is this place quiet or noisy?**

- Have students look at the picture and say what they see. Ask questions to prompt discussion; for example, *Where does the family live? What's in the house? What's outside?* Once students have talked about the picture, ask *Who can you see?* (Jake from Unit 4). Remind students of the challenge from the end of Unit 4: *What am I drinking?* and have them find the answer in the picture (tea / hot chocolate / a hot drink).
- Tell students they are going to listen to Jake talking to his grandpa. Ask a prediction question: *What do you think he can hear?* and elicit suggestions. Play the audio and have students point to the words or pictures as they listen.
- Ask the gist question *Is this place quiet or noisy?* and elicit the answer. Play the audio again for students to check.

**Answer**
It looks quiet but there are a lot of noises!

**B** TRACK 52 TB p. 219 **Listen, say, and number the pictures in A.**

- Play the audio and have students point to the pictures and say the words.
- Tell students to listen again and write numbers next to the words in the picture. Do the example together (crunch).
- Check answers by pointing to different people and actions in the picture and having students call out the words simultaneously. Alternatively, project the answers using the TTL.

**Answers**
1 *crunch* 2 crash 3 chirp 4 splash 5 bark
6 buzz 7 bang 8 squeak 9 whisper 10 whistle

**C** TRACK 53 TB p. 219 **Close your eyes. Listen, visualize, and say.**

- Prepare students for the visualization. (See TB p. 21.)
- Play the audio, allowing students to visualize the ideas as they listen. Make sure students know not to speak until they hear the word *say*. Put your finger to your lips if necessary.
- Have students choose their favorite sounds and tell their partner. Encourage them to try to make the sounds they chose.

**D Look and write.**

- Students are going to are going to consolidate understanding by deciding which noise word can be connected to each animal or thing in the box. Draw students' attention to the example and invite a volunteer to whistle a song. Then have them find an example of someone whistling a song in the picture.
- Have students complete the rest of the activity in pairs. Tell them to decide which is the most logical answer in each case and then use the picture to check. To check answers, invite one student to say a sentence and have the rest of the class make the noise.

**Answers**
1 *whistle* 2 buzz 3 chirp 4 whisper 5 splash
6 crunch 7 squeak 8 bark

**E** TRACK 54 TB p. 219 **Listen and complete. Then watch and sing.**

- Point to the song title *Are You Awake?* Ask *Do you sometimes stay awake at night? What noises do you hear?* and elicit suggestions. Then play the song once, allowing students to listen and enjoy it. Are students' ideas in the song?
- Ask *Can you guess what words are missing?* Play the song again, this time pausing where necessary for students to write their answers.
- Check answers as a class.
- Play the song video and encourage students to sing and move to the music as they watch.

**Answers**
1 *crunch* 2 whistle 3 squeak 4 whisper 5 bang
6 crash

### Cool Down

Play *Bingo* with sounds (see TB p. 26). Have students draw a 3 x 3 grid in their notebooks. They should choose six sounds from A and write them in their grid. Using sound effects, reproduce the sounds. When students hear a sound, they can cross it out on their grid. The first student to cross out all six sounds wins.



**Practice Student's App:** Vocabulary Practice; Song Video

# Explore Language

## Lesson Objectives

- to learn to use *going to* for future plans
- to practice noises vocabulary

**Materials**
Audio Tracks 55 and 56

## Warm Up

Ask students what time they usually get up. Ask *Do you ever get up very early in the morning? Why?* See if students have a special reason for getting up early or if they just wake up. Students may wake up early if they are excited or nervous about something, such as a birthday or a test.

**A** TRACK 55 TB p. 219 **Listen and read. What's Jake's plan?**

- Remind students of the scene on pp. 62–63. Ask *Where is Jake staying?* (in the country with his grandparents) Tell students that they are going to listen to Jake talking to his grandma early one morning. Play the audio and have students follow the dialogue in their books.
- Ask the gist question *What's Jake's plan?* and elicit the answer. Ask *Does he continue with his plan?* (no)

**Answer**
He's going to look for owls in the forest.

**B** **Look at A. Complete.**

- Write or project the table onto the board.
- Have students complete the grammar table in pairs using the dialogue.
- When they have completed the table, invite students to come up to the board and fill in one word each. Ask if everyone agrees. Students should now have the skills and strategies to be able to lead a discussion about the word order and verb forms they see in the table. If you feel that students need more guidance, the **ETB** provides a differentiation activity to help you support students as they explore the grammar table.
- Encourage students to notice the verb *to be* and review the difference between the first-person and third-person forms.
- Refer students to the Grammar tip *Remember.* Remind students about contractions. In Level 1 students studied the contractions *isn't* and *aren't*. Tell students that when the verb *to be* is followed by another verb (e.g. *going*) we can also contract the verb *be* instead of *not*. Then elicit example sentences using different subject pronouns: *We aren't going to make any noise* means the same as *We're not going to make any noise*. You may wish to point out that *I'm not* always works like this (i.e. you can't say *I amn't*).

**Answers**
'm; going to; going to

**C** **Think and discuss. Then choose.**

- Have students work in pairs to discuss the statement. Refer them to the table in B for examples of *going to*. Then check the answer.
- Ask students what Jake's plan is (to take pictures of owls). Ask *Do you think he decides to do that while he is talking to Grandma, or did he did he think about doing it before?* (before: he had all his equipment ready the night before) Explain that we use *going to* talk about plans we've already made.

**Answer**
1 a plan

**D** TRACK 56 TB p. 219 **Listen and say.**

- Tell students they're going to practice saying the structures. Play the audio, having students repeat each sentence chorally.
- For ideas on how to vary the drill, see TB p. 23.

**E** **Read and complete.**

- Look at the example together. Have students notice the verb *going to* and the main verb (in brackets). Write the sentence on the board and circle or underline these using different colors. Elicit the correct word order (*be* + *going to* + verb).
- Have students complete the activity individually. Remind them to use the correct form of *to be* and to use contractions. Check answers as a class.

**Answers**
1 *'s going to visit* 2 'm not going to bang
3 're going to play 4 'm going to whisper
5 isn't going to be / 's not going to be
6 aren't going to open

**F** **Play a game. Think about what you're going to do after school today. Mime and guess.**

- Ask *What do you do after school?* Have students suggest activities and write these on the board.
- Ask *What are you going to do after school today?* Ask two volunteers to demonstrate using the examples on the page: one student mimes playing soccer, and the other student guesses. Students can play in pairs or groups of three.
- Use a timer (preferably with a sound/buzzer). Allow three minutes for each round of the game. Whenever the timer goes off, have students rearrange into a new group/pair. Continue as long as time and interest allow. Additional rounds can have a new time period: the weekend, next Monday, next summer, when they grow up.

## Cool Down

Play *Versus* (see TB p. 27) for the procedure. For this version, call out a situation and two options; for example, *It's a sunny afternoon. Are you going to play video games or go to the park? It's a cold day. Are you going to wear a hat or gloves?* Students then turn to a friend and say what they are going to do.

**Practice** **Resource Bank:** Grammar Printout
**Student's App:** Grammar Practice

## Global Citizenship

### Lesson Objectives

- to learn musical instruments vocabulary: *cello, clarinet, conductor, drums, flute, harp, orchestra, piano, trumpet, violin, xylophone*
- to explore the importance of music in the community
- to practice listening for gist and details

**Materials**

Audio Tracks 57 to 59; Audio Track E; a globe or map of the world (D)

### Opening Question

Ask the opening question: *Why are there different kinds of music?* Write students' ideas on the board.

**A** TRACK 57 TB p. 219 **Listen. What does Rashid learn about the cello?**

- Have students name as many instruments as they can in English or in L1. Tell them they're going to listen to an interview with a conductor. Play the audio and have students point to the words or pictures as they listen.
- Ask the comprehension question *What does Rashid learn about the cello?* Play the audio again for students to check.

**Answers**

It looks like the violin, but it's bigger. It has to stand on the floor between the musician's knees.

**B** TRACK 58 TB p. 220 **Listen, say, and number the pictures in A.**

- Play the audio and have students point to the pictures and say the words.
- Tell students to listen again and write numbers next to the words in the picture. Do the example together (conductor).
- Check answers by pretending to play the musical instrument and having students call out the numbers.

**Answers**

1 *conductor* 2 orchestra 3 violin 4 cello 5 harp 6 flute 7 piano 8 trumpet 9 drums 10 clarinet 11 xylophone

TRACK E TB p. 220 **Visualization**

The TTL has a visualization audio track for this vocabulary set. (See TB p. 21.)

**C Read and choose.**

- Look at the example together. Ask *Which word can you play?* (cello) *Where do you play it?* (in an orchestra)
- Have students complete the activity individually. Then check answers as a class.

**Answers**

1 *cello; orchestra* 2 conductor 3 clarinet; flute 4 drums 5 harp

**D** TRACK 59 TB p. 220 **Now listen to Derick and María. What do they think about their music classes?**

- Tell students they are going to listen to two children talking about their music classes. Have students look at the two pictures and notice where each child is from. You could point out Venezuela and the USA on a globe or map. Tell students they are going to listen to two children talking about their music classes. Ask *Do you think their music classes will be similar or different?*
- Listening for gist: Ask the gist question *What do they think about their music classes?* Play the audio and elicit answers. Encourage students to justify their answers by asking them *What makes you say that?*
- Ask *What kind of music do they play?* Play the audio again so students can hear the clips of music. (Derick plays rock music; María plays classical music.)

**Suggested Answer**

They think their music programs are great. Derick gets to perform a lot and create his own music. María gets given an instrument and is taught how to play in an orchestra. She gets to play every day.

**E Listen again. Complete.**

- Listening for details: have students look at the sentences before they listen again to see how many things they remember. Then play the audio and have students complete the sentences. Check answers.

**Answers**

1 *violin* 2 drums 3 orchestra 4 buy 5 music

**International English**

Highlight the different spelling of the nouns (additional *–me*). Elicit which is American English and which is British English.

### Discussion Questions

- Draw students' attention to the discussion questions: *Is music important to you? Why? Where can people hear music in your community?* Have students discuss the questions in pairs. See **ETB**.
- Return to the opening question to ask again: *Why are there different kinds of music?* Recap ideas discussed at the beginning of the class and then encourage students to share any new ideas. Focus on the concept that music is personal: different people like different sounds and different instruments make different sounds: Encourage students to also think about the influence of local traditions on different kinds of music.

### Cool Down

Have students pretend to play different instruments as if they were a band. To make it more challenging, have the drummer set a rhythm that the others should follow!



**Practice** **Student's App:** Vocabulary Practice; Listening Practice

## Explore Language

### Lesson Objectives

- to learn questions with *going to*
- to practice musical instrument vocabulary

**Materials**
Audio Tracks 60 and 61

### Warm Up

Say *When you play an instrument, you make music.* Ask *What other things can you make?* Write students' suggestions on the board. Then ask students *Do you like making things? Do you ever make things out of old boxes, paper, etc.? What kinds of things do you make?* Elicit suggestions from students and write their ideas on the board.

**A** TRACK 60 TB p. 220 **Listen and read. What are Jen and Carla planning?**

- Tell students that they are going to listen to Jake's little sister, Jen, making something with her friend Carla. Have them look at the picture here and predict what the girls are making. Play the audio and have students follow the dialogue in their books.
- Ask the gist question *What are Jen and Carla planning?* and elicit the answer. Ask *Who is the show for?* (their moms).

**Answer**
They're planning a show.

**International English**

Have students notice the different verbs and elicit which phrase is American English and which is British English.

**B Look at A. Complete.**

- Review question words with the class, writing them on the board. Elicit that *what* is for objects/things, *when* is for times, and *who* is for people.
- Write or project the table onto the board.
- Have students discuss and complete the grammar table in pairs using the dialogue. Let your class guide the discussion. If you feel that students need more guidance, the **ETB** provides a differentiation activity to help you support students as they explore the grammar table.
- Check answers. Discuss the verb forms and word order together, but let your class guide the discussion.
- Make sure students are clear that they have to use the correct form of *be* and that this depends on the subject that comes after. Ask *How are the questions different from the sentences on p. 65?* Elicit that the word order changes so the structure is *be* + subject + *going to* + verb. Point out the short answer forms.
- Draw students' attention to the Grammar tip *Remember.* Write *What are you going to make?* on the board. Then listen to it on the audio track. Ask *Does it sound the same? Can you hear the three words "What are you"?* Elicit that the words sound like the contracted form, *What're you.* Explain that when we speak we often join words together, but we usually don't contract when we write the plural form.

**Answers**
are; is; going to; is; to; buy; Are; to; aren't

**C Think and discuss. Then choose.**

- Have students work in pairs to discuss the statement. Refer them to the table in B for example questions. Then check the answer.

**Answer**
1 future

**D** TRACK 61 TB p. 220 **Listen and say.**

- Tell students they're going to practice saying the new structures. Play the audio, having students repeat each sentence chorally. Encourage students to do actions to demonstrate making drums, moving chairs, playing an instrument in an orchestra.
- For ideas on how to vary the drill, see TB p. 23.

**E Read and complete.**

- Look at the example together. Elicit that the sentences are about a group of children playing music. Tell students to look at the picture and read the answers before completing the questions.
- Have students do the activity individually. Then check answers as a class.

**Answers**
1 *he going to play?* 2 Is she going to play
3 Are they going to play 4 is/'s going to play
5 Is he going to play

**F Play *I'm a Detective!* Each person writes sentences. Put them all in a pile. Then find out who's going to do it.**

- Play as a class, or with a large class, divide students into groups of approximately ten.
- Give each student a strip of paper. Tell students to write a sentence saying what they are going to do after dinner tonight. Then have each group mix up the pieces of paper, so that each student in the group has a different sentence. Students have to find the person who wrote the sentence by asking *going to* questions. Do the example with two volunteers.
- When students have guessed who wrote their sentence, they should write the name on the back of the piece of paper. If you are playing in groups, the first group to guess who wrote all the sentences wins. You can play again with sentences about other future plans.

### Cool Down

Play *Twenty Questions* (see TB p. 27). Choose an instrument.
Example questions: *Is it big? Does it have strings? Is it brown?*

**Practice** **Resource Bank:** Grammar Printout
**Student's App:** Grammar Practice

# Talk About It

## Lesson Objectives

- to prepare and practice a conversation discussing classes
- to use agreeing and disagreeing phrases
- to recognize and reproduce /θ/ and /ʧ/

**Materials**

Video; Audio Track 62

## Warm Up

Ask *Do you study music at school? What subjects do you study?* Elicit the subjects and write them on the board. Then ask students if they take any other classes. Students may attend after-school classes such as ballet or robotics. Add their ideas to the board.

**A** TB p. 238 **Watch and listen. Do Otis and Lewis agree in the end?**

- Tell students they are going to watch a video of a conversation between Otis and Lewis about classes. Show the picture using the TTL or have students look at the picture in their books. Ask the prediction question: *Do they think the same?* and elicit answers.
- Ask the gist question *Do Otis and Lewis agree in the end?* Have students predict the answer. With books closed, play the video and then check the answer. Ask further comprehension questions; for example, *Whose favorite class is music?* (Otis) Play the video again and have students notice the boys' body language.

**Answer**

Yes, they do.

**B Watch again. Check (✔) the phrases you hear.**

- Have students read the phrases. Play the video again and have students check the phrases they hear. Check answers as a class.
- Ask students which phrases you can use to agree with someone (*That's true; You're right; That's a good point*). Then have students identify the phrases you can use to disagree (*I disagree; That's not true*). Write these phrases on the board in two columns.
- Ask students which boy said *I think* (Lewis). Then ask *How did Otis give his opinion?* ("In my opinion …") Add a third column to the board for these two phrases. To help with categorizing the phrases, students could copy the table into their notebooks. Can they add any other phrases?
- Finally, ask students why Lewis asks *Why do you think that?* (to ask about Otis's reasons for his opinion)

**Answers**

*1*; 3; 4; 6; 8

## Pronunciation /θ/ and /ʧ/

TRACK 62 TB p. 220 **Listen and say.**

Demonstrate the two sounds first. Check the pronunciation of **/θ/**, which students practiced in Unit 4. Then show them how to pronounce **/ʧ/**, exaggerating the shape of your lips and mouth. Drill the two sounds one after the other so students can try to physically feel the difference.

Play the audio and have students repeat the words. Repeat if students need more practice.

Say *These words are used in the video. What other words do you know with these sounds?* Elicit ideas and write them on the board in two columns (e.g. *think*, *chirp*). Drill the pronunciation of each word.

**Suggested Answers**

/θ/ mouth; theater

/ʧ/ cheetah; cheese; chair; spinach; teach; choose; beach; catch; branch

**C Plan. Which class do you think is the most important? Complete.**

- Tell students they are going to plan a conversation about school subjects. Say *In the video, the boys say which class is the most important. They say why they think this.*
- Draw students' attention to the infographic. Do an example on the board with the class. Have them choose a subject. Then elicit reasons why that subject is important; for example, *English: we learn to communicate; we learn to read texts; we can talk to people from other countries.* Students could do a Rally Robin routine (see TB p. 20). Say *Math is the most important subject. Why?* Repeat with different subjects.
- Say *Now think about which class is the most important for you.* Have students complete their plans individually.

**D Prepare your conversation. Use your ideas from C and phrases from B.**

- Play the video again to remind students of the different stages in the conversation.
- Then have students work in pairs to prepare their conversation using their notes in C and phrases from B. Try to put students in pairs with someone who has a different opinion. Make sure students know that it is important to accept that other people have different opinions from our own and to respond politely when they disagree. It's OK to agree to disagree.

**E Practice with a friend.**

- Have students practice their conversation with their partner as many times as they like. Remind them to take turns and listen when their partner is speaking.
- Students can then change partners and have a different conversation.

## Cool Down

Do a *Gradient Line* (see TB p. 26). For this version, ask students how much they like different subjects.



**Practice** **Student's App:** Speaking Skills Practice; Speaking Video

# Write About It

## Lesson Objectives

- to learn to use quotation marks and commas before quotation marks
- to plan and write a soundscape
- to review sound words

**Materials**

(Optional) Support, Standard, and Challenge writing printouts from the Resource Bank, one per student (C and D)

## Warm Up

Have students do a quick senses scavenger hunt. If possible, allow them to go out of the classroom. Give them a list of five things to find using their different senses (e.g. something that smells good, something yellow, something that makes a crunch, something sweet, and something soft).

**A Read the paragraph. Underline the words people said and circle the sound words.**

- Ask students *What do you think a "soundscape" is?* and have students look at the title and the first sentence of the paragraph. Elicit the answer by asking *Where does the girl live?* (a city) *Where is she right now?* (by her apartment window) *What is she going to tell us about?* (the sounds from her window)
- Go through the paragraph sentence by sentence and show how the writer is constructing a "painting" of sounds. You may wish to have students draw the different types of sounds and their sources to help make the soundscape more tangible for them.
- Have students read the instructions. Ask *What do you have to underline?* (the words people say) *What do you have to circle?* (sound words) Have students work individually to do the activity. Then check answers as a class.
- Review why we use quotation marks (to identify what people say).

**Answers**

I'm going to tell you about the sounds from my apartment window on a hot, summer afternoon. I heard lots of cars go by. I heard tires squeak. Then a man shouted, "Watch where you're going!" Three dogs were barking loudly. A woman called, "Stop barking!" but the dogs didn't stop. Lots of children were shouting and laughing. One little kid said, "Wait for me!" I heard music in my friend's apartment, and a baby cried, "Mama! Mama!" Someone's door shut with a bang. Then my mom called, "Come and help with dinner," so I left my window.

**Practice Student's App:** Writing Practice

### International English

Elicit that *apartment* is American English and *flat* is British English. Ask *Which do we use?*

**B Rewrite. Add a comma and quotation marks.**

- Read the paragraph in A and have students call out anything that is in quotation marks. Then have students notice the comma before the opening quotation marks and that the first letter inside the quotation marks is capitalized.
- Look at the example together on the board. Explain that the comma helps signal that the quotation (what the person is saying) is about to start. Then have students copy the sentences, adding punctuation. Check answers as a class.

**Answers**

1 *The police officer shouted, "Look out!"*
2 His mother called, "Time for dinner!"
3 My little sister asked, "Can you help me?"
4 The boy said, "Hurry up!"
5 My dad said, "Please clean your room."

**C Plan. Think about your soundscape. Close your eyes and imagine. Complete.**

- Tell students they are going to plan their own soundscapes. Do a visualization activity. Have students close their eyes and ask them to imagine they are somewhere else. Ask *Where are you? What sounds can you hear? You hear some voices; who is with you? What are they saying?*
- Then have students plan their soundscape based on what they visualized. Challenge printouts can be handed out now.

**D Write about your soundscape.**

- Have students write a draft of their soundscapes in their notebooks or on paper, using their ideas from C. Support printouts can be handed out now.
- Students should self-correct or exchange their work with a friend and peer-correct. You can put a checklist of things for students to look for on the board (e.g. spelling, use of adjectives and adverbs, punctuation, conjunctions, quotation marks).
- Have students write their final versions on paper or hand out the Standard printouts. Give students time to draw a picture of what they imagined.

## Cool Down

Have students choose one of the picture dictionary scenes from the Vocabulary lessons (Units 1 to 5). In pairs, they should imagine what each person in the scene is saying and write it in their notebooks using quotation marks. They can then read their sentences and have another pair of students guess who said each one.

# Think It Over

## Lesson Objectives

- to review what has been learned in the unit
- to reflect on the unit and their own progress
- to think about learning strategies and how to continue learning at home

### Warm Up

Ask students what the unit theme was (noise) and write it in the middle of the board. Brainstorm any words or phrases students can think of that relate to the topic and write them on the board. Encourage students to think about the things we can hear around us every day in different places.

**Read the questions and draw or write your answers.**

- Give students time to think about and discuss activities in the unit before they complete each question. Explain that they can choose to either write a few words or sentences or to draw a picture. Allowing students to make a personal response will help them retain knowledge and engage with the learning points.

**What did I do?**

- Give students a few minutes to look back through the unit at the different activities they did. Ask questions about the unit, or write questions on the board for students to discuss in pairs or small groups; for example, *What sounds did Jake hear? What instruments do the children in the unit play?*
- Encourage students to identify something in the unit that they found challenging or something that was particularly memorable for them. Students can draw or write about their chosen activity.

**What did I learn?**

- Ask questions about the unit to help students think about what they learned; for example, *What did you learn about sounds and music? What sentences can you say using "going to"? Can you describe a soundscape? What else did you learn?* Have students discuss their ideas in pairs.
- Encourage students to draw a picture or write sentences about their learning outcomes.

**How did I learn?**

- Ask students how they learned the sound and noise vocabulary and the music vocabulary in Lessons 1 and 3. Elicit ideas (e.g. by connecting sound words to animals and things, by singing a song, by doing a visualization, by making predictions about the picture). Encourage students to think about the spelling and pronunciation of the words. Ask *What helped you remember how to say and write the new words?*
- Then encourage students to think about how they learned throughout the unit; for example, how did they develop their speaking skills?
- Have students draw or write about the activities that helped them learn.

**How well did I do?**

- Tell students to circle the number of musical notes that best expresses how well they have learned the unit content (i.e. the more notes they circle, the more they feel they have learned). Ask *What do you understand? What do you need to practice more?* Encourage students to look back through the unit to see how much they remember, what they did well, and what they found difficult.

**What can I do next?**

- Brainstorm ideas with the class about what they can do to continue to learn (e.g. think about benefits of music, find and pronounce words with /θ/ and /ʧ/, go to see some live music of their choice, research information about a composer (this could be a modern composer), listen to different types of music to see if there are other genres they like, pay attention to their listening skills, disagree politely in a discussion with friends or family). Students can look back at the previous units to get more ideas. Encourage students to suggest their own ideas for different activities they can do.
- Draw students' attention to the *What can I do next?* box. Encourage students to think about what they can do at home to improve their English. Have them suggest some verbs that they can use (e.g. listen, read, write, discuss, research) and write the verbs they choose in their books.
- Have students choose several activities that they would like to do and write them in their notebooks. They can then share their ideas with a partner.

### Looking Forward

- Draw students' attention to the character at the bottom of the page. Ask *Who's this?* and elicit what they remember about her (Carla appears in Explore Language 2, p. 68; she made instruments and had a show).
- Draw students' attention to Carla's question: *What's my favorite food?* Encourage students to make predictions about what her favorite food is and what Unit 6 is about. Tell students they will find the answer in Lesson 1 of the next unit.

## Play 1

To further review and recycle the language in Units 1 to 5, have students practice and perform the play, *The Grassland Orchestra* on pp. 140–141. See TB p. 211 for teaching notes.

**Practice** **Resource Bank:** Unit Test; Mid-year Test
**Student's App:** Vocabulary and Grammar Review

## Get Ready to Read

### Lesson Objectives

- to activate prior knowledge about noise and sounds
- to guide inquiry and deepen understanding through a Question Starts VTR
- to preview the reading skill of understanding cause and effect

**Materials**

Various music clips (WU) (Optional) VTR printout from the Resource Bank (Activities A, B, C)

### Warm Up

Play some clips of different types of music (e.g. pop, jazz, classical). Have students tell you how each one makes them feel.

### Question Starts

**A Look at the picture. Then brainstorm questions. Write a list.**

Students are going to do a Question Starts VTR to explore the image of the musicians.

- Have students look at the picture for a minute and then say what they can see. Help with vocabulary as necessary and write it on the board.
- Draw students' attention to the question words. *What questions do you have about the picture?* Give students a few minutes to write questions.
- Then bring the class back together and write all suggestions on the board, helping students correct their questions when needed.

**B Look at your list from A. Which questions seem the most interesting? Discuss them with the class.**

- Have students identify the questions they would most like to know the answers to from their own lists.
- Tell students that they are going to practice negotiation skills by working as a group to decide which three questions they want to ask. Have students work in groups of three to review the questions and discuss possible answers. This will help them decide which questions they think are the most interesting. Then discuss them as a class and decide on the most interesting questions.

Here's an example of this part of the routine:

**Teacher:** Which questions seem the most interesting? What do you really want to know?
**Student A:** What kind of music are they playing?
**Teacher:** Great. What do you think?
**Student B:** Happy music for a celebration.
**Student C:** Traditional music because they're wearing traditional costumes.
**Teacher:** OK, what other questions do you have?
**Student D:** Why aren't there any women?

**C What new ideas or questions do you have now? Talk about your ideas with your partner.**

- Encourage students to think about ideas and questions about music and performing globally: they shouldn't limit their ideas to what they see in the picture. Refer students to the example questions and give them a couple of minutes to think of their own questions. Then have students share their questions in pairs and discuss any possible answers.
- Encourage students to ask all the questions they want, including any generated in the discussion they had earlier in the lesson.

### Transition

Ask *What sounds do you think there are in the picture? What sounds do the instruments make? Is it a noisy place or a quiet place?*

**D Think and discuss. Imagine a noisy place and a quiet place. What things can you hear?**

- Students are going to think about the contrast between noise and silence. Remind them that places can be noisy and quiet at different times (e.g. a classroom when students are doing silent reading and when they are playing a game). Tell students to think of two places, then imagine the different sounds they might hear there.
- Students can draw as they discuss their ideas. The drawing of noisy and quiet spaces will show that there are different causes for sound and silence (e.g. classroom discussions, music performances, and building sites compared with libraries, bedrooms at night, and museums).
- Have students share their ideas with the class.

**E Think and discuss. What different sounds do these make? When are they loud? When are they quiet?**

In this activity students will preview the skill of understanding cause and effect: the causes of sound and the effects that they make.

- Have students look at the four items and decide if they are usually loud or quiet. Do an example with the class: a crowd at a soccer game. Ask *What different sounds does the crowd make?* (cheering, shouting, groaning, etc) *Is it usually loud or quiet?* (loud) *When does it make a very loud noise?* (after a goal is scored) *When is it quiet?* (when their team loses; when the game finishes)
- Give students a few minutes to discuss the other items in pairs. Then invite volunteers to share their ideas with the class.

**Answers**

Students' own answers

Now read **The Art of Sound**

# Nonfiction: *The Art of Sound*—Informational Text

## Lesson Objectives

- to read an informational text about sound effects in movies
- to make a personal connection to the reading

**Materials**

Audio Tracks 25 and 26; Video; a video clip of an action scene from a movie suitable for children (WU)

## Warm Up

Students are going to listen to a scene from a movie. Play the video clip on your computer but don't project it. Have students listen and discuss what's happening in pairs. Share ideas with the class. Then show students the clip. Ask *Were you right?*

### TRACK 25 TB p. 232 Reading Approach

**First Reading: Engage with the Text**

- Ask students to notice the title, text, and pictures on the page and use this information to predict ideas about the reading. Ask questions to elicit ideas; for example, *What are the people in the pictures doing?*
- Have students look at the picture of the knights. Ask *What sounds will you hear?* Then have students read the first paragraph. Encourage students to try to make the sound effects.
- Ask the gist question *What does a Foley artist do?* Then play the audio and have students listen and read. Elicit answers. (A Foley artist puts special sounds into movies.)
- To recap, ask students why the reading has the title *The Art of Sound*. Ask if students think the reading is interesting. *Why or why not?*
- Read the whole reading before looking at the Words in Context.

### TRACK 26 TB p. 233 Words in Context

- Play the audio and have students repeat the words.
- Have students race to find the words in the reading.
- Ask students what strategies they know to guess the meaning of new words. Play the video and encourage students to **use the pictures/actions/events in the video to help establish the meaning of new words** (see TB p. 13, Three-Stage Reading Approach).
- Bring the class together and use these discussion points to confirm the meanings.

**knight** (p. 74) Ask *Do you know of any famous knights?* Elicit that a *knight* is a soldier from the past who wore armor and rode a horse.

**swords** (p. 74) Ask *What do the man and the knight pull out and fight with?* Have students locate the swords in the picture.

**realistic** (p. 74) Ask students to identify another word in *realistic* (real). Say *A movie isn't real. It's fiction. What makes it realistic or believable?* (the sound effects, the scenery, etc.)

**artist** (p. 75) Say that *artist* can refer to a painter or any type of performer or creative person, such as a writer. Ask *What does a sound artist do?* (makes or re-creates sounds for movies)

**record** (p. 75) Ask *How do Foley artists keep the sounds they make to put in the movie later?* (They record them.) Ask students what they can use to record their voice (a cell phone, a computer).

**voices** (p. 75) Ask *What sounds are recorded in a movie?* Have students look in the reading to find the answer (the actors' voices). Say *Can I hear your voice?* and encourage students to say something.

**studio** (p. 76) Ask *Where do Foley artists work?* Elicit that a studio is a special room where they record the sounds (TV shows, music albums, etc.).

**Second Reading: Analyze the Text and Features**

- Play the video again to consolidate students' understanding of the story.
- Ask some questions to check comprehension; for example, *Why don't they record the sounds when they film?* (It's too noisy.) *What can you find in a Foley studio?* (many tools)
- Discuss the questions in the blue boxes.
  - **Language Focus** (p. 74): *Sound words like "crash" help us imagine what's happening.* Focus on the sentence *Their swords crash together with a loud smash.* Elicit other things that make a *crash*.
  - **Fact** (p. 75): *The name "Foley artist" comes from Jack Foley, one of the first people to work with sound in movies.* Ask students if they know of any objects named after people.
  - **Detail** (p. 76): *What are different ways a Foley artist makes sounds?* Have students scan the text to find how a Foley artist makes sounds and what he/she uses.
  - **Personalization** (p. 77): *Do you think it's fun being a Foley artist? Why or why not?* You could take a class vote on this question. Encourage students to give reasons for their answers.

**Third Reading: Interact with the Text**

- Have students take turns to read a section of the text in small groups. While one student reads the text, have the others do the actions. Encourage students to add their own sound effects.

## Cool Down

Ask *What was your favorite sound effect from the reading? Why?* Have students discuss their answers in pairs.

**Practice** **Student's App:** Nonfiction Video

## Explore the Reading

### Lesson Objectives

- to understand and analyze *The Art of Sound* through reading comprehension activities
- to make a personal connection to the reading
- to learn through CLIL (arts and humanities): exploring how we can use objects to re-create sounds
- to reproduce and write words with *ou*

**Materials**

(Optional) Video; Audio Tracks 25 and 27; sound effects (e.g. from an app) (WU); activities written on cards (CD)

### Warm Up

Play several different sound effects (e.g. footsteps, raindrops, a horse trotting). Have students identify the sound and where they might hear it. They could also think about how a Foley artist might make the different sounds.

**A Answer the questions.**

- If more than one day has passed since students read *The Art of Sound*, play the video again.
- With books closed, have students say what they remember about the reading. Encourage students to use simple structures in English, but allow some use of L1 if necessary.
- Have students open their books and look at the activity. Ask a volunteer to read the first question. Have students find the answer in the reading (a Foley artist puts special sounds into movies). Remind students that answers should be complete sentences.
- Have students do the rest of the activity individually, looking back at the reading to check their answers. Check answers as a class, having students say on which page they found their answer.

**Answers**

1 A Foley artist puts sounds into movies.
2 The name "Foley artist" comes from Jack Foley, one of the first people to work with sound in movies.
3 When the movie is made outside, small but important sounds are too quiet.
4 The Foley artist works in a special studio.
5 The Foley artist might use an old chair, coconut shells, or a book to make clear and crisp sounds.

**B Think and discuss. What makes a good Foley artist?**

- Have students use a Think, Pair, Share routine (see TB p. 20) to discuss the question.
- Ask *What skills do you need to be a good Foley artist?* Suggested answers: good hearing, good listening skills, attention to detail (they need to watch the movie carefully and see what the actors are doing; they need to decide how loud or quiet the sounds should be).
- After they have discussed their ideas, have pairs choose the most important skill and explain the reason for their choice to the class.

**C Think and write. Imagine a Foley artist copied sounds from your day. What sounds would they make?**

Students are going to connect the reading to their own lives. This draws on the CLIL arts and humanities concept of exploring how we can use objects to re-create sounds.

- Elicit what activities students do every day. Say *What do you do when you get up in the morning?* Brainstorm ideas on the board. Have students think about their morning routine, how they leave home to go to school, transportation they use, noises at school, and so on.
- Have students work individually to choose four actions and write them in their books. If they want to choose more, have them do the activity in their notebooks.
- Draw students' attention to the question in the blue box: *Can you imagine what could make those sounds?* Put students in pairs and have them look at their lists and decide together how a Foley artist could make those sounds. Have students write their ideas next to each activity.

**Answer**

Students' own answers

### Spelling Pattern *ou*

**TRACK 27** TB p. 233 **Listen and write. Then check your answers.**

- With books closed, write *ou* on the board.
- Play the first part of the audio and have students repeat each word. Then have them open their books. Play the first part of the audio again and have students complete as many words as they can.
- Then play the second part of the audio for students to check their spelling and complete the words correctly. Ask *Which sounds are the same?* (house, proud; and touch, cousin, young) and have them read the words aloud. Then have students underline *ou* in each word and notice that there is a consonant before and after these letters.
- Have students look back at the reading to find more words that contain *ou* and write them in a word cloud. Invite students to read a word from their cloud.

**Answers**

1 touch 2 house 3 cousin 4 proud 5 young
In the reading: through; out; loud; sound(s); outside; louder; you

### Cool Down

Play a game. Have one student come to the front. Show the student an activity. He/she should make sound effects for the activity. The other students should try to guess what the activity is.

Suggested activities: ice skating, swimming, drinking a can of soda, playing a guitar, bouncing a basketball

**Practice** **Resource Bank:** Spelling Printout
**Student's App:** Reading Practice; Spelling Pattern Practice

# Get Ready to Read

## Lesson Objectives

- to practice the reading skill of understanding cause and effect
- to activate prior knowledge about sounds and hearing
- to make a personal connection to the reading

**Materials**

(Optional) A piece of music by Beethoven (B); small cards, five blank and five with effects written on per group (CD)

### Warm Up

Play *Read My Lips*. In this game students pretend to say a word, but they don't make any sound. Do a few examples with the class first. Tell students to look at your mouth carefully. Say a simple word students will know slowly, exaggerating your mouth movements. Have students raise their hands to guess. Then have them play in pairs, choosing words connected to the unit for their partner to guess. Examples of words might be: *crash, noisy, quiet, bee, movie.*

**A Draw and discuss. What can cause each of these sounds?**

Students are going to practice the reading skill of understanding cause and effect.

- Write the three sound words on the board as column headings. Elicit the sound each one makes. Brainstorm one idea about what can cause each sound and write the ideas in the three columns.
- Encourage students to use their imaginations and think of a variety of different causes for each sound. Have them draw at least one idea in each of the boxes. When students have finished drawing, have them show their drawings and discuss their ideas in pairs.
- Draw students' attention to the skills box. Ask for volunteers to name the cause and effect of their drawings (the cause is the action and the sound is the effect). Then ask students to think of other examples of cause and effect connected to sounds; for example, crash (a plate dropping to the ground and breaking) and thud (someone walking with big boots).

**Suggested Answers**

*crunch*: stepping on a branch or autumn leaves, eating potato chips; *squeak*: a door in a haunted house, sneakers on the gym floor; *buzz*: a buzzer (kind of doorbell), a cell phone on vibration

**B Read these facts about Ludwig van Beethoven, a famous composer. Match the cause to the effect.**

- If you have a piece of music by Beethoven, play one or two minutes of it. Ask students to close their eyes and listen to the music. Ask *What sounds can you hear? Which pictures do you have in your mind when you listen to the music? How does it make you feel?* Ask volunteers to share their ideas with the class.
- Ask students if they have heard of Beethoven. Ask *Do you know anything about him?* Students will find out more about Beethoven in the next lesson.
- Draw students' attention to the instructions. Quickly review what *cause* and *effect* are (cause is why something happens; effect is what happens) and elicit an example from the class (this could be from A).
- Have students match the causes to the effects individually. Then check answers as a class.

**Answers**

1 b 2 a 3 d 4 c

**C Think and discuss. Do all people hear well? Do you know anyone who doesn't hear very well or who can't hear?**

- Ask students *Do you have good hearing? Do you always hear what people are saying? Do you sometimes need people to repeat?*
- Then have students discuss whether all people hear well in pairs or small groups. Encourage them to say if they know anyone who doesn't hear very well or who is deaf. Students may need some scaffolding with the language associated with hearing loss, such as *hearing aid, sign language, deaf,* and *hard of hearing.*
- Ask students to share their answers with the class. Elicit or point out that often people's hearing gets worse when they get old, while some people are born deaf and others develop hearing loss as the result of an illness. If students are interested, go on to discuss how people with hearing difficulties manage. Ask *How can we communicate with someone who can't hear?* Discuss sign language and the use of gesture as a means of communication.

### Cool Down

Prepare some cards with effects written on them, such as *getting wet, feeling angry,* and *a broken window.* Give small groups a set of cards with effects and the same number of blank cards. Have students discuss and write a possible cause for each effect on the cards. Students can then swap cards with another group and match the causes and effects.

Now read **Beethoven's 9th**

# Fiction: *Beethoven's 9th*—Poem

## Lesson Objectives

- to read a poem about the premiere of Beethoven's 9th Symphony
- to make a personal connection to the reading

**Materials**
Audio Tracks 28 and 29

## Warm Up

Read the first stanza of the poem. Use gesture to aid comprehension (e.g. mime playing the violin). Then say *Imagine you're at the concert. What are you wearing? How do you feel?* Students listen and visualize and then discuss their visualizations with their partner.

### TRACK 28 TB p. 233 **Reading Approach**

First Reading: Engage with the Text

- Ask students to notice the title, text, and pictures on the page. Ask *What do you think the poem will say about Beethoven?*
- Play the audio and have students read along as they listen. Pause after the first page and ask *Do you think the people will like the music?* and elicit answers.
- Read the whole poem before looking at the Words in Context.

### TRACK 29 TB p. 233 **Words in Context**

- Play the audio and have students repeat the words.
- Have students race to find the words in the reading.
- Tell students that sometimes the writer compares things using *like*. Encourage them to **think about how the two things are similar to help understand the words** (see TB p. 23). Have students discuss their ideas in pairs.
- Then bring the class together and use these questions to confirm the meanings.

**composer** (p. 80) Ask *What was Beethoven's job? What did he do?* (He wrote music.) Elicit that a composer is a person who writes music.

**eagle** (p. 82) Have students read the first two lines of the third stanza. Encourage students to do the actions with their arms. Elicit that this description helps us figure out that an eagle is a big bird.

**bends** (p. 83) Look at the line *First, he stands tall, then he bends down.* Ask students *When you bend down are you tall or small?* (small) Invite students to demonstrate standing tall and then bending down. Explain or elicit that the author is contrasting two ideas here.

**knees** (p. 83) Ask *Which part of the body is Beethoven bending?* Have one or two students demonstrate bending their knees.

**deaf** (p. 85) Have students find other phrases in the poem that mean the same as *deaf*. (can't hear; hearing long dead) Ask students to imagine not being able to listen to music.

Second Reading: Analyze the Text and Features

- Read the poem and have students follow along in their books. Use gesture and your voice to show emotion. If you prefer, play the audio again.
- Ask some questions to check comprehension e.g. *What is Beethoven doing on the stage?* (conducting / helping the orchestra to play the music). *Did the audience wait a long time to hear Beethoven's music?* (Yes, ten years.)
- Discuss the questions in the blue boxes.
  - **Fact** (p. 81): *Ludwig van Beethoven (1770–1827) was a famous composer from Germany.* Ask students if they know any other famous composers. You could have students find Germany on a map.
  - **Language Focus** (p. 82): *What words does the author use to help you see and hear more details?* Point out the simile *like an eagle that flies* and have students imagine how Beethoven moves his arms. Have students look for other words that help them see and hear (e.g. *soft and sweet, light shines, wind's in his hair, like a small boat sailing on stormy seas, drums boom*).
  - **Fact** (p. 84): *Beethoven was probably around 25 when he started losing his hearing.* Ask students how old they think Beethoven was in the poem (he was in his fifties when the 9th was first performed). Ask *Could he hear when he wrote the music?* (no)
  - **Making Connections** (p. 85): *Why is Beethoven crying? How would you feel?* Ask *Is Beethoven sad?* (No, he's happy/proud.) Ask students if they sometimes cry when they are happy.
- Discuss the text focus question: *Sensory details use your five senses to visualize a scene. Can you find some?* Elicit the five senses (sight, hearing, smell, taste, and touch). Give students two or three minutes to try to find examples of each sense in the poem.

Third Reading: Interact with the Text

- Ask *How do you feel before a performance? How do you feel at the end?* Discuss different emotions Beethoven might be feeling at each stage, e.g. excitement and nervousness before the performance; passion and pride as he conducts the orchestra; pride, happiness, and relief at the end. Have students read the poem to each other in pairs. They should try to use their voices to show some of the emotions they identified.

## Cool Down

Have students draw a picture to illustrate their favorite word or description in the poem. Then have them share their pictures with a friend.

# Explore the Reading

## Lesson Objectives

- to understand and analyze *Beethoven's 9th* through reading comprehension activities
- to make a personal connection to the reading
- to explore the SEL competency of social awareness by respecting others

**Materials**
(Optional) Audio Track 28

### Warm Up

Play a version of the *Yes/No Game* (see TB p. 27). For this version, assign one side of the classroom as *Beethoven* and the other *Audience*. Call out different things either the audience or Beethoven does in the poem; for example, *Wait* (audience); *Stands proud* (Beethoven); *Bends knees* (Beethoven); *Wear dresses and suits* (audience); *Clap and cheer* (audience); *Deaf* (Beethoven); *Like his music* (audience); *Waves arms* (Beethoven); *Happy* (note that students could stand on either side, as both Beethoven and the audience are happy).

**A** TRACK 28 **TB p. 233 Read and choose.**

- If more than one day has passed since students read *Beethoven's 9th*, play the audio again and have students follow in their books.
- With books closed, have a Group Time discussion (see TB p. 21) to check students' comprehension of the text. Have students say what they remember about the reading. Encourage students to use simple structures in English, but allow some use of L1 if necessary.
- Have students open their books and read the first question. Draw students' attention to the three options and elicit what you can do in each place; for example, watch a play, read / take out books, play sports. Remind students that the *setting* is the place where the story takes place.
- Have students do the rest of the activity individually. Remind students to look back at the reading quickly to find the answers. Check answers as a class.

**Answers**
1 a 2 b 3 a 4 c 5 b

**B Think and check (✔). What effects did Beethoven's music have on the audience?**

- Students are going to consider how the audience felt when they heard Beethoven's music and how they can recognize this. This draws on the SEL social awareness competencies of recognizing others' emotions (review from Unit 1) and respecting others.
- Say *How do you think the audience felt when they heard Beethoven's music?* Have students look back at the pictures in the poem. See if they can identify any emotions. Ask *How can we know what someone is feeling?* Elicit that we can look at their face and gestures, and we can listen to their voice. Draw students' attention to the picture in B. Ask *How are they feeling?*
- Have students check the sentences. Check answers as a class. Ask *Why did they clap and cheer?* (they enjoyed the music). Elicit that applause is a way of showing respect and appreciation for a performance.

**Answers**
They clapped and cheered. Time flew by for them. Everyone felt happy.

**C Think, circle, and discuss. Do you ever listen to live music? Who do you listen with? How do those people feel? How do you feel?**

- Students are going to connect the reading to their own lives. This builds on the SEL social awareness competency of recognizing one's own and others' emotions, introduced in Unit 1, and also on respecting others' feelings and emotions. Ask students the question *Do you ever listen to live music?* Explain that *live* means that you are in the place where the singer/musicians are performing, such as a theater or stadium. Ask *Do you go to concerts?* Encourage students to say who the performers were that they saw. If students have never been to a concert, ask them to think of music they have heard in school or on the street.
- Draw students' attention to the adjectives and check the meaning of each one. Ask *When you listen to live music, who do you go with? Do they like the music? How do you think it makes them feel?* Tell students to circle some of the adjectives with red. Then ask *How does the music make you feel?* Have students circle adjectives with blue. Tell them they can circle the same adjectives or different ones.
- Students are now going to discuss their ideas in pairs or small groups. Monitor and provide language help when needed. Then bring the class together and ask some students to share their ideas. Encourage students not to make judgments on what other students have seen, even if they don't like the music themselves. Different thoughts and opinions will produce a lively and interesting discussion, but students should also be respectful of what other students think. If necessary, discuss with students what facial expressions or gestures might mean that they are being disrespectful (e.g. laughing, looking very surprised or shocked, looking uninterested).

**Answers**
Students' own answers

### Cool Down

Play *Pass the Whisper!* with a line from the poem (see TB p. 26). Repeat as required.

**Practice** **Student's App:** Reading Practice

## Think Together

### Lesson Objectives

- to make connections between the readings
- to explore the key concept: What different types of sounds are in our world?
- to reflect on the unit and provide personal thoughts and opinions

### Warm Up

Have students look back at the VTR picture on pp. 72–73. If you are using the TTL, project the image onto the board. Ask students how they think the picture connects to the two readings in the unit. If necessary, write the following prompts on the board: *work/jobs, sounds, type of music, entertainment, performances/shows, audience, feelings.* Encourage students to be creative in their answers; for example, *They are performing music, like Beethoven. The instruments make different sounds; I think the people watching feel happy; Maybe they are playing Beethoven's music.*

**A Look at both readings. Find three different sound words. Write.**

- Remind students that sound words are words that sound like things we hear (e.g. *crash*). Review with students different things that might make a *crash*. Then give students a few minutes to look back through the readings to find other sound words.
- Students should write the sound words in the bubbles. They can use fun lettering to create a comic style.

**Suggested Answers**
Three of the following: crunch, squeak, crash, smash, noisy, buzzing, barking, thunder, bang, hum, boom, cry, clap, cheer

**B Sit quietly. Close your eyes. What can you hear? Listen very carefully. Then complete the graphic organizer.**

- Students are going to listen to the different sounds they can hear in their environment. If possible, take students to another place in the school (e.g. the cafeteria, playground, library, gym). If time permits, go to more than one place.
- Have students take notes while they listen. If you are taking students to more than one place, have them do this in their notebooks.
- Students are going to share their ideas in C.

**C Talk about the sounds you heard with your partner. Did any of them surprise you? Do a Think, Pair, Share.**

- Students are going to discuss their ideas about the key concept question *What different types of sounds are in our world?* using a Think, Pair, Share routine (see TB p. 20).
- Give students a couple of minutes to look at their graphic organizer and think about the sounds. If they have been to more than one place, tell them to compare and contrast the different sounds they heard.
- Then have students share their thoughts with a partner. Tell students to think about if they heard the same things as their partner. Ask *What sounds did you both notice?*
- Now have students share their partner's ideas with the rest of the class. Write their ideas in a list on the board.
- Finally, as a class, have students look at the list and decide whether the ideas represent the different types of sounds in our world. Can they add any others to the list?

### My Reading Journal

**Which is your favorite noise from the unit? Why?**

This question focuses on personalization. Write all the sounds (see answer key for A) on the board for reference. Point to each one and elicit from the class the sound it makes. Then have students choose their favorite. Ask a few students why they like the sounds they chose.

**Example Answer**
I liked the (boom) because (it's a loud noise that a drum makes).

**Look back at the unit. What questions do you have? What do you want to learn more about?**

This task encourages students to review and remember what they learned and think about what else they would like to know. Give students a few minutes to look back through the unit. Write the five *Wh-* question stems plus *How* on the board. Elicit one or two questions from the class; for example, *How did Beethoven write music if he was deaf?* Have students complete their reading journals individually, monitoring and providing language help when needed.

**Example Answers**
*How did Beethoven know if the music sounded good? How does a Foley artist make the sound of glass breaking? I want to know which sounds a Foley artist made in my favorite movie.*

### Cool Down

Have students work in groups of three to write three quiz questions about the unit. The questions can be about the two readings, the VTR picture, or the Spelling section. Students can choose to write true or false questions, multiple-choice questions, or challenge questions (e.g. Name five sounds). Then they get together with another group and quiz the students.

**Practice** **Resource Bank:** Unit Test; Mid-year Test
**Student's App:** Key Concept Practice

UNIT 6

# That Looks Good

## Unit Overview

### Themes

Preparing food and staying healthy

Food and our bodies

### Synopsis

In this unit, students will explore how important it is to have a balanced diet to stay healthy. They will learn about different types of food and their benefits to our bodies and think about different recipes. Students will prepare a conversation about a menu and write a report about an experiment.

## Language Book

**Vocabulary**
*cut up, fresh, fridge, fry, grill, microwave, mix, peel, sink, stove, throw out, trash can*
p. 128

**Explore Language**
Infinitives
p. 129

**Global Citizenship**
How do people stay healthy?
*beans, butter, carbohydrates, dairy, fat, grains, meat, nuts, protein, sugar*
p. 130

**Explore Language**
Gerunds
p. 131

**Talk About It**
Conversation: talking about a menu
p. 132

**Write About It**
Describing an Experiment
Text Features: using headings
p. 133

**Think It Over**
Review and Reflection
p. 134

# Literacy Book

### Think Together
Why is food important?
p. 141

### Visible Thinking
See, Think, Wonder
p. 135

### Nonfiction
Persuasive Text: *Too Young to Cook? True Stories of Young Chefs*

Words in Context: *successful, flaxseed, cookbook, experimented, discovered, elderly*
p. 139

### Fiction
Story: *Little Chef*

Words in Context: *delicious, frozen, caramel, winner, advice*
p. 136

### Reading Skill
Scanning for specific information
p. 138

### Spelling Pattern
*–old*
p. 140

## Language and Literacy Connections

The connecting theme in Unit 6 is food and cooking.

| | Language | Literacy |
|---|---|---|
| **Vocabulary** | **Set 1:** kitchen and food<br>**Set 2:** a balanced diet | **Fiction:** fresh, mix(ed), throw (it) out<br>**Nonfiction:** sugar |
| **Grammar** | **Infinitives**<br>I plan to make fruit salad.<br>I don't like to eat meat.<br>Would you like to have more potatoes?<br>**Gerunds**<br>I enjoy making new dishes.<br>Alec hates cutting up onions.<br>Do you like cooking? | **Fiction**<br>I also want to add cookie people.<br>I can't wait to see that!<br>**Nonfiction**<br>Mikaila Ulmer and Fraser Doherty love cooking.<br>She wanted to make a product.<br>How did she decide what to make?<br>Fraser began to make jam. |
| **Skills** | **Pronunciation:** /fr/ and /bl/ | **Reading:** scanning for specific information<br>**Spelling Pattern:** *–old* |
| **International English** | trash can/rubbish bin; server/waiter, waitress | |

## Vocabulary

### Lesson Objectives

- to learn kitchen and food vocabulary: *cut up, fresh, fridge, fry, grill, microwave, mix, peel, sink, stove, throw out, trash can*
- to sing a song that explores cooking and food

**Materials**
Audio Tracks 63 to 66; Video

### Warm Up

Play *Change Places* (see TB p. 25) with names of fruit.

**A** TRACK 63 TB p. 220 **Listen and find. What happened to the strawberries?**

- Project pp. 74–75 on the board for a minute for students to look at. Then use the masking tool to hide sections of the picture. Have students say what they can remember seeing in the picture. Do this several times with different parts of the picture.
- Display the complete picture or have students look in their books. Ask questions to prompt discussion; for example, *How many children can you see cooking? What do they look like? What food are they preparing? Are they working individually or in teams? Who are the adults? What are they doing? Where are they?*
- Then ask *Who can you see?* Remind students of the challenge in Unit 5: *What's my favorite food?* Tell students they are going to listen to Carla and her friends preparing food. Play the audio and have students point to the words or pictures as they listen. Ask *What's Carla's favorite food?* and elicit ideas.
- Ask the comprehension question *What happened to the strawberries?* and elicit the answer. Play the audio again for students to check.

**Answer**
Carla and Liz ate them.

**International English**

Highlight the different words and elicit *trash can* is American English and *rubbish bin* is British English. Ask *Which phrase do we use?*

**B** TRACK 64 TB p. 220 **Listen, say, and number the pictures in A.**

- Play the audio and have students point to the pictures and say the words.
- Tell students to listen again and write numbers next to the words in the picture. Do the example together (stove).
- Check answers by calling out a number and having volunteers call out the word. Alternatively, project the answers using the TTL.

**Answers**
1 *stove* 2 microwave 3 sink 4 fridge
5 trash can 6 peel 7 cut up 8 throw out
9 fry 10 grill 11 mix 12 fresh

**C** TRACK 65 TB p. 220 **Close your eyes. Listen, visualize, and say.**

- Prepare students for the visualization (see TB p. 21).
- Play the audio, allowing students to visualize and act out the ideas as they listen.
- Have students mime two or three of their visualizations for a partner to guess, making sure they include as many details as possible; for example, *How does hot water from the sink feel? How does the trash can smell?*

**D Look and write.**

- Students are going to categorize the vocabulary. This encourages critical thinking, and using a simple table is an effective way to organize vocabulary. Draw students' attention to the table and the word *trash can*. Write the two questions from the table on the board and elicit an example for each one. Remind students that we use *things* and we do *actions*.
- Tell students to write the words from A in the table. Then check answers as a class. Ask students why *fresh* can't go in either of the two columns (because it's an adjective). You could project the answers using the TTL.

**Answers**
What do I use?: *trash can*, microwave, stove, fridge, sink
What do I do?: throw out, peel, cut up, fry, grill, mix
The best food is fresh food!

**E** TRACK 66 TB p. 221 **Listen and complete. Then watch and sing.**

- Point to the song title *That Looks Good!* Ask *What food looks good?* and elicit suggestions, having students name foods from the picture. Then play the song once, allowing students to listen and enjoy it.
- Have students look at the song and unscramble the words. Play the song again, this time pausing where necessary for students to check their answers.
- Check answers with the class.
- Play the song video and encourage students to sing and move to the music as they watch.

**Answers**
1 *fridge* 2 fresh 3 Cut up 4 stove 5 Fry 6 Mix
7 grill 8 microwave

### Cool Down

Play the *Chain Game* (see TB p. 25). Have students make sentences using at least one word from A; for example, *I'm grilling fish.* Have students change the verb into third person as they repeat the previous sentences.

**Practice** **Student's App:** Vocabulary Practice; Song Video

## Explore Language

### Lesson Objectives

- to learn to use infinitives after certain verbs
- to practice kitchen and food vocabulary

**Materials**
Audio Tracks 67 and 68

### Warm Up

Ask students to remember the scene from the vocabulary lesson. Ask *What were the children doing? What were Carla's mom and dad cooking? Who do you think is going to eat the food?* Elicit that they are going to have a barbecue. Ask students *Do you have barbecues? What food do you eat? Is it your favorite way to eat? Why or why not?*

**A** TRACK 67 TB p. 221 **Listen and read. Who's going to wash the dishes?**

- Tell students that they are going to listen to Carla's family and friends again. Play the audio and have students follow the story in their books.
- Ask the comprehension question *Who's going to wash the dishes?* and elicit the answer. Ask *What kind of team do you think they are on?* (They are on a soccer team, but accept any responses that fit with the picture on pp. 74–75.)

**Answer**
Alec is going to wash them.

**B** **Look at A. Complete.**

- Write or project the table onto the board.
- Have students discuss and complete the grammar table in pairs using the story.
- Check answers on the board. Discuss the verb endings and word order in the sentences together, but let your class guide the discussion. Encourage students to notice whether each sentence is positive, negative, or a question and elicit that the second verb always stays the same (*to* + base verb). The first verb changes in positive sentences, to match the subject pronoun. If you feel that students need more guidance, the **ETB** provides a differentiation activity to help you support students as they explore the grammar table.
- Refer students to the Grammar tip *Remember.* Elicit different ways of completing *I like to …* Go around the class (or have students work in smaller groups), having each student give a different example. Point out that we never say *I enjoy to.*

**Answers**
make; like; to; eat; loves; like; have

**C** **Think and discuss. Then choose.**

- Write a sentence from B on the board (e.g. *Alec likes to wash dishes!*) and ask students to identify the two verbs. Circle them both. Then have a student underline *to* in the sentence.
- Have students work in pairs to discuss the first sentence in C. Refer them to the table in B for examples.
- Then write the question from the table on the board: *Would you like to have more potatoes?* Underline *Would you like to* and then ask *Do you know another verb to ask the question?* Elicit *want* and write the alternative question underneath: *Do you want more potatoes?* Ask students to decide which one is more polite.
- Have students discuss the second sentence in C. Check answers as a class.

**Answers**
1 before 2 more

**D** TRACK 68 TB p. 221 **Listen and say.**

- Tell students they're going to practice saying the structures. Play the audio, having students repeat each sentence chorally.
- For ideas on how to vary the drill, see TB p. 23.

**E** **Read and complete.**

- Ask *What fruits can you put in a fruit salad?* and elicit ideas from the class. Ask *How many fruits are there in the text?* Have students read the text quickly (scan) to find the answer. *What are they?* (mangoes, bananas, apples, peaches)
- Have students complete the activity individually. Remind them to look at the table in B to help them. Check answers as a class.

**Answers**
1 *love to eat* 2 try to eat 3 need to wash
4 don't need to wash 5 likes to peel
6 choose to cut up 7 like to mix

**F** **Choose and write sentences with infinitives. How many can you make? Compare.**

- Review the meaning of the verbs in the boxes. Then have students read the examples from the page.
- Divide the class into pairs. Each pair tries to create eight sentences using all the words in both boxes once each. Have them cross out each word as they use it. The first pair to hand in a correct list is the winner!
- Check that all eight sentences are correct before declaring winners. If there are any mistakes, the pair must correct their sentences and the game continues. If time and interest allow, the class can play another round with new partners. Can any pair make more than eight sentences?

### Cool Down

Have students play *Stand Up, Sit Down* in small groups (see TB p. 27). Have students make statements using the infinitive; for example, *I don't want to do homework.*

**Practice** **Resource Bank:** Grammar Printout
**Student's App:** Grammar Practice

# Global Citizenship

## Lesson Objectives

- to learn a balanced diet vocabulary: *beans, butter, carbohydrate, dairy, fat, grains, meat, nuts, protein, sugar*
- to explore healthy eating and the importance of a balanced diet
- to practice listening for gist and details

**Materials**
Audio Tracks 69 to 71; Audio Track F; a globe or map of the world (D)

### Opening Question

Ask the opening question: *How do people stay healthy?* Encourage students to think about the different things people do to be healthy, including diet (what people eat and drink) and exercise.

**A** TRACK 69 TB p. 221 **Listen to the food scientist. Which foods have protein?**

- Tell students they are going to listen to a food scientist talking about how to have a healthy diet. Ask *What is a food scientist?* Have students discuss their ideas in pairs and try to elicit the answer (a food scientist studies, researches, creates, or improves food and food processes so that they are safer for the public).
- Play the audio and have students point to the words or pictures as they listen.
- Ask the comprehension question *Which foods have protein?* Play the audio again for students to check. Then have them point to each of these types of food in the picture. Follow up by asking students which carbohydrates they can see in the picture (bread, pasta, grains, sugar), and which dairy items they can see (milk, cheese, and butter).

**Answer**
Meat, fish, eggs, nuts, and beans have protein in them.

**B** TRACK 70 TB p. 221 **Listen, say, and number the pictures in A.**

- Play the audio and have students point to the pictures and say the words.
- Tell students to listen again and write numbers next to the words in the picture. Do the example together (butter).
- Check answers by asking volunteers to come to the board and draw one of the food groups on the board; the class can call out which number it is.

**Answers**
1 *butter* 2 beans 3 sugar 4 meat 5 carbohydrates
6 fat 7 protein 8 grains 9 nuts 10 dairy

TRACK F TB p. 221 **Visualization**
The TTL has a visualization audio track for this vocabulary set. (See TB p. 21.)

**C Read and choose the correct answer.**

- Students are going to read sentences with the key vocabulary and choose the best word. Look at the example together. Ask *Which food group contains meat, fish, and eggs?* (protein).
- Have students do the activity individually. Then check answers as a class.

**Answers**
1 *protein* 2 every day 3 grains 4 Dairy
5 a little bit of 6 Strawberries

**D** TRACK 71 TB p. 221 **Now listen to Min-jun and Francesca. How are their lunches the same?**

- Have students look at the two pictures and say what they see. Ask *What foods are there? Which food groups do they belong to?* Tell students they are going to listen to two children talking about food. Draw their attention to the two countries: South Korea and Italy. You could point out the countries on a globe or map. Ask *Do you know any foods from these countries?* Have students share their ideas with the class.
- Listening for gist: Ask the gist question *How are their lunches the same?* Play the audio. Elicit answers from the class.

**Answer**
All students have the same lunch. They eat vegetables. They have fruit for dessert.

**E Listen again. Check (✔) what they eat.**

- Listening for details: have students look at the list of food to see what they remember. Then play the audio and have students check the foods.
- To check answers, read each question and have students raise their left hand for *Min-jun*, their right hand for *Francesca*, and both hands for both girls.

**Answers**
1 *Min-jun* 2 Min-jun, Francesca 3 Min-jun, Francesca
4 Min-jun, Francesca 5 Francesca 6 Min-jun, Francesca

### Discussion Questions

- Draw students' attention to the discussion questions: *What's your favorite meal? What can people do to eat healthier meals?* Have students discuss the questions in small groups. See **ETB**.
- Return to the opening question to ask again: *How do people stay healthy?* Review ideas discussed at the beginning of the class and then encourage students to share any new ideas. Focus on the concept of a balanced diet. Do students think their diet is balanced?

### Cool Down

Have students discuss this question: *If you could only eat one meal for the rest of your life, what would you eat?* Encourage them to think about how healthy the food they choose is. Will it help them have a long life?



**Practice** **Student's App:** Vocabulary Practice; Listening Practice

## Explore Language

### Lesson Objectives

- to learn to use gerunds after certain verbs
- to practice balanced diet vocabulary

**Materials**
Audio Tracks 72 and 73

### Warm Up

Draw a picture on the board of a face with tears falling from its eyes (it could be a simple emoji). Say *Look, he's crying!* Ask pairs to think of three reasons why somebody might cry. Then have students share their ideas with the class. If they feel comfortable, have students discuss what makes them cry.

**A** TRACK 72 TB p. 221 **Listen and read. Why doesn't Tim cry?**

- Tell students that they are going to listen to Tim and Alec while they are cooking. Have students find the boys in Explore Language 1 (Alec in picture 1, Tim in picture 3). Play the audio and have students follow the story in their books.
- Ask the gist question *Why doesn't Tim cry?* Have students look at the pictures to try to find the answer. Ask *Does Alec like cooking?* (yes)

**Answer**
Because he is wearing goggles.

**B** **Look at A. Complete.**

- Write or project the table onto the board.
- Have students discuss and complete the grammar table in pairs using the story.
- Check answers on the board. Discuss the word order and verb endings together, but let your class guide the discussion. If you feel that students need more guidance, the **ETB** provides a differentiation activity to help you support students as they explore the grammar table.
- Ask students if they notice any similarities between the verbs in the first verb column (they all express feelings about something). Have students read the Grammar tip *Remember.* Write the two example sentences *I like playing* and *I enjoy playing* on the board. Elicit that both sentences have the same meaning. Then write *I like to play* and ask students if it is correct (yes, and it has a similar meaning). Repeat for *I enjoy to play* and elicit that this is incorrect. Explain that some verbs (e.g. *like, love, hate*) can be followed by either the infinitive or an *–ing* verb. While some (e.g. *enjoy*) *must* be followed by an *–ing* verb and others (e.g. *plan, want*) must be followed by an infinitive.

**Answers**
enjoy; hates; cutting up; doesn't mind; cooking

**C** **Think and discuss. Then choose.**

- Ask students what they think the gerund verb form is. Have students call out gerunds from the table in B, but don't correct them at this point.
- Then have students work in pairs to discuss the sentences. Check answers as a class.
- Write *I enjoy eating* on the board. Ask students to suggest a noun that could replace eating (e.g. food). Ask *Can we say I enjoy happy?*

**Answers**
1 –ing 2 noun

**D** TRACK 73 TB p. 221 **Listen and say.**

- Tell students they're going to practice saying the new structures. Play the audio, having students repeat each sentence chorally. Encourage students to do actions to demonstrate each sentence after they say it.
- For ideas on how to vary the drill, see TB p. 23.

**E** **Read and complete.**

- Read out the example and elicit the missing word. (eating) Point out the verb *enjoys* and ask *do we need to use the infinitive or the gerund?* (gerund) Ask a volunteer to read out the full example sentence.
- Have students complete the sentences in their books individually. Then check answers as a class.

**Answers**
1 *eating* 2 putting 3 cooking 4 waiting 5 eating 6 shopping

**F** **Play *Who Is It?* Write about three friends. Then read and guess in groups of three.**

- Before students do the activity, review which verbs are followed by the infinitive with *to* (Lesson 2) and which are followed by a gerund. Make two lists on the board. Reinforce that the verbs *love, like,* and *hate* can be followed by either form, so students might like to use the lists to create a Venn diagram. Keep the lists on the board as reference.
- Draw students' attention to the example. Then have them write sentences about three classmates using the verbs on the board. Put students into groups of three. Have them take turns to read their sentences aloud and the others guess who they refer to.

### Cool Down

Have students work in pairs to make a Venn diagram about themselves. They should draw two overlapping circles in their notebooks and write their name at the top of one circle and their partner's name at the top of the other. They are going to ask each other questions to find out what they have in common. Encourage students to ask questions using the verbs in A and E and those in Explore Language 1. They should then write sentences in their Venn diagrams; for example, *I enjoy watching soccer; We hate cleaning up! She doesn't like watching soccer.*

**Practice** **Resource Bank:** Grammar Printout
**Student's App:** Grammar Practice

# Talk About It

## Lesson Objectives

- to prepare and practice a conversation about a menu
- to recognize and reproduce /fr/ and /bl/

**Materials**

Video; Audio Track 74

## Warm Up

Ask students if they ever eat at different places. Ask *Do you go for lunch at your grandma's or to your friend's house after school? Do you eat out in cafés or restaurants? Do you choose what to eat? Do you like trying new or different things, or do you always eat the same things?* Have students discuss them in pairs or small groups. Ask volunteers to share their ideas with the class.

**A** TB p. 238 **Watch and listen. What does Stephen choose for his salad?**

- Tell students they are going to watch a video of a conversation between a boy named Stephen and a server in a restaurant. Have students make some predictions about the types of phrases they might hear in the conversation.
- Ask the comprehension question *What does Stephen choose for his salad?* Ask students to suggest salad ingredients. Play the video and then check the answers. Ask further comprehension questions; for example, *What can you eat at the Happy Tomato?* (salad) *Do you think he's going to enjoy his meal?* (Yes—he sounds very happy/excited about it.) Play the video again and ask students to notice the body language of the server when she talks to Stephen.

**Answers**

He chooses lettuce, tomatoes, corn, mushrooms, black beans, and cheese.

**B Watch again. Check (✔) the phrases you hear.**

- Have students read the phrases.
- Play the video again and have students check the phrases they hear. Check answers as a class.
- Have students remember who says each phrase (or who would say it if it were in the video). Play the video again and have them correct the sentences that don't appear in the video. (Do you want some water? [3]; Cheese, please![6])

**Answers**

1; 2; 4; 5; 7

**International English**

Elicit *server* is American English and *waiter/waitress* is British English. Ask *Which word do we use?*

## Pronunciation /fr/ and /bl/

TRACK 74 TB p. 222 **Listen and say.**

Demonstrate the two sounds first. Isolate each phoneme in the cluster and elicit how to pronounce it (/f/; /r/). Then put the two sounds together to make /fr/ and have students repeat it. Do the same for /bl/.

Play the audio and have students repeat the words. Repeat if students need more practice.

Say *These words are used in the video. What other words do you know with these sounds?* Elicit ideas and write them on the board in two columns (e.g. *fry, blonde*). Drill the pronunciation of each word.

**Suggested Answers**

/fr/ fresh, fridge, friend, Friday, frog, Frisbee
/bl/ block, tablet, problem

**C Plan. Think about your restaurant. Complete.**

- Tell students they are going to plan a conversation about a restaurant.
- Complete a graphic organizer on the board for *The Happy Tomato* with the students' help.
- Then draw students' attention to the graphic organizer in their books. They need to think of a restaurant name, what kind of food they will have, and what choices they will offer to their guests. The name should reflect the food they sell. Remind them to include food from each of the six food groups. Students could do a Round Robin routine (see TB p. 20) to generate ideas.
- Have students complete the graphic organizer about their restaurants individually.

**D Prepare your conversation. Use your ideas from C and phrases from B.**

- Play the video again as a model.
- Have students work in pairs to prepare their conversation using their notes in C and the phrases from B. Tell them to choose the ideas they think work best. Encourage them to write in their notebooks so they can include more choices than in the template. Provide language help when needed.

**E Practice with a friend.**

- Have students practice their conversation with their partner as many times as they like. Remind them to smile and maintain eye contact.

## Cool Down

Play *Secret Letter.* Tell students that you have a restaurant with a strange rule, but you are **not** going to tell them the rule. They have to think critically to figure out the rule as they play. Have students ask for different food items. If the food begins with the same letter as the student's name, say *Yes, of course!* but if it begins with a different letter, say *Sorry, you can't have that!* Have students continue asking questions until they figure out the rule.



**Practice** **Student's App:** Speaking Skills Practice; Speaking Video

## Write About It

### Lesson Objectives

- to learn to use headings in a report
- to plan and write about an experiment

**Materials**

(Optional) Support, Standard, and Challenge writing printouts from the Resource Bank, one per student (C and D)

### Warm Up

Play *Crazy Recipes*. Each student needs a piece of paper. Students will play in groups of five. Call out a food group and have students write a food from that group at the top of their paper. They will then fold over the paper twice so that the next student can't read what they've written, and pass the paper to their left. Call out another food group and repeat until you have called out all five food groups (carbohydrate, protein, dairy, fat, and fruit and vegetables). At the end, students open up their pieces of paper and read all the ingredients their crazy recipe contains! Is there a recipe students want to try?

**A Read the report. Circle the four headings.**

- Introduce students to the concept of a report. Say *After you do an experiment, you can write about your results in a report.* Tell students they are going to read a report about a food experiment. Ask *What did the author want to know?* and *What did he/she do?* Give students one or two minutes to read the report and try to answer the questions. (Am I a healthy eater?; He/She kept a food diary.)
- Remind students why we use headings (to show what a paragraph is about). Point out that they are usually a different size or color from other parts of the text. Have students work individually to read the report again and circle the headings. Then check answers as a class. Ask students to explain what information goes under each heading (a question, a process, what the process showed, the things you decide are true after looking at the evidence).

**Answers**

Question; Method; Results; Conclusions

**B Match each heading to the correct sentence.**

- Have students match the headings to the sentences, looking back at A to help them. Then check answers as a class.

**Answers**

1 d 2 c 3 a 4 b

**C Plan. Keep a food diary for one day. Use the method in A. Then write down your results. What are your conclusions?**

- Tell students they are going to write their own food diaries and then write a report.
- Draw students' attention to the prompts in their books. Explain that they will need to take their books home to complete the food diary and that they will need to write down everything they eat and drink in one day.
- When they have their completed food diaries, students can complete the graphic organizer in their books with their data. Depending on students' level, you can explain that the food diary is their data, or information, and the graphic organizer helps them analyze, or think about, their data. This is what scientists do. The Challenge printouts can be handed out now.

**D Write about your experiment.**

- Have students write about their experiment. They should organize their ideas into sections with the four headings from A.
- Have students write a draft in their notebooks first, then self-correct or exchange their work with a friend and peer-correct. You can put a checklist of things to correct on the board (e.g. spelling, correct use of headings, verb forms, punctuation). Support printouts can be handed out now.
- Have students write their final reports on paper. Alternatively, hand out the Standard printouts from the Resource Bank. Students can add visuals such as bar graphs to their reports.
- Have students display their reports around the classroom and give them time to circulate and look at each other's work. Encourage them to identify any conclusions that are similar or the same. Are there any general conclusions about how students in the class eat? Are students generally healthy or unhealthy? What does the class need to eat more/less of?

### Cool Down

Play *Twenty Questions* (see TB p. 27). Start by asking a student to think of a kind of food. Encourage the class to ask questions, such as *Is it a protein? Do you cook it? Do you keep it in the fridge? Is it sweet?*

**Practice** **Student's App:** Writing Practice

# Think It Over

## Lesson Objectives

- to review what has been learned in the unit
- to reflect on the unit and their own progress
- to think about learning strategies and how to continue learning at home

### Warm Up

Ask students what the unit theme was (food / healthy eating) and write it in the middle of the board. Brainstorm any words or phrases students can think of that relate to the topic and write them on the board. Encourage students to think about how food is grouped together and how to have a healthy diet.

**Read the questions and draw or write your answers.**

- Give students time to think about and discuss activities in the unit before they complete each question. Explain that they can choose to either write a few words or sentences or to draw a picture. Allowing students to make a personal response will help them retain knowledge and engage with the learning points.

**What did I do?**

- Give students a few minutes to look back through the unit at the different activities they did. Ask questions about the unit, or write questions on the board, for students to discuss in pairs or small groups; for example, *What games did you play? What did you talk/write about? What different ways of cooking and preparing food do you know?*
- Encourage students to identify something in the unit that they found challenging or something that was particularly memorable for them, but tell them not to choose their favorite activity yet. Students can draw or write about their chosen activity.

**What did I learn?**

- Ask questions about the unit to help students think about what they learned; for example, *What did you learn about food and healthy eating? What sentences can you say using the infinitive? What did you learn about Italian food and Korean food? What else did you learn?* Have students discuss their ideas in pairs.
- Encourage students to draw a picture or write sentences about their learning outcomes.

**What was my favorite part?**

- Have students look back through the unit and decide what they enjoyed the most. Tell them it can be an activity they found interesting or fun, a dialogue they enjoyed reading, a favorite character, or a role-play activity. They should try to choose just one activity.
- Have students draw or write about the activity they liked the most.
- Remind students that when we like something, it is often easier to learn.

**How well did I do?**

- Tell students to color in the water bottle that best expresses how well they have learned they unit content (i.e., the bigger the water bottle, the more they feel they have learned). Ask *What do you understand? What do you need to practice more?* Encourage students to look back through the unit to see how much they remember what they did well and what they found difficult.

**What can I do next?**

- Brainstorm ideas with the class about what they can do to continue to learn (think about why and how they can eat healthily, find and pronounce words with **/fr/** and **/bl/**, go to the grocery store to identify healthy food, find and help cook or prepare healthy meals, watch a cooking show on TV or online and re-create the food, write a menu for the week, order a meal in café/restaurant, and speak politely). Students can look back at the previous units to get more ideas. Encourage students to suggest their own ideas for different activities they can do.
- Draw students' attention to the *What can I do next?* box. Encourage students to think about what they can do at home to improve their English. Have them suggest some verbs that they can use (e.g. listen, read, write, discuss, research) and write the verbs they choose in their books.
- Have students choose several activities that they would like to do and write them in their books. They can then share their ideas with a partner.

### Looking Forward

- Draw students' attention to the character at the bottom of the page. Ask *Who's this?* and elicit what they remember about him (Alec appears in the Vocabulary and Explore Language lessons on pp. 74, 76, and 80; he washed the apples and peaches; he loves to wash dishes; he likes cooking; onions make his eyes water).
- Draw students' attention to Alec's question: *How am I helping my dad?* Encourage students to make predictions about how Alec helps his dad in Unit 7. Tell students they will find the answer in Lesson 1 of the next unit.

# Put It Together

To further review and recycle the language in Units 5 and 6, play the game, *Say Three Things*, on pp. 86–87. See TB p. 208 for teaching notes.



**Practice** **Resource Bank:** Unit Test
**Student's App:** Vocabulary and Grammar Review

## Get Ready to Read

**Lesson Objectives**

- to activate prior knowledge about food and cooking
- to guide inquiry and deepen understanding through a See, Think, Wonder VTR
- to preview the reading skill of scanning for specific information

**Materials**

(Optional) VTR printout from the Resource Bank (Activities A, B, C)

### Warm Up

Ask *What kind of food do you usually eat? What meals do you like?* Then have students pretend to show each other their favorite meals in pairs, responding *That looks good!* or *Sorry, it's not my thing.*

### See, Think, Wonder

**A Look at the picture. What do you see?**

- Students are going to do a See, Think, Wonder VTR to explore the image of the lunch trays.
- Have students look at the image. Ask them to think of words connected to food. Elicit and write ideas on the board.
- Ask students *What do you see?* Then give students one minute to look at the picture before sharing answers in small groups and then as a class.

Here's an example of this part of the routine.
**Teacher:** What do you see?
**Student A:** I see food.
**Teacher:** What else do you see?
**Student B:** I see hands putting food on a plate.
**Teacher:** Good. What shapes do you see?
**Student C:** I see circles and squares.
**Student D:** I see semicircles!

**B What do you think?**

- Say *I think it's a special lunch. What do you think about the picture?* Elicit a response from a student and encourage the student to give a reason.
- Give students one to three minutes to think about the picture silently. Then have students work in small groups to share their ideas, before sharing as a class.

Here's an example of this part of the routine.
**Teacher:** What do you think about the picture?
**Student A:** (I think) the food is for kids.
**Teacher:** What makes you say that?
**Student A:** It looks cute.
**Teacher:** What else do you think?
**Student B:** (I think) it's for a party. It looks special.

**C What do you wonder?**

- Say *I wonder who the food is for. What do you wonder about the picture? What questions do you have?* Give students one to three minutes to think about the picture silently.
- Have students share their ideas in groups or as a class. Allow students to be creative and accept all their ideas.

Here's an example of this part of the routine.
**Teacher:** What do you wonder?
**Student A:** Who's going to eat the food?
**Teacher:** Good question! What else?
**Student B:** What is the food made of?
**Teacher:** What does everyone think?
**Student C:** (Maybe) rice.
**Student D:** I can see salad and fruit.
**Student B:** (Maybe) that's fish?

### Transition

Ask students who they think the person in the picture is. Ask *Is he/she a chef? What makes you say that? Who makes the food you eat?* Encourage students to think about the different places they eat in (e.g. home, school, restaurants) and who does the cooking.

**D Think and discuss. Do you like cooking? Why or why not?**

- Have students look at the picture again and ask *Is it fun to make pictures with food?*
- Ask students to think about times when they have cooked or helped prepare food. Ask *What did you make?* Write students' answers on the board. Ask *Was it easy or hard? Did it taste good?* Elicit a few answers, then have students discuss whether they like cooking in pairs. Encourage them to give reasons.

**E Look through *Little Chef* on the next page. What are the names of the characters? Write.**

In this activity students will preview the reading skill of scanning for specific information.

- Have students read the title of the story. Ask *What do you think the story is about?*
- Have them look at the pictures on pp. 90–91. Elicit that the children are taking part in a TV competition by asking questions such as *Who is the man in the suit?* (one of the presenters/hosts of the show) *Who are the people watching?* (the audience). Ask *Do you know any TV shows like this one?*
- Tell students to look for the names of the three characters. Tell them that they don't have to read the story. Elicit how students can quickly identify names (names start with a capital letter).
- Check answers as a class.

**Answers**

Marisa; Carlo; Amy (any order)

**Now read Little Chef**

# Fiction: *Little Chef—Cartoon*

## Lesson Objectives

- to read a cartoon about a cooking competition on TV
- to explore the SEL competency of responsible decision-making through implementing problem-solving skills
- to make a personal connection to the reading

**Materials**
Audio Tracks 30 and 31; Video

## Warm Up

Brainstorm types of competitions with the class (sporting, drawing, spelling bees, etc.). Ask students if they ever took part in a competition. Write questions on the board and have students discuss them in pairs: *What did you do? Did you have to work as a team? Did you win? Did you have a time limit? How did you feel?*

## TRACK 30 TB p. 233 Reading Approach

**First Reading: Engage with the Text**

- Ask students to notice the title, text, and pictures on the page and use this information to predict ideas about the reading.
- Ask students to close their books. Play the video, pausing where necessary to ask prediction questions; for example, *Which character will have a problem? What do you think the problem will be? Which character will win?*

## TRACK 31 TB p. 233 Words in Context

- Play the audio and have students repeat the words.
- Have students race to find the words in the reading.
- Remind students that sometimes they can **use the sentence or paragraph before to guess the meaning of the new words** (see p. TB 23).
- Have students work in pairs to try to figure out the meaning of each word in context. Bring the class together and use these discussion points to confirm the meanings.

**delicious** (p. 91) Say *The presenter says, "It sounds delicious!"* Have students read the previous bubble where Carlo describes his dessert. Ask *Do you think it sounds delicious? Why?*

**frozen** (p. 91) Have students describe Amy's dessert. Tell them to look at the picture. Ask *Where do we keep ice cream? Why?* Elicit that it needs to be very cold because ice cream is frozen.

**caramel** (p. 91) Have students look at the picture and notice the pan of caramel. Ask *What is she making?* Tell students that when we heat sugar, it turns into caramel.

**winner** (p. 95) Elicit the meaning of *win*. Remind students that we can add *–er* to a verb to make a person. Ask *Who is the winner of the competition?*

**advice** (p. 95) Ask students *How does Marisa's grandpa help her?* Explain that when people suggest ideas to help you, they are giving you advice.

**Second Reading: Analyze the Text and Features**

- Play the audio as students read along.
- Ask some questions to check comprehension, e.g. *What was Marisa's first dessert called?* (Caramel Tower) *Name two ingredients that were in it.* (cream, caramel, flour, chocolate) *What happened to it?* (It fell apart) *What did Marisa do next?* (turned it into a new dessert)
- Discuss the questions in the orange boxes.
  - **Detail** (p. 90): *How many sweet foods can you find?* Review the meaning of *sweet*. Then have students scan the pictures for sweet foods and count them. You could make this a race.
  - **Personalization** (p. 91): *Which do you think is the best dessert?* Have students imagine they are the judges and choose the winning dessert. Have them tell a partner which dessert they chose and why.
  - **Critical Thinking** (p. 93): *What does* When life gives you lemons, make lemonade *mean?* Elicit that lemons don't taste great on their own, but when they become lemonade, they taste good. The idea is that you can make something good out of a bad situation.
  - **SEL Competency** (p. 95): *Where do you get your ideas from?* This question explores the SEL competency of responsible decision-making through implementing problem-solving skills. Elicit that Marisa got her idea from her grandpa. Ask students to think about where their own ideas come from. Ask *Do you get advice from your family or friends?*
- Discuss the text focus: *The main events in a story make its plot. Can you find some important events?* Remind students that we use the word *plot* to talk about the story in books, movies, plays, and so on. Have students identify events in the plot of *Little Chef*.

**Third Reading: Interact with the Text**

- Have students do an interview role-play in groups. One student is a presenter, and the others are Carlo, Amy, and Marisa. Each group should brainstorm a list of questions the presenter can ask and the answers they think Carlo, Amy, and Marisa would give. Then give students time to role-play their interviews. See TB p. 23 for more about using role-play in the classroom.

## Cool Down

Elicit traditional recipe ideas from students and write them on the board. Have students work in pairs to choose one of the recipes and adapt it by changing some of the ingredients.

**Practice** **Student's App:** Fiction Video

# Explore the Reading

## Lesson Objectives

- to understand and analyze *Little Chef* through reading comprehension activities
- to explore the SEL competency of responsible decision-making through implementing problem-solving skills
- to make a personal connection to the reading

**Materials**
(Optional) Video or Audio Track 30

## Warm Up

Check students know the names of the three main characters in *Little Chef*. Then play *Who Said It?* (see TB p. 27). Example quotations: *Oh, no! It's falling apart.* (Marisa); *I got some good advice from my grandpa.* (Marisa); *It's shaped like a tree.* (Amy); *I mixed together this "Too Much Chocolate Cake."* (Carlo); *It's called the "Caramel Tower."* (Marisa)

**A Read and choose.**

- If more than one day has passed since students read *Little Chef*, play the video again.
- With books closed, have a Group Time discussion (see TB p. 21) to check students' comprehension of the reading. Ask *What's the name of the competition?* (Little Chef) *How many contestants were there?* (three; if necessary, clarify the term *contestant* by explaining it's someone who takes part in a competition) *What fruit can you find in the story?* (pineapple, strawberries, lemons) *What shape is Amy's dessert?* (a tree) *Why does Marisa change her recipe?* (because it's falling apart) *What do the TV hosts have to do?* (decide which dessert is the best) *Who wins the competition?* (Marisa)
- Have students open their books and look at the first sentence. Ask *Can you find this in the reading?* Have students look back and find the phrase (one hour).
- Have students do the rest of the activity individually. Check answers as a class.

**Answers**
1 60  2 chocolate  3 mango  4 cookies  5 delicious

**B Draw. Look through *Little Chef* for details about the desserts. What did they look like?**

- Brainstorm all the adjectives from the story first and write them on the board (dark, white, frozen, tall, fresh, delicious, creative). Can students remember which dessert each adjective described?
- Then have students look back at the pictures and draw the three desserts. Ask students which words in the text they used to help them draw their pictures.

**Answers**
Students' own answers

**Practice** **Student's App:** Reading Practice

**C Complete the story mountain for *Little Chef*. Then compare and discuss.**

- Draw students' attention to the story mountain and explain that it is a graphic organizer to help them write about the story. If possible, display the mountain on the board using the TTL.
- Have students look at the four boxes and notice what they represent. Remind students that these are four key areas in a story. Then have students fill in the boxes individually, looking back at the story to help them if necessary.
- Have students compare and discuss ideas in small groups.

**Suggested Answers**
Characters: Marisa, Carlo, Amy, two TV hosts (a woman and a man);
Setting: a game show kitchen
Problem: Marisa's dessert falls apart without time to start over
Solution: Marisa makes a new plan for a different dessert

**D Think and discuss. When Marisa had a problem, she thought about her grandpa. When you have a problem, who do you talk to?**

- This activity draws on the SEL competency of implementing problem-solving skills. Tell students to imagine they have problem with a school project. Ask *Who do you talk to about this problem. Why?* Give students a minute to think about their answer. Then say *Imagine you have a problem with a friend. Do you go to the same person about the problem or someone else?* Have students think silently for a minute about the people they talk to when they have a problem. Ask for volunteers to share their thoughts with the class. Do students generally talk to the same people each time, or do they talk to different people for different problems?

## Cool Down

Have students take part in a mini-debate. Divide the class into three groups and assign each group one of the three desserts from the story. Alternatively, they can be three different dishes (sweet or savory). Tell students that they have to convince you that their dessert/dish is the best. Give groups a few minutes to think of arguments. Each group chooses a spokesperson. Then ask each group to say why you should eat their dessert/dish. Finally, choose one (or all three!).

# Get Ready to Read

## Lesson Objectives

- to practice the reading skill of scanning for specific information
- to activate prior knowledge about children who develop their own companies
- to make a personal connection to the reading

**Materials**

Slips of paper, one per student (CD)

## Warm Up

Play *Odd Man Out* (see TB p. 26). If you have already completed the **Language Book** vocabulary lessons, call out kitchen and cooking items; for example:

*pineapple, strawberry, chocolate, lemon*

*microwave, stove, fridge*

*fry, cut up, peel, mix*

*meat, fish, vegetables*

If not, choose vocabulary from a previous unit.

**A Scan *Little Chef* and write the names of the desserts.**

Students are going to review and practice the reading skill of scanning for specific information.

- Draw students' attention to the instructions. Ask *Can you remember the three desserts?* Tell students to look back at the reading and find the names of the three desserts very quickly. Remind them not to read the whole story but to look for the information they need. To ensure students do this, set a time limit (e.g. 30 seconds) for them to find and write the names in their books.
- Then have students read the skills box. To focus students on the importance of scanning, ask them to think of texts where they scan for information. Write their ideas on the board (e.g. dictionaries, webpages, recipes). Reiterate that we often don't need to read the entire text to get the information we need. This allows us to read texts more quickly. Ask *After we have scanned, why is it important to read the whole sentence?* (to check we have found the information we need)

**Answers**

1 Too Much Chocolate Cake 2 The Frozen Tree
3 Caramel Tower 4 Lemonade

**B Read the questions. Scan the paragraphs for the answers and write.**

- Write *Mikaila's Lemonade Story* on the board and tell students that it is the title of a text. Ask *What do you think it's about?* and elicit suggestions from the class.
- Draw students' attention to the questions above the text. Ask students if they need to look for a name, thing, or number in each question.
- Then have students scan the text to find the answers. Again, give students a time limit (e.g. one minute). Check answers as a class, having students say where in the text they found their answers.

**Answers**

1 one 2 four 3 bees and honey 4 Ulmer

**C Think and discuss. Imagine there is a children's business competition near you. What product would you make?**

- Ask students *How did Mikaila decide what to make for the business competition?* Review what they know about Mikaila; for example, she wanted to make something for Austin Lemonade Day, a bee stung her twice, and she became interested in bees and honey.
- Ask *What things are important if you want to start a new business?* Have volunteers suggest some ideas (e.g. an original idea, a good product, some money, a name, a business plan, equipment, a website, a team of people). Then remind students of *Mikaila's Lemonade Story* and highlight that she became interested in bees and honey. Elicit that you need to have an interest or a passion in the product your company makes.
- Draw students' attention to the question *What product would you make?* Have students discuss some obvious ideas in small groups. They can write ideas down on a large piece of paper. Then encourage them to think of more unusual ideas. Monitor and ask questions to prompt students; for example, *What if you combined the two products?* Encourage students to be as imaginative as possible.
- Have students share their ideas with the class. Take a class vote to see which product they think is best for the children's business competition.

## Cool Down

Tell students that they will be reading an article about Mikaila and her product. Give each student a slip of paper as an exit pass. Have them write one question they think will be answered in the article. They should give you the paper as they leave the classroom.

Now read **Too Young to Cook?**

# **Nonfiction:** *Too Young to Cook?—* Article

## Lesson Objectives

- to read an article about two young entrepreneurs
- to make a personal connection to the reading
- to learn through CLIL (arts and humanities): exploring culinary arts

**Materials**
Audio Tracks 32 and 33

## Warm Up

Read or display the questions students wrote at the end of the previous lesson. Have students choose three questions (they don't have to choose their own) that they think will be answered. They will check these predictions during the first reading stage.

## TRACK 32 TB p. 234 **Reading Approach**

### First Reading: Engage with the Text

- Ask students to notice the title, text, and pictures on the page. See if the pictures answer any of the questions students had.
- Have students read the text individually, in silence. Have them try to find the answers to their three prediction questions from the Warm Up.
- Review the questions with the class to see how many were answered in the article. Ask volunteers to say one thing they found interesting or surprising about Mikaila's story.
- Then read the Words in Context.

## TRACK 33 TB p. 234 **Words in Context**

- Play the audio and have students repeat the words.
- Have students race to find the words in the reading.
- Remind students they can **use the pictures to guess the meaning of some words**.
- Bring the class together and use these discussion points to confirm the meanings.

**successful** (p. 98) Have students read the introductory sentences. Ask *What made Mikaila and Fraser successful?* (a great idea; people bought their products) Ask students to think of someone they know who's successful.

**flaxseed** (p. 99) Encourage students to look at the pictures. Students already know what lemons and honey are. Have students find a picture of flaxseeds, which is also labeled.

**cookbook** (p. 99) Ask students to say what things they can find in a cookbook (recipes/meals). Have students say if their family has a special cookbook or any traditional recipes they use.

**experimented** (p. 100) Ask *Who wrote the jam recipe?* (Fraser's grandmother) *Did Fraser change the recipe?* (yes) *Did he try out one idea, or many different ideas before he changed the recipe?* (many different ideas) Elicit that when we experiment we try out different ideas to see what works.

**discovered** (p. 100) Say *One day Fraser discovered a way to make the recipe without sugar.* Elicit that *discover* and *find* are synonyms.

**elderly** (p. 101) Encourage students to look at the picture of the tea party. Elicit that *elderly* and *old* are synonyms. Ask *Which one is more polite?*

### Second Reading: Analyze the Text and Features

- Play the audio and have students follow along in their books.
- Ask some questions to check comprehension; for example, *What's different about Mikaila's lemonade?* (It is made from lemons, flaxseed, and local honey.) *How many stores sold her lemonade in 2016?* (55) *What's different about Fraser's jam?* (It has no extra sugar.) *What happened in 2009?* (A large store agreed to sell his jam.)
- Discuss the questions in the orange boxes.
  - **Fact** (p. 98): *Austin is in Texas, USA.* You could have students identify Austin on a map. Ask *Who is from Austin?* (Mikaila)
  - **Making Connections** (p. 99): *Why are bees important to the environment?* Have students research this question online or give a simple explanation of how pollination works.
  - **Fact** (p. 100): *Edinburgh is in Scotland, UK.* Point out Edinburgh on a map. Ask *Who is from Edinburgh?* (Fraser)
  - **Personalization** (p. 101): *How often do you cook with your family?* Say *Mikaila and Fraser's grandmothers gave them recipes. Do you know any recipes from your grandparents?* Have students discuss with a partner their experiences of cooking.

### Third Reading: Interact with the Text

- Have students work in pairs to compare and contrast Mikaila and Fraser and their products. Ask them to create a Venn diagram, or other graphic organizer to show the similarities and differences. Have each pair join another pair to discuss their ideas.

## Cool Down

Ask students to stand up quickly and say either a type of jam or a type of drink. Explain that you will go first and say *strawberry jam*. Every time a student thinks of a jam or a drink, he/she stands up, gives his/her idea, and sits down again. This can be played in two teams or groups. Keep going until students have exhausted all ideas. Accept imaginative creations but nothing that is impossible!

# Explore the Reading

## Lesson Objectives

- to understand and analyze *Too Young to Cook?* through reading comprehension activities
- to make a personal connection to the reading
- to learn through CLIL (arts and humanities): exploring culinary arts
- to reproduce and write words with *–old*

**Materials**

Audio Tracks 32 and 34

## Warm Up

Play *Jump!* (see TB p. 26).

Suggested words from the story: *successful, bee, lemonade, flaxseed, cookbook, recipe, jam, experimented, business, sugar, factory, store, tea*

**A Read and complete.**

- If more than one day has passed since students read *Too Young to Cook?*, play the audio again.
- With books closed, ask *Wh-* questions to see what students remember about the reading; for example, *Who made jam with no sugar?* (Fraser) *When did Mikaila get her idea?* (when she was four) *What did Mikaila learn about bees?* (how important they are) *What are the three main ingredients of the lemonade?* (lemons, honey, and flaxseed) *Where does Fraser sell his jam?* (in stores)
- Have students open their books and look at the words in the box. Check they understand the words. Then have a student read the example sentence and notice the phrase crossed out in the box.
- Have students do the rest of the activity individually, looking back at the reading to find the answers. Check answers as a class, having students say on which page they found their answers.

**Answers**

1 bee stings 2 recipe 3 cookbook 4 honeybees
5 sugar 6 parties

**B Think and write. What did Mikaila and Fraser learn from their grandmothers? Who do you learn from in your family?**

- Write the two characters' names in large letters each on a piece of paper. Stick these on the walls on either side of the classroom. Have students stand in the middle of the classroom. Call out the following phrases. Students should go and stand next to the relevant character: *This person … got an idea at the age of 14 / got an idea from animals / lives in Texas / lives in the UK / learned from their grandmother* (both!).
- Have students sit down and open their books. Draw their attention to the activity. Ask *What did Mikaila learn? What did Fraser learn?* Tell students to think about something they learned and who they learned it from. Brainstorm some ideas with the class to help (e.g. ride a bike, knit/sew, bake a cake). Then have students complete the activity in their books.

**Answers**

1 to make lemonade 2 to make jam
3 Students' own answers

**C Think and discuss. Did you ever cook using a recipe? What did you make? How did it taste?**

- Students are going to connect the reading to their own experiences. This draws on the CLIL arts and humanities focus of exploring culinary arts.
- Draw students' attention to the first question, *Do you ever cook using a recipe?* Tell students that a recipe can be from a cookbook, a website, or a piece of paper or from memory. Perhaps a parent or grandparent showed them how to make something. Tell students that it could be a meal, a snack, or even a drink. Give them a few minutes to think and remember what they made.
- Then have students discuss their experiences in small groups. Did any of them make the same thing? Did it taste good? Have some volunteers share their ideas with the class.

## Spelling Pattern *–old*

TRACK 34 TB p. 234 **Listen and write. Then check your answers.**

- With books closed, write *–old* on the board and elicit the pronunciation.
- Play the first part of the audio and have students repeat each word. Then have them open their books. Play the first part of the audio again and have them complete as many of the words as they can.
- Then play the second part of the audio for students to check their spelling and complete the words correctly. Have them read the words aloud.
- Have students look back at the reading to find more words with *–old* and write them in a word cloud. Invite students to read a word from their cloud.

**Answers**

1 gold 2 cold 3 told 4 hold 5 fold
From the reading: old, cold, sold

## Cool Down

Do a *Gradient Line* (see TB p. 26). Call out questions about food and cooking; for example, *How much do you like eating vegetables? How much do you like making cupcakes?*

**Practice** **Resource Bank:** Spelling Printout
**Student's App:** Reading Practice; Spelling Pattern Practice

## Think Together

### Lesson Objectives

- to make connections between the readings
- to explore the key concept: Why is food important?
- to reflect on the unit and provide personal thoughts and opinions

**Materials**

Three pieces of construction paper with a different prompt written in the middle of each (CD)

### Warm Up

Have students look back at the VTR picture on pp. 88–89. Ask students how they think the picture connects to the two readings in the unit. If necessary, write prompts on the board: *types of food, food groups, recipes, presentation of food, tools and equipment, words to describe food.* Encourage students to be creative in their answers; for example, *The food is fun, like "The Frozen Tree"; I think kids will eat fruit and vegetables if it looks good; I think a kid had the idea to make faces; I think it's a competition to create the most beautiful food.*

**A Read and check (✔). What's true about the people from the readings?**

- With books closed, write the question on the board. Brainstorm ideas as a class and write a few suggestions.
- Have students open their books and look at the first sentence. Ask *Is it true for Marisa? For Mikaila? For Fraser?*
- Have students work individually to think and check the boxes. Check answers as a class.

**Suggested Answers**

1 Mikaila, Fraser 2 Marisa, Mikaila, Fraser
3 Mikaila, Fraser 4 Mikaila, Fraser

**B Think and write. Why is food important? Make a list.**

- Students are going to make connections and think critically about what they have learned in the unit to answer the key concept question *Why is food important?* If you have not yet done the **Language Book** unit, you may want to consider discussing food groups and how each kind of food is important.
- Have students look at the question and think for a few minutes. Have them write a list of their ideas in their notebook. Then have students discuss their ideas in pairs and add new ideas to the list. Finally, brainstorm ideas as a class, writing students' ideas on the board.
- Give students a few minutes to write their answers in the graphic organizer. They could decide which three ideas are the most important. If they have several ideas, have students draw and complete their own graphic organizer in their notebooks.

**Suggested Answers**

it feeds us / we need to eat; it gives us energy; it can help people; we can sell it and make money; it brings us close to our family and friends; it's delicious to eat

**C Think and discuss. What's your family's favorite recipe? What are the ingredients? Do a Three-step Interview.**

- Students are going to do a Three-step Interview to discuss and share their ideas (see TB p. 20).
- In Step 3, students share what they have learned about their friend with the class. With large classes, they can share their ideas in groups. Have the class (or group) vote for the recipe they most want to try.

### My Reading Journal

**Write three interesting things from this unit.**

This task encourages students to review and remember what they learned. Tell the class one thing you found interesting in the unit; for example, *I am interested in bees.* Give students a few minutes to look back through the unit and find things that interested them. Students should write their ideas in their reading journals.

**Example Answer**

I think the reading about Mikaila and Fraser is interesting. I am interested in the bees and helping them. I think my friends' recipes are interesting, too.

**What recipe do you want to make at home?**

Give students a few minutes to look back and identify the recipes. They can also think about the recipes their friends shared in this lesson. Have students complete the sentence about a recipe they want to make. Encourage students to give reasons for their choices. Ask volunteers to share their ideas with the class.

**Example Answer**

I want to make the Too Much Chocolate Cake because I love chocolate!

### Cool Down

Have students round up their ideas from the unit using a Chalk Talk routine (see TB p. 21). Give them the following prompts: *Food I want to learn to cook; Food that is important to me; Why food is important.* Remind students to write silently. When students have written on all the posters, hang them on the wall for the class to look at and comment on before they leave.

**Practice** **Resource Bank:** Unit Test
**Student's App:** Key Concept Practice

UNIT 7

# How Can We Help?

## Unit Overview

### Themes

Natural disasters

Emergencies

### Synopsis

In this unit, students will explore how we can help each other in a disaster. They will learn about different natural disasters and how to act in an emergency. They will discuss the theme of people who help us and think about how we can prepare for natural disasters. Students will plan and prepare a presentation about an important helper and write a story ending on the topic.

**Language Book**

**Vocabulary**
*ambulance, dangerous, emergency, flood, helicopter, rescue worker, safe, shelter, storm*
p. 144

**Explore Language**
Relative Clauses: *Who*
p. 145

**Global Citizenship**
How can we prepare before an emergency?
*avalanche, burn, cover, earthquake, forest fire, hurricane, tornado, tsunami, volcano*
p. 146

**Explore Language**
Relative Clauses: *That*
p. 147

**Take the Stage**
Presentation: describing a dream job
p. 148

**Write About It**
Finishing a Story
Punctuation: using exclamation points and quotation marks
p. 149

**Think It Over**
Review and Reflection
p. 150

## Literacy Book

### Think Together
How can we help each other in an emergency?

p. 157

### Visible Thinking
See, Think, Wonder

p. 151

### Nonfiction
Informational Text: *Animals to the Rescue*

Words in Context: *search, train, rubble, survivors, trapped, safety, stuck*

p. 155

### Fiction
Story: *What Happens Next?*

Words in Context: *gentle, crawl, hot-air balloon, rope, loudspeaker*

p. 152

### Reading Skill
Making inferences and predictions

p. 154

### Spelling Pattern
*–ly*

p. 156

## Language and Literacy Connections

The connecting theme in Unit 7 is responding to natural disasters.

| | Language | Literacy |
|---|---|---|
| **Vocabulary** | **Set 1:** emergency services<br>**Set 2:** natural disasters | **Fiction:** emergency, safe, earthquake<br>**Nonfiction:** rescue workers |
| **Grammar** | **Relative Clauses: *Who***<br>There's the woman who works in the café down the street.<br>He's the rescue worker who came to our store.<br>**Relative Clauses: *That***<br>This is the wall that stopped the flood.<br>Those are things that floated here.<br>There's a backpack that has someone's homework inside.<br>People that lost things can find them. | **Fiction**<br>I looked at Akiko, who was holding onto the legs of her desk.<br>**Nonfiction**<br>Rescue workers find people who are hurt.<br>Dog handlers are people who train search and rescue dogs.<br>Dogs helped to find a 15-year-old boy who was trapped. |
| **Skills** | **Pronunciation:** /str/ and /tr/ | **Reading:** making inferences and predictions<br>**Spelling Pattern:** *–ly* |
| **International English** | fire truck/fire engine; truck/lorry; student/pupil; named/called; exclamation point/exclamation mark | principal/head master; truck/lorry |

## Vocabulary

### Lesson Objectives

- to learn emergency services vocabulary: *ambulance, dangerous, emergency, helicopter, rescue worker, safe, shelter, storm*
- to sing a song about emergency helpers

**Materials**

Audio Tracks 75 to 78; Video; sound effects of sirens (WU); signs for each of the emergency services (CD)

### Warm Up

Play siren sound effects to the class. You can find these on sound effects apps and websites. Have students discuss in small groups what they think has happened. Then have groups share their answers with the class.

**A** TRACK 75 TB p. 222 **Listen and find. Where's the family going?**

- Display the picture for one minute only. Then hide it and ask students to remember what they saw. They can discuss this in pairs. Display the picture again to see how much they remembered. Ask questions to encourage students to find more things in the picture that they didn't notice before; for example, *What's the man in the yellow jacket carrying in his hand?* (a hat)
- Then ask students if they can see Alec and his sister. Remind students of the challenge from the end of Unit 6: *How am I helping my dad?* Have students make predictions about why they are moving the boxes, but do not confirm the answer at this stage.
- Tell students they are going to listen to Alec and his family in their shop. Play the audio and have students point to the words or pictures as they listen.
- Ask the gist question *Where's the family going?* and elicit the answer. Play the audio again for students to check. Then ask *What's the disaster?* (a storm)

**Answer**

to their house, high up on a hill

**B** TRACK 76 TB p. 222 **Listen, say, and number the pictures in A.**

- Play the audio and have students point to the pictures and say the words.
- Tell students to listen again and write numbers next to the words in the picture. Do the example together (safe).
- Check answers by calling out a number and having volunteers call out the word. Alternatively, project the answers using the TTL.

**Answers**

1 *safe* 2 dangerous 3 rescue worker 4 helicopter
5 ambulance 6 shelter 7 storm 8 emergency

**C** TRACK 77 TB p. 222 **Close your eyes. Listen, visualize, and say.**

- Prepare students for the visualization (see TB p. 21).
- Play the audio, allowing students to visualize the ideas as they listen.
- Have students draw a scene that includes some of the things they imagined during the visualization. They can then discuss their drawings in pairs.

**D** **Look and write.**

- Students are going to categorize some of the vocabulary. This encourages critical thinking and helps students organize the words in a logical way. Draw students' attention to the four sections. Elicit examples of words from each category (these don't have to be from A), for example, adjectives: *big*; person: *teacher*.
- Tell students to write the words from A in the table. Then check answers as a class.

**Answers**

Adjectives: safe, dangerous
Person: rescue worker
Place: shelter
Transportation: ambulance, helicopter

**E** TRACK 78 TB p. 222 **Listen and complete. Then watch and sing.**

- Point to the song title. Ask *Who are the emergency helpers? Who helps us in an emergency?* and elicit suggestions. Then play the song once, allowing students to listen and enjoy it.
- Have students notice the missing words. Can they guess what words they are? Play the song again, this time pausing where necessary for students to write their answers.
- Check answers as a class.
- Play the song video and encourage students to sing and move to the music as they watch.

**Answers**

1 *safe* 2 ambulance 3 helicopter 4 Rescue workers
5 emergency 6 shelter

### International English

Highlight the different words and elicit *fire truck* is American English and *fire engine* is British English. Ask *Which do we use?*

### Cool Down

Divide the classroom into three areas, each one representing a different emergency service: police, fire department, ambulance. Put a picture or sign up in each area. Call out a situation. Have students decide which emergency service to call and move to that area of the classroom.

Situations: *a house is on fire / a child has a broken leg / someone entered the school at night / a car had an accident / there's a flood*



**Practice** **Student's App:** Vocabulary Practice; Song Video

## Explore Language

### Lesson Objectives

- to learn to use relative clauses with *who*
- to practice emergency services vocabulary

**Materials**
Audio Tracks 79 and 80

### Warm Up

Ask students to remember the scene from pp. 88–89 by describing it. Encourage them to use as many adjectives as possible and to describe how the people are feeling. *What was Alec's family doing? Why? What was their plan?* Elicit that they were going to go home. Ask *Do you think they went home? Was there another safer place?*

**A** TRACK 79 TB p. 222 **Listen and read. What's Hassan doing?**

- Tell students that they are going to listen to Alec's family again. Have students look at the picture. Ask *Where are they now?* (in the emergency shelter) Play the audio and have students follow the dialogue in their books.
- Ask the gist question *What's Hassan doing?* and elicit the answer. Ask *Why does Alec's dad want to thank Hassan?* (because he helped them—and everyone else—get to safety) Ask *Why is it important to say "thank you"?* and have students share their ideas with the class.

**Answers**
He's telling a story to those kids. He's flying a helicopter!

**B Look at A. Complete.**

- Write or project the table onto the board.
- Have students discuss and complete the grammar table in pairs using the dialogue.
- Check answers on the board. Discuss the subject and word order of the *who* sentences. Let your class guide the discussion. If you feel that students need more guidance, the **ETB** provides a differentiation activity to help you support students as they explore the grammar table.
- Refer students to the Grammar tip *Watch Out*. Write the sentence on the board. Elicit that we never use a subject (*I, you, he, she, we, they*) after *who*. You may also want to point out that the relative pronoun comes directly after the noun it's giving more information about.

**Answers**
's; who; came; who; drive

**C Think and discuss. Then choose.**

- Have students work in pairs to discuss the sentence and answer options. Refer them to the table in B for examples. Then check the answer.

**Answer**
1 people

**Practice** **Resource Bank:** Grammar Printout
**Student's App:** Grammar Practice

**D** TRACK 80 TB p. 222 **Listen and say.**

- Tell students they're going to practice saying the structures. Play the audio, having students repeat each sentence chorally.
- For ideas on how to vary the drill, see TB p. 23.

**E Underline the relative clause in each sentence.**

- Have students read the sentences and underline the relative clauses. Remind them to look at the table in B to help them.
- Check answers as a class.

**Answers**
1 *who wants to be a firefighter*
2 who directs traffic
3 who drive the ambulance
4 who helps at the shelter
5 who wants to fly a helicopter
6 who keep us safe

**F Look around your classroom. Complete and compare. Do you agree?**

- Review the meanings of the superlative adjectives by playing a quick game of *Mime It!* (see TB p. 26) *or Draw It!* (see TB p. 25).
- Tell the class they are going to play a game called *The Student Who*, which is a similar to the game *Who Is It?* they played in Unit 6.
- Give students time to complete each sentence with the name of a classmate. Then have two students read the model on the page.
- Put students in pairs. Have them take turns sharing their answers, as in the model. Tell them to keep a tally of how many they agree on. At the end have a show of hands to see which pairs agreed on the most sentences. Did any pairs agree on all five? If time and interest allow, play another round with new partners.

**Answers**
Students' own answers

**International English**

Elicit that *truck* and *student* are American English and *lorry* and *pupil* are British English. Ask *Which words do we use?*

### Cool Down

Have students find a picture that contains at least one person in their books. They should show the picture to their partner and say something about one of the characters; for example, *She's the girl who ate the strawberries! He's the boy who wears goggles to cut onions! She's the girl who bought a lamp.*

## Global Citizenship

### Lesson Objectives

- to learn natural disasters vocabulary: *avalanche, burn, cover, earthquake, flood, forest fire, hurricane, tornado, tsunami, volcano*
- to explore how the community works together in natural disasters
- to learn how to prepare for an emergency
- to practice listening for gist and specific details

**Materials**
Audio Tracks 81 to 83; Audio Track G; a globe or map of the world (D)

### Opening Question

Ask the opening question: *How can we prepare before an emergency?* Then encourage students to think of the ways we can prepare for events such as a flood or a bad storm. They can use the information they learned in the Vocabulary lesson and draw on prior knowledge to discuss the question.

**A** TRACK 81 TB p. 222 **Listen to Jonas talking about natural disasters. Why does he want to be a storm chaser?**

- Tell students they are going to listen to a boy named Jonas talking about natural disasters. Play the audio and have students point to the words or pictures as they listen.
- Ask the comprehension question *Why does he want to be a storm chaser?* Play the audio again for students to check.

**Answers**
Because he's really interested in the weather.

**B** TRACK 82 TB p. 222 **Listen, say, and number the pictures in A.**

- Play the audio and have students point to the pictures and say the words.
- Tell students to listen again and write numbers next to the words in the pictures. Do the example together (earthquake).
- Check answers by writing the first letter of each word on the board for students to call out the word and then the number that it corresponds to in the audio.

**Answers**
1 *earthquake* 2 burn 3 flood 4 hurricane
5 volcano 6 avalanche 7 cover 8 tsunami
9 forest fire 10 tornado

TRACK G TB p. 223 **Visualization**
The TTL has a visualization audio track for this vocabulary set. (See TB p. 21.)

**C Read and match.**

- Look at the example together. Read the first definition and refer students to the pictures in A. Point out that they can look at the pictures to figure out which natural disaster is being described.
- Have students do the matching activity individually. Then check answers as a class.

**Answers**
1 *b* 2 d 3 a 4 f 5 e 6 c

**D** TRACK 83 TB p. 223 **Now listen to Mely and Dustin. What do they practice at school?**

- Have students look at the pictures of The Philippines and the USA and say what they see. You could point out the countries on a globe or a map. Ask *What natural disasters do you think each place has?* Elicit ideas from the class.
- Listening for gist: tell students they are going to listen to two children talking about natural disasters. Ask the gist question *What do they practice at school?* Play the audio and elicit answers.

**Answers**
Mely practices how to stay safe in an earthquake.
Dustin practices how to stay safe in a tornado.

**E Listen again. Write *True* or *False*.**

- Listening for details: have students read the sentences before they listen again to see what they remember. Then play the audio and have students write the answers.
- To check answers, read each question and have students nod their heads for *True* and shake their heads for *False*.

**Answers**
1 *True* 2 False 3 True 4 False 5 True 6 True

### Discussion Questions

- Draw students' attention to the discussion questions: *How can you and your family be ready for an emergency? What is your school's emergency plan?* Have students discuss the questions in pairs. See **ETB**.
- Return to the opening question to ask again: *How can we prepare before an emergency?* Review the ideas discussed at the beginning of the class and then encourage students to share any new ideas. Focus on the concept of working together and how everyone can use their skills to do something, however simple, to prepare. Ask *Why is it important to be prepared?*

### Cool Down

Elicit all the pieces of advice that students have heard about how to act in a disaster. Write these on the board. Have pairs rank them in order of importance for different natural disasters. Which advice is good for an earthquake? Which for a flood?

Possible advice: Move to higher ground. / Cover your head. / Stay under a desk or table. / Do what your teacher says. / Have a plan with your family. / Hide underground.

**Practice** **Student's App:** Vocabulary Practice; Listening Practice

## Explore Language

### Lesson Objectives

- to learn to use relative clauses with *that*
- to practice natural disasters vocabulary

**Materials**
Audio Tracks 84 and 85

### Warm Up

Tell students to imagine that there has been a flood but now it has gone. Ask *What does the playground look like?* Have students discuss their ideas. They can draw a picture if they wish to.

**A** TRACK 84 TB p. 223 **Listen and read. What do Hassan and Alec find?**

- Tell students that they are going to listen to Hassan and Alec after the flood. Have students look back at Explore Language 1 to help them remember Alec and Hassan. Play the audio and have students follow the story in their books.
- Ask the gist question *What do Hassan and Alec find?* and elicit suggestions. Ask *Who is Alec's friend?* and elicit the answer (Zack).

**Answer**
Zack's backpack

**International English**

Elicit *named* is American English and *called* is British English. Ask *Which word do we use?*

**B Look at A. Complete.**

- Write or project the table onto the board.
- Have students discuss and complete the grammar table in pairs using the story.
- Check answers on the board. Discuss the subject and word order of the *that* sentences together, but let your class guide the discussion. If you feel that students need more guidance, the **ETB** provides a differentiation activity to help you support students as they explore the grammar table.
- Students may notice that both present and past verb forms can be used after *that*. Tell students that we use relative pronouns like *that* to join two ideas in one sentence. Show this by writing *This is the wall. The wall stopped the flood.* Cross out *The wall* at the beginning of the second sentence and write *that* above it. Then write the new sentence below. Explain that we use relative pronouns so we don't need to repeat words.
- Refer students to the *Look* box. Point out that relative pronouns introduce relative clauses. Remind students of the other relative pronoun they know (*who*) and elicit an example sentence.

**Answers**
that; floated; that; has; that; lost

**Practice** **Resource Bank:** Grammar Printout
**Student's App:** Grammar Practice

**C Think and discuss. Then choose.**

- Refer students to the table in B and have them notice the sentence subjects. If you are using the TTL, circle these.
- Then have students work in pairs to discuss the answer options. Check answers as a class. Point out that we can only use *who* for people, but we can use *that* for people and things.

**Answer**
1 things or people

**D** TRACK 85 TB p. 223 **Listen and say.**

- Tell students they're going to practice saying the new structures. Play the audio, having students repeat each sentence chorally. For ideas on how to vary the drill, see TB p. 23.

**E Make new sentences with *that*.**

- Look at the example together and elicit what changes have been made (the subject *the helicopter* [the noun] is replaced with the pronoun *that*, and this joins the two sentence together to make one sentence [two clauses]). If necessary, write the first sentence on the board in one color, then make the changes to that sentences with another color, talking through what the changes are.
- Have students write sentences in their books. Then check answers as a class.

**Answers**
1 *This is the helicopter that stopped the forest fire.*
2 I heard the avalanche that covered our village with snow.
3 They remember the earthquake that shook their house.
4 We escaped the tsunami that came after the earthquake.
5 Hassan found a backpack that had Zack's homework in it.

**F Play *Silly Sentences*. Complete and say. Who has the silliest sentences?**

- Students are going to make up silly sentences using the prompts on the page. Encourage students to use their imaginations and have fun with this activity. Model the activity using the examples on the page. Elicit more ways of completing the sentence prompts. Make sure students understand that these sentences are supposed to be silly, not real, but they must be grammatically correct.
- Put students in pairs. Have them work together to write five silly sentences. When they finish, put pairs together with other pairs to share their silly sentences.
- Then ask each group of four to choose and read their silliest sentence to the class. Write them on the board, and have the class vote for the silliest sentence of all by a show of hands.

### Cool Down

Play *Backs to the Board* (see TB p. 25) using vocabulary from the unit (e.g. rescue worker).

# Take the Stage

## Lesson Objectives

- to prepare and practice a presentation about an important helper
- to recognize and reproduce /str/ and /tr/

**Materials**
Video; Audio Track 86

## Warm Up

Brainstorm jobs with the class (students studied these in Level 1). You could do this as a Venn diagram on the board with the categories *Inside*, *Outside*, or *Both*. Then ask *What do you want to be when you grow up? Why?* Write *I want to be a person who …* on the board. Have students call out sentences; for example, *I want to be a person who saves people*. The other students should guess which job it is.

**A** TB p. 239 **Watch and listen. Why does Otis want to be a rescue worker?**

- Tell students they are going to watch a presentation by a boy named Otis about the job he wants to do. Ask *What does Otis say about rescue workers?* Play the first scene of the video where Otis introduces his favorite job. (They are very important in an emergency.)
- Ask the gist question *Why does Otis want to be a rescue worker?* Have students predict possible reasons. Play the rest of the video and then check the answer, eliciting specific ideas of how rescue workers help people. Ask more comprehension questions (see **ETB**). Ask students what they noticed about Otis' body language.

**Answer**
Because he wants to help the world.

**B Watch again. Check (✔) the phrases you hear.**

- Have students read the phrases. Ask *Which phrases did Otis use?*
- Play the video again and have students check the phrases they hear. Check answers as a class.
- Have students classify the sentences into *Beginning*, *Middle*, and *End*. Then, with the class, build up the presentation on the board using the phrases.

**Answers**
1; 2; 4; 6; 7

### Pronunciation /str/ and /tr/

TRACK 86 TB p. 223 **Listen and say.**

Demonstrate the two sounds first. Isolate each phoneme in the cluster and elicit how to pronounce it (/s/; /t/; /r/). Then put the last two sounds together /tr/ and have students repeat it. Then add /s/ to make /str/. Have students practice this several times.

Play the audio and have students repeat the words. Repeat if students need more practice.

Say *These words are used in the video. What other words do you know with these sounds?* Elicit ideas and write them on the board in two columns (e.g. *orchestra*, *trash*). Drill the pronunciation of each word.

**Suggested Answers**
/str/ destroy, orchestra, strange, strawberries, striped, street, astronaut
/tr/ travel, tree, traditional, trap, treasure, triangle, trip, trumpet, electricity, entrance

**C Plan. Think about important helpers. Would you like to be one? Complete.**

- Ask *Would you like to be an important helper?* To prepare students, first brainstorm responses to the question *Who helps us?* If students have already completed Lesson 1 of **Literacy Book** Unit 7, they can recap some ideas they discussed in the Warm Up. Students should be encouraged to think about everyone who helps us.
- Then draw students' attention to the table in their books. Tell them that they are going to plan their own presentation. They need to choose a job or role and think about reasons why they would or wouldn't like to do that job.
- Have students complete the notes individually.

**D Prepare your presentation. Use your ideas from C and phrases from B.**

- Draw students' attention to the index cards they will use to plan their presentation. Ask *What will you say in the introduction?* (which job I have chosen to talk about) *How many reasons will you give?* (three) Tell students that their last sentence can be a general idea or reason.
- Have students prepare their presentations using their notes in C and phrases from B. Monitor and provide language help when needed.

**E Practice with a friend. Then share with your class.**

- Have students practice their presentation with their partner as many times as they like. They can use the information on their index cards the first few times they practice, but they should try not to read their cards.
- Ask one or two students to demonstrate their presentation in front of the class. Remind students to look at the faces in the audience and to smile!

## Cool Down

Play a game of *Ten Questions*. This is like *Twenty Questions* (see TB p. 27), but students can ask only ten questions. Choose an important helper (a firefighter, a police officer, a rescue worker, a doctor, an ambulance driver/paramedic, a nurse) and have students ask questions to guess; for example, *Do they wear uniforms? Do they drive a vehicle?*

**Practice** **Student's App:** Speaking Skills Practice; Speaking Video

# Write About It

## Lesson Objectives

- to learn to use exclamation points
- to review how to use quotation marks
- to plan and finish a story

**Materials**

(Optional) Support, Standard, and Challenge printouts from the Resource Bank, one per student (C and D)

## Warm Up

Ask *What makes a good story?* and elicit ideas from the class. Ask further questions to scaffold the discussion; for example, *Does a good story have an interesting start?* (yes) *Does it have an interesting ending?* (yes) *Does it have surprises or problems?* (yes) *Can people speak in a story?* (yes) *What words can you use to make sentences more interesting?* (adjectives and adverbs)

**A Read the story. Circle the quotation marks and underline the exclamation points.**

- Review the use quotation marks. Say *When someone speaks in a story, you write what they say in quotation marks.* Encourage a student to say something and write what they said on the board; for example, *Juan said, "I don't understand."*
- Have students look quickly at the story in their books and find the title (*Tornado!*). Looking at the picture, ask students to make some predictions about the story. Then have them read it quickly to see if their predictions are correct. Ask *What's the main idea?* and elicit the answer (a family goes to a shelter when they see a tornado).
- Point out the examples. Have students read the story, circle the quotation marks, and underline the exclamation points.
- Check answers as a class. Encourage students to notice that if a quotation doesn't end in an exclamation point, it ends in a comma or a period.
- Look at the sentence *It's a tornado!* and have students notice that Dad shouted this. Ask *How does Dad feel?* (excited or scared) Elicit when we use exclamation points (to show someone is surprised or excited, or when we shout).

**Answers**

Tornado!
"Look!"
"It's a tornado!"
"Quick! Into the shelter!"
"You go first!"
"I'm here, John," she said.
"Dad!" "Frosty's in the house!"
"Let me get him," said Dad. "Stay with Mom."

**International English**

Elicit that *exclamation point* is American English and *exclamation mark* is British English. Ask *Which do we use?*

**Practice** Student's App: Writing Practice

**B Read what John and his mom said later. Add the correct punctuation. Use (!) or (,). Then add quotation marks (" ").**

- Have students look at the first sentence and do it as an example on the board. Ask *What did Mom say?* (Be careful!) *How do you think she said it? Do we need a comma or an exclamation point?* (an exclamation point) *Why?* (because Mom is calling out a warning). Then ask *Do we need quotation marks? Where do we put them?* Elicit that we put quotation marks at the beginning and end of what someone says.
- Have students do the activity, looking back at A to help them. Then display the answers using the TTL for students to check.

**Answers**

1 *"Be careful!" called Mom.*
2 "I need to find Frosty!" I shouted.
3 "Please help us!" we called to the rescue worker.
4 "We're down here!" Mom and I shouted.
5 "You're safe now," I whispered to my cat.

**C Plan. How does the story end? Write.**

- Ask *What happens next?* Brainstorm ideas together. Think about the sequence of events that might come next, another character that might come, and what the characters might say. Use the questions in the table to elicit ideas.
- Give students enough time to think about their answers to the questions and complete the table. Challenge printouts can be handed out now.

**D Write your own ending to the story. Use your ideas from C.**

- Students are now going to write a draft ending to the story in their notebooks. Encourage students to use their imaginations to come up with original endings. Remind students that they are writing from John's point of view and they should use *I*. Students should write at least ten sentences, including a minimum of three quotations. Support printouts can be handed out now.
- Have students either self-correct or exchange their work with a friend and peer-correct. You can put a checklist of things to correct on the board (e.g. spelling; use of adjectives and adverbs; verb forms; and punctuation, including quotation marks and exclamation points).
- Have students write their final stories neatly on paper. Alternatively, hand out the Standard printouts. Students can draw a picture to illustrate the ending to their story. They can then get into small groups and read their stories to one another.

## Cool Down

Play *Pass the Whisper!* (see TB p. 26) using one of the quotations from the story.

# Think It Over

## Lesson Objectives

- to review what has been learned in the unit
- to reflect on the unit and their own progress
- to think about learning strategies and how to continue learning at home

## Warm Up

Ask students what the unit theme was (emergencies/natural disasters) and write it in the middle of the board. Brainstorm any words or phrases students can think of that relate to the topic and write them on the board. Encourage students to think about how people help each other during emergencies and natural disasters.

**Read the questions and draw or write your answers.**

- Give students time to think about and discuss activities in the unit before they complete each question. Explain that they can choose to either write a few words or sentences or to draw a picture. Allowing students to make a personal response will help them retain knowledge and engage with the learning points.

**What did I do?**

- Give students a few minutes to look back through the unit at the different activities they did. Ask questions about the unit or write questions on the board for students to discuss in pairs or small groups; for example, *What discussions did you have? What do you remember about Jonas?*
- Encourage students to identify something in the unit that they found challenging or something that was particularly memorable for them. Students can draw or write about their chosen activity.

**What did I learn?**

- Ask questions about the unit to help students think about what they learned; for example, *What did you learn about emergencies and natural disasters? What sentences can you say using defining relative clauses (who, that)? What did you learn about Philippines and the USA? What did you learn about writing a story? What else did you learn?* Have students look through the unit and discuss their ideas in pairs.
- Encourage students to draw a picture or write sentences about their learning outcomes.

**How did I learn?**

- Ask students how they learned the emergency and natural disaster vocabulary in Lessons 1 and 3. Elicit ideas (e.g. by categorizing words, by singing a song, by doing a visualization, by making predictions about the picture, by using prior knowledge). Encourage students to think about the spelling and pronunciation of the words. Ask *What helped you remember how to say and write the new words?*
- Then encourage students to think about how they learned throughout the unit; for example, how did they develop their presentation skills?
- Have students draw or write about the activities that helped them learn.

**How well did I do?**

- Tell students to color in the number of jackets that best expresses how well they have learned they unit content (i.e., the more uniforms they color, the more they feel they have learned). Ask *What do you understand? What do you need to practice more?* Encourage students to look back through the unit to see how much they remember, what they did well, and what they found difficult.

**What can I do next?**

- Brainstorm ideas with the class about what they can do to continue to learn (e.g. think about the effects of different natural disasters and what the consequences are; make a plan or be prepared for a natural disaster in the community; find and pronounce words with /str/ and /tr/; find a vocabulary app or game to play; research presentation skills by looking at other presentations online). Students can look back at the previous units to get more ideas. Encourage students to suggest their own ideas for different activities they can do.
- Draw students' attention to the *What can I do next?* box. Encourage students to think about what they can do at home to improve their English. Have them suggest some verbs that they can use (e.g. listen, read, write, discuss, research) and write the verbs they choose in their books.
- Have students choose several activities that they would like to do and write them in their notebooks. They can then share their ideas with a partner.

## Looking Forward

- Draw students' attention to the character at the bottom of the page. Ask *Who's this?* and elicit what they remember about him (Hassan appears in the Vocabulary and Explore Language lessons on pp. 88, 90, and 94; he helped Alec's family in the flood, he played/flew a helicopter with some children; he cleaned up after the flood; he found a backpack).
- Draw students' attention to Hassan's question: *Where do I go on vacation?* Encourage students to make predictions about where Hassan goes on his vacation and what Unit 8 is about. Tell students they will find the answer in Lesson 1 of the next unit.

**Practice** **Resource Bank:** Unit Test
**Student's App:** Vocabulary and Grammar Review

## Get Ready to Read

### Lesson Objectives

- to activate prior knowledge about natural disasters
- to guide enquiry and deepen understanding through a See, Think, Wonder VTR
- to preview the reading skill of making inferences and predictions

**Materials**

(Optional) VTR printout from the Resource Bank (Activities A, B, C)

### Warm Up

Write on the board *People Who Help Me* and have students brainstorm ideas in pairs. Encourage students to think about times when they may need help (e.g. at home, at school, when they're sick, when they're traveling). Have students make a list and report back to the class. Write the ideas on the board.

### See, Think, Wonder

**A Look at the picture. What do you see?**

Students are going to do a See, Think, Wonder VTR to explore the image of the mountain.

- Have students brainstorm any words they know connected to mountains.
- Ask students *What do you see?* Give students one minute to look at the picture before sharing answers in small groups and then as a class.

Here's an example of this part of the routine.
**Teacher:** What do you see?
**Student A:** I see a helicopter.
**Teacher:** Good! What else do you see?
**Student B:** I see people helping.
**Teacher:** Anything else?
**Student C:** They're in the mountains.

**B What do you think?**

- Say *I think they are going to take the man to the hospital. What do you think about the picture?* Elicit a response from a student. Then ask *What makes you say that?* and encourage the student to give a reason.
- Give students one to three minutes to think. Then have them work in small groups to share their ideas, before sharing as a class. Monitor and provide language help when needed.

Here's an example of this part of the routine.
**Teacher:** What do you think about the picture?
**Student A:** (I think) the man hurt his head.
**Teacher:** What makes you say that?
**Student A:** His head is red.
**Teacher:** What else do you think?
**Student B:** (I think) this person is the pilot.

**C What do you wonder?**

- Say *I wonder how long it takes to get to the hospital by helicopter. What do you wonder about the picture? What questions do you have?* Give students one to three minutes to think about the picture silently.
- Have students share their ideas in groups or as a class. Allow students to be creative and accept all their ideas and focus on the meaning of the questions rather than correcting any grammatical errors. Fun questions can generate interesting discussion.

Here's an example of this part of the routine.
**Teacher:** What do you wonder?
**Student A:** (I wonder) what happened to the man.
**Teacher:** Good question! Does anyone have any ideas?
**Student B:** I think he fell off the mountain.
**Teacher:** OK, what else do you wonder?
**Student C:** *Is (this person) a doctor?*

### Transition

Ask students what they think happened to the man. *What was he doing? Was he climbing the mountain or skiing? How did he fall?* Ask students to think about what dangers the mountain might have. They can discuss their ideas in pairs or small groups.

**D What types of natural disasters do you know about? Brainstorm with a group.**

- Have students look at the picture again and think about possible natural disasters that could occur (e.g. an avalanche). Then have students think about other natural disasters they know about. Students may have seen images on TV or videos online. Encourage them to talk about any natural disasters that have happened, the effects of them, what people do and how they feel, what help there is, and so on. Have students work in groups to collate their ideas on paper.
- Then have each group share their ideas with the class. Combine their prior knowledge to create a whole class list for reference throughout the unit. If appropriate, ask students if they have any stories they can share about natural disasters, for example anecdotes they heard from family members.

**E Think and discuss. Look at the pictures on the first page of the reading. What do you think it's about?**

In this activity students will preview the reading skill of making predictions and inferences.

- Display the pictures from the first page of the reading or have students look at them in their books. Ask *What do you think the reading is about? What type of text is it?*
- Give students a few minutes to discuss their ideas in pairs. Then have students share their ideas with the class.

Now read **What Happens Next?**

# Fiction: *What Happens Next?*— Realistic Fiction

## Lesson Objectives

- to read realistic fiction about an earthquake
- to make a personal connection to the reading

**Materials**

Audio Tracks 35 and 36; sticky notes (CD)

## Warm Up

Have students look at the opening spread of the reading. Ask *What's happening?* (an earthquake) Ask *What should you do in an earthquake?* and brainstorm suggestions from the class.

### TRACK 35 TB p. 234 Reading Approach

**First Reading: Engage with the Text**

- Have students sit in a circle to listen to the story the first time you read it.
- Ask prediction questions before turning the page; for example, *Where will they move?*
- Read the whole story before looking at the Words in Context.

### TRACK 36 TB p. 234 Words in Context

- Play the audio and have students repeat the words.
- Have students race to find the words in the reading.
- Remind students to look at sentences containing a target word, then **look at the pictures to help establish the meaning of the new words** (see TB p. 23).
- Use these discussion points to confirm the meanings.

**gentle** (p. 107) Ask students how the desk moved at first. Ask *Did it shake a lot?* Ask a student to use a desk or chair to demonstrate gentle shaking. Say *The shaking was gentle at first, but it got bigger and stronger.*

**crawl** (p. 108) Have students look at the picture. Ask *Where are the children?* (under the desks) *How did they get there?* Have a student demonstrate crawling under a desk.

**hot-air balloon** (p. 109) Say *In the story, Sophie climbed into the hot-air balloon.* Then have students look at the picture of the book and identify the hot-air balloon. Ask *Would you like to travel in a hot-air balloon?*

**rope** (p. 109) Refer students back to the picture. Have students read the sentence from the story where Sophie cuts the rope. Ask *What was the rope doing?* (tying the hot-air balloon to the ground) *What happened after she cut it?* (The hot-air balloon flew up into the sky.)

**loudspeaker** (p. 110) Ask *Where can the children hear the principal's voice? Is he in the classroom? How can they hear him?* Have students identify the loudspeaker in the picture.

### International English

Elicit *principal* is American English and *head teacher* is British English. Ask *Which word do we use?*

**Second Reading: Analyze the Text and Features**

- Play the audio and have students follow along in their books.
- Ask some questions to check comprehension: *Who is the students' favorite teacher?* (Mr. Carlson) *What got bigger and stronger?* (the shaking) *Which objects fell?* (pencils, books) *What did the students do?* (They got under their desks.) *What was strange?* (Mr. Carlson started reading again.) *How did the children feel?* (scared)
- Discuss the questions in the orange boxes.
  - **Critical Thinking** (p. 106): *What do you think* brought books to life *means?* Ask *Are stories real? Do the children feel like they are in the story?* Elicit that the teacher helps the students imagine that they are in the story.
  - **Gist** (p. 108): *What should you do in an earthquake?* If you discussed this in the Warm Up, ask students if they have changed their minds after reading the story.
  - **Personalization** (p. 109): *How can you use your imagination to stay calm?* Say *In the reading, the children listened to the story.* Elicit other ways students can use their imaginations.
  - **Making Connections** (p. 111): *Who or what can help you in an emergency?* Elicit ideas about people, animals, and actions that can help us or make us feel better.
- Discuss the text focus: *This kind of story is called* ***realistic fiction****. It's made up, but it could still happen.* Have students remember *The Beginning of Alice's Adventures* from Unit 1. Ask *What things in that story are not possible in real life?*

**Third Reading: Interact with the Text**

- Refer students to the hot-air balloon story. Say *Ken wants to know what happens next, can you tell him?* Have students discuss ideas in pairs, and then write and draw the next part of the story.

## Cool Down

Have students think of one thing they have learned during the lesson, write it on a sticky note, and stick it on the door. Keep these for the next lesson.

## Explore the Reading

### Lesson Objectives

- to understand and analyze *What Happens Next?* through reading comprehension activities
- to explore the SEL competency of self-management through exhibiting positive motivation, hope, and optimism

**Materials**

(Optional) Audio Track 35; completed sticky notes from the previous lesson (WU)

### Warm Up

Put students in groups of three. Hand out the sticky notes that students completed at the end of the previous lesson, giving each group three random notes. Have groups read the sticky notes and decide which is the most interesting fact.

**A Put these events from the story in order. Then retell the story to a partner.**

- If more than one day has passed since students read *What Happens Next?*, play the audio again.
- With books closed, have a Group Time discussion (see TB p. 21) to check students' comprehension of the reading. Ask *Where is the story set?* (at school) *Who's Mr. Carlson?* (the teacher) *Which natural disaster took place?* (an earthquake) *Where did the children hide?* (under their desks) *How did Aiko feel?* (scared)
- Have students open their books and look at the activity. Ask *Which happened first?* Tell students to read quickly (scan) the five events from the story to find the one that happened first. They should look in the story to help them. Check the answer.
- Have students order the events individually. Then have them retell the story in pairs. They can add more details if they wish. Check answers by having some students read their ordered sentences aloud.

**Answers**

4, 2, 3, 1, 5

**B Think and complete the graphic organizer. How did the class stay calm? Use details from the story.**

- Ask *Were the children scared?* (yes) *What do you do when you're scared?* Brainstorm ideas with the class. *Did the class panic or stay calm?* (They stayed calm.) *How did they stay calm? Did someone help them? How?* Elicit ideas from the class.
- Then have students draw three pictures showing how the class stayed calm. Tell students they can look at the pictures in the story to help them.
- Have them write a caption for each picture.

**Suggested Answers**

by following the three-step plan; by smiling at each other; by listening to the story; by getting lost in the story; by listening for more information

**C Write and discuss. When an emergency happens, what can you do to stay calm?**

- This activity develops the SEL competency of self-management through exhibiting positive motivation, hope, and optimism.
- Recap what Mr. Carlson did to stop his students from feeling afraid (he read to them). Highlight that this is a positive action in a difficult situation. Ask students to imagine being in the characters' situation. Would listening to a story stop them from feeling afraid? Why or why not?
- Ask *What is an emergency?* Brainstorm different types of emergencies with the class. Have students name the main emergency services and say what they do. It may be useful to categorize the emergencies by each service (police, ambulance, fire department) on the board. Make sure that students are aware that an emergency is when a person is in danger.
- Say *Imagine you are in an emergency situation. What can you do to stay calm?* Give students a few minutes to think. Encourage them to draw on personal experiences or emergencies they know about, have read about, or have seen.
- Then have students work in pairs to look at each of the emergencies on the board, describe how they might feel, and discuss ways to keep themselves calm. Remind students to think of positive ways to help the situation. Monitor and provide language help when needed.
- Ask students to write sentences about an emergency and what they do to keep calm. Remind them to write about actions and feelings.
- Have students share their sentences in groups. Encourage students to ask each other questions to find out more details.

**Answers**

Students' own answers

### Cool Down

Play *Bingo!* (see TB p. 25) for the procedure. For this version, use emergencies. Elicit and write a series of emergencies on the board. Instead of calling out *Bingo!* have students call out *Emergency!*

Suggested items: *hot water on your arm / a car accident / a house fire / a bank robbery / a child can't swim / a woman not breathing / a snake bite / an old man can't move*

**Practice** **Student's App:** Reading Practice

# Get Ready to Read

## Lesson Objectives

- to practice the reading skill of making inferences and predictions
- to activate prior knowledge about natural disasters
- to make a personal connection to the reading

**Materials**
Pictures of a natural disaster (WU); a ball(s) (CD)

## Warm Up

Ask students if they know of any natural disasters that have happened in their country. Ask *What happened? Did you see it? Do you know anyone who was there?* You could do some online research with the class and look for pictures. If you have not yet done the **Language Book** unit, pre-teach any vocabulary connected to natural disasters: tsunami, tornado, earthquake, volcano, hurricane, avalanche, forest fire, flood.

**A Look at the title and picture below. Write what the reading is about. Then read and write why the reading is useful.**

Students are going to practice the reading skill of making inferences and predictions.

- Have students look the title and the picture. Ask *What can you see?* Draw students' attention to the sign and the word *HAZARD*. Ask *Can you think of a similar word?* (danger) Do a quick See, Think, Wonder routine with the class (see TB p. 20).
- Ask *What is the title?* (*Tsunamis*) Point out that *tsunami* has a silent *t*. Note: the word *tsunami* comes from the Japanese word for harbor wave. Have students write what they think the reading is about.
- Give students one or two minutes to read the text to identify useful information. Students can underline any information they think is useful. Ask *What are tsunamis? What useful information did you learn?* Then have students use their ideas to complete the sentence about why the reading is useful.
- Have students read the skills box. Tell students that they made predictions about the text before they read it. Ask *How did you do this?* (They looked at the picture and the title.) Then tell students that they made inferences when they completed the sentence. Ask *Did you do this before or after you read the paragraph?* (after) Explain that an inference is an opinion that you form about something that is based on information you already have. Ask *What opinion did you form about the text?* Elicit that students formed the opinion that the text was useful because they learned about how to prepare for a tsunami.

**Answers**
This reading is about tsunamis. This reading is useful because it tells you how to prepare for a tsunami.

**B Think and write. Look at *Animals to the Rescue*. Predict what the reading is about.**

- Give students a minute to look at the next page. Remind them that pictures and the title can help them predict what a text is about. Then have students discuss their predictions in pairs or small groups and write their ideas in their books.

**Answer**
Students' own answers

**C Scan *Animals to the Rescue*. Write two animals that work. Predict their jobs.**

- Review how to scan a text with the class. Remind students that when we scan, we read quickly to find specific information (e.g. answers to questions). Ask *Do we read every word?* (no)
- Ask *What information do we need to look for?* (two animals) Ask *Do you think we can find this information in the pictures or in the text?* (The animals can be found in the pictures, but students will need to read the text to find out more information about them.)
- Have students quickly look and find two of the animals from the reading and write them in the table. Then have students predict what job each animal does. Remind students to look for clues in the pictures (e.g. what the people are wearing might give them a clue about what job the dog does).

**Suggested Answers**
Dogs rescue people in the mountains; horses carry people and things.

## Cool Down

Play *Pass the Ball* (see TB p. 26) to encourage students to think about the different abilities animals may have. The student with the ball calls out the name of an animal and throws the ball to someone else. That student must make a sentence about the animal using *can*; for example, *Dolphins can swim*. The student then chooses another animal and the game continues. With large classes, have students play in smaller groups.

Now read **Animals to the Rescue**

# Nonfiction: *Animals to the Rescue*—Informational Text

## Lesson Objectives

- to read an informational text about animals that help people
- to make a personal connection to the reading

**Materials**

Audio Tracks 37 and 38; Video; slips of paper (CD)

## Warm Up

Display and enlarge the first image on p. 114 if you are using the TTL or have students look at the picture in their books. Have students describe what they see. Then have them make predictions about what happened before this picture was taken, what is happening now, and what will happen next.

### TRACK 37 TB p. 234 Reading Approach

**First Reading: Engage with the Text**

- Have students look at the title and pictures in the reading. Ask *What's one thing you want to find out about these animals?* Have students discuss this in pairs.
- Play the video and ask how many students found the answer to their question.
- Then look at the Words in Context.

### TRACK 38 TB p. 235 Words in Context

- Play the audio and have students repeat the words. Then have them race to find the words in the reading.
- Review the strategies learned so far for working out the meaning of new words (see TB p. 23). Have students work in pairs to discuss the words in context.
- Use these discussion points to confirm the meanings.

**search** (p. 114) Ask *What do the dogs do?* Elicit that they look for people who are trapped. *What role do the dogs have?* (search and rescue) Elicit that *search for* and *look for* are synonyms.

**train** (p. 114) Have students look at the sentence. Ask *What kind of word is "train" in this sentence?* (a verb) *Can you think of a similar word?* (teach)

**rubble** (p. 115) Remind students to look at what has come before in the reading to figure out the meaning of new words. If necessary, refer them to the first paragraph. Say *When a building falls down, search and rescue dogs are sent in because they can get into small places. What do you think rubble is in this context?* Elicit that it is the remains of the building (usually stone, brick, concrete). Can they point to rubble in the first picture?

**survivors** (p. 115) Say *Many people died, but the dogs worked hard to find survivors.* Elicit that *survivors* are people who are still alive after a disaster. Have students find an example of a survivor in the reading (the 15-year-old boy).

**trapped** (p. 115) Ask *Where are some people after a building falls down?* Elicit that people are under the buildings and ruins. Ask *Can they move?* (no) Say *When you can't move or get out, you're trapped.*

**safety** (p. 116) Elicit that the horses take people to a safe place. Remind students of the meaning of *safe* by contrasting it with *dangerous*. Tell students that *safe* is an adjective but *safety* is a noun.

**stuck** (p. 117) Remind students to read the next sentence after they find a word. Here the next sentence tells us the meaning of *stuck*. Elicit that if you are *stuck*, you can't move.

- Ask students which strategies they used to figure out the meanings of the words.

**Second Reading: Analyze the Text and Features**

- Play the audio and have students follow along in their books.
- Ask some questions to check comprehension, e.g. *Why are the dogs special?* (They are trained and can smell very well.) *Why are horses used?* (They can travel a long way; they can see, hear, and smell well; and they carry useful things.)
- Discuss the questions in the orange boxes.
  - **Fact** (p. 114): *Some scientists think a dog's sense of smell is 10,000 times stronger than a human's!* Ask *Would you like to have a better sense of smell?*
  - **Gist** (p. 115): *Why do people sometimes need animals in a natural disaster?* Ask students *What can animals do better than humans?* Elicit that they have better senses and they can access difficult/small places.
  - **Fact** (p. 116): Horses' ears can turn to hear noises better. Ask students if they have noticed how a horse's ears turn. Ask *Do other animals have ears that do this?*
  - **Inference** (p. 117): Ask *Do you think dolphins and whales make good rescue animals?* You could have students research this question online to find out more about how sea animals can help us.

### International English

Have students find *trucks* in the reading. Elicit that this is the plural form of *truck*. Can they guess what the plural of lorry is? (lorries)

**Third Reading: Interact with the Text**

- Have students work in pairs to compare and contrast the three animals and what they do. Encourage them to draw a Venn diagram to show their ideas.

## Cool Down

Tell students that all the animals in the text are entered for the award for the *Best Helper of the Year*. Have students write down the animal they think should win the award on a slip of paper. They should include reasons why this animal should win. Then collect the papers, count the votes, and reveal the winner.

**Practice** **Student's App:** Nonfiction Video

## Explore the Reading

### Lesson Objectives

- to understand and analyze *Animals to the Rescue* through reading comprehension activities
- to learn through CLIL (social studies): exploring how people help in the community
- to make a personal connection to the reading
- to reproduce and write words with *ly*

**Materials**
Audio Tracks 37 and 39

TRACK 37 TB p. 234 **Warm Up**
Have students brainstorm all the words they can remember from the reading. Then play the audio and have students check off any words they hear mentioned. Ask students how many words they checked off and what they were.

**A Think and check (✔). Why are these animals good for search and rescue?**

- With books closed, ask questions to see what students remember about the reading; for example, *Which animals are "search and rescue" animals?* (dogs and horses) *How do dogs find people?* (with their noses) *Why can dogs search in rubble more easily than people?* (because they are smaller) *When did the dog find the boy in Nepal?* (five days after the earthquake) *How did a whale save a swimmer?* (by pushing her up out of the water)
- Have students open their books and look at the first statement: *Dogs are good for search and rescue because … they have a strong sense of smell.* Ask *Do dogs have a strong sense of smell?* (yes) *Does it help them search and rescue people?* (yes) Tell students to check the circle.
- Have students do the rest of the activity individually, looking back at the reading to find the answers. Make sure that students know they only have to choose the options that help the animals with their job. Check answers as a class.

**Suggested Answers**
Dogs are good for search and rescue because: a, c, d
Horses are good for search and rescue because: b, c, d

**B Think and discuss. Look back at your predictions on page 113. Were they correct?**

- Tell students to look back at the jobs they wrote in the table on p. 113 and check if their predictions were correct. They can look back at the reading if they need to.
- Students are going to discuss their predictions in pairs. Have two students demonstrate using the examples on the page; for example, *Yes, I was right because I wrote "dogs" and "rescue people".* Then have students talk in pairs about which predictions were or weren't correct.

**C Think, write, and discuss. How do you think the author feels about animals? Make an inference and give an example from the reading.**

- Draw students' attention to the question *How do you think the author feels about animals?* Have students look back at the text and try to infer how the author feels about animals. They should write their ideas with an example from the reading in their books.

**Answer**
Students' own answers

**D Choose and write. Do you think being a rescue worker is hard work? Why or why not?**

Students are going to connect the reading with their own understanding of their communities. This draws on the CLIL social studies focus of exploring how people help in the community.

- Have students work in pairs to brainstorm some situations in their communities that might require rescue workers. Ask *What do rescue workers do?* and have students list some ideas. Ask *Do you think being a rescue worker is hard work? Why or why not?* Have students look at their list and decide which things are hard work and which ones aren't. Encourage students to justify their opinions by giving as many reasons as possible.
- Have students write their ideas in their books or notebooks.

**Answers**
Students' own answers

### Spelling Pattern *–ly*

TRACK 39 TB p. 235 **Listen and write. Then check your answers.**

- With books closed, write *ly* on the board and elicit the pronunciation.
- Play the first part of the audio and have students repeat each word. Then have them open their books. Play the first part of the audio again and have them complete as many words as they can.
- Then play the second part of the audio for students to check their spelling and complete the words correctly. Have them read the words aloud.
- Have students look back at the reading to find more words with *ly* and write them in a spidergram. Invite students to read a word from their spidergram.

**Answers**
1 family 2 friendly 3 quietly 4 early 5 happily
From the reading: quickly, easily, carefully, really, only

### Cool Down

Play *Shark* with *-ly* words (see TB p. 27). Students then swap roles.



**Practice** **Resource Bank:** Spelling Printout
**Student's App:** Reading Practice; Spelling Pattern Practice

## Think Together

### Lesson Objectives

- to make connections between the readings
- to explore the key concept: How can we help each other in an emergency?
- to reflect on the unit and provide personal thoughts and opinions

### Warm Up

Have students look back at the VTR picture on pages 104–105. Ask students how they think the picture connects to the two readings in the unit. *What would you do if you found an injured person in the mountains?* Encourage students to be creative in their answers; for example, *We could call an ambulance; We could put our coats on him/her to keep him/her warm.*

**A Think and discuss. Look at both readings. How do people or animals work together in an emergency?**

- Elicit some examples of people or animals working together. Then give students a few minutes to look back at the two readings in the unit and identify examples of animals and humans working together.
- Have students work in pairs to discuss their ideas. Monitor and help students with the discussion if necessary by asking questions; for example, *So why is the dog better in that situation? How do the dog handlers and dogs work together?*
- Then bring the class together and have students share their ideas.

**B Think about natural disasters. How can you help? Complete the graphic organizer with a partner.**

Students are going to make personal connections and think critically about the key concept in the unit: *How can we help each other in an emergency?*

- Do an example together. Have the class choose a natural disaster. This will be most effective if this is a natural disaster that affects the students' country. Then ask *How can you help before? How can you help during the disaster? How can you help after?* Brainstorm ideas with the class. Encourage students to apply what they have learned during the unit.
- Then have students work with a partner to choose a disaster, discuss their ideas, and write them in the graphic organizer.

**Answers**
Students' own answers

**C Look at the graphic organizer in B. Do a Rally Robin.**

- Set students up for a Rally Robin routine (see TB p. 20). Students are going to use their ideas from B to have a discussion with a different partner on the different things they can do before, during, and after a natural disaster.
- Have students share some of their ideas with the class.

### My Reading Journal

**Look back at the unit. Which part did you find the most interesting? What did you learn?**

This question helps students review and remember what they learned. Tell the class one interesting thing that you learned from the unit; for example, *I learned that dolphins and whales helped rescue humans.* Give students a few minutes to look back through the unit and find one thing that interested them and one thing that they learned. Students should write their ideas in their reading journals. They can then compare their ideas with a friend.

**Example Answers**
The most interesting part was how the animals helped people in a disaster.
I learned that dogs can smell 10,000 times better than me!

**Now look back at the activities. How did you do? Color one face. Then write why.**

This activity allows students to evaluate their own learning. Give students a few minutes to look back at the activities they have done and consider how well they did them. Ask *Did you do the activities well? Did you find them difficult? Did you try your best?* Tell students to color in the face that best expresses their feelings about their progress then write why they chose that face. Students are used to doing this type of self-evaluation in the **Language Book**.

### Cool Down

Encourage students to do further self-reflection by choosing three of the following questions and asking other students in groups. Write the questions on the board:

*Which reading did you like best? Why?*

*Which picture do you think best represents the unit?*

*Which activity did you like the most?*

*Which activity did you find difficult?*

**Practice** **Resource Bank:** Unit Test
**Student's App:** Key Concept Practice

UNIT 8

# Under the Sea

## Unit Overview

### Themes

Sea creatures

Endangered sea life

### Synopsis

In this unit, students will explore the theme of sea life and how we can protect it. They will learn about different kinds of fish and sea creatures and examine their patterns. They will also discuss the dangers to coral reefs and how we can protect the sea and its life. Students will plan and prepare a presentation about an endangered animal and write a concrete poem.

## Language Book

### Vocabulary

*angelfish, clownfish, coral, dolphin, jellyfish, octopus, seahorse, sea turtle, shark, starfish, whale*

p. 160

### Explore Language

Simple Present and Present Progressive

p. 161

### Global Citizenship

Why is sea life important?

*aquarium, clear, flat, horizontal, protect, round, save, spotted, striped, vertical*

p. 162

### Explore Language

Future: Predictions with *Will*

p. 163

### Take the Stage

Presentation: an endangered animal

p. 164

### Write About It

A Concrete Poem

Word Building: synonyms

p. 165

### Think It Over

Review and Reflection

p. 166

# Literacy Book

## Think Together
What is life like under the sea?
p. 173

## Visible Thinking
Question Starts
p. 167

## Fiction
Fantasy: *The Lost Camera*

Words in Context: *divers, surface, slipped, noticed, tag, everywhere*
p. 171

## Nonfiction
Persuasive Text: *Coral Reefs*

Words in Context: *stick, shallow, creatures, waste, damage, marine park*
p. 168

## Reading Skill
Identifying perspective
p. 170

## Spelling Pattern
*–ight*
p. 169

## Language and Literacy Connections

The connecting theme in Unit 8 is understanding and protecting sea life.

| | Language | Literacy |
|---|---|---|
| **Vocabulary** | **Set 1:** marine life<br>**Set 2:** patterns | **Nonfiction:** coral, jellyfish, sea turtle(s), shark(s), starfish, whale(s), protect<br>**Fiction:** angelfish |
| **Grammar** | **Simple Present and Present Progressive**<br>They often swim into the coral and hide.<br>Is that a coral reef?<br>They're swimming through the coral right now!<br>Why are the fish swimming together?<br>**Future: Predictions with *Will***<br>We'll catch some lionfish!<br>We won't catch any other fish.<br>What will happen to the fish that live here?<br>Will they have food? Yes, they will. No, they won't. | **Nonfiction**<br>There are fish, sharks, and whales in the world's oceans.<br>The sea is getting warmer.<br>The coral are losing their color.<br>Without protection, the coral reefs will die.<br>**Fiction**<br>I'm feeling sick. |
| **Skills** | **Pronunciation:** /h/ and /w/ | **Reading:** identifying perspective<br>**Spelling Pattern:** *–ight* |
| **International English** | ocean floor/seabed | ocean floor/seabed |

## Vocabulary

### Lesson Objectives

- to learn sea life vocabulary: *angelfish, clownfish, coral, dolphin, jellyfish, octopus, seahorse, sea turtle, shark, starfish, whale*
- to sing a song that explores watching sea life during a boat trip

**Materials**
Audio Tracks 87 to 90; Video

### Warm Up

With books closed, write the unit title, *Under the Sea*, on the board. Have students work in pairs to predict words they think will be in the unit. They could draw a picture of the ocean to use as a graphic organizer and write all their words under the ocean in different categories (e.g. animals, plants, objects).

**A** TRACK 87 TB p. 223 **Listen and find. Why do the fish swim away?**

- Have students look at the pictures and say what they can see. Ask *Can you find Hassan from Unit 7?* Allocate each person in the picture to a group of students and have them brainstorm what that person is seeing and thinking; for example, what questions do they want to ask? They can also make some predictions about the person (the group doing Hassan can build on what they have learned about him already). Give them a few minutes to discuss and then have them share their ideas with the class.
- Tell students they are going to listen to Hassan and his family on the boat. Play the audio and have students point to the words or pictures as they listen. Remind students of the challenge from the end of Unit 7: *Where do I go on vacation?* and elicit that he goes to the ocean. Ask *Does this look like a fun vacation?* and ask volunteers to give their opinion.
- Ask the comprehension question *Why do the fish swim away?* and elicit the answer. Play the audio again for students to check.

**Answer**
Because a shark comes.

**B** TRACK 88 TB p. 223 **Listen, say, and number the pictures in A.**

- Play the audio and have students point to the pictures and say the words.
- Tell students to listen again and write numbers next to the words in the picture. Do the example together (dolphin).
- Check answers by describing each of the sea creatures in turn and having students call out the word and the corresponding number. Alternatively, project the answers using the TTL.

**Answers**
1 *dolphin* 2 clownfish 3 coral 4 angelfish
5 starfish 6 jellyfish 7 seahorse 8 octopus
9 shark 10 whale 11 sea turtle

**C** TRACK 89 TB p. 223 **Close your eyes. Listen, visualize, and say.**

- Prepare students for the visualization (see TB p. 21).
- Play the audio, allowing students to visualize the ideas as they listen.
- Have students choose their favorite visualization and describe it to a partner.

**D Look and write.**

- Students are going to classify the vocabulary into two sets. This encourages critical thinking and helps organize the words in a logical way. Draw students' attention to the table. Say *Some of the sea creatures are fish, but some aren't fish.* It may be useful to discuss what a fish is with the class (a fish has gills, scales, and fins).
- Tell students to write the words from A in the table. Then check answers as a class. You could project the answers using the TTL.

**Answers**
Fish: *seahorse*, angelfish, clownfish, shark
Not Fish: *octopus*, whale, dolphin, coral, jellyfish, starfish, sea turtle

**E** TRACK 90 TB p. 224 **Listen and complete. Then watch and sing.**

- Point to the song title *Under the Sea* and read the lyrics from the chorus. Ask *What sea creatures do you see?* and elicit suggestions, having students name sea creatures from the picture. Then play the song once, allowing students to listen and enjoy it.
- Ask *Can you remember what the missing words are?* Play the song again, this time pausing where necessary for students to write their answers.
- Check answers as a class.
- Play the video and encourage students to sing and move to the music as they watch.

**Answers**
1 *whale* 2 dolphins 3 jellyfish 4 seahorse
5 starfish 6 clownfish

**International English**

Elicit that *ocean floor* is American English and *seabed* is British English. Ask *Which do we use?*

### Cool Down

Play *Backs to the Board* (see TB p. 25) with the sea creatures from A.

**Practice** **Student's App:** Vocabulary Practice; Song Video

# Explore Language

## Lesson Objectives

- to review simple present and present progressive
- to practice sea life vocabulary

**Materials**

Audio Tracks 91 and 92

## Warm Up

Ask students to remember the scene from the vocabulary lesson. Ask *What was Hassan's family doing? What sea life did they see? What do you think they are going to see next?*

**A** TRACK 91 TB p. 224 **Listen and read. What's the word for a group of fish that swims together?**

- Tell students that they are going to listen to Hassan's family on the boat again. Ask *What are they looking at?* Play the audio and have students follow the dialogue in their books. Elicit the answer (a coral reef).
- Ask the comprehension question *What's the word for a group of fish that swims together?* and elicit the answer. Ask *What fish can they see?* and play the audio again. Check answers as a class (coral, small fish, sharks, large fish, angelfish).

**Answers**

a school

**B** **Look at A. Complete.**

- Write or project the table onto the board.
- Have students discuss the grammar and complete the table in pairs using the dialogue.
- Check answers on the board. Discuss the differences between the verb forms together. Let your class guide the discussion. If you feel that students need more guidance, the **ETB** provides a differentiation activity to help you support students as they explore the grammar table.
- Refer students to the *Look* box. Review adverbs of frequency with the class. Write the first sentence from the table on the board. Underline *often*. Ask *Do you know any more words like this?* (always, usually, never) Point out that we use the simple present with adverbs of frequency. Ask *Which time words do we use with present progressive?* (now, today)

**Answers**

swim; Is; swimming; are; swimming

**C** **Think and discuss. Then choose.**

- Have students work in pairs to discuss the sentences and answer options.
- Refer students to the table in B for examples. Then check answers. Ask students which words helped them figure out the answers (often, now).

**Answers**

1 simple present 2 present progressive

**Practice** **Resource Bank:** Grammar Printout
**Student's App:** Grammar Practice

**D** TRACK 92 TB p. 224 **Listen and say.**

- Tell students they're going to practice saying the structures. Play the audio, having students repeat each sentence chorally. For ideas on how to vary the drill, see TB p. 23.
- You may wish to remind students that *fish* can be either singular or plural and that they need to look for context clues in the sentence to tell them which one it is. Say *Can you replace the word "fish" with "they," as in item 3? Then it is plural. Can you replace the word "fish" with "it"? Then it is singular.*

**E** **Read and complete.**

- Tell students they are going to complete the sentences with verbs in the simple present or present progressive.
- Have students do the activity individually. Remind them to look at the table in B to help them. Check answers as a class by asking volunteers to read individual sentences aloud.

**Answers**

1 go; 're going 2 swims; 's swimming 3 hide; 're hiding
4 're swimming; swim

**F** **Play *Under the Sea*. You're a fish. Mime an activity you do often. Guess and ask.**

- Ask *What activities do fish do?* Brainstorm ideas with the class (e.g. look for food, sleep, play, swim, splash).
- Students are going to pretend they are fish and this is a day in their life under the sea. Have the class play in groups. One student in each group mimes an activity. The other students in the group guess the activity using the present progressive. The student who guesses correctly asks *How often do you …?* and the student who is miming answers. Students can think of any activity, even if it is not something a fish would normally do.
- Students continue to play in groups as long as time and interest allow.

## Cool Down

Have students play a TPR game in pairs. One student describes a series of events using the present progressive and simple present, and the other student acts it out; for example, *You're playing ball on the beach. You're running and jumping. The ball goes in the water. You're running into the water to get the ball. You see a jellyfish!*

## Global Citizenship

### Lesson Objectives

- to learn patterns vocabulary: *aquarium; clear, flat, horizontal, round, spotted, striped, vertical; protect, save*
- to explore why sea life is important and how we can protect the sea and its life
- to practice listening for gist and specific details

**Materials**

Audio Tracks 93 to 95; Audio Track H; a globe or map of the world (D)

### Opening Question

Ask the opening question: *Why is sea life important?* Remind students of their discussion of trees and plants in Unit 2. Say *Forests and other biomes are important for our planet. Oceans are also important. Why?* Have students suggest ideas. Don't correct them or give much feedback; students will find out more about the topic during the lesson.

**A** TRACK 93 TB p. 224 **Listen to Anya and Dean talk about fish. Why are they different shapes and colors?**

- Tell students they are going to listen to two children talking about fish. Elicit the answer, then play the audio and have students point to the words or pictures as they listen. Check the answer. (They're in an aquarium.)
- Ask the gist question *Why are they different shapes and colors?* Elicit the answer, then play the audio again for students to check. Ask *Does the aquarium help fish?* (Yes, it keeps them safe.)

**Answer**

Their shapes and colors protect them.

**B** TRACK 94 TB p. 224 **Listen, say, and number the pictures in A.**

- Play the audio and have students point to the pictures and say the words.
- Tell students to listen again and write numbers next to the words in the pictures. Do the example together (striped).
- Check answers by calling out the numbers and having students "buzz" to answer the question. Alternatively, project the answers using the TTL.

**Answers**

1 *striped* 2 spotted 3 vertical 4 horizontal 5 flat 6 round 7 clear 8 save 9 protect 10 aquarium

TRACK H TB p. 224 **Visualization**

The TTL has a visualization audio track for this vocabulary set. (See TB p. 21.)

**C Read and complete. Then match.**

- Students are going to match two sentence halves containing the key vocabulary. Write the example on the board and remind students of the meaning of *so*. Say *We use "so" to talk about the cause of something. A jellyfish is clear so big fish can't see it. This means that big fish can't see it because it is clear.*
- Have students do the activity individually. Then check answers as a class.

**Answers**

1 *clear; b* 2 flat; c 3 striped; d 4 Vertical; a 5 aquarium; e

**D** TRACK 95 TB p. 224 **Now listen to Yasmin and Li Li. What's special about their aquariums?**

- Have students look at the two pictures and say what they see. Ask *What does the shark look like? Do you think it's dangerous?*
- Listening for gist: tell students they are going to listen to two children talking about aquariums. Draw students' attention to the countries: United Arab Emirates and China. You could point out the countries on a globe or map. Ask *Do you think the two aquariums will be similar or different?* Have students share their ideas.
- Ask the gist question *What's special about their aquariums?* Play the audio. Elicit answers from the class.

**Answers**

The Dubai Aquarium is one of the biggest aquariums in the world. The Shanghai Ocean Aquarium has one of the longest underwater tunnels in the world.

**E Listen again. Check (✔) the correct city.**

- Listening for details: have students look at the questions before they listen again to see what they remember. Then play the audio and have students check the correct city.
- To check answers, read each question and have students raise their left hand for *Shanghai* and their right hand for *Dubai*. Then ask *Which aquarium would you like to visit more? Why?*

**Answers**

1 *Shanghai* 2 Dubai 3 Shanghai 4 Dubai 5 Dubai 6 Dubai

### Discussion Questions

- Draw students' attention to the discussion questions: *What can you do to help protect the sea? Where can people learn more about the sea?* Have students discuss the questions in pairs or small groups. See **ETB**.
- Return to the opening question to ask again: *Why is sea life important?* Review the ideas discussed at the beginning of the class and then encourage students to share any new ideas. Focus on how the oceans and sea life are the biggest ecosystem and we depend on it for water, oxygen to breathe, food, and some medicines.

### Cool Down

Play a word association game. Give an example. Say *shark* and ask a volunteer to say a word associated with shark. The next student then continues; for example, *Shark, teeth, dentist, chair, table, …* Play as a whole class or in groups.

**Practice** **Student's App:** Vocabulary Practice; Listening Practice

## Explore Language

### Lesson Objectives

- to learn to make simple future predictions: *will*
- to practice patterns vocabulary

**Materials**

Audio Tracks 96 and 97; a ball (CD)

### Warm Up

With books closed, tell students that you are going to tell them about a new kind of fish. Say *It's a lionfish! What does it look like? What color is it? Is it big or small? Is it round or flat? Is it striped or spotted? Does it look like a lion?* Ask volunteers to share their ideas with the class.

**A** TRACK 96 TB p. 224 **Listen and read. What are the boys going to do?**

- Have students open their books and look at the picture of the lionfish. Ask *Is it how you imagined?* Tell students that they are going to listen to Ahmad and his friend Daniel after they get off the boat. Have students look back at p. 102 to find the two boys. Play the audio and have students follow the dialogue in their books.
- Ask the gist question *What are the boys going to do?* and elicit answers.

**Answer**

They're going to try to catch a lot of lionfish.

**B Look at A. Complete.**

- Write or project the table onto the board.
- Have students discuss and complete the grammar table in pairs, using the dialogue in A.
- Check answers on the board. Discuss the word order, word forms, and meaning of the sentences and questions, but let your class guide the discussion. If you feel that students need more guidance, the **ETB** provides a differentiation activity to help you support students as they explore the grammar table.
- Encourage students to notice that there is only one form of *will* and *won't*. Elicit that in questions *will* goes before the subject and that we don't contract *will* in questions.
- Finally, review the short answer forms.
- Refer students to the *Look* box. Drill the pronunciation of the contractions. Have students suggest example sentences using different verbs. Write these on the board and drill them.

**Answers**

won't; will; Will; have; will; won't

**C Think and discuss. Then choose.**

- Ask students what a prediction is (they should know this from the **Literacy Book**). Write an example from the table on the board: *We'll catch some lionfish.* Ask *Do they know this for sure?* Elicit that they don't know but they think it is going to be true.
- Then have students work in pairs to discuss the sentence. Check the answer as a class.

**Answer**

1 the future

**D** TRACK 97 TB p. 224 **Listen and say.**

- Tell students they're going to practice saying the new structures. Play the audio, having students repeat each sentence chorally. For ideas on how to vary the drill, see TB p. 23.

**E Put the words in order.**

- Look at the example with students. Elicit that the beginning and end of each sentence are easy to identify: a sentence begins with a capital letter and ends with a period, question mark, or exclamation point.
- Say *Now write the words in order to make sentences.* Have students do the activity individually. Check answers by asking volunteers to write individual sentences on the board or by projecting them using the TTL.

**Answers**

1 *In three years, the seawater will be clean again.*
2 You won't catch many fish tomorrow.
3 Will you visit the aquarium again next year?
4 People who care about sea life will save the coral reefs in the future.
5 Next week, the sand will be warmer at the beach.
6 Next summer, my family will go on vacation.

**F Play a game. Predict the future. What will sea life be like in ten years?**

- Do a quick visualization. Have students close their eyes. Say *Imagine it's ten years into the future. You take a boat trip. What will your boat be like? Look through the glass bottom of the boat. What will you see? Will there be new animals? Will there be any animals missing? Will any be in danger?*
- Give students time to write a prediction, using *will* or *won't*. Then divide the class into two teams, standing in two lines. The first person on each team has to say their prediction about sea life in the future. If the sentence is correct, the team gets a point. The first person of each team goes to the back and the next student on each team makes a statement. Continue until all team members have contributed. The team with the most points wins.

### Cool Down

Play *Pass the Ball* (see TB p. 25). Students have to make a prediction using *will* or *won't*.

**Practice** Resource Bank: Grammar Printout
Student's App: Grammar Practice

# Take the Stage

## Lesson Objectives

- to prepare and practice a presentation about an endangered animal
- to recognize and reproduce /h/ and /w/

**Materials**
Video; Audio Track 98

## Warm Up

Ask students which sea creature is their favorite. Ask *Why do you like it? What do you know about it?* Have students talk about their favorite sea creatures in pairs.

**A** TB p. 239 **Watch and listen. What happened after people stopped catching blue whales?**

- Tell students they are going to watch a video of a girl named Anya giving a presentation about a sea creature. Have students look at the picture. Ask *Which animal is she going to talk about?* (a blue whale) Ask volunteers to give any information they know about blue whales. Then play the video and ask students to notice Anya's body language when she gives the presentation.
- Ask the comprehension question *What happened after people stopped catching blue whales?* Play the video again and then check the answer. Ask further comprehension questions; for example, *What color are blue whales? How heavy are they?*

**Answer**
The number of whales began to grow again.

**B** **Watch again. Check (✔) the phrases you hear.**

- Have students read the phrases.
- Play the video again and have students check the phrases they hear. Check answers as a class.
- Have students classify the sentences into *Beginning, Middle,* and *End.* Then, with the class, build up the presentation on the board, using the phrases.

**Answers**
*l*; 3; 5; 6; 7

### Pronunciation /h/ and /w/

TRACK 98 TB p. 225 **Listen and say.**

Demonstrate the two sounds first. Point out that both sounds are soft sounds. Show students how air comes out of your mouth as you say **/h/**. Have students put their hand in front of their mouth to feel the air. Have students notice that they don't need to move their mouth to say this sound.

To make **/w/**, students need to round their mouths to make a narrow space for the air to come out.

Play the audio and have students repeat the words. Repeat if students need more practice.

Say *These words are used in the video. What other words do you know with these sounds?* Elicit ideas and write them on the board in two columns (e.g. *horizontal, will*). Drill the pronunciation of each word.

**Suggested Answers**
/h/ harp, harvest, hat, head, heavy, help, helicopter, hit, hold
/w/ work, winter, whistle, when, wet

**C** **Plan. Think about a sea creature you learned about in this unit. How can we protect it? Check (✔) and complete.**

- Complete a graphic organizer on the board for Anya's presentation with the students' help. Elicit a description of the blue whale, the problem, and solutions.
- Then draw students' attention to the table in their books. Tell them that they are going to plan their own presentation. They need to choose a sea creature they're interested in, describe it, and think about the problems it may face and how we can help. Ask *How can you describe your sea creature?* (color, size, etc.) They may want to do additional research, if time allows.
- If students have chosen the same sea creature, they could do a Rally Robin routine to generate ideas (see TB p. 20).
- Have students complete the table individually.

**D** **Prepare your presentation. Use your ideas from C and phrases from B.**

- Draw students' attention to the index cards they will use to plan their presentation. Ask *How many parts will your presentation have?* (three) *What is the first part?* (introduction) *What will you say here?* (which sea creature I am talking about) *What will you say next?* (a brief description of the animal) Elicit the two middle stages (problem and solution), then ask how students can end their presentation (saying what the situation is now).
- Have students prepare their presentations using their notes in C and phrases from B. Monitor and provide language help as needed.

**E** **Practice with a friend. Then share with your class.**

- Have students practice their presentation with their partner as many times as they like. They can use the information on their index cards the first few times they practice, but they should try not to read their cards.
- Have one or two students demonstrate their presentation in front of the class. Remind students to look at the faces in the audience and to smile!

## Cool Down

Play *Silly Sentence.* Have students work in pairs to make up a sentence containing as many words beginning with **/h/** and **/w/** as they can. This could be a question beginning with a *Wh–* word, e.g.: *What will the happy whales have for lunch on the weekend?*



**Practice** **Student's App:** Speaking Skills Practice; Speaking Video

## Write About It

### Lesson Objectives

- to learn to use synonyms
- to plan and write a concrete poem

**Materials**
A short poem about a sea creature (WU); (optional) Support, Standard, and Challenge writing printouts from the Resource Bank, one per student (C and D)

### Warm Up

Find a short poem that is of a suitable level and topic for students. An example might be Meish Goldish's *Sea Animals* or his *Sea Creatures*. Read the poem to the class. Then ask *What did you imagine? What words do you remember? Did you like the poem?*

**A Read the concrete poems. Why do they look like this?**

- Introduce students to the concept of a concrete poem. Ask *What is a poem?* and elicit suggestions. Students read a poem in Levels 1 and 2. Elicit some features of poems such as a title, rhyme (e.g. *cat, sat, mat*), stanzas (the equivalent of a paragraph in prose writing), imagery (similes, e.g. as big as an elephant, hot like the sun), and metaphors (e.g. my life is an open book). Point out that although some poems rhyme, they don't have to. Have students open their books and look at the poems on the page. Ask *What do you notice about these poems?*
- Have students read the poems silently, then read them to the class. Ask *What are the poems about?* (The first one is about fish; the second is about starfish.) Ask *Why do they look like this?* Elicit that the poems take the shape of what the poem is about. Then ask students' opinions: *Do you like these poems? Does the shape make the poems more interesting to read? Which one do you like best? Why?*

**Answer**
Because the first poem is about a fish and the second poem is about a starfish.

**B Look at A. Find synonyms for these words and phrases. Write.**

- Remind students of the meaning of *synonym*: a word with the same meaning. Draw their attention to the example to illustrate this.
- Have students look at the words in B and try to find words with the same meaning in A. Then check answers as a class. Ask *Why do we use synonyms?* Elicit that it is good to use different words rather than repeating the same words. Have students think of other synonyms they might know. Common synonyms are smart / clever; noisy / loud; little / small; angry / mad; frightened / scared.

**Answers**
1 *fast* 2 tiny 3 ocean 4 beautiful 5 colorful

**Practice** Student's App: Writing Practice

**C Plan. Think about a topic for your concrete poem. Complete.**

- Tell students they are going to write their own concrete poems, using a table to help them plan.
- Draw students' attention to the table. Brainstorm a few topics with the class. These could be sea creatures from the unit or anything the students are interested in. Encourage students to think about topics they know about or any hobbies or interests they have. Tell students to choose a shape that represents their topic (e.g. a poem about spring could be in the shape of a flower).
- Then have students work individually to brainstorm words, phrases, and ideas that they have about their topic. Encourage them to think of as many things as possible so they will have plenty of ideas to choose from when they go on to write their concrete poem. Remind them to think of synonyms. Students have the opportunity to write down anything they wish, providing it is connected to the topic. Encourage them to be as imaginative as possible. Challenge printouts can be handed now.

**D Write your concrete poem.**

- Have students read the steps for the instructions. Make sure students know that their shape needs to be big enough to write the entire poem in. Remind them to use at least one synonym. Students write their poems, editing as they go. This first version is a draft, so students can experiment with size and shape. Ask students to use a pencil, not a pen, so they have the option to erase and rewrite or redraw as they edit. Support printouts can be handed out now.
- Students should either self-correct or exchange their work with a friend and peer-correct. You can put a checklist of things to correct on the board (e.g. spelling, use of adjectives and adverbs, punctuation, synonyms).
- Have students write their poems neatly on paper. Alternatively, hand out the Standard printouts from the Resource Bank. Students can add small illustrations or a frame around their concrete poem.

### Cool Down

Display the poems around the classroom and give students time to circulate and read each other's work. Have students choose their favorite poem, try to learn the poem, and recite it to the student who wrote it.

# Think It Over

## Lesson Objectives

- to review what has been learned in the unit
- to reflect on the unit and their own progress
- to think about learning strategies and how to continue learning at home

### Warm Up

Ask students what the unit theme was (sea life) and write it in the middle of the board. Brainstorm any words or phrases students can think of that relate to the topic and write them on the board. Encourage students to think about the different patterns sea creatures have and the dangers they face.

**Read the questions and draw or write your answers.**

- Give students time to think about and discuss activities in the unit before they complete each question. Explain that they can choose either to write a few words or sentences, or to draw a picture. Allowing students to make a personal response will help them retain knowledge and engage with the learning points.

**What did I do?**

- Give students a few minutes to look back through the unit at the different activities they did. Ask questions about the unit or write questions on the board; for example, *What sea creatures can you remember? Where are Anya and Dean?* Have them discuss their ideas in pairs or small groups.
- Encourage students to identify something in the unit that they found challenging or something that was particularly memorable for them, but tell them not to choose their favorite activity yet. Students can draw or write about their chosen activity.

**What did I learn?**

- Ask questions about the unit to help students think about what they learned; for example, *What did you learn about sea life? What sentences can you say using "will"? What did you learn about poems? What did you learn about different aquariums in the world? What else did you learn?* Have students discuss their ideas in pairs.
- Encourage students to draw a picture or write sentences about their learning outcomes.

**What was my favorite part?**

- Have students look back through the unit and decide what they enjoyed the most. Tell them it can be a funny dialogue, an interesting text, a favorite character, a speaking game, or a role-play activity. They should try to choose just one activity. Have students write or draw about the thing they liked the most. Remind students when we like something, it's often easier to learn.

**How well did I do?**

- Tell students to color the number of schools of fish that best expresses how well they have learned the unit content. Ask *What do you understand? What do you need to practice more?* Encourage students to look back through the unit to see how much they remember, what they did well, and what they found difficult.

**What can I do next?**

- Brainstorm ideas with the class about what they can do to continue to learn (e.g. think about how we can help protect sea creatures, find and pronounce words with **/h/** and **/w/**, visit an aquarium, write another concrete poem, make predictions about next week).
- Draw students' attention to the *What can I do next?* box. Encourage students to think about what they can do at home to improve their English. Have them suggest some verbs that they can use (e.g. make, visit, write, discuss, research) and write the verbs they choose in their books. Students can look back at the previous units to get more ideas. Encourage students to suggest their own ideas for different activities they can do.
- Have students choose several activities that they would like to do and write them in their notebooks. They can then share their ideas with a friend.

### Looking Forward

Draw students' attention to the character at the bottom of the page. Ask *Who's this?* and elicit what they remember about him (Daniel appears in the Vocabulary and second Explore Language lesson, p. 100 and p. 106; he was on a boat looking at sea creatures; he wanted to catch lionfish).

Draw students' attention to Daniel's question: *How do I feel?* Encourage students to make predictions about how he feels in Unit 9. Have them notice how he has his hand on his stomach and think about why he might be doing that.

Ask *What do you think Unit 9 is about?* and elicit suggestions from the class. Tell students they will find the answer in Lesson 1 of the next unit.

## Put It Together

To further review and recycle the language in Units 7 and 8, play the game, *Crossword Clues*, on pp. 112–113. See TB p. 209 for teaching notes.

**Practice** **Resource Bank:** Unit Test
**Student's App:** Vocabulary and Grammar Review

## Get Ready to Read

### Lesson Objectives

- to activate prior knowledge about sea life
- to guide inquiry and deepen understanding through a Question Starts VTR
- to preview the reading skill of identifying perspective

**Materials**

(Optional) VTR printout from the Resource Bank (Activities A, B, C)

### Warm Up

Pre-teach *diver* by drawing a simple picture on the board. Tell students to imagine they are a diver. Ask them to close their eyes and imagine everything they can see during their dive. Encourage them to think of animals and plants, as well as things that have been left behind by people. Then have them open their eyes and share their ideas with the class. Write their ideas on the board.

### Question Starts

**A Look at the picture. Then brainstorm questions. Write a list.**

Students are going to do a Question Starts VTR to explore the image of the seabed.

- Have students look at the picture for a minute and then say what they can see. If students don't know a word in English, ask them to describe what they see so you can provide the word.
- Draw students' attention to the question words.
- Give students a few minutes to write questions in their notebooks, based on the prompts.
- Encourage students to raise their hands to suggest questions. Write all the suggestions on the board, helping students correct their questions, when needed.

**B Look at your list from A. Which questions seem the most interesting? Discuss them with the class.**

- Ask students to look at their list of questions individually and identify the questions they would most like to know the answers to.
- Tell students that they are going to work as a group to decide which three questions they want to ask. Have students work in groups of three to review the questions and discuss possible answers. This will help them decide which questions they think are the most interesting. Have students write the questions in their books. Then discuss them as a class and decide on the most interesting questions.

Here's an example of this part of the routine.

**Teacher:** Which questions seem the most interesting? What do you really want to know?
**Student A:** Why is he holding his hand up?
**Teacher:** Good question! Why do you think?
**Student A:** To stop the shark.
**Teacher:** Does everyone agree?
**Student B:** I think he's going to touch the shark.
**Teacher:** Why do you say that?
**Student B:** He doesn't look scared.
**Teacher:** Great. What other questions do you have?
**Student C:** What's in that box?

**C What new ideas or questions do you have now? Talk about your ideas with your partner.**

- Encourage students to think about ideas and questions about the sea and sea animals globally. They shouldn't limit their ideas to what they see in the picture. Refer students to the example questions and give them a couple of minutes to think of their own questions. Then have students share their questions in pairs and discuss any possible answers.
- Encourage students to ask all the questions they want, including any generated in the discussion they had earlier in the lesson.

### Transition

Ask students who they think the diver is. Ask *What's his job? What makes you say that?* Then ask *Do you think he is scared? Why or why not?*

**D Think and discuss. Which animal in the ocean is the scariest?**

- Encourage students to look at the picture again and decide if the shark is scary. Have students work in pairs to think of other sea creatures and decide if they are scary. They should then decide which is the scariest. They can do this by ranking in order, from the least scary to the scariest.
- Have pairs share their ideas with the class and write them on the board. You could then take a vote to find out which animal the class thinks is the scariest.

**E Think, write, and share. Choose an animal that lives in the ocean. Imagine you are that animal. How do you feel?**

In this activity students will preview the reading skill of identifying perspective.

- Brainstorm sea creatures and write them on the board. Choose an animal together. Tell students to imagine they are that animal, living in the ocean. Ask *How do you feel?* Encourage students to think of different things that might affect the animal's feelings (e.g. access to food, relationships with other animals, human interventions).
- Have students work individually to choose an animal and write their ideas about how it feels.
- Then have students share their ideas in small groups.

**Answer**
Students' own answers

Now read **Coral Reefs**

# Nonfiction: *Coral Reefs*—Persuasive Text

## Lesson Objectives

- to read a persuasive text about coral reefs
- to make a personal connection to the reading

**Materials**
Audio Tracks 40 and 41; Video; pictures of coral (WU); large pieces of paper (one for each group) (CD)

## Warm Up

Ask students to find the title of the reading, *Coral Reefs*. Ask *What's coral? Is it a plant or an animal?* Show them pictures of coral as an organism and in jewelry. Encourage students to make a connection between the two. Ask *Which picture shows coral before? Where does coral live?* Don't tell students if they are right or wrong at this stage; they will find out when they read the text.

### TRACK 40 TB p. 235 Reading Approach

**First Reading: Engage with the Text**

- Ask students to notice the text and pictures, and use this information to predict ideas about the reading.
- Have students close their books. Play the video and ask students to listen for the answer to the gist question *Is coral an animal or a plant?* (an animal) Elicit the answer. Ask *Does coral swim?* (no)
- Then look at the Words in Context.

### TRACK 41 TB p. 235 Words in Context

- Play the audio and have students repeat the words.
- Have students race to find the words in the reading.
- Remind students to **read the next words to get clues to explain the meaning of a new word** (see TB p. 23). Have students work in pairs to try to figure out the meaning of each word in context
- Use these discussion points to confirm the meanings.

**stick** (p. 122) Say *A polyp is a tiny creature. It sticks to rocks and later this becomes coral.* Use gesture to demonstrate *stick*. Make a fist with one hand to represent a rock and use your other hand to represent polyps. Have students copy you. Ask *Do polyps fall off the rocks?* (no)

**shallow** (p. 122) Tell students that we say *shallow* when there isn't a lot of water. Say *When you go to the beach and put your feet in the water, is it shallow or deep?*

**creatures** (p. 122) Have students notice the conjunction *such as*. Tell students that we use this to give examples. Ask *Can you find another word for "creatures"?* Elicit *animals*.

**waste** (p. 123) Ask *What comes from big cities and goes into the sea?* (waste/dangerous chemicals) Explain that *including* tells us that *dangerous chemicals* are connected to *waste*. Tell students that *waste* is like *trash* but it can be in a liquid or a gas form.

**damage** (p. 123) Read the sentence *People who visit the reefs can touch the coral and damage them.* Ask *Do you think it is good to touch the coral?* Explain that when you touch or stand on coral, it can get hurt or die.

**marine park** (p. 123) Have students notice the example of the marine park ("The Gardens of the Queen"). Ask *What does the marine park do?* (It protects the coral reef.)

**Second Reading: Analyze the Text and Features**

- Have students open their books. Play the audio and have students follow along.
- Ask some questions to check comprehension: *How do coral get their bright colors?* (from algae) *Which animals need coral?* (sea turtles, starfish, urchins) *How do big cities affect the sea?* (The waste they produce goes into the sea.)
- Discuss the questions in the blue boxes.
  - **Fact** (p. 122): *About two million species live in, on, and around coral reefs. That's 25 percent of all sea creatures!* Elicit that 25 percent is one-quarter of something and draw a pie chart on the board to make this more visual. Ask *What kinds of animals live near coral reefs?* and elicit suggestions from the class.
  - **Making Connections** (p. 123): *What can people do to protect coral reefs?* Recap how people are protecting the reef in Cuba (no one can go fishing there, and very few tourists can visit it). Ask students to think of other things we can do; for example, take part in clean-up days, don't leave trash on the beach, and don't buy coral jewelry.
- Point out the text focus *Look for captions under pictures. What information do they give you?* Have students identify the captions in the text. Ask *How do the captions help you?* Elicit that captions help us understand what we see in the pictures.

**Third Reading: Interact with the Text**

- Play the video on mute and have students take turns narrating it in pairs or small groups as if they were a documentary presenter.

## Cool Down

Have students sit in groups of four. Give each group a large piece of paper. Each group then draws five boxes (one on each side of the paper, and one large box in the middle. Each student writes three things they learned from the lesson in one box of the graphic organizer. Students then share their ideas with the rest of the group and choose three ideas they have in common. They write these ideas in the middle box.

**Practice** **Student's App:** Nonfiction Video

# Explore the Reading

## Lesson Objectives

- to understand and analyze *Coral Reefs* through reading comprehension activities
- to learn about marine biology through CLIL (science) focus: exploring the importance of protecting coral reefs
- to reproduce and write words with *–ght*.

**Materials**
Video; Audio Tracks 40 and 42

## Warm Up

Play *Unscramble* with words from the reading (see TB p. 27).

Suggested anagrams and words: *yoplps* (polyps), *lnigusht* (sunlight), *stiasrfh* (starfish), *eratsucre* (creatures) *setwa* (waste) *mgdeaa* (damage)

**A Write *True* or *False*. Write the page where you found the answer.**

- If more than one day has passed since students read *Coral Reefs*, play the video again.
- With books closed, have a Group Time discussion (see TB p. 21) to check students' comprehension of the reading. Ask *What do coral look like?* (mushrooms, trees, brains, and fingers) *How many types of coral are there?* (two—soft and hard) *When do polyps turn into coral?* (after hundreds of years) *Why do animals live in or near coral?* (for shelter/food) *Where are people protecting coral?* (in Abu Dhabi and Cuba)
- Have students open their books and look at the example sentence. Say *Is it true or false? Can you find this in the reading?* Have students look back and find the information on p. 122.
- Have students do the rest of the activity individually. Check answers as a class.

**Answers**
1 *True; 122* 2 False; 122 3 True; 122 4 False; 122
5 True; 123

**B Find the headings in *Coral Reefs*. Write. Then match to the main idea.**

- Recap what a heading is (students looked at headings in the text focus in Unit 2). Elicit that it is a sentence or question that tells us what a part of the text is about. Give students a few seconds to underline the headings in the reading. Then review *main idea* and elicit that it is the main point or most important thought about a topic.
- Have students read the example heading. Point out that b is the main idea of this heading. Tell students to match the headings they underlined to the other main idea sentences, and write them in their books.

**Answers**
1 *A World of Tiny Animals; b* 2 Reefs as Shelter; d
3 Are Coral Reefs in Danger?; a 4 Protecting Coral Reefs; c

**C Read and complete. Why are coral reefs in danger?**

- With books closed, ask the question and elicit suggestions.
- Then have students open their books and look at the phrases in the box. Check students' comprehension of the phrases by asking questions; for example, *What is sunlight? What's another word for damage? What are algae?*
- Have students complete the sentences in their books, looking back at the reading, where necessary. Then check answers as a class.

**Answers**
1 the algae leave 2 there isn't enough sunlight
3 they can damage them

**D Think and discuss. Why is it important to protect coral reefs?**

Students are going to explore the CLIL science focus: the importance of protecting coral reefs.

- Ask *Why is it important to protect coral reefs?* and elicit one or two answers from the class. Then have students discuss their ideas in pairs.
- Bring the class together and recap how and why we should help protect coral reefs. If necessary, draw students' attention to the prompt *It's important because …*

## Spelling Pattern *–ight*

TRACK 42 TB p. 235 **Listen and write. Then check your answers.**

- With books closed, write *–ight* on the board and elicit the pronunciation.
- Play the first part of the audio and have students repeat each word. Then have them open their books. Play the audio again and have them complete as many words as they can.
- Then play the second part of the audio for students to check their spelling and complete the words correctly. Have them read the words aloud.
- Have students look back at the reading to find more words with *–ight* and read them aloud. Have students write all the *–ght* words from this lesson in a spidergram. Encourage them to add to the spidergram as they come across more *–ight* words.

**Answers**
1 night 2 right 3 tight 4 fight 5 lightning
From the reading: bright, sunlight

## Cool Down

Play *60 Seconds* (see TB p. 25).

**Practice** **Resource Bank:** Spelling Printout
**Student's App:** Reading Practice; Spelling Pattern Practice

# Get Ready to Read

## Lesson Objectives

- to practice the reading skill of identifying perspective
- to activate prior knowledge about different characters in stories
- to make a personal connection to the reading

## Warm Up

Show students a picture of one of the characters in the story. If you are using the TTL, project and enlarge one of the images from p. 125. Alternatively, have students look at the pictures in their books and choose one. Ask *What can you guess about this character? How old is he/she? What does he/ she like? Does he/she have brothers and sisters?* Have students build up a profile of the character using their imaginations. Students could complete a fact file about the character including the following information: name, age, nationality/ species (depending on which character it is), family, likes and dislikes, personality, and interesting fact. Have students share their ideas with the class.

**A Think and discuss. Look back at *What Happens Next?* on page 106. Who's telling the story about the earthquake? Imagine Mr. Carlson tells the story. How does the story change?**

Students are going to practice the reading skill of identifying perspective.

- Recap what students remember about the story from Unit 7. Ask *What happened? Who tells the story?* (Ken) *How does Ken feel?*
- Tell students to imagine that Mr. Carlson is telling the story, not Ken. Ask *What does Mr. Carlson say? How does he feel? Is he scared? What does he say to the students?* Have students discuss their ideas in pairs.
- Then help students understand that sometimes an outsider might be telling the story rather than a character. Tell students that this person knows everything and can give us information about a lot of different characters.
- Draw students' attention to the skills box and have them read it silently. Check comprehension by asking *Do all the characters in a story have the same opinions? Do they feel the same? Why not?*

**B Scan *The Lost Camera*. Which characters speak? Check (✔).**

- Draw students' attention to the instructions. Recap what *scan* means (to read quickly to identify specific information). Ask *How do we know someone is speaking in a reading?* Elicit that we can see quotation marks or speech bubbles and words like *said*, *told*, *asked*, and *whispered*. Tell students to look at the story very quickly to find out which characters speak. To ensure students don't read the story, set a time limit (e.g. one minute) for them to find and check the names in their books.
- Check answers as a class. Ask *Why do you think Dollie doesn't speak?* (possible answer: she's a pet)

**Answers**

Sandy, Fin, Dr. Crab

**C Read and write. Who's telling the story?**

Students are going to practice the reading skill of identifying perspective. Tell them to read the text.

- Draw students' attention to the phrase *My sister and I*. Ask *Who is "I"?* Have students write the character's name in their books.
- Ask *How do we know? Which part of the story gives us the answer?* Have students discuss their answers in pairs. Then check answers as a class. ("I'm coming Fin," she said to me.)
- Point out that Fin is telling the story here and he has his own version of how things happened and why. Ask students if they always feel the same as their brothers/ sisters/cousins/friends. Explain that in the same way Fin's feelings and experiences aren't the same as his sister's. If his sister was telling the story she might tell it differently!

**Answer**

Fin

## Cool Down

Tell students they are going to think about what different characters might be thinking in different stories in the **Literacy Book**. Show a scene from the stories and ask *What is* (name) *thinking?* Have students discuss their ideas in pairs.

Suggested scenes: p. 34 Wen Shu has just seen the coins; p. 36 Wen Shu at the vet; p. 48 Jodie when she laughs at Paige; p. 53 Paige's dad in the kitchen; p. 63 Harry's dad when the car gets stuck in traffic; p. 67 Harry's mom watching the play; p. 84 the audience; p. 95 Amy after losing the competition.

**Now read The Lost Camera**

# Fiction: *The Lost Camera—Story*

## Lesson Objectives

- to read a story about a city under the sea
- to make a personal connection to the reading

**Materials**
Audio Tracks 43 and 44

## Warm Up

Review what students know about Fin from *The Lost Camera.* Ask *What do you know about Fin's family? Where is he going?* Encourage students to make predictions about what will happen in the story. Ask *Will Fin find the camera? What will he do with it? Will he take pictures?*

## TRACK 43 TB p. 235 Reading Approach

### First Reading: Engage with the Text

- Ask students to notice the title, text, and pictures on the page and use this information to predict further ideas about the reading.
- Play the audio and have students read along as they listen. Ask the prediction question in the blue box (p. 126) before moving on to the next page: *Do you think the diver will get her camera back?* Pause again at the end of p. 129 and ask *How can Fin and Sandy get to Mexico?* You could use an Option Explosion routine to generate ideas (see TB p. 21). Then finish reading the story and ask if any of their predictions were correct.
- Read the whole text before looking at the Words in Context.

## TRACK 44 TB p. 236 Words in Context

- Play the audio and have students repeat the words.
- Have students race to find the words in the reading.
- Remind students that sometimes they can **use words around the new words to guess their meaning** (see TB p. 23). Encourage students to identify synonyms, or to look for words that have some kind of connection to the new words.
- Use these discussion points to confirm the meanings.

**divers** (p. 126) Remind students where they have seen divers before (the shark picture). Ask *How many divers can you see in the picture?* (six) Point out that *diver* is the noun (the person) and *dive* is the verb (the action).

**surface** (p. 126) Ask *Where were the divers? Were they up at the top or at the bottom of the sea?* Elicit or explain that the surface is where the water ends and the air begins. Ask *Are Fin and Sandy near the surface?* (no)

**slipped** (p. 126) Have students read the sentence containing the word, and the following sentence. Remind students that sometimes the explanation comes in the next sentence. Which words are similar in the next sentence? (fell down)

**noticed** (p. 127) Encourage students to look at the pictures. Ask *Did anyone see the camera? Did the divers see it?* (no) Ask *Which word means "see"?*

**tag** (p. 128) Ask students to look at the camera strap (it's purple). Can they identify the tag? What information is written on the tag? Ask students *Do you use name tags on your clothes/things?*

**everywhere** (p. 130) Ask *Where did the diver look for her camera? Did she look in one place or a lot of places?* Elicit that *everywhere* means in *all* places.

### Second Reading: Analyze the Text and Features

- Play the audio again and have students read along chorally.
- Ask some questions to check comprehension: *Where do Fin and Sandy live?* (in Seaville, a city under the sea) *What did they find?* (a camera) *Where does Fin want to go?* (Mexico).
- Discuss the questions in the blue boxes. Use a Think, Pair, Share routine (see TB p. 20).
  - **Gist** (p. 127): *How do the creatures in Seaville travel around?* Have students look at the pictures to find the answer (they swim or ride dolphins).
  - **Language Focus** (p. 131): *Can you answer Sandy's question?* Have students look at the picture and identify what the children are making. Ask *Do you know this word?*
  - **Detail** (p. 131): *Why are they feeling sick?* Say *Sometimes when people are on a boat they feel sick. They are seasick. Why do Fin and Sandy feel sick? Where do they live? Do they usually breathe air?*

### Third Reading: Interact with the Text

- Tell students they are going to adapt the story into a play script. Elicit some features of a play script, such as stage directions, character names followed by colons, no quotation marks, etc. Explain that students will have to add dialogue to show what Fin is thinking, or include stage directions, e.g. Stage direction: Fin points.
  Fin: Look, there's a boat!
- Have students work in small groups and give each group a few lines of the story to work on. Help them change past tense thoughts into present tense dialogue, where appropriate.

## Cool Down

Have each group act out their section of the play to create a whole class performance.

## Explore the Reading

### Lesson Objectives

- to understand and analyze *The Lost Camera* through reading comprehension activities
- to make a personal connection to the reading
- to explore the SEL competency of social awareness by identifying social cues to determine how others feel

**Materials**

(Optional) Audio Track 43; handwritten cards with quotations from the reading (WU)

### Warm Up

Play *Who Said It?* (see TB p. 27). Example quotations: *Where's Mexico?* (Fin); *Let's take the camera back to Mexico!* (Sandy); *Dollie! Take us to the surface, please!* (Fin); *Let's swim to the boat!* (Sandy); *What are the children making?* (Sandy); *I'm feeling sick.* (Sandy); *Tell us what happened, Fin—EVERYTHING!* (Fin's mom); *It's a long story, Mom.* (Fin)

**A Read and choose.**

- If more than one day has passed since students read *The Lost Camera*, play the audio again.
- With books closed, ask questions about the reading; for example, *Where do Fin and Sandy live?* (Seaville) *What did Fin and Sandy find?* (a camera) *What did they decide to do?* (go to Mexico and give the camera back) *How did they travel?* (on a dolphin) *How did Sandy feel after?* (sick)
- Have students open their books and read the first sentence. Have them look back at the picture on pp. 126–127 to find out why no one saw the camera. Have students read the three options and choose the correct one. Ask students to explain why b and c are wrong. (The camera is the same size as the fish; it's easy to see the camera in the picture, so it isn't too dark.)
- Have students do the rest of the activity individually, looking back at the text to find the answers. Check answers as if it were a TV game show. Put students in teams and have them "buzz in" to answer each question.

**Answers**

1 a 2 c 3 a 4 b 5 c

**International English**

Refer students to the box on p. 127. Ask *Is this story written in American or British English? How do we know?* (American English because the author says the camera landed on the ocean *floor*).

**B Read and match. Imagine there's another scene of *The Lost Camera*. Who says each sentence?**

- Have students act out emotions for the class to guess. As they guess, write the adjectives on the board.
- Discuss with the class how the different characters felt in the story. Ask *How did Sandy and Fin feel when they went to Mexico? How did Sandy feel after staying above the surface? Was Dad angry? How did Mom react?*
- Draw students' attention to the activity. Say *Imagine the story continues and there's another scene.* Tell students to think about what might happen next. Brainstorm some ideas with the class. Then have students read the sentences and match them to the characters.
- Check answers as a class.

**Answers**

1 Sandy 2 Dr. Crab 3 Fin 4 Mom

**C Think and discuss. How would the story be different from Sandy's perspective?**

- Say *Now imagine Sandy is telling the story. How is it different? Does she see the same things as Fin or different things? What does Sandy think are the most important parts of the story?* Do a Think, Pair, Share routine (see TB p. 20).

**D Think, write, and discuss. Choose a character. How does he or she feel at the beginning, middle, and end of the story?**

- Students are going to use creative thinking skills and the SEL competency of identifying social cues to determine how others feel to adapt the story.
- Tell students they will choose one character and decide how he/she is feeling at the beginning, middle, and end of the story. Do an example with the class. Choose a character from the story (e.g. the diver). Make a spidergram on the board of what you and the class know about this character; for example, *She was diving in the ocean. / She was taking pictures of sea creatures. / She dropped her camera. / She was happy to get her camera back. / She was surprised when she saw the picture of Fin and Sandy.*
- Then have students help you classify the ideas into *Beginning, Middle,* and *End.*
- Tell students to choose a different character and think about what he/she did and how he/she felt at each stage of the story. Remind them to look back at the story and the pictures to help them.
- Have students work individually to complete the notes in their books. Then have them discuss their ideas in pairs.

**Answers**

Students' own answers

### Cool Down

Tell students to choose their favorite scene from the story and think about why they like it. Have students stand up and walk around the classroom talking to other students about their favorite scene and why they like it.



**Practice** **Student's App:** Reading Practice

## Think Together

### Lesson Objectives

- to make connections between the readings
- to explore the key concept: What is life like under the sea?
- to reflect on the unit and provide personal thoughts and opinions

### Warm Up

Have students look back at the VTR picture on pp. 120–121. Ask them to talk about similarities and differences between the VTR picture and each of the readings; e.g. *All the divers explore under the sea. I think this diver wants to know how sharks live, but the diver on p. 123 wants to learn about corals. Divers go down under the sea, but the children in the story go up to the surface.* Point out that the story is a *fantasy*. Have students make a Venn diagram to show the similarities and differences between the world in the story and the real world.

**A Think, discuss, and write. Look at the pictures in the unit. Complete the graphic organizer about what lives under the sea.**

- With books closed, write *Under the sea* on the board. Brainstorm a few ideas as a class about what lives under the sea and write their suggestions on the board.
- Have students work in pairs or small groups to look back through the unit. Tell them to look closely at the pictures and find examples of animals and other beings that live under the sea. Students should write their own ideas in the graphic organizer.

**Answers**
Students' own answers

**B Think and discuss. How is life under the sea different from life on land or in the air? Do an Inside–Outside Circle.**

Students are going to do some comparative thinking and build on the key concept in the unit: *What is life like under the sea?*

- Brainstorm ideas with the class first. Ask *How is life under the sea different from life on land or in the air?* Encourage students to think of different animals that live in the sea, on land, or in the air and how they live. Draw a table on the board and divide it into three columns: *Land, Sea, Air.* Every time students suggest an idea, write it in the correct column in the table.
- Ask two volunteers to complete the prompts in the book, using the information from the table; for example, *Under the sea there's coral, but on land there are bugs.*
- Then have students do an Inside–Outside Circle routine to share their ideas (see TB p. 20).

### My Reading Journal

**Which setting from this unit would you like to visit—a coral reef or Seaville?**

This question focuses on personalization. Ask students which place from the unit they would like to visit. Give students a few minutes to look back through the unit and decide which of the two places they would prefer to visit and think about why. Have students complete the sentence in their books and then compare with a partner.

**Example Answer**
I'd like to visit (a coral reef) because (it's real. I want to see all the different colors.)

**How can we help protect sea life? Make a list.**

This task encourages students to review what they learned and make connections to the real world. Give students time to look back through the unit and find ideas. You could allow them to do some online research on endangered sea creatures, such as Great White Sharks, to find out what we can do to help protect sea life. Have students write their ideas in their books.

**Example Answers**
Don't throw trash on the beach. Recycle as much as possible. Don't touch or walk on coral. Don't catch too many fish. Keep the beaches clean. Be careful where you swim.

### Cool Down

Play *Test the Teacher.* Students work in groups to write questions about information from the two readings. Encourage them to write questions with a variety of *Wh-* question words rather than writing yes/no questions. Make sure students write the answer next to the question. Each group then takes turns asking you a question. You must answer the question from memory! If you answer correctly, you get one point. If the answer is incorrect, the group gets one point.

**Practice** **Resource Bank:** Unit Test
**Student's App:** Key Concept Practice

UNIT 9

# What's the Matter?

## Unit Overview

### Themes

Illnesses, symptoms, and treatments

The history of medicine

### Synopsis

In this unit, students will explore the topic of health. They will learn about different illnesses and treatments and how to give advice. They will discuss the importance of keeping clean and what to do when we're sick. Students will plan and prepare a conversation giving health advice and write a letter to a friend.

**Language Book**

**Vocabulary**

*cold, cough, dizzy, earache, fever, headache, sick, sneeze, sore throat, stomachache*

p. 176

**Explore Language**

Past Progressive with *When*

p. 177

**Global Citizenship**

Why are doctors and nurses important?

*bandage, blood, broken arm, cast, germs, medicine, nurse, shot*

p. 178

**Explore Language**

Past Progressive with *While*

p. 179

**Talk About It**

Conversation: giving health advice

p. 180

**Write About It**

A Letter to a Friend

Spelling: simple past irregular verb forms

p. 181

**Think It Over**

Review and Reflection

p. 182

## Literacy Book

### Think Together
What do we do when we're sick?

p. 189

### Visible Thinking
Think, Pair, Share

p. 183

### Fiction
Story: *A Surprise Cure*

Words in Context: *scientist, bacteria, laboratory, mess, attack, liquid, penicillin*

p. 187

### Nonfiction
Informational Text: *Take Your Medicine*

Words in Context: *cure, treatments, patient, grind, opposites, disease*

p. 184

### Reading Skill
Understanding the main idea and details

p. 186

### Spelling Pattern
*ur*

p. 185

## Language and Literacy Connections

The connecting theme in Unit 9 is identifying health issues and how to treat them.

| | Language | Literacy |
|---|---|---|
| **Vocabulary** | **Set 1:** illnesses<br>**Set 2:** treatments | **Nonfiction:** earache, fever, sick, sore throat, bandage, blood, medicine, shot<br>**Fiction:** germs |
| **Grammar** | **Past Progressive with *When***<br>What were you doing when that sign fell down?<br>I was listening to the doctor when it fell down.<br>Were you holding the skeleton when the sign hit you?<br>Yes, I was. No, I wasn't.<br>**Past Progressive with *While***<br>Were you feeling sick while you were working with the children?<br>I was feeling hot and cold while I was helping you at the clinic.<br>While we were working, I was washing my hands a lot. | **Fiction**<br>When I looked in the dishes, something strange was happening.<br>While Dr. Fleming was working in hospitals, he saw many people die because of bacteria.<br>While the scientists were trying to make penicillin into medicine, they worked hard. |
| **Skills** | **Pronunciation:** /kw/ and /kr/ | **Reading:** understanding the main idea and details<br>**Spelling Pattern:** *ur* |
| **International English** | have a fever/have a temperature; sick/ill; clinic/health centre; shot/injection | shot/injection; sick/ill; mold/mould |

# Vocabulary

## Lesson Objectives

- to learn illnesses vocabulary: *cold, cough, dizzy, earache, fever, headache, sick, sneeze, sore throat, stomachache*
- to sing a song about feeling sick

**Materials**
Audio Tracks 99 to 102; Video

## Warm Up

Have students stand up behind their desks. Then call out instructions for students to shake different parts of their bodies, starting from the extremities—for example, *Shake your fingers, shake your hands, shake your arms, shake your feet*—until students are shaking their whole bodies. Then have them slowly relax each part of the body. Ask *Did that make you feel good?*

**A** TRACK 99 TB p. 225 **Listen and find. What's the matter with number three?**

- Have students work in pairs. Ask them to look at the picture and say *Imagine you're in this room. Walk around and describe what you can see and hear.* Have students take turns describing what they can see. They should try to describe different details (e.g. the spider on the window, the pictures on the wall).
- Tell students they are going to listen to two children, George and Heather, playing a game with the doctor. Have students find the game in the picture. Play the audio and have students point to the words or pictures as they listen.
- Ask the comprehension question *What's the matter with number three?* and elicit the answer.
- Ask *Can you see Daniel?* Remind students of the challenge from the end of Unit 8: *How do I feel?* If necessary, play the audio again and elicit the answer (sick, he has a stomachache).

**Answer**
She has a headache.

**International English**

Highlight the different phrases and encourage students to choose one of the two varieties of English and practice saying how they feel; for example, *I'm sick. I have a fever.*

**B** TRACK 100 TB p. 225 **Listen, say, and number the pictures in A.**

- Play the audio and have students point to the pictures and say the words.
- Tell students to listen again and write numbers next to the words in the picture. Do the example together (cough).
- Check answers by miming the illnesses and having students call out the corresponding number and word.

**Answers**
1 *cough* 2 sneeze 3 sore throat 4 cold
5 headache 6 earache 7 stomachache 8 dizzy
9 fever 10 sick

**C** TRACK 101 TB p. 225 **Close your eyes. Listen, visualize, and say.**

- Prepare students for the visualization (see TB p. 21).
- Play the audio, allowing students to visualize the ideas and do the actions as they listen.
- Have students draw picture a picture showing two things they visualized and tell a partner how they felt.

**D Look and write. Some words are used twice.**

- Students are going to classify the vocabulary by identifying which words are nouns, adjectives, or verbs. Draw students' attention to the table. Have them look at the example. Ask *What kind of word is "stomachache"?* (noun) Elicit that we use *I have …* with nouns. Then say *What do we always put after "going to"?* (a verb) Tell students that one of the words can be used here as both a noun *and* verb. Finally, point out that we use *I feel …* with adjectives. Explain that one word can be both a noun and adjective.
- Tell students to write the words from A in the table. Check answers as a class.

**Answers**
I have: *a stomachache*, a fever, a sore throat, a headache, a cold, a cough, an earache
I'm going to: sneeze, cough
I'm / I feel: sick, dizzy, cold

**E** TRACK 102 TB p. 225 **Listen and complete. Then watch and sing.**

- Point to the song title. Ask *What's the matter?* and elicit possible answers to the question. Encourage students to use phrases from D. Then play the song once, allowing students to listen and enjoy it.
- Have students try to remember the missing words. Play the song again, this time pausing where necessary for students to complete the words.
- Check answers as a class.
- Play the song video and encourage students to sing and do the actions like the children in the video.

**Answers**
1 cold 2 headache 3 coughing 4 sneezing
5 stomachache 6 dizzy 7 fever 8 earache

## Cool Down

Have students play *Mime It!* in pairs (see TB p. 26). Students take turns being the doctor and the patient. The patient mimes the illness, and the doctor diagnoses it.

**Practice** **Student's App:** Vocabulary Practice; Song Video

# Explore Language

## Lesson Objectives

- to review simple past and learn to use the past progressive with *when*
- to practice illnesses vocabulary

**Materials**
Audio Tracks 103 and 104

## Warm Up

Ask students to remember the scene from the previous lesson. Ask *What were the children doing? What was the matter with Daniel?* Tell students to remember a time when they felt sick. Ask *Can you remember what happened? Where were you? What did you do?* Have students discuss their ideas in pairs.

**A** TRACK 103 TB p. 225 **Listen and read. What happened to the sign and the skeleton?**

- Tell students that they are going to listen to Daniel talking to his friend George. Ask students to remember the scene from the previous lesson. Ask *What was George doing?* and elicit the answer. (He was standing next to the skeleton.) Play the audio and have students follow the dialogue in their books.
- Ask the gist question *What happened to the sign and the skeleton?* and elicit the answer. Ask *Why do you think George fell down?* and elicit suggestions from the class (the sign hit him).

**Answer**
They fell down.

**B** **Look at A. Complete.**

- Write or project the table onto the board.
- Have students discuss and complete the grammar table in pairs using the dialogue.
- Check answers on the board. Review the verb forms (past progressive and past simple) and how each one is made, subject–verb agreement for *be*, and word order for questions and statements. Let your class guide the discussion. Point out that there are two parts to each statement/question and elicit which word separates the two parts. If you feel that students need more guidance, the **ETB** provides a differentiation activity to help you support students as they explore the grammar table.
- Refer students to the Grammar tip *Remember.* Write on the board *I wasn't holding the skeleton.* and *The sign didn't fall on my leg.* Have a student underline the negative verb forms. Elicit more examples of negative sentences in the past progressive and simple past and write these on the board.

**Answers**
were; doing; fell; was; when; fell; weren't; holding; when; fell; holding; when; hit; was; wasn't

**C** **Think and discuss. Then choose.**

- Draw a timeline on the board using an everyday example to show what happens when that event is interrupted by another event; for example, *I was eating dinner when the cat jumped onto the table.* Use different colored chalk or markers to show the overlapping events.
- Have students work in pairs to discuss the sentences and answer options. Refer them to the table in B for examples. Then check answers.

**Answers**
1 past progressive 2 when

**D** TRACK 104 TB p. 225 **Listen and say.**

- Tell students they're going to practice saying the structures. Play the audio, having students repeat each sentence chorally.
- For ideas on how to vary the drill, see TB p. 23.

**E** **Read and complete. Write about you.**

- Students are going to complete the sentences with their own ideas. Look at the example together. Have students change the beginning of the sentence with a different idea; for example, *My mom was singing.*
- Have students complete the sentences individually. Remind them to look at the table in B to help them. Then have a few students share some of their answers with the class.

**Answers**
Students' own answers (must use the correct past form)

**F** **Play *Silly Conversation*. Complete and say. Who has the silliest sentences?**

- Explain to students that they are going to play a make-believe game. Ask them to take a minute and think of silly things they can do. Brainstorm ideas and write them on the board.
- Write *What were you doing when the cheetah ran by?* on the board. Ask two volunteers to read the examples on the page. Then have a student ask you the question and make up a funny statement about what you were doing when the cheetah ran by.
- After demonstrating a couple of times, put students in pairs. They take turns asking and answering the questions. When they finish, have them find new partners. Continue as long as time and interest allow.

## Cool Down

Play a variation of *Never-Ending Sentence* (see TB p. 26). Have students make up a short story (with several sentences) where each student contributes one word. The story should use past progressive and simple past sentences with *when.* Each student adds one word to the story; for example, Teacher: *Yesterday*; Student A: *I*; Student B: *was*; Student C: *reading*; Student D: *a*; Student E: *book*; Student F: *when …* (*Yesterday I was reading a book when …*).

**Practice** **Resource Bank:** Grammar Printout
**Student's App:** Grammar Practice

# Global Citizenship

## Lesson Objectives

- to learn treatments vocabulary: *bandage, blood, broken arm, cast, germs, medicine, nurse, shot*
- to explore the importance of doctors and staying clean
- to practice listening for gist and specific details

**Materials**

Audio Tracks 105 to 107; Audio Track I; a globe or map of the world (D)

## Opening Question

Ask the opening question: *Why are doctors and nurses important?* Then encourage students to think about the different times when people might need a doctor or nurse.

**A** TRACK 105 TB p. 225 **Listen to a nurse who works at a community clinic. When do people go to the hospital?**

- Tell students they are going to listen to a nurse talking about the clinic where he works. Check the meaning of *clinic* by reminding students of the clinic they looked at in Lesson 1. Ask *Do clinics usually have a lot of people?* (yes) Play the audio and have students point to the words or pictures as they listen.
- Ask the gist question *When do people go to the hospital?* Elicit answers, then play the audio again for students to check. Have students give more responses based on their personal experience; for example, *I went to the hospital when I hurt my leg.*

**Answers**

once a year, when they have an emergency, when they're sick, and sometimes just to say "thank you"

**B** TRACK 106 TB p. 225 **Listen, say, and number the pictures in A.**

- Play the audio and have students point to the pictures and say the words.
- Tell students to listen again and write numbers next to the words in the pictures. Do the example together (shot).
- Check answers by giving definitions of the words and having students call out the correct number and word.

**Answers**

1 *shot* 2 broken arm 3 cast 4 nurse 5 medicine 6 germs 7 blood 8 bandage

TRACK I TB p. 226 **Visualization**

The TTL has a visualization audio track for this vocabulary set. (See TB p. 21.)

**International English**

Elicit which words are American English and which are British English. Ask *Which words do we use?* Play the audio again if necessary.

**C Read and complete.**

- Students are going to complete sentences with the key vocabulary. Look at the example together. Ask *What do you take when you're sick?* (medicine)
- Have students do the activity individually. Then check answers as a class.

**Answers**

1 *medicine* 2 nurse; shot 3 blood 4 bandage 5 broken arm; cast

**D** TRACK 107 TB p. 226 **Now listen to Jorge and Olivia. Which museum has nurses' uniforms and hospital beds?**

- Have students look at the two pictures. Ask *What do you see? Where do you think they are?*
- Tell students they are going to listen to two children talking about field trips to museums. Draw students' attention to the countries: Ecuador and the UK. You could point out the countries on a globe or map. Ask *What other things might be in these museums?*
- Listening for gist: Ask the gist question *Which museum has nurses' uniforms and hospital beds?* Play the audio. Elicit the answer from the class.

**Answer**

the Florence Nightingale Museum, in London

**E Listen again. Write *True* or *False*.**

- Listening for details: have students read the sentences before they listen again to see what they remember. Then play the audio and have students write *True* or *False*.
- To check answers, read each question and have students raise their left hand for *True* and their right hand for *False*.

**Answers**

1 *True* 2 False 3 True 4 False 5 True 6 True

## Discussion Questions

- Draw students' attention to the discussion questions: *When do you see a doctor or nurse? How can people stay healthy?* Have students discuss the questions in small groups. See **ETB**.
- Return to the opening question to ask: *Why are doctors and nurses important?* Recap ideas discussed at the beginning of the class and then encourage students to share any new ideas. Focus on the concept of how important it is to get treated quickly when you are sick so that you get better and don't pass the illness on to other people, as well as the importance of prevention (i.e., what you can do to help yourself not get sick).

## Cool Down

Play *Snowballs* (see TB p. 27).



**Practice Student's App:** Vocabulary Practice; Listening Practice

# Explore Language

## Lesson Objectives

- to learn to use the past progressive with *while*
- to practice treatments vocabulary

**Materials**
Audio Tracks 108 and 109

## Warm Up

Ask *When do you wash your hands?* Have students do a Rally Robin routine (see TB p. 20) to think of answers in pairs. Then elicit ideas from the class.

**A** TRACK 108 TB p. 226 **Listen and read. How long was Heather sick?**

- Tell students that they are going to listen to Heather, a girl who appeared in the Vocabulary lesson, talking to the nurse. Have students look back in their books to see if they can find her (she's by the pictures on the back wall). Ask *What do you think is the matter with Heather?* and have students make predictions. Play the audio and have students follow the dialogue in their books. Check to see if students' predictions were correct.
- Ask the comprehension question *When did Heather wash her hands a lot?* and elicit suggestions. Ask *Is Heather feeling better now?*

**Answer**
for three days

**B Look at A. Complete.**

- Review the use of the past progressive and simple past. Write a question on the board: *Were you holding the skeleton when the sign hit you?* Have a student underline the two verb forms in different colors. Students can later compare this with the example on the page.
- Write or project the table onto the board.
- Have students complete and discuss the grammar table in pairs using the dialogue.
- Check answers on the board. Discuss the verb forms in each statement/question, but let your class guide the discussion. Make sure that students notice the use of *while* in the sentences. If you feel that students need more guidance, the **ETB** provides a differentiation activity to help you support students as they explore the grammar table.
- Refer students to the *Look* box. Write two example sentences on the board, one with *while* beginning the first clause and one with *while* beginning the second clause. Point out that we can change the order of the verbs if we want to. Then have students notice the comma in the example from the table. Explain that we use a comma to separate the two parts of the sentence when *While* is in the first part.

**Answers**
feeling; while; was; Were; feeling; working; were; working; was; washing

**C Think and discuss. Then choose.**

- Draw two timelines on the board. One should show an action that interrupted another (past progressive and simple past); for example, *I was watching TV when my dad got home from work.* The other should show two simultaneous actions (both in the past progressive); for example, *I was watching TV while my sister was eating her lunch.*
- Then have students work in pairs to discuss the answer options. Check the answer as a class.

**Answer**
1 at the same time as

**D** TRACK 109 TB p. 226 **Listen and say.**

- Tell students they're going to practice saying the new structures. Play the audio, having students repeat each sentence chorally. Encourage students to do actions to demonstrate each sentence after they say it.
- For ideas on how to vary the drill, see TB p. 23.

**E Read and complete. Write about you.**

- Students are going to complete the sentences with their own ideas. Look at the example together. Have students change the ending with a different idea (e.g. *my dad was working*). Point out the comma between the clauses.
- Have students complete the sentences individually. Remind them to look at the table in B to help them. Then ask a few volunteers to share some of their answers with the class.

**Answers**
1 *my cat was playing with my toys* 2–6 Students' own answers (using the past progressive correctly)

**F Play a chain game. What were you doing?**

- Play the *Chain Game* (see TB p. 25). Ask three students to read out the examples on the page. Then have students sit in a circle. Start by saying *Last night, I was sleeping. While I was sleeping, what were you doing?* Each student must use the previous person's activity for his/her *While* clause.
- Then have students play in groups. The group that continues for the longest is the winner!

## Cool Down

Play *Pass the Whisper!* (see TB p. 26). For this version, use a sentence that contains the past progressive and *while*; for example, *The boy was singing while I was doing my homework.*

**Practice** **Resource Bank:** Grammar Printout
**Student's App:** Grammar Practice

# Talk About It

## Lesson Objectives

- to prepare and practice a conversation giving health advice
- to recognize and reproduce /kw/ and /kr/

**Materials**
Video; Audio Track 110

### Warm Up

Ask students if their friends or families are ever sick. Ask *What do you say?* Have students share a few examples of things they say when someone is sick. Then ask *Do you give them advice?* Pretend you have an illness and ask students for advice. Ask *What should I do?* and elicit ideas from the class.

**A** TB p. 239 **Watch and listen. What is Natalia going to do?**

- Tell students they are going to watch a video of a conversation between two girls named Rania and Natalia at school. Play the first scene of the video where Natalia says she feels sick. Ask *What's the matter with Natalia?* and elicit suggestions from the class.
- Ask the gist question *What is Natalia going to do?* Have students suggest ideas. Play the video and then check the answer. Ask further comprehension questions; for example, *What is Natalia drinking?* Play the video again and have students notice the girls' body language.

**Answer**
She's going to go home, lie down, and put ice on the back of her neck.

**B** **Watch again. Check (✔) the phrases you hear.**

- Have students read the phrases.
- Play the video again and have students check the phrases they hear. Check answers as a class.
- Have students remember who says each phrase (or who would say it if it isn't in the video). Then, with the class, build up a simple conversation on the board using the phrases. Ask students to identify the phrases used at the beginning, middle, and end of the conversation. Ask *What does Rania say and do to show she cares?* (she says *Oh, I'm sorry*; she makes suggestions to help Natalia get better)

**Answers**
1; 2; 3; 5; 6

**Pronunciation /kw/ and /kr/**

TRACK 110 TB p. 226 **Listen and say.**

Demonstrate the two sounds first. Isolate each phoneme in the cluster and elicit how to pronounce it (/k/; /w/). Then put the two sounds together /kw/ and have students repeat it. Do the same for /kr/.

Play the audio and have students repeat the words. Repeat if students need more practice.

Say *These words are used in the video. What other words do you know with these sounds?* Elicit ideas and write them on the board in two columns (e.g. *question*, *crossword*). Drill the pronunciation of each word.

**Suggested Answers**
/kw/ quarter, earthquake, squeak, equals, aquarium, square
/kr/ crocodile, creature, script, (ice) cream, microwave, cross

**C** **Plan. Choose two illnesses. Complete.**

- Tell students they are going to plan a conversation about illnesses. Draw students' attention to the graphic organizer in their books. Do an example together using *headache*. Say *If you have a headache, you can do these things: …* and ask a volunteer to give two pieces of advice. (The student can use the advice that Rania gave Natalia in A.) Tell students to choose two more illnesses and think of advice they could give.
- To generate some interesting ideas for advice, do a Chalk Talk routine with the different illnesses (see TB p. 21).
- Have students complete the graphic organizers in their books individually. Monitor and provide language help when necessary.

**D** **Prepare your conversation. Use your ideas from C and sentences from B.**

- Play the video again as a model.
- Have students work in pairs to prepare their conversation using their notes in C and phrases from B. Remind them to always include a response after each person speaks.
- Monitor and provide language help when needed.

**E** **Practice with a friend.**

- Have students practice their conversation with their partner as many times as they like. Remind them to take turns and listen when their partner is speaking. Note that students can give as much or as little advice as they want.
- Students should then change partners and have a different conversation so that they experience both roles.

### Cool Down

Play a game. Have each student secretly write an illness on a sticky note and stick the note to a friend's back, or somewhere their friend can't see it. Then have students walk around the classroom giving advice to each person they meet related to the illness on their back. The objective is for students to guess what illness they have, based on the advice; for example,

Student A: *You should drink a lot of water.*
Student B: *Do I have a fever?*
Student A: *No!*
Student C: *You should sit in a dark room.*



**Practice** **Student's App:** Speaking Skills Practice; Speaking Video

# Write About It

## Lesson Objectives

- to learn to use simple past irregular verb forms
- to plan and write a letter to a friend

**Materials**

(Optional) Support, Standard, and Challenge writing printouts from the Resource Bank, one per student (C and D)

## Warm Up

Do a Mad Lib letter. First, have students write down a word for each of the following:

1 an adjective; 2 a place; 3 a natural place; 4 a school subject; 5 a topic/theme; 6 a past verb; 7 a noun

Then write the following text on the board. Students should read the text to their partner, saying their chosen words where the numbers are.

Dear Laura/Lee, Today I'm feeling (1). I went to the (2), and I fell in the (3). At school we had (4) homework, so I read a book about (5). Then I (6), and it was time for (7).

Ask one or two volunteers to read their letters to the class. Who has the craziest letter?

**A Read the letter. Underline the simple past irregular verbs.**

- Ask students if they've ever written a letter. Ask *Who was it to? What information did you include?* Then draw their attention to the letter on the page. Have students read the letter silently. Then ask one or two comprehension questions; for example, *Who wrote the letter? What does he talk about?* Elicit that Alexis is sick and that his classmates sent him letters to help him feel better.
- Ask *Why does Nasim write some verbs in the simple past?* Elicit that he was talking about what they did today (earlier in the day). Review the simple past with the class.
- Tell students to find and underline the simple past irregular verbs in the letter. Give students a few minutes to do this. Then check answers as a class.

**Answers**

Mr. Wolski <u>said</u> …
School <u>was</u> OK …
We <u>built</u> volcanoes …
we <u>went</u> to the library …
I <u>found</u> a great book …
I <u>read</u> it …
I <u>gave</u> it to Macio …
we <u>had</u> a rehearsal …
Everybody <u>knew</u> the script!
Mr. Wolski <u>was</u> surprised!
I <u>felt</u> really tired …
I <u>slept</u> badly …
I <u>had</u> bad dreams.

**Practice** **Student's App:** Writing Practice

**B Complete.**

- Have students look at the list of verbs. Elicit that the verbs are in the simple present. Students have to write these verbs in the simple past.
- Have students complete the blanks, looking back at A to help them. Then check answers as a class. Remind students of the different pronunciations of present *read* /riːd/ and past *read* /red/. They reviewed this in Unit 1.

**Answers**

1 *found* 2 built 3 knew 4 got 5 read 6 slept

**C Plan. Think about writing a letter to a friend. Complete.**

- Tell students they are all going to write letters to a sick classmate. Ask students if they know anyone who is sick or in the hospital. If not, they can choose to write a letter simply as a kind gesture.
- Draw students' attention to the plan. Discuss the five stages of the letter with the class. Have them look back at the letter in A to find examples of each part of the letter.
- Remind them to use greetings at the beginning (e.g. Dear, Hi, or Hello) and closings at the end (e.g. Your friend, From, or Love—if it's a relative).
- Have students complete their plans individually. Challenge printouts can be handed out now.

**D Write your letter. Decorate it with pictures.**

- Have students write up their letters neatly. They should write at least ten sentences and three (short) paragraphs. They should include at least three sentences about their friend, and they should give him/her advice. They should write at least three sentences about what happened today. Support printouts can be handed out now.
- Students should either self-correct or exchange their work with a friend and peer-correct. You can put a checklist of things to correct on the board (e.g. spelling, use of adjectives and adverbs, verb forms, punctuation).
- Have students write their final letters on paper and add pictures to decorate them. Alternatively, hand out the Standard printouts from the Resource Bank.

## Cool Down

Play a collocation *Word Tennis* game using simple past verbs (see TB p. 27). For example,

Teacher: She built
Student A: She built a house
Student B: She built a tower
Student A: She built a hospital
Student B: …

# Think It Over

## Lesson Objectives

- to review what has been learned in the unit
- to reflect on the unit and students' own progress
- to think about learning strategies and how to continue learning at home

## Warm Up

Ask students what the unit theme was (illnesses and treatments) and write it in the middle of the board. Brainstorm any words or phrases students can think of that relate to the topic and write them on the board. Encourage students to think about how diet and hygiene (keeping clean) are linked to staying healthy.

**Read the questions and draw or write your answers.**

- Give students time to think about and discuss activities in the unit before they complete each question. Explain that they can choose to either write a few words or sentences or to draw a picture. Allowing students to make a personal response will help them retain knowledge and engage with the learning points.

**What did I do?**

- Give students a few minutes to look back through the unit at the different activities they did. Ask questions about the unit or write questions on the board; for example, *What illnesses do you know? What was wrong with Daniel and Heather? What advice did you give to a friend?* Have them discuss their ideas in pairs or small groups.
- Encourage students to identify something in the unit that they found challenging or something that was particularly memorable for them. Students can draw or write about their chosen activity.

**What did I learn?**

- Ask questions about the unit to help students think about what they learned; for example, *What did you learn about illnesses and treatments? What sentences can you say using the past progressive? What did you learn about being clean? What did you learn about Ecuador and the UK?* Have students look through the unit and discuss their ideas in pairs.
- Encourage students to draw a picture or write sentences about their learning outcomes.

**How did I learn?**

- Ask students how they learned the illnesses and treatment vocabulary in Lessons 1 and 3. Elicit ideas (e.g. by using mime; by categorizing phrases by verb, noun, and adjective; by talking about personal experiences; by watching a video). Encourage students to think about the spelling and pronunciation of the words. Ask *What helped you remember how to say and write the new words?*
- Then encourage students to think about how they learned throughout the unit; for example, how did they develop their conversational and writing skills?
- Have students draw or write about the activities that helped them learn.

**How well did I do?**

- Tell students to color in the face that best expresses how well they have learned they unit content. Ask *What do you understand? What do you need to practice more?* Encourage students to look back through the unit to see how much they remember, what they did well, and what they found difficult.

**What can I do next?**

- Brainstorm ideas with the class about what they can do to continue to learn (e.g. think about health and hygiene and how to avoid getting sick, find out about different museums to visit in the area, look at different kinds of letters, write a letter to a friend, watch a show in English about a hospital).
- Draw students' attention to the *What can I do next?* box. Encourage students to think about what they can do at home to improve their English. Have them suggest some verbs that they can use (e.g. visit, watch, read, write, discuss, research) and write the verbs they choose in their books. Students can look back at the previous units to get more ideas. Encourage students to suggest their own ideas for different activities they can do.
- Have students choose several activities that they would like to do and write them in their notebooks. They can then share their ideas with a partner.

## Looking Forward

Draw students' attention to the character at the bottom of the page. Ask *Who's this?* and elicit what they remember about her. (Nurse Hayes appears in the Vocabulary and second Explore Language lessons, pp. 115 and 120; she works at the community clinic; she showed children how to wash their hands; she talked to Heather)

Draw students' attention to Nurse Hayes's question: *What did you learn about staying healthy?* Elicit suggestions from the class, then point out her instruction: *Look for something huge in Unit 10!* Ask students to make predictions about what it is and what Unit 10 is about. Tell students they will find the answer in Lesson 1 of the next unit.

**Practice** **Resource Bank:** Unit Test
**Student's App:** Vocabulary and Grammar Review

## Get Ready to Read

### Lesson Objectives

- to activate prior knowledge about health and illnesses
- to guide inquiry and deepen understanding through a Think, Pair, Share VTR
- to preview the reading skill of understanding the main idea and details

**Materials**

VTR printout from the Resource Bank (Activities A, B, C)

### Warm Up

Pretend you are sick using mime (e.g. holding your head and rubbing it, saying *Ouch!*). Elicit the question *What's the matter?* from students and write it in the board. Have students guess what is the matter (you have a headache). Make sure students know that you are not really sick! Drink some water and then say *That's better!*

### Think, Pair, Share

**A Look at the picture. Imagine you're the doctor. What's the matter? Think about it.**

Students are going to do a Think, Pair, Share VTR to explore the image of an X-ray.

- Have students say what they can see in the picture. If students don't know a word in English, ask them to describe what they see for you to provide the word.
- Tell students to imagine they are doctors. Ask them to look at the picture and read the question *What's the matter?*
- Give students a couple of minutes to think about their ideas silently.
- Tell them to cross their arms when they have thought of some ideas.

**B Discuss with your partner.**

- Ask two volunteers to read the example dialogue in B.
- Divide the class into pairs and have students share their ideas about the picture.
- Monitor and support students as they discuss their ideas. Encourage them to listen to each other and to give reasons for their opinions.

**C Share your ideas with the class.**

- Ask pairs to share their ideas about the picture with the class. Encourage students to use *we*, as they are talking about the opinion of a partner, too. When you ask a student a question, encourage other students to say if they agree or not: *Us too. / We agree. / We don't agree. / Really?* Encourage the class to lead the discussion.

Here's an example of this part of the routine.

**Teacher:** What do you and your friend think?
**Student A:** We think the white thing is fixing the arm.
**Teacher:** OK. Why do you think that?
**Student A:** Because the bones look OK. They aren't broken.
**Student B:** We don't agree. We think the wrist is broken!
**Teacher:** What makes you say that?

### Transition

Ask students how the doctor helped the patient. Say *The patient hurt his/her arm. What do you think the doctor did to fix it?* Elicit suggestions from the class.

**D Think about a time when you were sick. What was wrong? What made you well?**

- Give students one or two minutes to think about a time when they were sick. You could have students draw a quick picture.
- Ask one or two students *What was the matter?* and help them express their ideas. Encourage them to use gesture if they don't know the words. Then ask *What made you well?* Write their answers on the board. Brainstorm more ideas about illnesses and treatments on the board to help students with their discussion.
- Have students discuss their ideas in small groups.

**E Think, write, and discuss. Look at the next page. What is the reading about? What are two interesting details you can see?**

In this activity students will preview the reading skill of understanding the main idea and then the details.

- Have students read the title *Take Your Medicine*. Ask *What do you think the reading is about?*
- Give students one or two minutes to look at the next page. Ask *Now what do you think the reading is about?* and elicit suggestions (types of medicine through different times in the past). Then have students write what they think the main idea is in their books.
- Ask students to find two interesting details on the next page. Tell students that they shouldn't read every word, but they can look for something they find interesting and read that part. Remind students that pictures can help us decide if the information looks interesting. Students then write the two details in their books.
- Have students discuss and compare their ideas in pairs.

**Suggested Answers**

1 It's about ancient times. / It's about medicine.
2 Students' own answers

Now read **Take Your Medicine**

# Nonfiction: *Take Your Medicine*—Informational Text

## Lesson Objectives

- to read an informational text about the history of medicine
- to learn through CLIL (science): exploring illnesses and treatments
- to make a personal connection to the reading

**Materials**

Audio Tracks 45 and 46; card or paper for students to make their own pelmanism cards

### Warm Up

Review parts of the body with the class with a game of *Simon Says* (see TB p. 27).

### TRACK 45 TB p. 236 Reading Approach

**First Reading: Engage with the Text**

- Ask students to notice the title, text, and pictures on the page and use this information to predict ideas about the reading. Ask *What can you see?*
- Have students open their books. Ask prediction questions before they start to read; for example, *What strange ideas do you think doctors had in the past? What kinds of things do you think they used?* Then have students read the text silently. Remind them not to worry if there are parts of the text they don't understand.
- Then look at the Words in Context.

### TRACK 46 TB p. 236 Words in Context

- Play the audio and have students repeat the words.
- Have students race to find the words in the reading.
- Remind students to **read the next words or sentence to get clues to explain the meaning of a new word** (see TB p. 23).
- Use these discussion points to confirm the meanings.

**cure** (p. 138) Ask *What do you think doctors had different ideas about? What do doctors do?* Elicit that doctors can cure people. and that *make better* is a synonym.

**treatments** (p. 138) This word appears several times in the reading. With the class, make a list of all the treatments mentioned. Elicit that a *treatment* is a way of curing or helping an illness or injury.

**patient** (p. 139) Have students look at the picture of the doctor and patient on p. 140. Ask *Who is the doctor? Who is the other person?* (the patient)

**grind** (p. 139) Have students read the sentence containing *grind*. Ask *What do some people do with their teeth when they sleep?* Demonstrate *grinding* your teeth. Ask *What food and drink can you grind?* (pepper, coffee)

**opposites** (p. 140) Have students read the sentence *The ancient Romans thought opposites were good treatments.* Then identify the two health problems in the next two sentences of the paragraph: a fever and feeling cold. Ask *What did Romans put on people who had a fever / were hot? What did they tell cold people to eat? Why?* Elicit that they put cold things on hot people and vice versa. Elicit that opposites are completely different.
Refer students to the blue box on p. 140 and ask *What other opposites can you think of?* Have students suggest more opposites, competing in pairs/groups to make the longest list (e.g. big/small, good/bad).

**disease** (p. 141) You may wish to give some background information about the plague. Elicit or explain that *disease* is a synonym of *illness*.

### International English

Elicit which words are American English and which words are British English. Ask *Which words do we use?*

**Second Reading: Analyze the Text and Features**

- Play the audio as students read along in their books.
- Ask some questions to check comprehension: *What did people put on cuts?* (moss—a kind of plant found near rocks and trees) *Why did the Chinese eat gold?* (to stay healthy and live forever) *What did a cooked potato cure?* (earache)
- Discuss the questions in the blue boxes.
  - **CLIL Focus (Science)** (p. 139): *Do you think any of these treatments worked?* Elicit the illnesses and treatments mentioned on p. 139. Ask *Do you think this worked?* for each one. Have students explain why or why not.
  - **Critical Thinking** (p. 141): *Why do you think people in the past had such different ideas about medicine?* Ask *Where did people in the past get their information from?* Elicit that people had to use trial and error. They would use things they could find to try and treat illnesses.

**Third Reading: Interact with the Text**

- Have students work in pairs to make cards: One person makes a set of illnesses and the other a set with the treatments. They can write the word and draw a quick picture as a visual aid. Then have them play pelmanism (see TB p. 26).

### Cool Down

Do a survey to find out which treatment students think is the craziest. Take a vote and tally the students' responses on the board.

## Explore the Reading

### Lesson Objectives

- to understand and analyze *Take Your Medicine* through reading comprehension activities
- to learn through CLIL (science): exploring illnesses and treatments
- to make a personal connection to the reading

**Materials**
Audio Tracks 45 and 47

### Warm Up

Have students work in pairs to make a list of all the things they remember from the reading that were used as treatments. Do they remember what illnesses they were for?

**A Complete the table.**

- If more than one day has passed since students read *Take Your Medicine*, play the audio again or have students quickly read the text in their books.
- With books closed, have a Group Time discussion (see TB p. 21) to check students' comprehension of the reading. Ask *When did people use plants?* (3300 BCE) *What animals did the Egyptians use?* (birds, mice, and flies) *How did the ancient Greeks help with pain?* (They used wet sponges.) *What disease killed millions of people in Europe in the 1300s?* (the plague)
- Do number 1 (a toothache) together. Encourage students to look at the timeline, as well as the paragraphs.
- Have students do the rest of the activity individually. Remind students not to read every word. Check answers as a class.

**Answers**
1 take medicine from dead mice; 2500–2000 BCE; Ancient Egypt
2 cucumbers on the body; 20 BCE–400 CE; Ancient Rome
3 put a dirty sock around neck; 1800s, Britain
4 tie a cooked potato to head; 1800s; Britain
5 wear a dead toad around neck, put chicken feathers on sores; 1300s; Europe

**B Think and discuss. Do you think any of those treatments cured people? Why or why not?**

- The aim for this activity is for students to discuss how the cures were unlikely to work, as they were based on superstition and unresearched science. Contrast this with our greater understanding of the human body and disease today based on research and study. It is worth noting that in some instances science now agrees that leeches are useful (they can get the blood flowing post-operation) but they are unlikely to cure a fever. Note: there is a further opportunity to discuss these issues in the final lesson.
- Write on the board *I think (leeches) cured people because …* and *I don't think (dirty socks) cured people because …*
- Direct students to the questions in the book and ask a volunteer to give his/her opinion. Give students a few minutes to look back at the treatments, think, and discuss their ideas with a partner.

**C Write and discuss. What happens when you go to the doctor? Make a list.**

- Students are going to connect the reading with their own experiences. This draws on the CLIL science focus of exploring illnesses and treatments.
- Draw students' attention to the question *What happens when you go to the doctor?* Elicit some suggestions from the class and write these on the board; for example, *The doctor asks me, "What's the problem?"*
- Then give students a few minutes to think about their own experiences of going to the doctor and then tell their partner. Have them think about the order of events so that they are in a logical order. Finally, have students share their partner's ideas with the class.

**Answers**
Students' own answers

### Spelling Pattern *ur*

TRACK 47 TB p. 236 **Listen and write. Then check your answers.**

- With books closed, write the letters *ur* on the board.
- Play the first part of the audio and have students repeat each word. Then have them open their books. Play the first part of the audio again and have them complete as many words as they can.
- Then play the second part of the audio for students to check their spelling and complete the words correctly. Have them underline *ur* in each word and encourage them to notice where the letters appear in the word. Ask students to read the words aloud.
- Have students look back at the reading to find more words with *ur* and write them in a word cloud. Invite students to share a word from their cloud. Ask *Do these words sound like the others?* Note: *cure* and *Europe* have the same spelling but a different sound from the other words.

**Answers**
1 fur 2 curtain 3 surfing 4 turn 5 purple
From the reading: cure, hurt, Europe

### Cool Down

Play *Stand Up, Sit Down* (see TB p. 27) using the following sentences: *Doctors in the past had similar ideas to doctors now.* (False) *The ancient Egyptians didn't use medicines.* (False) *The cure for grinding your teeth was to sleep next to a skull.* (True) *A dirty sock helped cure earache.* (False) *The Romans used food to cure people.* (True)

**Practice** **Resource Bank:** Spelling Printout
**Student's App:** Reading Practice; Spelling Pattern Practice

# Get Ready to Read

## Lesson Objectives

- to practice the reading skill of understanding the main idea and details
- to activate prior knowledge about treatments and cures

**Materials**
Slips of paper, one per student (CD)

## Warm Up

Ask *Did you ever break your arm or leg?* Use gesture to teach/review *broken*. Have any students who have suffered a broken bone describe their experience to the class. Ask questions to guide; for example, *How did you break it? What were you doing? Did it hurt a lot? How long did it take to get better? Did you wear a cast?* Again, use gesture to teach/review *cast*. Encourage other students to ask questions.

**A Read. Then write the main idea and two details.**

This lesson reviews the reading skill of understanding the main idea and details in a text.

- Have students look at the picture and say what they think is happening. Ask *Where is the girl? Why is she there? What's the matter? What do you think the doctor is saying?*
- Draw students' attention to the instructions. Ask *What is the main idea?* Tell students to quickly read (skim) the text on the page and try to identify what it is about. Elicit ideas from the class. Refer students to the table and have them write their answer.
- Then tell students that we want to know more details about the text. This time they will scan the text to find two pieces of information (note: there are more than two, so students can identify any two). Give students a time limit of two minutes to read the text and write the details in the table.
- Now have students read the skills box. Ask *What is the important idea called?* (main idea) *What are the details called?* (supporting ideas) Point out that a text always has a main idea and that the other details in the text help us understand it.
- Review students' answers with the class. Ask volunteers to say which details they found the most interesting (e.g. it takes 6–8 weeks for the bone to heal).

**Answers**
Main idea: the process of mending/fixing a broken arm
Details: doctors take an X-ray; they find the broken bone; they put a cast on your arm; you have to wait 6–8 weeks for the bone to heal

**B Think and discuss. Look at the reading on the next page. Look at the title and the pictures. What do you think the main idea is?**

- The aim of this activity is for students to predict the main idea in a text. To activate prior knowledge, see if students know anything about Alexander Fleming or what he's famous for.
- Tell students to look at the opening pages of the reading on pp. 144–145 and try to identify what the main idea is. Remind them to look at the title, the pictures, and the text but not to read every word. Give students a maximum of two to three minutes to do this.
- Have students discuss their ideas in pairs or small groups. Then have one or two students share their ideas with the class. Ask *Do you agree?*

**Suggested Answers**
Note: these answers can be inferred from the opening spread. A scientist works hard to find a cure. / A scientist finds a cure for bacteria. / A scientist wants to find a way to stop bacteria.

**C How does it feel when you discover something or solve a problem? Do a Think, Pair, Share.**

- Say *Alexander Fleming wants to find a new medicine to cure sick people. If he discovers a solution to his problem, how will he feel?* Elicit suggestions from the class.
- Say *Think about a time when you solved a problem or discovered something new.* With the class, brainstorm a few problems students have or had; for example, *I didn't understand my science project.* Ask *Did you find a solution? How did you feel?* Remind students that they can use any of the ideas discussed in Unit 3 (problems and solutions).
- Give students a few minutes to think and share their ideas in pairs. Then have them share their partner's ideas with the class.

## Cool Down

Give each student a slip of paper as an exit pass. Have them predict one thing they think will happen in the reading. They should give you the paper as they leave the classroom.

Now read **A Surprise Cure**

# Fiction: *A Surprise Cure*—Historical Recount

## Lesson Objectives

- to read a story about how Alexander Fleming discovered penicillin
- to make a personal connection to the reading

**Materials**

Audio Tracks 48 and 49; Video

## Warm Up

Read aloud or display the predictions students made at the end of the previous lesson. Have students work in pairs to choose three predictions that they think will be true. They will check these predictions during the first reading.

## TRACK 48 TB p. 236 Reading Approach

**First Reading: Engage with the Text**

- Students have already looked at this page and made predictions. Have students look more carefully to try to check their predictions from the Warm Up.
- Have students open their books and read the text aloud in pairs. Students can take turns reading a paragraph. Have pairs try to find the answers to their three prediction questions from the Warm Up.
- Confirm with the class which predictions were correct and which weren't.
- Read the whole story before looking at the Words in Context.

## TRACK 49 TB p. 236 Words in Context

- Play the audio and have students repeat the words.
- Have students race to find the words in the reading.
- **Use negative sentences nearby to help decode the meaning of a new word** (see TB p. 23).Have students work in pairs to try to figure out the meaning of each word.
- Use these discussion points to confirm the meanings.

**scientist** (p. 144) Have students read the sentence. Ask *What kind of word is "scientist"?* Elicit that it is a noun. Compare *scientist* with *science*, which students studied in Unit 1. Ask *What's the difference?*

**bacteria** (p. 144) Have students read the first sentence with the word. Ask *Can you find a synonym of "bacteria" in the same sentence?* (germs)

**laboratory** (p. 144) If possible, enlarge the picture using the TTL. Elicit that there are bottles, a microscope, papers, and so on. Ask *Where do scientists work? What do they do there?*

**mess** (p. 145) Encourage students to look at the pictures. Ask *Is the laboratory organized?* Remind students that sometimes a text gives us clues by saying what something isn't—*Fleming isn't the neatest*. Elicit that *neat* and *messy* are antonyms, or opposites.

**attack** (p. 146) Ask *The mold says, "Attack!" Why?* Elicit that *attack* is a synonym of *fight*. Ask *Who won—the mold or the bacteria?*

**liquid** (p. 148) Refer students to the picture of what Fleming can see through the microscope. Ask *What can you see?* Ask *What does Fleming call this liquid?* (mold juice) Elicit other kinds of liquid.

**penicillin** (p. 149) Ask What does penicillin kill? (bacteria) Who does it cure? (sick people) So what is penicillin? Elicit that it is a medicine.

**Practice** **Student's App:** Fiction Video

## International English

Elicit which spelling is American English and which spelling is British English. Ask *Which spelling do we use?*

**Second Reading: Analyze the Text and Features**

- Play the video, pausing to ask questions to check comprehension: *Why did Fleming study bacteria?* (He wanted to find a cure.) *Did he clean his laboratory before he went on vacation?* (no) *What did he find when he got back?* (There was mold on the dishes.) *What did the mold do?* (It killed the bacteria.)
- Discuss the questions in the blue boxes.
  - **Making Connections** (p. 144): *How do scientists and doctors find new medicines?* Have students recall that Dr. Fleming found penicillin by mistake. Ask *Is this how scientists usually discover new medicines?* Elicit that scientists spend a lot of time trying different things to get a result.
  - **Fact** (p. 146): *Mold is a fungus. Mushrooms and yeast in bread are both types of fungi.* Draw a mushroom on the board. Tell students that mold, like mushrooms, grows. Ask if students ever saw mold on bread or other foods.
  - **Making Connections** (p. 149): *What other medicines do you know?* Have students discuss this question in pairs using a Rally Robin routine (see TB p. 20).
- Point out the text focus. (p. 144): *This kind of story is historical fiction. It uses people and places from history.* Ask *Are there any other readings about famous people?* (*Beethoven's 9th* from Unit 5). Ask students which other texts are historical but not fictional (*The History of Money, Take Your Medicine*).

**Third Reading: Interact with the Text**

- Have students discuss in pairs how the story would be different if it were told by Dr. Fleming instead of the spider. This links to the idea of perspective developed in Unit 8.

## Cool Down

Play *Snowballs* (see TB p. 27).

## Explore the Reading

### Lesson Objectives

- to understand and analyze *A Surprise Cure* through reading comprehension activities
- to make a personal connection to the reading
- to explore the SEL competency of self-management through setting plans and working toward goals

**Materials**
(Optional) Video or Audio Track 48; pictures related to health, medicine, and science (WU); sticky notes (CD)

### Warm Up

Display the pictures you have prepared. Tell students to work in pairs to decide which pictures have a connection to *A Surprise Cure*. Then elicit suggestions, asking *What makes you say that?* to encourage students to justify their answers.

**A Complete the story map.**

- If more than one day has passed since students read *A Surprise Cure*, play the video or audio again.
- Display the story map using the TTL or copy it onto the board. Ask students what information they should include in each section. Point out the question words and elicit possible answers.
- Have students complete the story map in their books. Encourage them to look back at the reading to help them find the details. Remind them to answer the question in each box.
- Check answers as a class, asking one or two students to share their ideas for each section of the map.

**Suggested Answers**
Title: *A Surprise Cure*
Characters: Dr. Fleming, Dr. Fleming's assistant, Spider, Bacteria, Mold
Setting: Dr. Fleming's laboratory, London; 1928
Problem: Dr. Fleming was trying to find a way to fight bacteria; Fleming left his lab a mess
Solution: Mold grew in the dishes and killed the bacteria; Fleming identified penicillin; scientists made penicillin into medicine

**B Think and write. What is the main idea of *A Surprise Cure*? What are some supporting details? Complete the graphic organizer.**

- Students are going to practice the reading skill of identifying the main idea and details. Ask *What's the main idea of "A Surprise Cure"?* Give students a few minutes to look back at the reading if they need to.
- Then have students look back at their predictions on p. 143. Ask *Did you correctly identify the main idea?* Reinforce the idea that it doesn't matter if your predictions are wrong; it can help you understand a text if you think about it and make predictions before you read.
- Ask *What are the supporting details in the story?* Have students suggest some ideas and write them on the board. Then draw students' attention to the graphic organizer on the page and have them complete it with their ideas.

**Suggested Answers**
Main Idea: The discovery of penicillin
Details: Dr. Fleming was a medical doctor. / Dr. Fleming did experiments to fight bacteria. / Dr. Fleming went on vacation and left the bacteria in the dishes. / Mold grew in the dishes, and the bacteria died. This led to the discovery of penicillin.

**C Think and discuss. What was Dr. Fleming's goal? How did he work toward it? What goal do you have? How do you work toward it?**

Students are going to connect the reading to their own lives. This draws on the SEL competency of self-management through setting plans and working toward goals.

- Ask *What was Dr. Fleming's goal?* and elicit suggestions from the class. *How did he work toward it?* Have students discuss the question in pairs before sharing their ideas with the class.
- Tell students that people can have different goals, some big (like Dr. Fleming's) and some small. Elicit a few goals that students may have. These could be related to their future career, family life, free time, and so on. Ask *What do you want to do in the future?* Remind students that they can have long-term and short-term goals.
- Have students discuss their goals in pairs. Together, they should come up with one or more ways in which they can work toward their goals. Then have some students share their ideas with the class.

**Suggested Answers**
Dr. Fleming's goal was to find a way to kill bacteria and cure sick people.
He kept dishes of bacteria and studied them. He worked long and hard. He looked carefully at the dishes and discovered a cure.
Students' own answers

### Cool Down

Have students think of one question they have about the story of Dr. Fleming and write it on a sticky note. Put all the notes on the wall near the door. As students leave the classroom, have them take one of the sticky notes. They should investigate the question and try to find out the answer. They can look online or go to the library to find the answer. Students can share what they have learned at the beginning or end of the next lesson.

**Practice** **Student's App:** Reading Practice

## Think Together

### Lesson Objectives

- to make connections between the readings
- to explore the key concept: What do we do when we're sick?
- to reflect on the unit and provide personal thoughts and opinions

**Materials**
Three pieces of construction paper with a different prompt written in the middle of each (CD)

### Warm Up

Have students look back at the VTR picture on pp. 136–137. Ask students how they think the picture connects to the two readings in the unit. If necessary, write the following prompts on the board: *patient, time, sickness, problem, treatment, pain, doctor, scientist, bacteria, medicine*. Encourage students to be creative in their answers; for example, *I think this treatment is better than the ones in the reading; I don't think doctors gave him/her penicillin.*

**A Think and discuss. Complete the table.**

- Students are going to make connections to the key concept in the unit: *What do we do when we're sick?* by comparing and contrasting the various treatments students have learned about.
- Have students open their books. Elicit what kind of information we need to complete the table. Have students work individually to look back at the readings and complete the table. Check answers as a class.
- Have students compare the information in the table to any problems and treatments that are common in today's society. Ask *How are they different? Are there new problems and sicknesses today?* This may generate an interesting class discussion.

**Answers**
2500–2000 BCE; Ancient Egypt; toothache; *dead mouse medicine*
*20 BCE–400 CE*; Ancient Rome; fever, cold; put cool cucumbers on your body, eat hot peppers
1300s; Europe; *the plague*; wear a toad around your neck or put chicken feathers on your sores
1928; London; *bacteria*; penicillin

**B We should do our best to stay healthy. What can we do? What can we eat or drink? Do a Numbered Heads Together routine.**

- Ask *What can we do to stop getting sick?* If students focus just on treatments and cures, present the concept of prevention being better than a cure. Remind students about the importance of a healthy diet (students studied this in Unit 6). Elicit examples of prevention being better than a cure and the idea that taking good care of our health is the best way to avoid getting sick.
- Give students some time to think about the questions *What can we do to stay healthy? What can we eat or drink?* Have students discuss their ideas in groups and then share with the class through a Numbered Heads Together routine (see TB p. 20).

**C Think about your ideas from B. Make a list of the top three and share.**

- Students are now going to choose the best three ideas as a group. Give them a few minutes to discuss their ideas and decide which ones are more important.
- Students then write their three ideas in their books.
- Have groups share their top three ideas with the class. While students are sharing their ideas, encourage other students to say if they agree or not and why.

**Answers**
Students' own answers

### My Reading Journal

**Write three questions about illnesses or medicine. What do you want to know?**

This task encourages students to think about what they learned and what they want to know. Tell students about a question you have. Then give students a few minutes to look back through the unit and think of three questions they have.

**Example Answers**
1 Do leeches hurt?
2 Do we use cold things when we have a fever now?
3 What do we use penicillin for?

**Who do you think might find this unit interesting? Why?**

Give students a few minutes to look back at the topics in the unit. Ask *Did you like this unit? Why or why not? Who might like it?*

**Example Answer**
People who like science might find it interesting because the stories are about science.

### Cool Down

Have students round up their ideas from the unit with a Chalk Talk routine (see TB p. 21), using the prompts: *What did you think about* Take your Medicine? *What did you think about* A Surprise Cure?; *What did you like best about Unit 9?*

**Practice** **Resource Bank:** Unit Test
**Student's App:** Key Concept Practice

UNIT 10

# Don't Push the Button

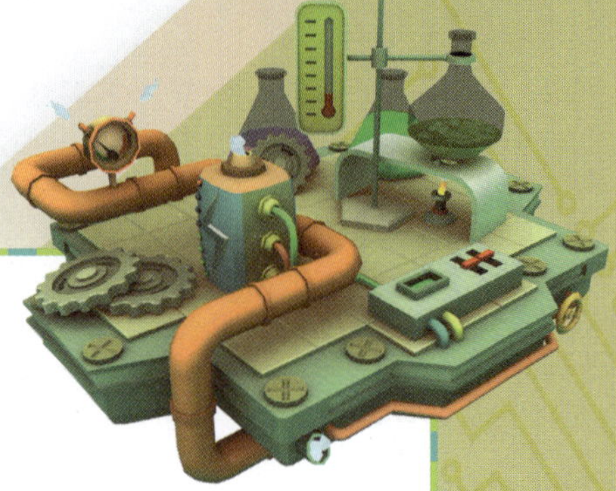

## Unit Overview

### Themes

Machines, materials, and inventions

How machines help us

### Synopsis

In this unit, students will explore how technology can make our lives easier. They will learn about machines and how they work, and how people invent new things. Students will plan and prepare a presentation about something they made and write a story about a girl who makes something.

**Language Book**

**Vocabulary**

*button, flip, gear, lever, pull, push, switch, turn, wheel*

p. 192

**Explore Language**

Comparatives with *Than* and *as ... as*

p. 193

**Global Citizenship**

Why do people invent new things?

*cotton, gold, leather, metal, plastic, silver, wood, wool*

p. 194

**Explore Language**

Modal Verbs

p. 195

**Take the Stage**

Presentation: telling a story about something you made

p. 196

**Write About It**

A Story

Paragraph Building: transition, words and phrases

p. 197

**Think It Over**

Review and Reflection

p. 198

## Think Together
Does technology make our lives easier?
p. 205

## Visible Thinking
Question Starts
p. 199

## Literacy Book

## Fiction
Science Fiction: *Searching for Sterling*
Words in Context: *cowboys, cattle, shuts down, motorcycle, fell asleep, tough*
p. 203

## Nonfiction
Informational Text: *Moving Machines*
Words in Context: *basic, rod, support, either, wind-up, swan*
p. 200

## Reading Skill
Understanding facts and opinions
p. 202

## Spelling Pattern
*ough*
p. 204

## Language and Literacy Connections

The connecting theme in Unit 10 is talking about family.

| | Language | Literacy |
|---|---|---|
| **Vocabulary** | **Set 1:** how machines work vocab<br>**Set 2:** materials vocab | **Nonfiction:** button, gear(s), lever, pull, turn, wheel, silver<br>**Fiction:** button, push |
| **Grammar** | **Comparatives with *Than* and *as … as***<br>This machine's even bigger than the first one.<br>This machine's as big as that house!<br>It isn't as exciting as the big machines.<br>**Modal Verbs**<br>We have to move this machine. We don't have to take it apart!<br>You should find a metal wheel. We shouldn't use plastic wheels.<br>Where could I put it? You could put it there. | **Nonfiction**<br>Someone has to press a button.<br>**Fiction**<br>It's better than all your horses.<br>Jules rode back as fast as he could.<br>I have to find Sterling!<br>You have to bring it back. |
| **Skills** | **Pronunciation:** /br/ and /fl/ | **Reading:** understanding facts and opinions<br>**Spelling Pattern:** *ough* |

## Vocabulary

### Lesson Objectives

- to learn vocabulary and verbs to describe how machines work: *button, gear, lever, switch, wheel; flip, pull, push, turn*
- to sing a song that explores a machine

**Materials**
Audio Tracks 111 to 114; Video

### Warm Up

Ask students if they used any machines this morning. If students have already completed the **Literacy Book**, students will have a lot of ideas about machines they use. If not, you may need to guide students with questions; for example, *What did you have for breakfast? Did you make toast? Did you wash your face? Was the water hot? How did you open the door?*

Note: students may not think of a door handle or other mechanisms as machines. Explain that a machine is anything that helps us do something (e.g. open a door). Tell them that a machine is not necessarily electronic; it can also be mechanical.

**A** TRACK 111 TB p. 226 **Listen and find. What does the machine make?**

- Play *Guess Who*. Display the picture using the TTL or have students look in their books. Tell them that you are going to describe someone in the picture and they have to try to find him or her. Encourage students to raise their hands rather than shouting out. Say *She has red hair. She's wearing a blue shirt.* (girl on the far left) Describe a few more people, then have students work in pairs to describe people in the picture to each other and guess who.
- Ask *Which characters do students recognize?* Remind students of the challenge from the end of Unit 9, *Look for something huge*, and have students find it on the page.
- Tell students they are going to listen to some of the people in the picture talking about a machine. Have them look at the machine in the picture and predict what it makes. Then play the audio and have students point to the words or pictures as they listen.
- Ask the gist question *What does the machine make?* and elicit the answer.

**Answer**
It makes colored paper.

**B** TRACK 112 TB p. 226 **Listen, say, and number the pictures in A.**

- Play the audio and have students point to the pictures and say the words.
- Tell students to listen again and write numbers next to the words in the picture. Do the example together (button).
- Check answers by calling out a number and acting out the corresponding word at the same time. Students should call out the word. Alternatively, project the answers using the TTL.

**Answers**
1 *button* 2 push 3 lever 4 pull 5 switch 6 flip
7 wheel 8 turn 9 gear

**C** TRACK 113 TB p. 226 **Close your eyes. Listen, visualize, and say.**

- Prepare students for the visualization (see TB p. 21).
- Play the audio, allowing students to visualize and act out the ideas as they listen.
- Have students draw a picture of the things they imagined during the visualization. They can then discuss their drawings in pairs.

**D Look and write.**

- Students are going to categorize the vocabulary. This encourages critical thinking and allows students to record the vocabulary clearly. Draw students' attention to the table. Write the two headings on the board and the example and elicit an example for *Actions*.
- Tell students to write the words from A in the table. Have students look at the pictures to help them.
- Check answers as a class. Students may be familiar with the verb form of the word *switch* from other contexts. If this comes up, explain both the noun and verb forms to the class and tell them it's OK to put the word in both categories.

**Answers**
Parts of a machine: *switch*, button, lever, wheel, gear
Actions: pull, turn, push, flip, switch

**E** TRACK 114 TB p. 226 **Listen and complete. Then watch and sing.**

- Point to the song title, *This Huge Machine*, and ask students which machine they think it means. Ask *What does the machine do?* Then play the song once, allowing students to listen and enjoy it.
- See if students can remember what the missing words are. Play the song again, this time pausing where necessary for students to write their answers.
- Check answers as a class.
- Play the song video and encourage students to sing and move to the music as they watch.

**Answers**
1 *pull* 2 flip 3 push 4 turn 5 gears 6 lever
7 wheels

### Cool Down

Play *Twenty Questions* (see TB p. 27). For this version, choose a machine (e.g. a computer).

**Practice Student's App:** Vocabulary Practice; Song Video

# Explore Language

## Lesson Objectives

- to review and practice comparisons with *than*
- to review and practice comparisons with *as … as*
- to practice parts of machines vocabulary and verbs

**Materials**

Audio Tracks 115 and 116

## Warm Up

Ask students to remember the scene from pp. 126–127. Ask *What were the children doing? What did the machine make? What parts did the machine have? Was the machine big? What other machines do you think there are?*

**A** TRACK 115 TB p. 227 **Listen and read. What does Ting want to know?**

- Tell students that they are going to listen to Carla and Ting talking about another machine. Ask *Are all the machines really big?* Play the audio and have students follow the story in their books. Check the answer with the class. (No, there's a little machine, too.)
- Ask the comprehension question *What does Ting want to know?* and elicit the answer.

**Answer**

She wants to know how the very small machine works.

**B Look at A. Complete.**

- Write or project the table onto the board.
- Have students discuss and complete the grammar table in pairs by looking at the story.
- Check answers on the board. Discuss word order and meaning of the comparative sentences together, but let your class guide the discussion. Make sure students notice that the *than* sentences include a comparative adjective and the *as … as* sentences include a normal adjective. Point out that we compare using *as … as*. Encourage students to notice that we can express the same idea using a *than* comparison and an *as … as* comparison; for example, *The small machine is quieter than the big one. The big machine isn't as quiet as the small one.* If you feel that students need more guidance, the **ETB** provides a differentiation activity to help you support students as they explore the grammar table.
- Refer students to the Grammar tip *Watch Out*. Write on the board *This machine's even bigger* ***then*** *the first one* and have students correct the mistake. Point out that in connected speech, *than* can sound like *then*.

**Answers**

's; bigger; than; interesting; big; as; as; exciting

**C Think and discuss. Then choose.**

- Write the first and third sentences from B on the board and have a student come to the front and draw a picture to illustrate each sentence.
- Have students work in pairs to discuss the sentences and answer options. Refer them to the table in B for examples. Then check answers.

**Answers**

1 different 2 the same

**D** TRACK 116 TB p. 227 **Listen and say.**

- Tell students they're going to practice saying the structures. Play the audio, having students repeat each sentence chorally.
- For ideas on how to vary the drill, see TB p. 23.

**E Look and complete.**

- Ask *What animals can you see?* Have students look at the picture of the two machines. *What parts do they have?*
- Have students do the activity individually. Remind them to look at the table in B to help them. Check answers as a class.

**Answers**

1 *as important as* 2 smaller than 3 bigger than
4 more complicated than 5 more simple than

**F Draw inventions and compare. How are they the same and different?**

- Tell students they are going to create some new inventions and draw them.
- Review the machine vocabulary by writing scrambled words on the board for students to guess.
- Refer students to the adjectives in the box. Tell students to use these words for ideas to create a machine; for example, *Is your machine tall or short? Does it have a long lever? Does it have big wheels? Does it have a small button?* Encourage students to use their imaginations with their drawings.
- Ask two volunteers to read the examples. Then have students work in pairs to show their drawings and make comparisons. If time and interest allow, have students switch partners and compare their drawings again.

## Cool Down

Play *Stand Up, Sit Down* in small groups (see TB p. 27). Make comparative sentences; for example, *A car isn't as fast as a helicopter.*

**Practice** **Resource Bank:** Grammar Printout
**Student's App:** Grammar Practice

# Global Citizenship

## Lesson Objectives

- to learn materials vocabulary: *cotton, gold, leather, metal, plastic, silver, wood, wool*
- to explore why people invent things
- to learn about inventions that help us
- to think about why it is important to share ideas
- to practice listening for gist and details

**Materials**

Audio Tracks 117 to 119; Audio Track J; world map (D)

## Opening Question

Ask the opening question: *Why do people invent new things?* Then encourage students to think about the different kinds of things people invent. Don't correct them or give much feedback; students will find out more about the topic during the lesson.

**A** TRACK 117 TB p. 227 **Listen to Lily talking to Grandpa José. What's special about his chair?**

- Tell students they are going to listen to a girl named Lily talking to her grandpa about his chair. Ask *Do you think Lily likes the chair?* Play the audio and have students point to the words or pictures as they listen. Check the answer with the class. (Yes, she does.)
- Ask the gist question *What's special about his chair?* Elicit answers, then play the audio again for students to check.

**Answer**

It folds up and fits/goes in his backpack.

**B** TRACK 118 TB p. 227 **Listen, say, and number the pictures in A.**

- Play the audio and have students point to the pictures and say the words.
- Tell students to listen again and write numbers next to the words in the pictures. Do the example together (cotton).
- Check answers by asking volunteers to call out the numbers and asking others to respond. Alternatively, project the answers using the TTL.

**Answers**

1 *cotton* 2 wool 3 leather 4 gold 5 silver
6 metal 7 plastic 8 wood

TRACK J TB p. 227 **Visualization**

The TTL has a visualization audio track for this vocabulary set. (See TB p. 21.)

**C Read and complete.**

- Look at the example together. Ask *What is the sentence describing?* and have students notice *jewelry*. Ask *What materials can jewelry be made of?*
- Have students do the activity individually. Then check answers as a class.

**Answers**

1 *gold*; silver 2 cotton 3 plastic 4 wool; leather
5 metal 6 wood

**D** TRACK 119 TB p. 227 **Now listen to Laura from Colombia. How old were the kids that she talks about?**

- Have students look at the two pictures and say what they see. Tell students they are going to listen to a girl called Laura from Colombia talking about inventions made by children in the USA. Have students find Colombia and the USA on a map. Ask some prediction questions: *Who is Laura? Why do you think she's talking about inventions? What do you think the children invented?* Give students time to discuss ideas and make predictions.
- Listening for gist: Ask the gist question *How old were the kids that she talks about?* Play the audio again. Elicit the answer from the class.

**Answer**

Cassidy was 11. CJ was 9.

**E Listen again. Answer the questions.**

- Listening for details: have students read the sentences before they listen again to see what they remember. Then play the audio and have students write their answers. Pause the audio where necessary to give students time to write.
- Check answers as a class.

**Answers**

1 *She invented crayon holders.* 2 It's made of plastic.
3 She made her invention because crayons break easily.
4 He made them for kids. 5 His cousin helped him make his first video. 6 You can see his videos online.

## Discussion Questions

- Draw students' attention to the discussion questions: *What invention do you want to make? Why is it important to share our ideas and inventions?* Have students discuss the questions in pairs or small groups. See **ETB**.
- Return to the opening question to ask again: *Why do people invent new things?* Recap ideas discussed at the beginning of the class and then encourage students to share any new ideas. Focus on the concept of how technology can help us in many different areas of our lives.

## Cool Down

Play *Describe It!* (see TB p. 25). Have students choose and describe inventions.



**Practice** **Student's App:** Vocabulary Practice; Listening Practice

## Explore Language

### Lesson Objectives

- to review modal verbs
- to practice materials vocabulary

**Materials**
Audio Tracks 120 and 121

### Warm Up

Tell students to think about all the different machines they know that have wheels. Give them two or three minutes to make a list in pairs. Have a volunteer pair read their list while the other students check off the same ones on their list. Have another pair add any additional ideas until the class has shared all their ideas. Which pair had the longest list?

**A** TRACK 120 TB p. 227 **Listen and read. What kind of wheels does the machine have?**

- Tell students that they are going to listen to the children in the picture finish making a machine. Have students look back at on pp. 126–127 to find all the characters. Ask *What do you think the machine does?* and elicit ideas from the class. Play the audio and have students follow the dialogue in their books.
- Ask the comprehension question *What kind of wheels does the machine have?* and elicit answers.

**Answer**
metal wheels

**B** **Look at A. Complete.**

- Write or project the table onto the board.
- Have students discuss and complete the grammar table in pairs by looking at the dialogue.
- Check answers on the board. Discuss the sentences together, but let your class guide the discussion. If you feel that students need more guidance, the **ETB** provides a differentiation activity to help you support students as they explore the grammar table.
- Encourage students to notice that there is only one form of *should* and *could* for all subjects, but *have* is *has* in third-person singular.
- Refer students to the Grammar tip *Watch Out*. Drill the pronunciation of *could* and *should* both isolated and in a sentence. Remind students that we don't pronounce the *l*.

**Answers**
have to; don't have to; should; shouldn't; could; could

**C** **Think and discuss. Then choose.**

- Have students underline the key point in each sentence (necessary, advice, possible, not necessary).
- Then have students work in pairs to discuss the sentences and circle the answers. Check answers as a class.

**Answers**
1 *have to* 2 should 3 could 4 don't have to

**D** TRACK 121 TB p. 227 **Listen and say.**

- Tell students they're going to practice saying the new structures. Play the audio, having students repeat each sentence chorally.
- For ideas on how to vary the drill, see TB p. 23.

**E** **Read and complete. Write about you.**

- Read the two examples to the class. Ask *Do you have to help your parents make dinner? What do you have to do?* Elicit some suggestions from the class. Encourage other students to say if they don't have to do those things.
- Have students complete the sentences with their own ideas in their books. Then have a few students share their ideas with the class.

**Answers**
Students' own answers

**F** **Play *Modal Madness*. Ask and answer about an imaginary machine.**

- Put students into pairs and give them a minute to think about a machine they could invent that does chores. Tell them they are going to ask each other questions to decide what it's made from and how it works.
- Have a pair of students read the example, then explain to students that they must use modal verbs (*should, could, have to*) in their discussion. Tell them they can also make suggestions using the modal verbs, as well as ask questions, e.g. *The machine could have wheels. Do you have to push a button to turn it on? No, you have to pull a lever.*
- Give students time to discuss their machines, then have them draw and present their ideas to another group.

### Cool Down

Have students role-play the dialogue in A in groups. Students can do the role-play in groups of five. Encourage students to improvise and change some of the dialogue by using different machine parts and different adjectives.

**Practice** **Resource Bank:** Grammar Printout
**Student's App:** Grammar Practice

# Take the Stage

## Lesson Objectives

- to prepare and practice a presentation about something you made
- to recognize and reproduce /br/ and /fl/

**Materials**

Video; Audio Track 122

## Warm Up

Ask students if they enjoy making things. Ask *What do you like making? Do you like to make things out of paper or other materials? Do you know how to do any special crafts, like origami or knitting? Do you like making models from kits?* Discuss these questions with the class. Try to open the discussion to include everyone and help students think of ideas for their presentations later. Remind students of any school projects they have done where they have made something.

**A** TB p. 239 **Watch and listen. Who helped Lewis?**

- Tell students they are going to watch a presentation by a boy named Lewis about something he made. Play the first scene of the video where Lewis talks about his noisy sisters. Ask *What do you think he made?* Play the rest of the video for students to find out and encourage students to notice Lewis's voice and body language.
- Ask the comprehension question *Who helped Lewis?* Elicit the answer. Ask a personalization question: *Do you like Lewis's tree house? Who do you ask for help when you make things?*

**Answer**

his dad

**B Watch again. Check (✔) the phrases you hear.**

- Have students read the phrases.
- Play the video again and have students check the phrases they hear. Check answers as a class.
- Have students classify the sentences into *Beginning, Middle,* and *End.* Then, with the class, build up the presentation on the board using the phrases.

**Answers**

1; 4; 5; 6; 8

### Pronunciation /br/ and /fl/

TRACK 122 TB p. 227 **Listen and say.**

Demonstrate the two sounds first. Isolate each phoneme in the cluster and elicit how to pronounce it (/b/; /r/). Then put the two sounds together /br/ and have students repeat it. Do the same for /fl/.

Play the audio and have students repeat the words. Repeat if students need more practice.

Say *These words are used in the video. What other words do you know with these sounds?* Elicit ideas and write them on the board in two columns (e.g. *broken, flip*). Drill the pronunciation of each word.

**Suggested Answers**

/br/ brush, brother, brown, broccoli, breathe, bread, zebra
/fl/ flower, flip, fly, flap, butterfly, cauliflower

**C Plan. Think about something you made. Complete.**

- Project the table in C onto the board. Complete it together, using the information from Lewis's presentation.
- Then draw students' attention to the table in their books. Tell them that they are going to plan their own presentation. They need to think of something they made and answer the questions.
- Have students complete the table individually.

**Answers**

Students' own answers

**D Prepare your presentation. Use your ideas from C and phrases from B.**

- Draw students' attention to the index cards they will use to plan their presentation. Ask *How many parts will your presentation have?* (three) *What is the first part?* (introduction) *What will you say here?* (that I made something) *What will you say next?* (what I made and when) Elicit the next two stages (why I made it and how I made it), then ask students how they can end their presentation (what happened after I made it).
- Have students prepare their presentations using their notes in C and phrases from B. Monitor and provide language help when needed.

**E Practice with a friend. Then share with your class.**

- Have students practice their presentation with their partner as many times as they like. They can use the information on their index cards the first few times they practice, but they should try not to read their cards.
- Invite students to demonstrate their presentation in front of the class. Remind students to sound enthusiastic and excited about their topic, to look at the faces in the audience, and to smile! Encourage the class to give a round of applause after each presentation.

## Cool Down

Ask students if they ever went in a tree house. Tell them to imagine they can go to Lewis's tree house. Write the following questions on the board and have students think and discuss their ideas with a partner. *Do you go alone or with Lewis? What do you take? What do you do there?*



**Practice** **Student's App:** Speaking Skills Practice; Speaking Video

## Write About It

### Lesson Objectives

- to learn to use transition words and phrases
- to plan and write a story

**Materials**

Cardboard box (WU); (optional) Support, Standard, and Challenge writing printouts downloaded from the Resource Bank, one per student (C and D)

### Warm Up

Play *Different Uses*. Show students a cardboard box. Put students in pairs and give them two or three minutes to think of as many possible uses for the box. Encourage them to use their imaginations and think of how they could use it to make different things.

**A Read the story. Circle the words that begin each paragraph.**

- Tell students they are going to read a story. Have students read the title and predict what the rainy day fun might be. Ask *What do you do on a rainy day? Do you have fun on rainy days?*
- Give students one or two minutes to read the story. Check students' predictions by asking *What did Luiza do on the rainy day?* (She made a slide.)
- Draw students' attention to the instructions. Ask *What do you have to circle?* (the first words in each paragraph) Have students work individually to read the story again and circle the words that begin each paragraph. Then check answers as a class.

**Answers**

*One rainy day,*
Suddenly,
In the end,

**B Look at A. Answer the questions.**

- Have students look at the questions. Discuss the first question together. Ask students if they can think of any other ways of starting a story. Then say *Imagine the title was* Windy Day Fun. *What words could the writer use to begin the story?*
- Have students answer the questions individually, looking back at A to help them. Then check answers as a class. Ask further questions to encourage students to think about the meaning of the phrases and possible alternatives; for example, *If something happens "suddenly," is it quick or slow? What things can happen suddenly?*

**Answers**

1 One rainy day 2 Luiza makes her slide.
3 First, Next, Then 4 In the end

**C Plan a story about these three pictures. Write.**

- Tell students they are going to think about three pictures and write a story about them. First, have students look at the pictures and say what they see.
- Tell students to write a sentence for each picture. These sentences will act as topic sentences that will help students identify the three main events in the story and where they fit in the story structure.
- Draw three columns on the board, with the headings *Beginning*, *Middle*, and *End*. Ask a few volunteers to read their sentences out loud. Write some of these on the board in the appropriate columns. Challenge printouts can be handed out now.

**Answers**

Students' own answers

**D Write your story.**

- Students are now going to write their stories. The stories should have three paragraphs. They should also use transition phrases and could use other conjunctions and time phrases. Have them use the three sentences they wrote in C as a basic idea and encourage them to think of other information and details they want to include in each paragraph. Remind students to think about how the characters are feeling, as well as what they're saying. Support printouts can be handed out now.
- Students should either self-correct or exchange their work with a friend and peer-correct. You can put a checklist of things to correct on the board (e.g. spelling, use of adjectives and adverbs, transition phrases, verb forms, punctuation).
- Have students write up their final stories on paper. Remind them to write three separate paragraphs. Alternatively, hand out the Standard printouts from the Resource Bank. Give students time to illustrate their stories.

### Cool Down

Have a storytelling session with the class. Have students sit in a circle, or in whatever routine you normally use with students when you read them stories. Place a chair at the front for the storyteller. Any student who wishes to read his/her story can sit in the chair and read it to the class. Encourage students to show emotion and excitement in their voices as they read, just like they did with their presentations in the previous lesson. If some students don't want to read their stories out loud, that's OK. They can sit and listen to the other stories, or perhaps they would prefer someone else to read their stories (another student or you).

**Practice** **Student's App:** Writing Practice

# Think It Over

## Lesson Objectives

- to review what has been learned in the unit
- to reflect on the unit and their own progress
- to think about learning strategies and how to continue learning at home

### Warm Up

Ask students what the unit theme was (machines and technology) and write it in the middle of the board. Brainstorm any words or phrases students can think of that relate to the topic and write them on the board. Encourage students to think about how important machines are in our everyday lives.

**Read the questions and draw or write your answers.**

- Give students time to think about and discuss activities in the unit before they complete each question. Explain that they can choose to either write a few words or sentences or to draw a picture. Allowing students to make a personal response will help them retain knowledge and engage with the learning points.

**What did I do?**

- Give students a few minutes to look back through the unit at the different activities they did. Ask questions about the unit or write them on the board; for example, *What machines do you remember? What did you write about?* Have them discuss their ideas in pairs or small groups.
- Encourage students to identify something in the unit that they found challenging or something that was particularly memorable for them, but tell them not to choose their favorite activity yet. Students can draw or write about their chosen activity.

**What did I learn?**

- Ask questions about the unit to help students think about what they learned; for example, *What did you learn about different machines? What did you learn about inventions created by children? What did you learn about making comparisons? What else did you learn? What sounds did you learn?* Have students discuss their ideas in pairs.
- Encourage students to draw a picture or write sentences about their learning outcomes.

**What was my favorite part?**

- Have students look back through the unit and decide what they enjoyed the most. Tell them it can be a text they found interesting, a fun pair work activity, a favorite character, a funny incident, or a speaking game. They should try to choose just one activity. Have students draw or write about the activity they liked the most. Remind them that when we like something, it is often easier to learn.

**How well did I do?**

- Tell students to color the model that best expresses how well they have learned the unit content. Ask *What do you understand? What do you need to practice more?* Encourage students to look back through the unit to see how much they remember, what they did well, and what they found difficult.

**What can I do next?**

- Brainstorm ideas with the class about what they can do to continue to learn (e.g. think about machines and technology and how they affect our everyday lives, find and pronounce words with /br/ and /fl/, identify different machines in the home and research how they work, do an arts and crafts or design technology activity).
- Draw students' attention to the *What can I do next?* box. Encourage students to think about what they can do at home to improve their English. Have them suggest some verbs that they can use (e.g. listen, read, write, discuss, research, make) and write the verbs they choose in their books. Students can look back at the previous units to get more ideas. Encourage students to suggest their own ideas for different activities they can do.
- Have students choose several activities that they would like to do and write them in their notebooks. They can then share their ideas with a friend.

### Reflection

Draw students' attention to the characters at the bottom of the page. Ask *Who are they* and elicit what they remember about the characters (they appear in various units throughout the book).

Ask *What did you like best in this unit and the book?* Give students five to ten minutes to look back through their books and remember the different activities they did during the year. They can discuss the things they remember with a partner or in small groups.

# Put It Together

To further review and recycle the language in Units 9 and 10, play the game, *Inside the Machine*, on pp. 138–139. See TB p. 210 for teaching notes.

# Play 2

To further review and recycle the language in Units 6 to 10 have students practice and perform the play, *Into the Future* on pp. 142–143. See TB p. 212 for teaching notes.



**Practice** **Resource Bank:** Unit Test; End-of-year Test
**Student's App:** Vocabulary and Grammar Review

## Get Ready to Read

### Lesson Objectives

- to activate prior knowledge about machines
- to guide inquiry and deepen understanding through a Question Starts VTR
- to preview the reading skill of understanding facts and opinions

**Materials**

A box (WU) (Optional) VTR printout from the Resource Bank (Activities A, B, C)

### Warm Up

Write the unit title *Don't Push the Button* on the board. Ask *Where might you see this? Who might say it? What does the button do?* Show students a box. Say *Imagine there's a button. What color is it? Do you want to push it?* Have students discuss their ideas in small groups. Then have groups share their ideas with the class.

### Question Starts

**A Look at the picture. Then brainstorm questions. Write a list.**

Students are going to do a Question Starts VTR to explore the image of a homemade machine.

- Have students look at the picture for a minute and then say what they can see. If students don't know a word in English, ask them to describe what they see so you can provide the word.
- Draw students' attention to the question words. Ask *What questions do you have about the picture?*
- Give students a few minutes to write questions in their notebooks.
- Encourage students to raise their hands to suggest questions. Write all suggestions on the board, helping students correct their questions.

**B Look at your list from A. Which questions seem most interesting? Discuss them with the class. Then discuss them as a class and decide on the most interesting questions.**

- Ask students to look at their list of questions individually and identify the questions they would most like to know the answers to.
- Tell students that they are going to practice negotiating skills by working as a group to decide which three questions they want to ask. Have students work in groups of three to review the questions and discuss possible answers. This will help them decide which questions they think are the most interesting.

Here's an example of this part of the routine:

**Teacher:** What questions are the most interesting? What do you want to know?
**Student A:** How does the machine start?
**Teacher:** Good question! What do you think?
**Student A:** I think there's a button behind the red glove.
**Teacher:** What does the button do?
**Student B:** I think it makes the spring come out.
**Teacher:** Great. What other questions do you have?
**Student C:** How long does it take to make this machine?
**Teacher:** What do you think?
**Student C:** A year!
**Student D:** I think you can make it quickly. You need a plan!

**C What new ideas or questions do you have now? Talk about your ideas with your partner.**

- Have students think of more ideas and questions about machines and how they work referring to the picture and their previous questions. Give students a couple of minutes to think of their own questions. Then have students share their questions in pairs and discuss any possible answers. Encourage them to be as creative as possible.

### Transition

Ask students if they think this machine is old or modern. Have them justify their answers by asking *What makes you say that?*

**D Think and discuss. What machines did you see on your way to school today?**

- Say *We use machines for a lot of different things in our lives. Did a machine bring you to school today?*
- Ask students to think about their morning routine and journey to school. Say *What machines did you see? What machines did you hear?* Have students discuss their ideas in pairs before sharing with the class.
- Make a spidergram on the board with their ideas.

**E Think and discuss. Choose one of the machines you saw. Say one true thing about it. Then say what you think about it.**

In this activity students will preview the reading skill of understanding facts and opinions.

- Do an example with the class, choosing one of the machines from the spidergram. Say *What do you know about this machine?* Elicit one or two facts from the class; for example, *The elevator goes up and down.*
- Then ask *Do you think the machine works well? Do you like it?* For example, *I don't like using elevators—I worry I'll get stuck.*
- Tell students to choose a machine, think of one thing they know about it, and what they think about it. Have them share their ideas in small groups and then as a class.

Now read **Moving Machines**

# Nonfiction: *Moving Machines*—Informational Text

## Lesson Objectives

- to read an article about the parts that make up a machine
- to learn about engineering through CLIL (science): exploring how parts work together to make a machine

**Materials**

Audio Tracks 50 and 51; mechanical toys or clickable ballpoint pens (one for each group)

## Warm Up

Ask *What is a machine?* Elicit that a machine is an object that does a job for us. Ask students to identify machines in the classroom. They may say electronic devices (computer, tablet, projector, interactive whiteboard, etc.) or classroom tools (clock, stapler, scissors, etc.).

## TRACK 50 TB p. 237 Reading Approach

**First Reading: Engage with the Text**

- Ask students to notice the title, subheadings, text, and pictures on the page and use this information to predict ideas about the reading. Ask *What machines can you see? What do you think they do?*
- Have students open their books and read silently. Remind students that they don't need to understand every word.

## TRACK 51 TB p. 237 Words in Context

- Play the audio and have students repeat the words.
- Have students race to find the words in the reading.
- Review all the strategies students have learned so far for working out the meaning of new words (see TB p. 23).
- Use these discussion points to confirm the meanings.

**basic** (p. 154) Refer students to the picture of the watch. Ask *How many parts does it have?* (a lot!) *Which parts does the reading tell us about?* Elicit that these *basic* parts are the main or most important parts.

**rod** (p. 154) Have students look at the picture and point to the rod. Ask *How do you know which part it is?* Elicit that the text describes the rod as *thin*.

**support** (p. 154) Explain that a support is something that holds something up or in place so it doesn't move. Have students identify the supports in the picture of the crank. Ask *What do they hold in place?* (the rod)

**either** (p. 155) Have students identify the lever in the picture and point to one end. Elicit what happens if we push it down and what happens if we push down the other end. Explain that here *either* shows us there is a choice: we can push down one end or the other end and get the same result.

**wind-up** (p. 156) Refer students to the words *wind-up doll*. Ask *How do we make the wind-up doll move?* Have students mime the action of turning the key to wind up the doll.

**swan** (p. 157) Have students look at the picture to identify the swan. Ask students what kind of animal it is (a bird). Ask *Did you ever see a real swan?*

- Ask students which strategies they used to figure out the meanings.

**Second Reading: Analyze the Text and Features**

- Play the audio and have students read along in their books.
- Ask some comprehension questions: *What does the belt do in a pulley?* (It connects the wheels and makes them move.) *What does the author think about machines?* (They are useful, fun, or both.)
- Discuss the questions in the pink boxes.
  - **Making Connections** (p. 155): *Where else can you find these parts?* Have students work in small groups to think of as many machines or devices as they can that have one or more of the four basic parts. Some examples are mechanical toys (e.g. clockwork cars), a toilet (flushing mechanism), a bicycle, and an office chair.
  - **Making Connections** (p. 156): *Which of the four parts can you see?* For homework, ask students to look at home and see how many objects they can find with cranks, gears, levers, or pulleys. Tell them to take a photo of the objects they find and share these in groups in the next lesson. You could award points to the student who finds the most objects, students who find an object with each of the four parts, and the student with the most interesting object!
  - **CLIL Focus (science)** (p. 157): *Do you like to take things apart and see how they work?* Have students discuss what things they have taken apart. Ask *Did you put it back together? Was it easy?* To extend the CLIL focus bring in a few small mechanical toys or clickable ballpoint pens and have students examine them and think about what parts they might have. If possible, allow them to take them apart and look at the different parts. Then have students try to put the pieces back together.

**Third Reading: Interact with the Text**

- In pairs, have students write down four things they now know about machines. Have them share their sentences with another pair. If they have a similar sentence, they should decide which one to keep. Then have the group organize their sentences into categories and add more sentences if necessary if they feel key information from the reading is missing.

## Cool Down

Play *Describe It!* (see TB p. 25) by choosing different machines.

## Explore the Reading

### Lesson Objectives

- to understand and analyze *Moving Machines* through reading comprehension activities
- to learn about engineering through CLIL (science): thinking about the purpose of machines

**Materials**
(Optional) Audio Track 50

### Warm Up

Play *Unscramble* (see TB p. 27).

Anagrams: *rackn* (crank); *elerv* (lever); *llupey* (pulley); *egar* (gear)

Then have students think of a machine that has each of these parts ( e.g. the inside of a clock).

**B A Read and answer.**

- If more than one day has passed since students read *Moving Machines*, play the audio again and have students follow in their books.
- With books closed, have a Group Time discussion (see TB p. 21) to check students' comprehension of the reading. Ask *What moving parts do you know?* (crank, gear, lever, pulley) *Why were people excited about automata?* (because they were new and fun) *How does the swan move* (It turns its head and catches a fish.) *When do automata start to move?* (when you push a button)
- Have students open their books and read the first question. Ask *Can you find this in the reading?* Have students look back and find the answer (a gear). Remind students not to read every word.
- Have students do the rest of the activity individually. Check answers as a class.

**Answers**
1 a gear 2 a crank 3 a lever 4 a pulley

**B Think and discuss. What parts can you see? How do you think it works?**

- Project the image of the bicycle onto the board. Ask students if they often ride a bike.
- Ask students if they can find the machine parts from their answers in A in the picture of the bike. Point to the gears and ask *What's this part? What does it do?*
- Give students one or two minutes to think about the parts and how they work. Remind them to look back at the reading if they wish. Then have them share their ideas with a partner. Invite some pairs to share their ideas with the class.

**Suggested Answers**
I can see gears, levers, cranks, and a pulley. I think the gears help these (pedals) turn. Here are the cranks. I think they turn the gears. There's a pulley. It connects the gears and help them move. There are two levers (in the hand brakes). They help you to stop.

**Practice** **Student's App:** Reading Practice

**C Think and discuss. Imagine you are building a machine. What would you like it to do?**

- This activity will draw on the CLIL science focus of thinking about the purpose of machines. Discuss with the class what machines are for. Ask *Why do we need or use different machines? What do we use them for? Do they help us? How?* Encourage students to give ideas; for example, *We use elevators to go up and down in a building so that we don't have to walk up stairs.* Elicit several ideas and write them on the board.
- Ask *Can you think of something that you would like a new machine to do? Is there something in your everyday life that could be easier if a machine did it?* Ask students to think of a moving machine they would like to invent. This could be as simple or as complex as they like. It could be a simple machine or an automaton. Have them think for a few minutes and write down their ideas.
- Then have students discuss their ideas in pairs or small groups.

### Cool Down

Have students work in small groups to rank the following list of machines in order from most complex to simplest. This develops students' critical thinking skills.

*an airplane, a bicycle, a pencil sharpener, a door handle, a vacuum cleaner, a microscope*

Then have students rank the machines in order from most useful to least useful. Students can see if there is a relationship between how complex and how useful the machines are.

Note: there are no right or wrong answers. Encourage students to explain their reasons for the order they have chosen.

# Get Ready to Read

## Lesson Objectives

- to practice the reading skill of understanding facts and opinions
- to activate prior knowledge about cowboys
- to make a personal connection to the reading

**Materials:**
Slips of paper, six per pair (CD)

## Warm Up

Play a version of the *Yes/No Game* (see TB p. 27) with facts and opinions. Assign one side of the classroom as *agree* and the other as *disagree*. For the facts, everyone should move to the same side of the room, whereas for the opinions, students may go to different sides.

Example statements: *A car is a machine. / My car is beautiful. / A car has four wheels. / Cars are faster than horses. / Sports cars are better than family cars. / Traveling by car is more comfortable than traveling by train. / Traveling by motorcycle is more dangerous than traveling by plane.*

Note: statistically it is more dangerous to travel by car than by plane. Traveling by motorcycle is even more dangerous.

**A Read and choose. Then write *Fact* or *Opinion*.**

Students are going to practice the reading skill of understanding facts and opinions.

- Draw students' attention to the picture. Ask *What's this?* Tell students to read the paragraph quickly. Then ask them what they learned from the text.
- Have students read the first part of the skills box: *A fact is a piece of information that is true. An opinion is what someone thinks.* Look at the example. Say *If someone says it is cool, is it a fact or their opinion?* Ask students if everyone thinks the toy is cool. Point out that some people might not like it. This means that *cool* is someone's opinion. Then have students find a fact in the paragraph. Remind them that a fact is something we know is true.
- Have students choose whether each sentence is a fact or an opinion. Then check answers as a class.
- Direct students back to the skills box and have them read more about opinions. Ask *Which words in the text tell us that it's an opinion?* (cool, want)

**Answers**
1 Opinion 2 Fact 3 Fact 4 Fact 5 Opinion

**B Read this text from *Searching for Sterling*. Underline the opinions.**

- Draw students' attention to the picture. Ask *What do you see?* What do you think the story is about?
- Ask three volunteers to read the text aloud: one student is the narrator, one is Ed, and the other is Jules.
- Tell students they are going to practice the reading skill of understanding facts and opinions. Tell students to read the text again and underline the opinions. Remind them that opinions are what people think.
- Check answers as a class, having students say where in the text they found the answer.

**Answers**
That was a hard day. Oh, Sterling's great.

**C Think and discuss. Look in your notebooks and find something you wrote. Where did you include facts and opinions?**

- Tell students that they are going to look in their notebooks to find facts and opinions. A good place to look is the work they did in the writing lessons, especially the book report (which should contain both), the anecdotal paragraph, the diary entry, and the letter to a friend.
- Tell students to underline examples of both facts and opinions. They can look at more than one piece of writing if necessary.
- Then have students share the facts and opinions they found and discuss where they found them.
- Discuss with students the importance of differentiating facts from opinion. Explain that a good reader must always think about the opinions expressed in a text rather than accept them as facts. This is an important critical literacy skill.

## Cool Down

Ask students to work in pairs to write one fact and one opinion about three of the following topics on slips of paper: reading, biomes, vegetables, coral reefs, an animal (of their choice). For example, *Reading is good for your brain.* (fact); *Comic books are funny.* (opinion) They should write one sentence on each piece of paper.

Collect the sentences and then hand them out randomly to students. In pairs, have them decide which are facts and which are opinions.

Now read **Searching for Sterling**

# Fiction: *Searching for Sterling—* Science Fiction

## Lesson Objectives

- to read a science-fiction story about a cowboy and his horse
- to make a personal connection to the reading

**Materials**

Audio Tracks 52 and 53; Video; a short clip of a Western movie suitable for children (WU)

## Warm Up

Play a short clip of a Western to introduce the topic of cowboys and to activate schema. Then have students discuss what they noticed about the scene. You could ask questions to help generate discussion; for example, *What were the people wearing? What were they doing? How did they travel? When do you think the movie was set? Do you think they had machines? What were they like?*

### TRACK 52 TB p. 237 Reading Approach

**First Reading: Engage with the Text**

- Ask students to notice the title, text, and pictures on the page and use this information to predict ideas about the reading.
- Ask the first question in the pink box (p. 160): *What do you know about cowboys?* Have students work in pairs to make a spidergram about cowboys. They can compare their ideas with what they learn from the story at the end of the lesson.
- Ask the gist questions *Where does Sterling go? Does the story have a happy ending?* Play the video and elicit answers.
- Then look at the Words in Context.

### TRACK 53 TB p. 237 Words in Context

- Play the audio and have students repeat the words.
- Have students race to find the words in the reading.
- Review all the strategies students have learned so far for working out the meaning of new words (see TB p. 23). Have students discuss the words in pairs.
- Then use these discussion points to confirm the meanings.

**cowboys** (p. 160) Have students look at the picture to find the cowboys. Ask *How do you think they got their name?* Ask *What do these boys do?* Elicit that they take care of the cows. Tell students that sometimes we can guess a word's meaning from its parts.

**cattle** (p. 160) Ask *What were they moving?* (cows) *Why do you think it says "cattle" and not "cows"?* Tell students that cows and bulls are called cattle. A cowboy's job is to take care of the cattle.

**shuts down** (p. 160) Refer students to the sentence *"When I push the Go to Sleep button he shuts down,."* Ask *Do robots sleep? When you aren't using a machine, what do you do?* Elicit that you *turn it off* and that this is a synonym of *shut down.*

**motorcycle** (p. 161) Students might already know this word. Ask students *What's the difference between a bicycle and a motorcycle?* Elicit that a motorcycle has a motor (an engine).

**fell asleep** (p. 162) Ask students if they know a similar word to *asleep*. Elicit that Jules went to *sleep*. Explain that *fall asleep* and *go to sleep* are synonyms.

**tough** (p. 163) Ask *Do you think it was an easy day for Jules? Why not?* Elicit that he was sad because he lost his horse, he had no food, and it was cold. Say *Do you think "tough" means easy or difficult?*

- Ask students which strategies they used to figure out the meanings.

**Second Reading: Analyze the Text and Features**

- Play the audio and have students follow along in their books.
- Ask some questions to check comprehension: *How is Jules's horse different from the others?* (He's a robot.) *How does Jules make Sterling go to sleep?* (He pushes a button.) *Who does Jules ask for help?* (the Sheriff) *When does Jules have to bring back the motorcycle?* (tonight) *Where did Sterling go?* (He went home.)
- Discuss the questions in the pink boxes. Use the Think, Pair, Share routine (see TB p. 20).
  - **Making Connections** (p. 162): *What do you think* under the stars *means?* Ask *Where are the stars?* (in the sky) Say *Jules sleeps under the stars. Does he sleep inside or outside?* (outside)
- Point out the text focus: *A big problem in a story is called **conflict**.* Have students identify the conflict in the story (Jules loses his horse).

**Third Reading: Interact with the Text**

- Have students work in pairs to summarize the story in three sentences using the sequencers *First, Next, Finally.* Have them share their summary with a different pair. Do they have the same or different points?

## Cool Down

Tell students that you are going to give them some answers to questions about the story, but they have to think of the questions. Explain that an answer could have many different questions, so they can use their imagination. Have students work in pairs. Answers: cattle; he goes to sleep; a motorcycle; it was too dark; because he lost his horse.

**Practice** Student's App: Fiction Video

## Explore the Reading

### Lesson Objectives

- to understand and analyze *Searching for Sterling* through reading comprehension activities
- to make a personal connection to the reading
- to explore the SEL competency of self-management through overcoming obstacles and creating strategies for more long-term goals
- to reproduce and write words with *ough*

**Materials**
Audio Track 54

### Warm Up

Do a visualization, having students do actions as they imagine. Say *Imagine you're a cowboy like Jules. You get on your horse. What's its name? You push a button and your horse starts to run. You're riding your horse across the fields. It's very hot and your horse needs a drink. You see a river. Get off your horse and let it drink. Now you're hungry. Make a fire and cook your dinner. What are you eating? Now you and your horse are tired—go to sleep.*

**A Read and write *True* or *False*. Write the page where you found the answer.**

- Have students read the summaries of *Searching for Sterling* that they wrote at the end of the previous lesson.
- With books closed, ask questions to see what students remember about the reading; for example, *Where were the cowboys going?* (south/home) *When did Jules know Sterling was gone?* (very early the next morning) *Why did Jules need a motorcycle?* (because Sterling wasn't a normal horse / was very fast) *How did Jules feel?* (tired, hungry, and sad) *Who found Sterling?* (Sheriff Ada)
- Have students open their books and read the sentences. Then ask a volunteer to read aloud the example sentence. Have students look back at the story and find the answer.
- Have students do the rest of the activity individually, by looking back at the reading to find the answers. Check answers as a class and ask students to tell you where they found the answer.

**Answers**
1 *False; 160* 2 False; 161 3 True; 162 4 False; 164
5 True; 165 6 False; 165

**B Write one fact and one opinion.**

- Tell students they are going to practice the reading skill of understanding facts and opinions. Review what facts and opinions are by playing *Stand Up, Sit Down* (see TB p. 27). Call out a variety of facts and opinions; for example, *It was almost winter.* (fact) *You're the best sheriff.* (opinion) See **ETB**.
- Have students look at the pictures. Ask *What fact do you know about Sterling?* Elicit answers. Ask *What's Jules's opinion about Sterling?* Have students complete the activity individually and then compare answers in pairs. Let them know there may be more than one possible answer and it's fine to answer the questions differently. Do they agree with their partner's answers?

**Suggested Answers**
1 Fact: He left the campsite because Jules didn't press the Go to Sleep button.; Opinion: He's better than all the other horses. 2 Fact: You have to press a button to start it.; Opinion: It's a great motorcycle. 3 Fact: It ate all of Jules's food.; Opinion: It made a strange noise.

**C Think and discuss. Imagine you are Jules. Would you return the motorcycle to the Sheriff on time? Why or why not?**

- Students are going to make a personal connection to the reading and explore the SEL competency of self-management through overcoming obstacles and creating strategies for more long-term goals.
- Give students a few minutes to think about the question individually. Then have them discuss their ideas in pairs, giving reasons for their answer.
- To check answers with the class, have students raise their hands if they would return the motorcycle on time. Choose a few students with their hands raised to explain their reasons. Then repeat with those who would keep the motorcycle for longer.

### Spelling Pattern *ough*

TRACK 54 TB p. 237 **Listen and write. Then check your answers.**

- With books closed write *ough* on the board.
- Play the first part of the audio and have students repeat each word. Then have them open their books. Play the first part of the audio again and have them complete as many words as they can.
- Then play the second part of the audio for students to check their spelling and complete the words correctly. Have them underline *ough* in each word and read the words aloud.
- Ask *Do they all rhyme?* (no—in fact, they all have different sounds!) Have students notice that the *gh* sound is pronounced **/f/** in cough and rough but is silent in dough, through, and thoughtful.
- Have students look back at the reading to find more words with *ough*. Check answers with the class and correct pronunciation as necessary.

**Answers**
1 cough 2 rough 3 thoughtful 4 dough 5 though
From the reading: thought, tough

### Cool Down

Have students choose their favorite image, scene, word or phrase from the story. Then have them share why they like it; e.g. *I like how it sounds.*

**Practice**
**Resource Bank:** Spelling Printout
**Student's App:** Reading Practice; Spelling Pattern Practice

## Think Together

### Lesson Objectives

- to make connections between the readings
- to explore the key concept: Does technology make our lives easier?
- to reflect on the unit and provide personal thoughts and opinions

**Materials**

(Optional): Stickers (CD)

### Warm Up

Ask students how they think the VTR picture on pp. 152–153 connects to the two readings in the unit. If necessary, write the following prompts on the board: *machine parts / how the machine works / what the machine is for / how useful the machine is / machines in the future.* Encourage students to be creative in their answers; for example, *Machines have a lot of parts and are complicated; Machines help us do things faster; It's important to design new machines for the future.*

**A Think and write. What machines are there in the two readings? What does each one do?**

- With books closed, brainstorm the machines that appear in the unit as a class and write their suggestions on the board. Then choose one and ask *What does it do?* Elicit ideas from the class.
- Have students open their books and look at the graphic organizer. Use the first idea you discussed to complete the table together.
- Have students work individually to write their ideas about the different machines. Then have a few students share their ideas with the class.

**Suggested Answers**

Clock: it tells the time; Automaton: it can move on its own; Sterling: it can go home and go to sleep; Sheriff's motorcycle: it can go fast; it moves on two wheels

**B Think and discuss. What are three useful machines you use at home? Do a Round Robin.**

Students are going to make connections to the key concept in the unit *Does technology make our lives easier?* using a Round Robin routine (see TB p. 20).

- Have students look at the question. Do an example: *I think the fridge is really useful because it keeps food fresh and we don't get sick.* Give students a few minutes to think silently.
- Then have students do the Round Robin to think of three (or more) machines they use at home. Students should say why each machine is useful.
- Ask *Do all these machines make our lives easier?* Ask volunteers to use the examples they discussed in the Round Robin routine to say how they do or don't make their lives easier.

**Practice** **Resource Bank:** Unit Test; End-of-year Test
**Student's App:** Key Concept Practice

### My Reading Journal

**Which machine from this unit would you like to build? Who would you ask for help?**

This question focuses on personalization. Tell students which machine you would like to build. Give students a few minutes to look back through the unit and find a machine that they would like to build. Ask *Will it be easy or hard? What will you need to build it? Who might be able to help you?* Have students discuss their ideas with a friend. Then have them complete the sentences in their books.

**Example Answer**

I'd like to build a robot pet like Sterling. I'd ask my uncle Jim.

**Which reading was your favorite in the whole book?**

Tell students which reading was your favorite. Give students a few minutes to look back through the whole book to find their favorite reading. Encourage students to give reasons for their choices. Ask *What did you like about it?* Have them complete the sentence in their books.

**Example Answer**

My favorite was *A Surprise Cure* because the spider was funny.

### Cool Down

Tell students that they have now finished the **Literacy Book**. They should give themselves a round of applause for finishing! You could have students evaluate their progress throughout the year. How happy are they with what they have learned? You could bring in some stickers and have students choose one to reflect their feelings.

## Where in the World?

### Lesson Objectives

- to review vocabulary from Units 1 and 2, focusing on book genres, adjectives, school subjects, and the world around us
- to review grammar from Units 1 and 2, focusing on the past simple, comparatives, and superlatives
- to practice communication and fluency skills

### Warm Up

Put students into teams to review comparative and superlative adjectives and adverbs. Say *Make a (comparative) sentence using (quick)* and have teams race to write a grammatically correct sentence. The first team to do so wins a point. The first team to get five points wins the game.

### How to Play

- Project the game onto the board using the TTL or hold up your book.
- Put students in teams of four and assign each student a biome (or let them choose). Each student takes turns to choose a square in their biome and answer the question or make a comparison using the words or pictures.
- Do an example with the class and choose a question. Elicit an answer and write it on the board. Ask *Is it correct? Are there any mistakes?* Let students know that sentences and answers must be grammatically correct.
- Draw students' attention to the images and elicit what each one shows, so that they will be able to make comparisons more easily. Remind them that they can use either adjectives or adverbs to make comparisons.
- Show students the flower and how to color it in. Explain that each time someone answers all the questions in their biome, they can color part of the flower (roots, stem, leaves, and petals). Demonstrate using the TTL.
- Tell students that the first team to color in the whole flower wins the game.

### Answers

Students' own answers.

### Playtime Practice

Have students work in their teams to write or draw three more questions/comparisons for each biome.

Tell them to pass their questions/comparisons to a different team. Let students know that this time they will be playing against the other students in their team. Students should take turns to answer the new questions for their biome. They get a point for each grammatically correct sentence. If another student thinks the sentence is incorrect, they can challenge and gain a bonus point. The winner is the student with the most points.

### Cool Down

Play *Draw It!* (see TB p. 25) using words from Units 1 and 2.

## Come to the Show!

### Lesson Objectives

- to review vocabulary from Units 3 and 4, focusing on money, time, and performance
- to review grammar from Units 3 and 4, focusing on modal verbs and past progressive questions and answers
- to practice communication and fluency skills

**Materials**

Coins (one per group); *Spinner and Counters* printout from the Resource Bank (one counter per player)

### Warm Up

Write *Come to the Show!* on the board and elicit its meaning. Ask *What kinds of shows do you know?* and elicit suggestions.

Then have students look at the pictures on the page and name the things they see. Ask *What kind of show is it?* (a school play)

### How to Play

- Cut out the counters before the lesson.
- Review language for playing board games before students play. Ask students what phrases they use when they play a board game. Write their suggestions on the board. Examples: *It's my turn. / Flip! / One, two … / Who's first? / Where's the coin? / Move two squares.*
- Project the board game onto the board using the TTL.
- Put students in pairs or small groups with one book between them. Give each student a counter. Have students color their counters a different color from other members of their group. Show students how to flip a coin and explain that if it lands on heads, they should move one square. If it lands on the other side, they should move two squares. Do an example with the class and point to the square you land on. Depending on the type of square, follow the directions or answer the question.
- Tell students that the winner is the first student to reach the Finish square.

**Answers**

Students' own answers.

Square 17, math symbols: + plus, - minus, = equals

### Playtime Practice

In pairs, have students choose one of the questions from the game and try to think of as many possible answers as possible; for example,

*What was your teacher doing five minutes ago?*

*She was listening to the class.*

*She was writing on the board.*

*She was thinking about the game.*

*She was giving instructions.*

*She was showing us how to play.*

### Cool Down

Play *Mime It!* (see TB p. 26) using words from Units 3 and 4.

## Say Three Things!

### Lesson Objectives

- to review vocabulary from Units 5 and 6, focusing on noises, musical instruments, kitchen and food, and a balanced diet
- to review grammar from Units 5 and 6, focusing on *going to*, infinitives, and gerunds
- to practice communication and fluency skills

**Materials**

*Spinner and Counters* printout from the Resource Bank (one spinner per group; one counter per player)

### Warm Up

Write *food* on the board. Then put students in pairs and have them play *Word Tennis* (see TB p. 27) with words on the topic of food. Repeat with the topic of sounds.

Then have students look at the pictures on the page and name the things they see.

### How to Play

- Make the spinners and cut out the counters before the lesson (or reuse them from the previous Put It Together lesson).
- Review language for playing board games before students play. Ask students what phrases they use when they play a board game. Write their suggestions on the board. Examples: *It's my turn. / Spin! / One, two, three, four … / Who's first? / Where's the spinner? / Move four squares.*
- Project the board game onto the board using the TTL.
- Put students in pairs or small groups with one book between them and one spinner. Have each student color their counter a different color from the other students in their group. Say *Place your counters on Start. Use your spinners. Look at the number and move your counter.* Do an example with the class and point to the square you land on. Elicit examples of the three phrases.
- Show students the points chart and how to complete it. Say *Each time you say a sentence, color one square.* Demonstrate using the TTL.
- Tell students that the winner is the first student in each group to get 20 points. They should carry on spinning and moving around the board until this happens.

**Answers**

Students' own answers.

### Playtime Practice

Have students write new questions and prompts for the game in groups. They can base these on Units 1 to 4. Do an example with the class first: *Talk about your school schedule. On Monday mornings I have …*

*On Thursdays I don't have …*

*My favorite subject is …*

Have students make a new board game with their questions. Students can either play their own game or exchange it with another group.

### Cool Down

Play *Describe It!* (see TB p. 25) using words from Units 5 and 6.

## Crossword Clues

### Lesson Objectives

- to review vocabulary from Units 7 and 8, focusing on emergency services, natural disasters, marine life, and patterns
- to review grammar from Units 7 and 8 focusing on relative clauses and the simple present
- to practice fluency and communication skills

**Materials**
Grids or graph paper

### Warm Up

Ask students if they ever do crossword puzzles. Elicit the features of a crossword (there are clues, there are squares for the letters, words can go across or down). Tell students to imagine they have to write clues for a crossword. Give them the following words (not in the activity) and have them suggest clues.

fridge / microwave / carbohydrate / stage / wallet / rehearsal

### How to Play

- Tell students they are going to solve a crossword puzzle by giving each other clues.
- Put students in pairs and have them decide who is Student A and B. Say *Raise your hand if you are Student A.* Tell them to look at the crossword puzzle on p. 112. Do the same with Students B, telling them to look at the one on p. 113. Make sure students fold their books so they can only see their page.
- Have students complete as much of the crossword as they can by looking at the pictures at the top of the page. Say *Your partner has the other words. You have to ask questions to find out what the words are. Take turns.*
- Do an example using the speech bubbles. Elicit how to complete the examples: *It's something that fish swim in* (aquarium). *It's an animal that lives in the sea and is very big* (whale).
- Tell students to take turns asking their partner for clues and giving explanations until both students in the pair have completed their crosswords, or written as many words as they can. When they have finished, students should compare crosswords and check that all the answers are the same.

**Answers**
Across: 1 round 6 seahorse 9 aquarium 10 avalanche 11 tsunami 12 striped
Down: octopus 3 dolphin 4 shark 5 clownfish 7 whale 8 ambulance

### Playtime Practice

Have students make their own crossword puzzles. You could give them a grid or graph paper on which to design their crosswords. Students can choose vocabulary from any of the previous units. You could assign a vocabulary set to each student or allow students to choose their own words.

### Cool Down

Play *Describe It!* (see TB p. 25) using words from Units 7 and 8.

# Inside the Machine

## Lesson Objectives

- to review vocabulary from Units 9 and 10, focusing on illnesses, treatments, how machines work, and materials
- to review grammar from Units 9 and 10, focusing on the past progressive with *when* and *while*, comparatives with *than* and *as … as*, and modal verbs
- to practice communication and fluency skills

**Materials**

*Spinner and Counters* printout from the Resource Bank (one spinner per group; one counter per player)

## Warm Up

Write *Machines* on the board. Then put students in pairs and have them play *Word Tennis* (see TB p. 27) with words on the topics of machines and health.

Then have students look at the pictures on the page and name the parts of the machine they see.

## How to Play

- Make the spinners and cut out the counters before the lesson (or reuse them from previous Put It Together lessons).
- Review language for playing board games. Ask students what phrases they use when they play a board game. Write their suggestions on the board. Examples: *It's my turn. / Spin! / One, two, three, four … / Who's first? / Where's the spinner? / Move four squares. / Miss a turn.*
- Project the board game onto the board using the TTL.
- Put students in small groups with one book between them and one spinner. Have them color their counters a different color from the other students in their group. Say *Put your counters on START. Use your spinners. Look at the number and move your counter.* Do an example with the class and point to the square you land on. Elicit an answer to the question. Ask *Is the sentence correct?*
- Write on the board *That's correct! / You made a mistake.* Ask students when they might say these phrases during the game. Tell students they must listen carefully to their teammates during this game, as only a grammatically correct answer will allow them to move on to the next square and wait for their next turn. If their answer is grammatically incorrect, they must stay on that square and try again on their next turn.
- Point out the pipes and gears. Say *The pipes go down, but the gears go up.* Show students how to move down or up as they land on one of the squares with a pipe or gear. If students are familiar with the game *Snakes and Ladders*, explain that the pipes are the snakes and the gears are the ladders.
- Tell students that the winner is the first student in each group to reach the *FINISH* square.

**Answers**

1 pull the lever 2 He sneezed. 3 Nurse Hayes 4 (move up) 5 He's sick. He has earache and a cough. 6 Push (stop) the button. 7 The jacket is warmer than the T-shirt. 8 dizzy / nervous 9 (move down to 1) 10 Students' own answers 11 (move up to 13) 12 (miss a turn) 13 Her dad was reading a book while she was visiting the doctor. 14 Students' own answers. 15 (move up to 19) 16 medicine 17 (move down to 7) 18 leather 19 pull the lever down 20 She shouldn't be at work. She should be at home (in bed) 21 He's pulling the lever 22 (move up to 26) 23 Yes, plastic is as strong as wood. 24 He has a cast. 25 (miss a turn) 26 He should cover his mouth to stop germs spreading. 27 (move down to 20) 28 Students' own answers.

**Playtime Practice**

Have students design their own game in groups. It could be a board game like this one based on *Snakes and Ladders* or a different kind of game. Encourage students to be creative and invent a new game or design. They can choose a theme for their game and use this to design the board. They can write questions or challenges on the board or make cards.

## Cool Down

Play *Draw It!* (see TB p. 25) using words from the whole book.

# The Grassland Orchestra

**Materials**
**Audio Track 123; pieces of paper (WU); simple props and scenery, e.g. an old book, masks for the animals, colored paper and pens to create a forest scene, paper to make programs**

## Warm Up

Play *Pass the Paper* (see TB p. 26) using the following lexical sets: forest, tundra, desert, grassland. Encourage students to think of animals, plants, and climate vocabulary.

## Teacher's Notes

**Setting:** A library and a theater stage in the grasslands.
**Characters and action:** The children in the play are first in a library reading a book, then in a fun African grassland scene. They travel into the book and become part of the story. The grassland animals act as a Chorus in the play.

## TRACK 123 TB p. 227 Listen and Engage

- Show students the title of the play. Ask them to predict what it is about. Ask *What animals live in the grassland? What animals do you think are in the play? Can the animals play instruments?* Have students share their ideas using a Think, Pair, Share routine (see TB p. 20).
- Have students open their books and look at the pictures on the page and check their answers.
- Draw students' attention to the character list. Ask *How many characters are there?* (five main characters and other animals) Point out that the animals are a group of characters that act as a chorus. Then have students find each character's name in the script.
- Play the audio and have students listen and follow in their books. At the end of the play Isabella says *That was exciting!* Ask if students agree with her.

## Interact

- Act out different sections of the play and have students guess which part it is. Then play the audio again and encourage students to do actions as they listen; for example, *Look at this old book!* (picking up and opening a book) and *I think we're in the book!* (looking at yourself, then around with a puzzled expression)
- Play the audio again and have students repeat each line chorally. Students can do actions if they wish.

## Practice and Prepare

- Tell students that they are going to practice the play to perform to an audience. Decide whether you want to have students perform the play in class or if you want to organize a performance with a live audience. If you are just going to perform the play in class, you could have students perform in groups.
- Assign roles to students. You could ask for volunteers and have students choose roles, or you could have students audition for specific parts.
- Practice once with the audio track. Play each section of the play, pausing after every few lines. Have the actors repeat their lines after hearing them. This will give them a chance to copy the pronunciation and intonation. Students can highlight or underline their parts in the script.
- Refer students to the stage directions on the page. Ask students what each character should do at each stage in the play and encourage them to think about how the characters are feeling. Have students who are playing each role demonstrate how they can follow the directions. Encourage other students to make suggestions.
- Have students practice their lines with a partner. They should listen to each other and make sure they are pronouncing their lines correctly. Monitor and help with pronunciation and intonation and give students a lot of encouragement and praise!
- Practice the play with all the actors without the audio. It is a good idea to rehearse once every day, at the end of the lesson. The more times students practice, the better their performance will be.
- Note: All students should be involved in some way. Some students may not wish to act. These students can have behind-the-scenes roles: stage manager (responsible for all props and everything needed for the play), costume director, makeup director, scenery painter, prop designer, camera director, prompter. They can be involved in organizing and creating simple props, scenery, invitations and programs while the others are rehearsing.

## Perform

- Invite parents or other classes to the performance. You may wish to use the school auditorium for this. An end-of-term performance can be a good way to show what students have learned.
- Designate some students to be in charge of welcoming the audience and showing them to their seats, and others to introduce the play. Remind students that the most important thing is to enjoy themselves!

## Cool Down

Have students look at the final stage direction of the play where Marco picks up a science-fiction book. Say *Imagine they fall into a book again. What adventures will they have?* Have students discuss their ideas in pairs or small groups.

# Into the Future

**Materials**

Audio Track 124; simple props and scenery, e.g. clothes or equipment for the different jobs: snorkel or goggles (Diego), a white coat (Noor), a bag with tools (Eli), a chef's hat (Laura), aluminum foil and cardboard for the time machine, paper for programs

## Warm Up

Tell students to think about the future of the people in their class. They should write three predictions about their classmates' lives; for example, *Luisa will be a doctor.* Then have students share their ideas in small groups. Do they agree?

## Teacher's Notes

**Setting:** An empty factory warehouse. Large, futuristic time machine is center stage.

**Characters and action:** Jin has invented a time machine and is showing it to his friends (Diego, Noor, Eli, Laura, and Kelsey), who want to travel to the future to save the world. The Chorus is a mix of boys and girls—they play a supporting role but do not appear as individual characters.

## TRACK 124 TB p. 228 Listen and Engage

- Show students the title of the play. Ask *How can we travel into the future? What questions do you have about the future? What is a time machine? What does it look like?* Have students share their ideas using a Round Robin routine (see TB p. 20).
- Have students open their books and look at the pictures. Encourage students to compare them with the time machine they imagined.
- Draw students' attention to the character list. Ask *How many characters are there?* (six main characters, and the chorus) Then have students find each character's name in the script.
- Play the audio and have students listen and follow in their books. Then ask *What happens in the story?* Encourage a few students to contribute to a brief summary of the story. Have them say which character they think seems the most interesting and why.

## Interact

- Play the audio again and encourage students to do actions as they listen; for example, *I'm ready!* (raising your hand) and *Go in!* (pointing to the machine).
- Play the audio again and have students repeat each line chorally. Students can do actions if they wish.

## Practice and Prepare

- Tell students that they are going to practice the play to perform to an audience. Decide whether you want to have students perform the play in class or if you want to organize a performance with a live audience.
- Assign roles to students. You could ask for volunteers and have students choose roles, or you could have students audition for specific parts.
- Practice once with the audio track, focusing on pronunciation and intonation. Students can highlight or underline their parts in the script.
- Have students practice their lines with a partner. They should listen to each other and make sure they are pronouncing their lines correctly.
- Have students notice the stage directions. Ask students what each character should do at each stage in the play and encourage them to think about how their character is feeling. Have students who are playing each role demonstrate how they can follow the directions. Encourage other students to make more suggestions. Remind students that the audience will want to see some action, so it is important to think about how they will be moving on stage.
- Practice the play with all the actors without the audio. It is a good idea to rehearse regularly. The more times students practice, the better their performance will be.
- Note: All students should be involved in some way. Students can have behind-the-scenes roles: stage manager (responsible for all props and everything needed for the play), costume director, makeup director, scenery painter, prop designer, sound manager (re-creates sound effects), prompter. They can be involved in organizing and creating simple props, scenery, invitations and programs while the others are rehearsing.

## Perform

- Invite parents or other classes to the performance. An end-of-term/-year performance can be a good way to show what students have learned during the year.
- Have students set up the area for the play. This includes placing scenery and props on stage, getting costumes ready, and setting up chairs for the audience. Remind students that the most important thing is for them to have fun!

## Cool Down

After the performance, congratulate students and ask them if they enjoyed performing the play. Review all the different things they had to do to prepare and write them on the board (e.g. practicing the lines, thinking of actions for the characters, creating the props and scenery). Ask students to put the things in order from what they found most difficult to what they found easiest. Invite pairs to share their answers and encourage them to give reasons.

# Audio Scripts

## Language Book

For the vocabulary drills, where an alternative exists in British English, this is noted in parentheses next to the corresponding American English word/phrase. Audio recordings of the British English pronunciation and words/phrases are available through the **Teacher's App** on **Navio**.

## Language Review

### TRACK 1

Language Review

**A Listen and write. What's beautiful?**

1 **Kareem:** Look at those mountains! Let's go there.
**Arthur:** No, that's a long walk. I'm tired.

2 **Kareem:** Oh, but the snow is soft and beautiful.
**Arthur:** Yes, and cold—very cold!

3 **Kareem:** Let's go for a shorter walk then.
**Arthur:** OK. We can swim under the waterfall! That's fun!

4 **Kareem:** Or we can go to the forest. I love those tall trees.
**Arthur:** I don't know. There are bears over there.

5 **Kareem:** Wait! Let's go to the lake. We can swim there, too.
**Arthur:** But I forgot my towel!

6 **Kareem:** Hmm, I don't know. What can we do?
**Arthur:** Well, there's a nice beach. We can play there.

7 **Kareem:** Oh, no! Do you see the rain over there?
**Arthur:** Yes, but it's OK. It isn't raining here.

8 **Kareem:** Look! There's a rainbow in the sky!
**Arthur:** Now *that's* beautiful!

### TRACK 2

Language Review

**B Listen and complete.**

**Ted:** Look at those boats! There's a kayak and a sailboat.
**Sadie:** The sailboat is faster than the kayak.
**Jeff:** Yes. The kayak is slower, and it's also smaller.
**Sadie:** I think sailing is more exciting than kayaking.
**Ted:** I went sailing and kayaking with my cousin last summer. Sailing was more difficult than kayaking!
**Jeff:** Really? Why?
**Ted:** I needed help. I was strong, but my cousin was stronger!
**Sadie:** So kayaking was better for you?
**Ted:** Yes. I really liked it. It was quieter and more interesting. And I did it by myself!

## Unit 1

### TRACK 3

Unit 1, Vocabulary

**A Listen and find. Who gets books for Kareem?**

**Millie:** Kareem, I found a book about robots in the future!
**Kareem:** That looks interesting, Millie! Where did you find it?
**Millie:** Over there, with the science-fiction books.
**Kareem:** Can you find some true stories? We need a lot of information for our project.
**Millie:** Sure! I saw one about how to build a robot.
**Kareem:** That sounds complicated! Are there pictures to help us understand?
**Millie:** Yes, of course!
**Adam:** Kareem, here's a biography about a man who builds robots! It's all about his life.
**Kareem:** Cool! We need that, too. Who is he?
**Adam:** Daniel Pérez. He's famous! Everybody knows him.
**Lucy:** How about this novel, Kareem? I found it in the fiction section.
**Kareem:** What's it about?
**Lucy:** It's a fantasy about the future. Robots can sail ships in the sky!
**Kareem:** That is a fantasy!
**Millie:** What books did you find, Kareem?
**Kareem:** Oh, I'm waiting for Robo. He's helping me.
**Robo:** I'm ROBO, the library robot. I can find any book. Kareem, here are your… Woah! … books…

### TRACK 4

Unit 1, Vocabulary

**B Listen, say, and number the pictures in A.**

1 interesting
2 science fiction
3 complicated
4 novel
5 popular
6 biography
7 exciting
8 fantasy
9 famous
10 adventure
11 boring

### TRACK 5

Unit 1, Vocabulary

**C Close your eyes. Listen, visualize, and say.**

Interesting. Your friend is telling you a story, and you don't want to stop listening. What is your friend talking about? Say "interesting."
Science fiction. Imagine you're reading a book about the future set in the year 3,000. What does a school look like? Say "science fiction."
Complicated. Imagine a long list of instructions for a new game. It is very difficult! Say "complicated."
Novel. Think about a book you read that *wasn't* a true story. Who was the main character? Say "novel."
Popular. Think about a teacher that all the students like a lot. That teacher is very popular! Say "popular."
Biography. Did you ever read a book about the life of a real person? Who was it about? Say "biography."
Exciting. Think of a sport or a game where things happen fast. What is it? Say "exciting."
Fantasy. Imagine you're flying above the trees. What kind of book is this? Say "fantasy."
Famous. Think of a real person that everybody knows from TV shows or movies. Why is this person famous? Say "famous."
Adventure. Think about a story where the main character goes somewhere very cool. Where did the character go? Say "adventure."
Boring. You're reading a book that *isn't* interesting. You're falling asleep! Say "boring."

### TRACK 6

Unit 1, Vocabulary

**E Listen and complete. Then watch and sing.**

*The Library*

*There's a world of information for you and me—*
*Everything you want at the library.*
*Books, games, computers, and movies you can see.*
*There's a lot to learn and do at the library!*

You can sit and read a novel at the library
Go on an adventure through the pictures you see.
You can find exciting stories or a fantasy
The library's never boring, and it's all free!

You can listen to great music at the library
And find a famous person's biography.
You can meet interesting people—maybe two or three
The library's very popular, and it's all free!

TRACK 7

**Unit 1, Explore Language**

**A Listen and read. What's Gavin's project about?**

**Gavin:** Where did you go yesterday after school, Kareem?

**Kareem:** I went to the library with my project group.

**Gavin:** What did you do there?

**Kareem:** We looked for books about robots.

**Gavin:** Did you find anything?

**Kareem:** Yes, we did. We read about the very first robot!

**Gavin:** Cool! I worked on my project, too.

**Kareem:** I didn't see you there, Gavin.

**Gavin:** Oh, I didn't go to the library.

**Kareem:** Where did you go?

**Gavin:** My project's about frogs, so I went to the river. And I found this!

TRACK 8

**Unit 1, Explore Language**

**D Listen and say.**

1 We looked for books about robots.
2 He didn't look for a biography.
3 They found some interesting fantasy books.
4 Where did you find that adventure novel?
5 Did she like that novel? Yes, she did.

TRACK 9

**Unit 1, Global Citizenship**

**A Listen to Linda talk about her library. How does it grow?**

**Linda:** I live in a small town in the United States. It doesn't have a library. But I love books! In the past, my friends and I always shared books, but last year we wanted more. So, my mom and I made a small library in our house. Many people gave us books. At first, we just had story books, but soon kids asked for nonfiction books to help with their school subjects, too. Now we have science books about animals and plants, and geography books about other countries and people. I have a lot of history books, fiction and nonfiction, about life in the past. We even have books about math for kids who love numbers. We have books about health—how to eat well and keep your body healthy. The kids can see famous paintings in art books, and listen to music. They can learn about technology, too. Kids and their parents come to our library every day. Sometimes they borrow books, and sometimes they stay and read. They often give us books they don't want anymore. That's how our library grows!

TRACK 10

**Unit 1, Global Citizenship**

**B Listen, say, and number the pictures in A.**

1 science
2 math
3 history
4 geography
5 English
6 technology
7 art
8 music
9 health
10 P.E. (physical education)

TRACK A

**Unit 1, Global Citizenship**

**Close your eyes. Listen, visualize, and say.**

Science. Do you like learning about plants and animals? What animal are you studying? Say "science."
Math. Mime adding numbers for homework. Is it easy or is it hard? Say "math."
History. Imagine you're learning about life a long time ago. Is it interesting? Say "history."
Geography. Imagine you're looking at a large map of the world. Can you find your country? Say "geography."
English. Think about the class are you in now. What language are you learning? Say "English."
Technology. Think about technology in your life—phones, tablets, computers, the internet. Which do you use a lot? Say "technology."
Art. Imagine you are in an art class. Are you painting or drawing a picture? What colors are you using? Say "art."
Music. Mime listening to music. What kind of music is it? Say "music."
Health. Think about how you feel. Do you eat well and play sports? Say "health."
P.E. Imagine your favorite P.E. class. Are you outside or in the gym? What sport are you playing? Say "P.E."

TRACK 11

**Unit 1, Global Citizenship**

**D Now listen to Skyla and Rishi. Why do these libraries travel to different places?**

**Skyla:** Here in the Netherlands, some towns don't have a library, and many schools don't either. In my town, there's a library on a bus, and it visits one school each day. Yesterday, it came to my school. My classmates and I visited during school with our teacher, and we went back after school too. Downstairs, there were books, and upstairs there were comfortable places to read. We liked reading together and talking about our favorite books. My favorite book at the moment is about music.

**Rishi:** People speak many languages in India and it isn't always easy to find books in your language. In my part of India, there's a library in a van with books in different languages. My dad drives the library van to small towns and villages. Sometimes, he travels for hours. Last week, I went with him. We stopped in the middle of a small town. Many people came to the van. They think it's exciting. It was great—everyone was reading or talking about books! I often borrow books from the van. I love history and science.

TRACK 12

**Unit 1, Explore Language**

**A Listen and read. What did Lena learn about penguins?**

**Millie:** Is that a science book, Lena?

**Lena:** Yes. It's all about animals.

**Millie:** Cool! I just read a book about penguins yesterday.

**Lena:** You read a whole book in one day? That was quick!

**Millie:** Well, I read quickly.

**Lena:** I don't. I read very slowly.

**Millie:** Why?

**Lena:** So I can remember every word.

**Millie:** Can you really remember *everything*? What's the first sentence?

**Lena:** "Penguins are birds, but they can't fly."

**Millie:** Wow, you really do read carefully!

TRACK 13

**Unit 1, Explore Language**

**D Listen and say.**

1 I read really quickly.
2 He writes carefully.
3 They can do math easily.
4 The children are playing happily.

TRACK 14

**Unit 1, Talk About It**

**Pronunciation. Listen and say.**

/sk/ ask scary school
/gr/ great grows agree

# Unit 2

TRACK 15

**Unit 2, Vocabulary**

**A Listen and find. Which four biomes do the girls see?**

**Tess:** Look, Millie! We can see all the biomes!

**Millie:** Here's the forest. Look at all the trees! The forest has the most trees and plants.

**Tess:** That's because it rains a lot. The wet weather helps everything grow.

**Millie:** Tess, is that a wolf?

**Tess:** Yes, it is. It looks like a dog!

**Millie:** Next is the tundra. It doesn't have any trees!

**Tess:** Just rocks and snow. It looks very cold!

**Millie:** Do you see the polar bear?

**Tess:** Yeah! It's white, like the snow.

**Millie:** And there's the desert. It looks really hot!

**Tess:** Yeah. Not many plants, but *lots* of sand.
**Millie:** And camels! They're so big!
**Tess:** The grassland doesn't have many trees. It doesn't rain much, so it's really dry.
**Millie:** What's that?
**Tess:** It's a cheetah! It's running in the grass.
**Millie:** Let's go there first! I want to see that cheetah.

TRACK 16
**Unit 2, Vocabulary**
**B Listen, say, and number the pictures in A.**
1 desert
2 forest
3 tundra
4 grassland
5 camel
6 cheetah
7 wolf
8 polar bear
9 wet
10 dry
11 biome
12 plants

TRACK 17
**Unit 2, Vocabulary**
**C Close your eyes. Listen, visualize, and say.**
Desert. Think about a hot, sunny desert. What animals live here? Say "desert."
Forest. Imagine you're sitting in a cool, shady forest. What can you see? Say "forest."
Tundra. Mime walking on the tundra. It's so cold! What are you wearing? Say "tundra."
Grassland. Imagine you're walking through tall grass in the grassland. What animals live here? Say "grassland."
Camel. Mime riding high up on a camel. Where are you sitting? Say "camel."
Cheetah. Imagine you see a cheetah in the grassland. What other animal does it look like? Say "cheetah."
Wolf. Think about seeing a wolf in the forest. What other animal does it look like? Say "wolf."
Polar bear. Imagine you meet a polar bear outside. What color is it? Say "polar bear."
Wet. It's raining and you don't have an umbrella. What happens to your clothes? Say "wet."
Dry. Now you put your wet clothes near a big fire. What happens to your clothes? Say "dry."
Biome. This biome has many trees. The climate is warm and wet. What animals can you see? Say "biome."
Plants. Think about the plants growing outside your school. Are they short or tall? Say "plants."

TRACK 18
**Unit 2, Vocabulary**
**E Listen and complete. Then watch and sing.**
*Different Homes*

*Where on Earth do you live?*
*Where on Earth is your home?*
*The climate, plants, and animals*
*Make your biome your home.*

The desert is hot and dry
Not much can grow on the land
But the camel walks through the sand.

The tundra has no trees
It's cold but small flowers grow
And the polar bear plays in the snow.

The grassland has tall, tall grass
It's dry and the wind is strong
And the cheetah runs all day long.

The forest is full of green trees
The sun shines warm and bright
But the wolf sleeps until night.

TRACK 19
**Unit 2, Explore Language**
**A Listen and read. Which animals do the girls talk about?**
**Millie:** Look at this cheetah! It's so big!
**Ava:** But this lion's bigger than the cheetah. Much bigger!
**Tess:** Wow, Ava, it is. Is the lion the biggest animal in the grassland?
**Ava:** No, wait. The biggest animal is coming in a minute.
**Tess:** Really? Is it dangerous?
**Ava:** Yes, it is! There—the biggest animal is the elephant.
**Tess:** The elephant? Are elephants dangerous?
**Ava:** Yes, some people say elephants are more dangerous than lions. They say elephants are the most dangerous animals of all!

TRACK 20
**Unit 2, Explore Language**
**D Listen and say.**
1 That lion's bigger than the cheetah.
2 The tundra is the coldest biome.
3 The forest is more beautiful than the desert.

TRACK 21
**Unit 2, Global Citizenship**
**A Listen to Iqaluk talk about a flower on the tundra. What color is it?**
**Seba:** Where do you live, Iqaluk?
**Iqaluk:** I live in Nunavut, in the Canadian Arctic. The land there is tundra, so there aren't any trees. But in the summer, there are purple flowers everywhere!
**Seba:** Really?
**Iqaluk:** Yes! The plants are small, but they grow close together. The ground looks purple!
**Seba:** Can you describe the flowers?
**Iqaluk:** Sure. They're beautiful. They have five petals like a star. In the middle, there's orange pollen. The stem has lots of tiny round leaves. They're gray and green. The stem is short, but the roots are long. They don't go into the ground. They grow on top of the rocks, and new shoots grow across the rocks. In the fall, after the first snow, the wind blows the seeds across the tundra.
**Seba:** But the summer is very short on the tundra. How do the flowers grow?
**Iqaluk:** The flower buds grow in fall, before the snow comes. They're under the snow all winter. Then a few days after the snow melts in the summer, the new flowers come out! Purple means the end of winter for us!

TRACK 22
**Unit 2, Global Citizenship**
**B Listen, say, and number the pictures in A.**
1 ground
2 bud
3 seeds
4 flower
5 roots
6 petal
7 shoot
8 leaves
9 stem
10 pollen

TRACK B
**Unit 2, Global Citizenship**
**Close your eyes. Listen, visualize, and say.**
Ground. Mime digging with a shovel. Is the ground hard or soft? Say "ground."
Bud. Imagine you are walking through a garden in early spring. There aren't any flowers yet, but you see a lot of buds waiting to become flowers. Say "bud."
Seeds. Imagine you want to grow some new plants. Hold the seeds in your hand. Mime planting them in the ground. Say "seeds."
Flower. Mime smelling a beautiful flower. What does it smell like? Say "flower."
Roots. Think about the roots on a big tree. How long are they? Say "roots."
Petal. How many petals does your flower have? What shape are they? Say "petal."
Shoot. Imagine you're walking in the forest. You see a tiny green shoot. Say "shoot."
Leaves. Does the stem of your flower have lots of leaves? What color are they? Say "leaves."
Stem. Does your flower have a long stem or a short stem? Is it thick or thin? Say "stem."
Pollen. Look closely at the middle of a flower. What color is the pollen? Do you see a bee? Say "pollen."

TRACK 23

**Unit 2, Global Citizenship**

**D Now listen to Amadou and Seba. Which plant grows in the water?**

**Amadou:** I'm Amadou, and I live in Tambacounda, in Senegal. A very special tree grows here. The baobab tree grows in many African countries, and it can live for 5,000 years! It's nickname is the "tree of life." It is very tall and very wide. It keeps a lot of water in its trunk. When the climate is dry, the tree can still grow. It also has a delicious fruit called "monkey bread." My mom works for a small company that makes juice from that fruit. She makes the juice in our home and then takes it to the market. It's a very important tree to our family.

**Seba:** My name is Seba, and I'm from Cairo in Egypt. Most of Egypt is a desert, so not many flowers can grow here. But a very special flower grows in the river Nile. It's called the blue water lily and it's the flower of Egypt. The flower is blue with yellow in the middle. It opens every morning and closes every afternoon. It's one of the oldest flowers in the world, and you can see it in pictures from thousands of years ago. Today people grow blue water lilies in water at home. We have some in our garden!

TRACK 24

**Unit 2, Explore Language**

**A Listen and read. What happened to Ava?**

**Ava:** Owen, do you see that plant? I like it!

**Owen:** I have one at home, Ava. It grows very quickly!

**Ava:** Really?

**Owen:** Well, it grows more quickly than the plant next to it.

**Ava:** Do any plants grow slowly?

**Owen:** Yes! Desert plants grow the most slowly of all. I have three of those.

**Ava:** Like this one?

**Owen:** Smaller, but don't …

**Ava:** OUCH!

**Owen:** You need to listen more carefully! Desert plants can be very sharp!

TRACK 25

**Unit 2, Explore Language**

**D Listen and say.**

1 Desert plants grow the most slowly of all.
2 This plant grows more quickly than that one.
3 You write more carefully than I do.
4 I answered the last question the most easily of all.

TRACK 26

**Unit 2, Take the Stage**

**Pronunciation. Listen and say.**

**/pl/** plants play place
**/kl/** climate clouds close

# Unit 3

TRACK 27

**Unit 3, Vocabulary**

**A Listen and find. How much does the shirt cost?**

**Owen:** Charlie, look at this lizard toy. I really like it.

**Charlie:** It's not just a toy, Owen. Look, it's a phone case.

**Owen:** Cool!

**Charlie:** Are you going to buy it?

**Owen:** Maybe. It's only $10.

**Charlie:** Wow, that's pretty cheap.

**Victor:** Oh, no! Billy, where's my wallet?

**Billy:** There it is, Victor! On the floor!

**Victor:** Thanks.

**Jodie:** I like this little box. Look, Nina! I can keep my allowance in it.

**Nina:** Good idea. I need something to save my money in, too.

**Jodie:** Great! Nina, where's Fatima? I can't see her.

**Nina:** She's talking to the cashier. I think she's buying something.

**Fatima:** I'd like to buy this shirt, please.

**Cashier:** OK. That's $9 and 25¢.

**Fatima:** Here's $10.

**Cashier:** And here's your change—75¢.

**Fatima:** Thank you! What can I do with 75¢?

**Cashier:** Take it home and save it!

TRACK 28

**Unit 3, Vocabulary**

**B Listen, say, and number the pictures in A.**

1 save
2 spend
3 sell
4 customer
5 buy
6 expensive
7 cheap
8 cashier
9 pay
10 change
11 wallet
12 allowance (British English: pocket money)

TRACK 29

**Unit 3, Vocabulary**

**C Close your eyes. Listen, visualize, and say.**

Save. Imagine you are holding a big jar of money. This is all the money you saved last year. Say "save."
Spend. Think about spending your jar of money. What store do you want to spend it in? Say "spend."
Sell. Think about that store. What's in the window? What does it sell? Say "sell."
Customer. Imagine you're inside the store. Someone asks, "Can I help you?" What are you looking for? Say "customer."
Buy. You need to get something at the store. What do you need to buy? Say "buy."
Expensive. Imagine you see something really expensive in the store. You love it, but it costs a lot of money. What is it? Say "expensive."
Cheap. Imagine you see something you want, and it doesn't cost much money. Are you going to buy it? Say "cheap."
Cashier. Think about taking your things to the cashier. The cashier tells you how much they are. Say "cashier."
Pay. Mime giving the cashier the money. How much is it? You're paying for your things. Say "pay."
Change. Imagine the cashier is giving you some change. Is it bills, coins, or both? Say "change."
Wallet. Mime opening your wallet and putting change inside. What color is your wallet? Say "wallet."
Allowance. Imagine your parents give you some money for the week. What will you do with your allowance? Say "allowance."

TRACK 30

**Unit 3, Vocabulary**

**E Listen and complete. Then watch and sing.**

*Money! Money! Money!*

Money! Money! Money!
We spend some every day!
We take our wallets to the store,
We buy things and we pay!

*Toys! Snacks! Video games!*
*Lunch! Drinks! Ice cream!*

Money! Money! Money!
We get some every day!
The customers come to our store,
We sell things and they pay!

Money! Money! Money!
We save some every day!
We count our money carefully,
And put it all away!
YAY!

TRACK 31

**Unit 3, Explore Language**

**A Listen and read. How does Owen get his money?**

**Charlie:** Let's get a snack.

**Owen:** I can't. I spent all my money.

**Charlie:** I have some. Do your parents give you money often?

**Owen:** Well, I get an allowance, but I have to help at home.

**Charlie:** Oh, really? What do you have to do?

**Owen:** I have to make my bed and wash the dishes. What about you?

**Charlie:** I have to clean my room and help with dinner, but I don't get an allowance.

**Owen:** Do you have to make your bed?

**Charlie:** Yes, I do. But I don't have to wash the dishes.

**Owen:** Why not?

**Charlie:** Because we have a dishwasher!

TRACK 32

**Unit 3, Explore Language**

**D Listen and say.**

1 I have to help at home.
2 He has to save his money.
3 You don't have to wash the car.
4 They don't have to buy anything at the store.
5 Do we have to pay the cashier?
6 Does she have to go to school on Saturdays?

TRACK 33

**Unit 3, Global Citizenship**

**A Listen to Annette talk about her American coins. Why does Sumiko like coins?**

**Sumiko:** Annette, can you tell me about your coins? Where are they from?

**Annette:** They're American. This brown one's a penny. It's only worth one cent.

**Sumiko:** What can you buy with one cent?

**Annette:** Nothing really.

**Sumiko:** OK. What's next?

**Annette:** Next is a nickel. It's five cents. It has a huge house on the back.

**Sumiko:** I know what's next. A dime! A dime is ten cents!

**Annette:** You're right. Dimes are the smallest coins. They're the same color as nickels but smaller than pennies. Next is a quarter.

**Sumiko:** How much is a quarter?

**Annette:** Twenty-five cents. It's called a quarter because it's a quarter of a dollar. Four quarters is 100 cents, or one dollar. It's bigger than a nickel.

**Sumiko:** Is it the biggest coin?

**Annette:** No, this dollar coin's the biggest.

**Sumiko:** Let's add them! Twelve pennies, three nickels, five dimes, eight quarters, one dollar coin … That's $3.77.

**Annette:** I also have these dollar bills!

**Sumiko:** I like coins better. Collecting them sounds like fun!

TRACK 34

**Unit 3, Global Citizenship**

**B Listen, say, and number the pictures in A.**

1 penny
2 cents
3 quarter
4 bills (British English: notes)
5 dollar
6 nickel
7 coins
8 equals
9 subtract
10 add
11 dime

TRACK C

**Unit 3, Global Citizenship**

**Close your eyes. Listen, visualize, and say.**

Penny. Imagine you find a penny. How much is it worth? Say "penny."
Cents. Imagine one dollar. Now imagine one hundred cents. They're worth the same amount. Are they the same size? Say "cents."
Quarter. Imagine a quarter. It's twenty-five cents. Do you know why it's called a quarter? Say "quarter."
Bills. Now imagine paper money. These are dollar bills. Which do you want—a dollar coin or a dollar bill? Say "bills."
Dollar. Can you find a dollar coin? Which do you want—four quarters or a dollar coin? Say "dollar."
Nickel. Now imagine a nickel. It's worth five cents. Is it bigger than a penny? Say "nickel."
Coins. Imagine you have lots of coins on your desk. How are they different? Say "coins."
Equals. Imagine you have 10 pennies in one hand and a dime in the other. Are they the same amount of money? Say "equals."
Subtract. Imagine you have 85 cents, and you give your friend a quarter. Subtract 25 cents. How much money do you have now? Write the number in the air. Say "subtract."
Add. Imagine you have three quarters. Add a dime. How much money do you have now? Write the number in the air. Say "add."
Dime. Now imagine a dime. Is a dime smaller than a nickel? Say "dime."

TRACK 35

**Unit 3, Global Citizenship**

**D Now listen to Leena and Davi. Why does Leena save her coins?**

**Leena:** I'm Leena, and I'm from Jordan. Whenever I get a coin, I save it for my future. Every night, I put my coins in a big jar, just like my dad. When the jar is full, I sort the coins and take them to the bank. The people at the bank count the coins and put them in the bank for me. Those coins are going to help me pay for college. I want to go to the University of Jordan in Amman when I'm older. Every cent helps!

**Davi:** I'm Davi from Brazil, and I use my coins to help people. I save them up for a long time, then I give them away! My teacher liked this idea, so we had a coin drive at my school. In just two weeks, our class collected $54.86. Our teacher gave the money to the library in São Paolo, and we got a thank-you letter from them! I'm really happy that our coins made a difference! Now it's time to start saving more coins! You can do it too!

TRACK 36

**Unit 3, Explore Language**

**A Listen and read. How much money does Andie spend?**

**Ting:** Andie, should I buy this lamp? It's $25. That's all my money.

**Andie:** You shouldn't spend it all on a lamp, Ting. You should save some money for later.

**Ting:** I know, but it's so cool. Look at the colors!

**Andie:** You could buy these lights. They're only $10.

**Ting:** I could, but …

**Andie:** You could even buy two sets of lights!

**Ting:** Yes, but …

**Andie:** You know, maybe you *should* buy the lamp. You love it. I'm going to buy a set of these lights for my room!

TRACK 37

**Unit 3, Explore Language**

**D Listen and say.**

1 You should buy the lamp.
2 She shouldn't spend all her money.
3 We could buy these lights, too.
4 They could pay with coins or bills.
5 Should he save his money?

TRACK 38

**Unit 3, Talk About It**

**Pronunciation. Listen and say.**

/pr/ present pretty surprised
/dr/ drinks draw drive

# Unit 4

TRACK 39

**Unit 4, Vocabulary**

**A Listen and find. What time does the curtain open?**

**Ting:** Tommy! Can you practice the script with me? Just once more?

**Tommy:** Sure, Ting! But I think you know the script really well ….

**Ting:** know, but I want to practice one more time.

**Tommy:** OK. Let's start on page 4. I say "Good morning …"

**Fred:** Wow! There are a lot of people in the audience!

**Zora:** What are they doing?

**Fred:** They're talking and laughing. They look excited, too!

**Zora:** My parents and my grandparents are out there.

**Fred:** Yeah, mine too. I hope they like the performance!

**Nasir:** Eddie! We have to finish the set right now! Where's that tree?

**Eddie:** Here it is! Coming!

**Nasir:** OK, great. Where's the rest of the crew? Is everybody ready?

**Eddie:** Yes, everybody's backstage. Let's go.

**Director:** Quiet down! It's 7:00. It's time for the curtain to open. Are all the actors on stage?

**All:** Yes!

**Director:** Wonderful! We worked very hard on this play, and we practiced a lot. Don't be nervous. It's really good! So please enjoy the performance! Let's do this!

TRACK 40

**Unit 4, Vocabulary**

**B Listen, say, and number the pictures in A.**

1 stage
2 nervous
3 backstage
4 costume
5 actor
6 director
7 script
8 set
9 crew
10 curtain
11 audience
12 performance

TRACK 41

**Unit 4, Vocabulary**

**C Close your eyes. Listen, visualize, and say.**

Stage. Imagine a stage. Where is it? Are you at school or at a theater? Say "stage."

Nervous. Imagine you're waiting to go on stage. You feel excited and happy, but also a bit frightened. Shake your knees. Say "nervous."

Backstage. Imagine you are standing backstage. Are there other actors standing with you? Say "backstage."

Costume. You're wearing a costume for the play. What does it look like? Say "costume."

Actor. Imagine you're an actor on stage in a play. Are you scared or is it fun? Say "actor."

Director. The director tells the actors what to do in the play. Do you want to be one? Say "director."

Script. Think about the script for the play. Do you know all your lines in the script? Say "script."

Set. Imagine the set on the stage. What does it look like? Say "set."

Crew. Mime carrying a set piece. What are you carrying? Say "crew."

Curtain. Imagine the stage has a big curtain. What color is it? Is it open or closed? Say "curtain."

Audience. You are sitting in the audience and waiting for the curtain to open. How do you feel? Say "audience."

Performance. Imagine your play is almost over. Was it a good performance? Say "performance."

TRACK 42

**Unit 4, Vocabulary**

**E Listen and complete. Then watch and sing.**

*Are You Ready?*

*Are you ready?*
*We're ready!*
*We're ready to perform!*

We're backstage and feeling nervous
We're going on stage soon. The play begins at eight.
We're behind the curtain in our costumes, and we look great!
We practiced hard and learned the script
We listened to our director and painted all the sets.
We hope no one forgets!

TRACK 43

**Unit 4, Explore Language**

**A Listen and read. Where was Fred?**

**Zora:** Oh, no! What happened to the lights? Fred? Where are you? I can't see! Fred?
OK, let me think. At seven o'clock …
Fred was standing by the curtain.
Tommy and Ting were practicing the script.
Nasir was checking the set.
The director was saying, "Places, everyone!" The actors weren't performing on stage. And it wasn't raining!
Oh good! There's Tommy, and Ting, and Nasir!
But where's Fred?

**Fred:** Here I am! I was getting a candle.

TRACK 44

**Unit 4, Explore Language**

**D Listen and say.**

1 Fred was standing by the curtain.
2 At 5:30, I was working with the crew.
3 The actors were practicing the script.
4 It wasn't snowing at five o'clock.
5 She was sitting in the audience at seven-thirty.

TRACK 45

**Unit 4, Global Citizenship**

**A Listen to the interview. What important thing did the performers learn?**

**Leah:** Hello, Simon. You have been involved in some really huge performances in the past. Can you tell us about one of them?

**Simon:** Yes, Leah. The biggest performance I've been involved in was the Opening Ceremony at the London Olympics. It was directed by Danny Boyle, who is a famous movie director! It was fun, but very busy! Ten thousand actors and dancers were practicing their parts every day for four months!

**Leah:** Wow! How many rehearsals did you have?

**Simon:** Hundreds. We had a complicated schedule. Everyone learned their parts in teams first. Then the teams had rehearsals together in London. We had rehearsals every day for a week before the Olympics.

**Leah:** What was one thing the performers learned from the schedule?

**Simon:** We learned to be on time for rehearsals. When someone was late, everyone had to wait. I tried to be early.

**Leah:** How was the performance?

**Simon:** It was amazing! We all worked together and performed our parts perfectly!

**Leah:** Are you going to do something like that again?

**Simon:** Uh, no, I don't think so! I was very tired after that performance. I slept from midnight until noon the next day!

TRACK 46

**Unit 4, Global Citizenship**

**B Listen, say, and number the pictures in A.**

1 late
2 early
3 on time
4 midnight
5 schedule
6 noon
7 rehearsal
8 lasts
9 team

TRACK D

**Unit 4, Global Citizenship**

**Close your eyes. Listen, visualize, and say.**

Late. Imagine you're late for school. Pretend you're running fast to the school door. How do you feel? Say "late."

Early. Imagine you're waiting at your desk because you're early for class. What can you do while you wait? Say "early."

On time. Class starts at 9 o'clock. Imagine you sit down and check the clock. It's one minute before 9! How do you feel? Say on "time."

Midnight. Imagine checking the clock again. Both hands are at 12. It is very dark outside. What time is it? Say "midnight."

Schedule. Mime checking your schedule. When does school start? When is English class? Say "schedule."

Noon. Imagine the clock again. Both hands are at 12, but it is sunny outside. What time is it now? Say "noon."

Rehearsal. Imagine you're at the last rehearsal for a big performance. Where are you? What are you doing? Say "rehearsal."

Lasts. The show starts at 1 o'clock and ends at 2 o'clock. It lasts one hour. Say "lasts."

Team. Imagine you are playing a sport with other people. You are all wearing the same shirts. You are on a team. Say "team."

TRACK 47

**Unit 4, Global Citizenship**

**D Now listen to Li Min and Adam. How did Li Min feel?**

**Li Min:** I'm Li Min, and I live in China. I performed in the Opening Ceremony of the 2008 Beijing Olympics! My acting group carried the Chinese flag into the stadium. We were all wearing special costumes from all over China. Before the ceremony, we practiced our parts many times with the other actors. It was hard work, but it was the most exciting time of my life! After the ceremony, I said to my mother, "I did this for my country. I'm very proud." I like to watch the video of the ceremony sometimes.

**Adam:** I'm Adam, and I acted in the Closing Ceremony of the 2012 London Olympics. There were 380 schoolchildren, including me! We were water in a river, so our costumes were blue. There was a singer on stage, and we ran out to move like the river during his song. Then we ran off again. We were on stage for just a few minutes. My family was watching, but they didn't see me. I was just one drop of water in the river!

TRACK 48

**Unit 4, Explore Language**

**A Listen and read. Why did the set fall down at the dance rehearsal?**

**Mr. Gates:** Wow! What happened here?

**Riya:** Sorry, Mr. Gates. We were practicing our dance.

**Marcus:** And suddenly the set fell down.

**Mr. Gates:** What were you doing?

**Ting:** We were dancing!

**Mr. Gates:** Were you dancing over there?

**All:** No, we weren't!

**Mr. Gates:** Who was watching the dance?

**Jake:** I was. I'm in the crew. I was finishing the lights.

**Mr. Gates:** Did you see anything?

**Jake:** Yes! A cat was climbing up the set.

**Mr. Gates:** A white cat?

**Jake:** Yes, and then all the boxes fell down.

**Mr. Gates:** Muffin! There you are! OK, kids! Let's fix the set!

TRACK 49

**Unit 4, Explore Language**

**D Listen and say.**

1 Were you dancing over there?
2 Yes, I was dancing.
3 Who was he talking to at two o'clock?
4 He was talking to the crew.
5 Were they practicing at midnight?

TRACK 50

**Unit 4, Take the Stage**

**Pronunciation. Listen and say.**

/ð/ there they then
/θ/ think three things

# Unit 5

TRACK 51

**Unit 5, Vocabulary**

**A Listen and find. Is this place quiet or noisy?**

**Jake:** Grandpa, it's so quiet here.
**Grandpa:** Yes, it is, Jake. I like it.
**Jake:** Me too! It's so noisy in the city. This is nice.
**Grandpa:** There's noise here, too! It's just different.
**Jake:** Really? I don't hear any noise.
**Grandpa:** Let's be quiet. Close your eyes and listen. No talking.
**Jake:** OK!
**Grandpa:** Well?
**Jake:** You're right! There's a lot to listen to … the wind and the leaves in the trees. And all the birds are chirping.
**Grandpa:** Yes! What else?
**Jake:** Bees are buzzing and a dog's barking over there.
**Grandpa:** Good. Keep going!
**Jake:** Something's splashing in the water—maybe a frog? In the house there was a crash, and a door banged open. And somebody's whistling.
**Grandpa:** That's Grandma. She's making dinner. Anything else?
**Jake:** Well, Grandpa, you're noisy, too! Your chair's squeaking, and you're crunching those cookies! [laughing] This isn't a quiet place. It's really noisy!
**Grandpa:** How can your sister sleep?
**Jake:** Shh. Don't wake her! We should whisper!

TRACK 52

**Unit 5, Vocabulary**

**B Listen, say, and number the pictures in A.**

1 crunch
2 crash
3 chirp
4 splash
5 bark
6 buzz
7 bang
8 squeak
9 whisper
10 whistle

TRACK 53

**Unit 5, Vocabulary**

**C Close your eyes. Listen, visualize, and say.**

Crunch. Imagine you're eating potato chips. What sound do the potato chips make? Say "crunch."
Crash. Mime carrying lots of toys! Suddenly you drop them. What noise do the toys make on the floor? Say "crash."
Chirp. Imagine it's early in the morning and you just woke up. Listen to the birds outside your window. What sound do they make? Say "chirp."
Splash. Imagine you're jumping into a lake. What sound does the water make? Say "splash."
Bark. Imagine there is a dog in your neighborhood. Does it bark a lot? Say "bark."
Buzz. Imagine a bee flying around you. What sound does it make? Say "buzz."
Bang. Think about an open door. The wind blows it shut. What sound does it make? Say "bang."
Squeak. Imagine you wake up at midnight. You open your bedroom door very quietly. The door squeaks, and it scares you! Say "squeak."
Whisper. Whisper the name of the person beside you. Can you hear someone whispering your name? Say "whisper."
Whistle. Put your lips together, like you're about to whistle. What tune do you want to whistle? Say "whistle."

TRACK 54

**Unit 5, Vocabulary**

**E Listen and complete. Then watch and sing.**

*Are You Awake?*

*Are you awake?*
*I hear a crunch. What is it?*
*I hear a whistle. What's that sound?*

I'm awake at midnight
I'm listening carefully
I hear scary noises all around me.
There's a squeak on the stairs
What's happening?
I'm scared! My eyes are big and round.

"Are you awake?"
I whisper in my sister's ear.
There's a bang on the door
I'm hugging my pillow
I'm listening carefully
I'm quiet and I don't make any noise.
There's a really loud crash and the light comes on!
"Oh! Mom! Sorry, you fell on our toys!"

TRACK 55

**Unit 5, Explore Language**

**A Listen and read. What's Jake's plan?**

**Grandma:** Jake! What are you doing?
**Jake:** I'm going to look for birds in the forest. Birds wake up early.
**Grandma:** Are you going to come back for breakfast?
**Jake:** No, I'm going to stay there all morning. Can I take my breakfast with me?
**Grandma:** Sure. So, what are you going to do in the forest all morning?
**Jake:** I'm going to sit quietly and look for owls. I'm not going to make any noise. Then I'm going to take pictures.
**Grandma:** But most owls are awake only at night.
**Jake:** Oh! Then, I'm going back to bed!

TRACK 56

**Unit 5, Explore Language**

**D Listen and say.**

1 I'm going to look for birds.
2 Are you going to play with me tomorrow?
3 We aren't going home for lunch today.
4 She's going to swim with us this afternoon.
5 I'm not going to stay at my grandma's house tonight.
6 Is he going to take pictures of birds?

TRACK 57

**Unit 5, Global Citizenship**

**A Listen. What does Rashid learn about the cello?**

**Rashid:** I'm Rashid Khan, and today I'm talking to Penélope Sánchez, the conductor of our city's orchestra. I want to find out about the orchestra for our music club. Ms. Sánchez, please tell us about the orchestra. What instruments are there and how do musicians play them?
**Ms. Sánchez:** There are many different kinds of instruments. First, there are the strings—for example, the violins and cellos. The cello looks like the violin, but it's bigger. It has to stand on the floor between the musician's knees.
**Rashid:** Is there a harp?
**Ms. Sánchez:** Yes, there is. It's is a beautiful, tall instrument. You play it with your fingers.
**Rashid:** Can you tell me about some of the other instruments?
**Ms. Sánchez:** Well, we also have flutes, clarinets and trumpets. You have to blow into them to make a sound.
**Rashid:** Do you have any really loud instruments?
**Ms. Sánchez:** Yes, we have lots of different kinds of drums. Do like playing the drums, Rashid?
**Rashid:** Yes, I do. And I'd like to play the xylophone, too. Do you have one in the orchestra?
**Ms. Sánchez:** Yes, we do.
**Rashid:** And is there a piano?
**Ms. Sánchez:** Of course! Every orchestra has to have a piano!

TRACK 58
**Unit 5, Global Citizenship**
**B Listen, say, and number the pictures in A.**
1 conductor
2 orchestra
3 violin
4 cello
5 harp
6 flute
7 piano
8 trumpet
9 drums
10 clarinet
11 xylophone

TRACK E
**Unit 5, Global Citizenship**
**Close your eyes. Listen, visualize, and say.**
Conductor. Imagine you're the conductor of the orchestra. Mime conducting the musicians with your arms. Say "conductor."
Orchestra. Mime playing an instrument in an orchestra. Which instrument do you play? Say "orchestra."
Violin. Mime holding a violin in your left hand. Now play it with your right hand. Say "violin."
Cello. Mime holding a cello between your knees. Now play! Say "cello."
Harp. Mime playing the harp. Pull the strings with your fingers. Say "harp."
Flute. Imagine holding a flute. Is the metal cold? Now blow! Say "flute."
Piano. Imagine you're sitting in front of a piano. Move your fingers. Take a deep breath. Now play! Say "piano."
Trumpet. Mime playing a trumpet. Is your trumpet loud? Say "trumpet."
Drums. Imagine you're in a rock band. Mime playing the drums. One, two, three, four! Say "drums."
Clarinet. Now imagine holding a clarinet. Hold it in front of you, pointing down. How does it sound? Say "clarinet."
Xylophone. Imagine you have two sticks in your hands. Now play the xylophone. Say "xylophone."

TRACK 59
**Unit 5, Global Citizenship**
**D Now listen to Derick and María. What do they think about their music classes?**
**Derick:** Hi, I'm Derick. Hey, listen to this! Did you like that? That's my music class at school! We learn rock music in our music classes. I play the drums. Some kids play the keyboard. It's an electric piano. Some kids sing. We create our own music and we perform a lot. Many schools in the USA teach rock music. The school gives us our instruments, but I'm going to buy my own drums some day. I'm saving all my money. Our music program's great! Do you want to hear some more? Listen!
**María:** Hello, my name's María. Listen to this! That's my after-school music program. I play the violin with my friends there every day and on weekends too. There are music programs like this all over Venezuela. They give us our instruments and teach us how to play in an orchestra. I chose the violin because it's small, like me! I love our music program! Some day, I'm going to play in the Simón Bolívar Youth Orchestra. It's from Venezuela, and it's the most famous youth orchestra in the world! Do you want to hear it? Listen!

TRACK 60
**Unit 5, Explore Language**
**A Listen and read. What are Jen and Carla Planning?**
**Mom:** What are you going to make?
**Jen:** Drums and a guitar. Then we're going to have a show!
**Mom:** Really! Where is it going to be?
**Jen:** Here. I'm going to move these chairs.
**Carla:** I'm going to make tickets.
**Mom:** When is the show going to be?
**Jen:** Tomorrow!
**Mom:** Are you going to practice the music now?
**Jen:** No, we aren't. We have to make everything first.
**Mom:** I see. Who's going to buy the tickets?
**Jen:** Oh. We didn't think about that.
**Carla:** Maybe our moms?
**Mom:** Good idea!

TRACK 61
**Unit 5, Explore Language**
**D Listen and say.**
1 What're you going to make?
2 We're going to make drums.
3 What's she going to do?
4 She's going to move the chairs.
5 Are they going to play in an orchestra?
6 Yes, they are.

TRACK 62
**Unit 5, Talk About It**
**Pronunciation. Listen and say**
/θ/ math with both
/tʃ/ much watch each

# Unit 6

TRACK 63
**Unit 6, Vocabulary**
**A Listen and find. What happened to the strawberries?**
**Mom:** OK, team, we're going to make a fresh fruit salad to go with dinner. Alec, can you and Aaron wash and peel the apples and peaches? They're in the sink.
**Alec and Aaron:** OK.
**Mom:** Marisa, you and Kate can cut up the watermelon and put the pieces in this bowl for the salad.
**Marisa and Kate:** OK.
**Mom:** Can you boys peel the oranges, mangos, and bananas? Then cut them up.
**Jake and Santiago:** No problem.
**Carla:** Where are the strawberries?
**Mom:** They're in the fridge. Can you and Liz wash them and mix them into the salad with the watermelon?
**Carla:** OK. Come on, Liz!
**Mom:** I'm frying mushrooms now. Next, I'll fry some potatoes on the stove. And Dad's grilling the chicken outside.
**Alec:** Excuse me. Where's the trash can? We have to throw out these pieces.
**Mom:** Oh, it's by Jake and Santiago at the end of the counter. Carla, can you please take the peas and carrots out of the microwave?
**Carla:** Sure, Mom.
**Dad:** Here's the chicken. Dinner looks delicious!
**Mom:** Wait! There aren't any strawberries! Where are they?
**Carla:** Sorry, Mom. We ate them all. They were *so* good!

TRACK 64
**Unit 6, Vocabulary**
**B Listen, say, and number the pictures in A.**
1 stove
2 microwave
3 sink
4 fridge
5 trash can (British English: rubbish bin)
6 peel
7 cut up
8 throw out
9 fry
10 grill
11 mix
12 fresh

TRACK 65
**Unit 6, Vocabulary**
**C Close your eyes. Listen, visualize, and say.**
Stove. Imagine you are turning on the stove. Don't touch it! Is it hot or cold? Say "stove."
Microwave. Imagine you're putting something in the microwave. What sound does it make when it's done? Say "microwave."
Sink. Wash your hands in the sink. Is the water hot or cold? Say "sink."
Fridge. Open the fridge door. Is it hot or cold inside? Say "fridge."
Trash can. Put some trash in the trash can. How does the trash can smell? Say "trash can."
Peel. Think about peeling an apple. Can you peel it in one piece? Say "peel."
Cut up. Now you're cutting up the apple for lunch. Be careful! Are the pieces big or small? Say "cut up."
Throw out. Now you're throwing out the rest of the apple in the trash can. What else is in there? Say "throw out."
Fry. Imagine you're frying an egg in a pan. Is the pan hot or cold? Say "fry."

Grill. Where is the grill? Go outside and put a piece of chicken on the grill. Turn the chicken over carefully. Say "grill."
Mix. Imagine you're making cookies. Mix everything together in a big bowl with a spoon. Go faster and faster! Say "mix."
Fresh. Think about a fresh strawberry. What does it look like? How does it smell? Say "fresh."

TRACK 66

**Unit 6, Vocabulary**

**E Listen and complete. Then watch and sing.**

*That Looks Good!*

Look in the fridge. What do you see?
I see fruit and vegetables calling to me!
All the fruit and vegetables, cold and fresh
Cut up into pieces—they're the best!
Look on the stove. What do you see?
You're cooking something special, just for me!
Fry some eggs and potatoes, delicious and hot
Mix it with cheese—I like it a lot!
Look on the grill. What do you see?
A piece of meat and vegetables there for me!
*Ping* goes the microwave. My food is done.
Choosing what I want to eat is so much fun!

TRACK 67

**Unit 6, Explore Language**

**A Listen and read. Who's going to wash the dishes?**

**Mom:** Would you like to have more potatoes?
**Alec:** Yes, please!
**Kate:** I'm glad we decided to have a team dinner.
**Jake:** And we learned to make fruit salad!
**Santiago:** I plan to make fruit salad for my family.
**Tim:** Me too! It's easy.
**Liz:** This chicken's good!
**Carla:** Yeah. Usually, I don't like to eat meat, but this is delicious!
**Marisa:** Let's start to clean up. Alec loves to wash dishes!
**Dad:** Not yet, Marisa! We need to enjoy the food first!

TRACK 68

**Unit 6, Explore Language**

**D Listen and say.**

1 Would you like to have more potatoes?
2 They love to eat fruit salad.
3 I plan to grill the chicken.
4 They don't want to throw that food out.
5 She doesn't need to grill the meat.

TRACK 69

**Unit 6, Global Citizenship**

**A Listen to the food scientist. Which foods have protein?**

**Food Scientist:** I'm a food scientist, and it's my job to study how different foods give you energy and help you grow and stay healthy.
First, you need to eat lots of fresh fruit and vegetables every day. Drinking some fruit juice is good, but eating fruit and vegetables is better!
Next, you need to eat protein. This can be a piece of meat, fish, eggs, nuts, or beans. Protein is important because it helps your body stay strong.
Next, you need to eat carbohydrates. Many of these foods come from grains. Bread, rice, and pasta are all carbohydrates.
Next is dairy. Most people should drink milk or eat some cheese or yogurt every day. All of these keep your bones strong.
You also need some fat, like butter or oil, but not too much!
Finally, let's talk about sugar. Sugar is a carbohydrate, like bread, but it doesn't come from grains, and it's not good for you. You probably love candy, but remember: fruit is sweet too, and it's healthier!

TRACK 70

**Unit 6, Global Citizenship**

**B Listen, say, and number the pictures in A.**

1 butter
2 beans
3 sugar
4 meat
5 carbohydrates
6 fat
7 protein
8 grains
9 nuts
10 dairy

TRACK F

**Unit 6, Global Citizenship**

**Close your eyes. Listen, visualize, and say.**

Butter. Put some butter on your bread. How does it taste? Do you like it? Say "butter."
Beans. Imagine a bowl of hard, black beans. Mime pouring water over them. You leave them in the water all night. In the morning, are they soft or hard? Say "beans."
Sugar. Mime putting a spoonful of sugar into a cup of hot tea. Stir it well and take a sip. Say "sugar."
Meat. Imagine you're making a sandwich with meat. Where does the meat come from? Say "meat."
Carbohydrates. You can have bread or pasta for your lunch. Which kind of carbohydrate do you choose? Say "carbohydrates."
Fat. You're in the supermarket. Cheese, avocados, and cookies all have fat. Which will you choose? Say "fat."
Protein. Imagine you're ordering a salad. You can add chicken, fish, or eggs to it. Which kind of protein do you choose? Say "protein."
Grains. Pour a bowl of healthy cereal. Add the milk and take a bite. How does it taste? Say "grains."
Nuts. Open a bag of mixed nuts. What do they taste like? Which type of nut is your favorite? Say "nuts."
Dairy. Mime opening your fridge. Take out the milk and cheese. What color is the cheese? Say "dairy."

TRACK 71

**Unit 6, Global Citizenship**

**D Now listen to Min-jun and Francesca. How are their lunches the same?**

**Min-jun:** My name is Min-jun, and I live in Busan in South Korea. At my school, we have a hot lunch every day. All the students eat the same lunch, and we sit with our teachers. School lunch is always delicious! It's different every day. There's always soup and rice. They're the biggest bowls. Then there are smaller bowls of kimchi, vegetables, and meat or fish. Often there's fruit, too. We eat with chopsticks and a spoon. I think about lunch all morning!
**Francesca:** I'm Francesca, and I live in Italy. I eat my lunch at school with my class. A truck brings the lunches to the schools, and then the schools serve them. So, every student in my city has the same lunch! We always have three courses. First, we have fresh pasta with sauce, or sometimes rice. Next, we have fish or meat with salad or vegetables. Sometimes, we eat salad *and* vegetables! We usually have cheese, too. Then, we have fruit for dessert. It's a very good lunch, and it gives me energy for the afternoon!

TRACK 72

**Unit 6, Explore Language**

**A Listen and read. Why doesn't Tim cry?**

**Tim:** So, Alec, do you like cooking?
**Alec:** Yes, Tim, I do. I enjoy making new dishes. It's fun.
**Tim:** Then, why are you crying?
**Alec:** I'm not crying! I love cooking, but I hate cutting up onions. They make my eyes water.
**Tim:** I don't mind cutting up onions. Let me do it.
**Alec:** Sure! Here you go. My eyes are hurting.
**Tim:** I like wearing these goggles. Then I never cry. I can cut up 100 onions!
**Alec:** Thanks, Tim!

TRACK 73

**Unit 6, Explore Language**

**D Listen and say.**

1 I hate cutting up onions.
2 She doesn't mind peeling potatoes.
3 We enjoy making new dishes.
4 They don't like frying vegetables.
5 He keeps cleaning up the kitchen.

TRACK 74
**Unit 6, Talk About It**
**Pronunciation. Listen and say.**
**/fr/** friendly fruit from
**/bl/** blog black blue

# Unit 7

TRACK 75
**Unit 7, Vocabulary**
**A Listen and find. Where's the family going?**
**Dad:** Alec, can you help me? We have to put these toys up high on these shelves. If the storm comes here, our store might flood. There could be water everywhere! The toys will be safe up here.
**Alec:** Sure, Dad.
**Mom:** It looks like it could be a real emergency.
**Leah:** Mom, someone's coming to the door.
**Hassan:** Hi, I'm Hassan. I'm a rescue worker and I'm helping with the storm. I want to make sure you have a plan.
**Dad:** Thanks. We're moving things up high so they won't get wet. Then we're going home. We live on a hill. Our house is up high.
**Hassan:** Good plan. Is your car here?
**Mom:** Yes. Can we drive through the streets?
**Hassan:** Yes, but you should leave right now. We need to close this street. Police officers are helping us.
**Alec:** Does everyone have to leave?
**Hassan:** Yes, but there's a shelter at the school where people are going to be safe. There are beds and lots of food and water. Well, I need to keep going. Stay safe!
**Dad:** Thanks, Hassan!
**Alec:** I can hear an ambulance!
**Leah:** And a helicopter!
**Dad:** Come on. Take your backpacks. Let's go!

TRACK 76
**Unit 7, Vocabulary**
**B Listen, say, and number the pictures in A.**
**1** safe
**2** dangerous
**3** rescue worker
**4** helicopter
**5** ambulance
**6** shelter
**7** storm
**8** emergency

TRACK 77
**Unit 7, Vocabulary**
**C Close your eyes. Listen, visualize, and say.**
Safe. There's a very bad storm, but you're inside your house with your family. You're warm and dry. How do you feel? Say "safe."
Dangerous. You can hear the wind outside. It's very strong. Could a tree fall down? Say "dangerous."
Rescue worker. Who comes to help you in the flood? What kind of jacket does he or she wear? Say "rescue worker."
Helicopter. Imagine a helicopter's in the air above you. What does it sound like? Say "helicopter."
Ambulance. You can hear an ambulance getting closer and closer. What happens to the sound? Say "ambulance."
Shelter. Imagine you are outside and it starts to rain. You're getting wet. Where can you find shelter? Say "shelter."
Storm. It's raining very hard. The sky is dark and the wind is strong. What does it sound like? Say "storm."
Emergency. You can hear ambulances and fire trucks outside. What's happening? Say "emergency."

TRACK 78
**Unit 7, Vocabulary**
**E Listen and complete. Then watch and sing.**
*Emergency Helpers*

*They're coming! They're coming! They're answering our call!*
*They're coming here to help us in no time at all!*

Police officers tell the drivers what to do,
They keep us safe at home and school and in bad weather, too!
The drivers of the ambulance go very, very fast.
They care for us and get us to the hospital at last!

Firefighters put out fires day and night
On a fire truck or a helicopter, they hold on tight!
Rescue workers come to help in an emergency
They take us to a shelter, a clean, warm place to be.

TRACK 79
**Unit 7, Explore Language**
**A Listen and read. What's Hassan doing?**
**Dad:** Everyone from Main Street is here!
**Alec:** There's the woman who works in the café down the street.
**Dad:** And that man drives a truck.
**Alec:** The people who drive the ambulance are here, too. I think everyone's safe.
**Dad:** I'm glad about that. Do you see Hassan?
**Alec:** Who's he?
**Dad:** He's the rescue worker who came to our store.
**Alec:** Look, he's telling a story to those kids. He's flying a helicopter!
**Dad:** Let's go and thank him again. He did a great job!

TRACK 80
**Unit 7, Explore Language**
**D Listen and say.**
**1** There's the woman who works in the café.
**2** The man who drives the ambulance is kind.
**3** The person who helped me was you.
**4** The families who left their homes are here.
**5** That's the person who brought me some juice.

TRACK 81
**Unit 7, Global Citizenship**
**A Listen to Jonas talking about natural disasters. Why does he want to be a storm chaser?**
**Jonas:** Ashley, guess what I'm going to be when I grow up?
**Ashley:** What?
**Jonas:** I'm going to be a storm chaser!
**Ashley:** A storm chaser? What's that?
**Jonas:** Storm chasers are people who study the weather. They watch the wind and clouds and rain, and they go to see big storms like tornadoes and hurricanes.
**Ashley:** That sounds dangerous!
**Jonas:** Not really. Most storm chasers stay near their cars and take pictures.
**Ashley:** Why do you want to do that?
**Jonas:** I'm really interested in the weather. What makes a flood happen? Why do we get earthquakes and tsunamis? I want to know!
**Ashley:** Do storm chasers have to travel a lot?
**Jonas:** Yes! They follow the storms across the country. In the mountains, they can see avalanches, and in other places, there are volcanoes. It's very exciting!
**Ashley:** What about forest fires? Do they watch those, too?
**Jonas:** Yes, and they see how quickly or how slowly they burn. This information helps scientists know more about the weather.
**Ashley:** Well, good luck, Jonas! I like watching the weather from inside my house!

TRACK 82
**Unit 7, Global Citizenship**
**B Listen, say, and number the pictures in A.**
**1** earthquake
**2** burn
**3** flood
**4** hurricane
**5** volcano
**6** avalanche
**7** cover
**8** tsunami
**9** forest fire
**10** tornado

TRACK G

**Unit 7, Global Citizenship**

**Close your eyes. Listen, visualize, and say.**

Earthquake. Imagine the floor is moving and buildings are falling. How do you feel? Say "earthquake."

Burn. Imagine you're watching a fire. What color is it? Say "burn."

Flood. The rain is very strong. The water starts to come inside the house. Is there water on the floor? Say "flood."

Hurricane. Imagine a very bad storm, with lots of wind, rain and floods. What does it sound like? Say "hurricane."

Volcano. Imagine a beautiful mountain. Suddenly fire comes out the top of it! How hot is it? Say "volcano."

Avalanche. Imagine a lot of snow moving down a mountain. How does it sound? Say "avalanche."

Cover. Imagine it is snowing outside. The snow covers everything! What does it look like? Say "cover."

Tsunami. Imagine a very big wave. It is higher than a house! How far do you think it will go? Say "tsunami."

Forest fire. Imagine a forest of green trees. The fire gets bigger and moves from one tree to another. Say *forest* "fire."

Tornado. Imagine it's windy and the sky is dark. There's a tall black cloud in the sky. Say "tornado."

TRACK 83

**Unit 7, Global Citizenship**

**D Now listen to Mely and Dustin. What do they practice at school?**

**Mely:** I'm Mely, and I live in The Philippines. We have lots of small earthquakes. The ground shakes and things fall off the shelves. Sometimes buildings fall down! An earthquake can cause a huge wave from the ocean, called a tsunami. My country has many small islands, so tsunamis can be dangerous. At school, we learn how to stay safe in an earthquake. Cover your head. Stay under a desk or table. Do what your teacher says. And have a plan with your family. We're always ready for earthquakes!

**Dustin:** I'm Dustin and I'm American. My part of the USA has tornadoes in the fall. A tornado is a very strong, dangerous wind. You can see it spinning around and around. It comes very quickly. At home, we have a shelter under the ground to hide in during a tornado. At school, we have another plan. We go to the basement and sit by the walls. We practice this a lot. A police officer comes to our classroom to talk about tornadoes, too. We need to stay safe!

TRACK 84

**Unit 7, Explore Language**

**A Listen and read. What do Hassan and Alec find?**

**Alec:** Hassan, what are you doing here? The flood is over!

**Hassan:** I'm helping to clean, Alec.

**Alec:** Rescue workers clean up, too?

**Hassan:** Yes, we do. This is the wall that stopped the flood. We're taking it down now.

**Alec:** What's on the ground?

**Hassan:** Those are things that floated here. We're going to take them to the police station. People that lost things can find them.

**Hassan:** Look! There's a backpack that has someone's homework inside. Someone named … Zack?

**Alec:** Zack's my friend! I'm going to call him.

TRACK 85

**Unit 7, Explore Language**

**D Listen and say.**

1 This is the wall that stopped the flood.
2 That's the building that fell down in the earthquake.
3 The people that live on the mountain are friendly.
4 The tornado that hit the town wasn't very strong.

TRACK 86

**Unit 7, Take the Stage**

**Pronunciation. Listen and say.**

/str/ straight stressed strong
/tr/ travel truck try

## Unit 8

TRACK 87

**Unit 8, Vocabulary**

**A Listen and find. Why do the fish swim away?**

**Guide:** Over there, you can see a clownfish. They like to hide on the ocean floor.

**Hassan:** Is it the fish that is orange, black, and white?

**Guide:** Yes, that's right.

**Hassan:** What is that pink plant?

**Guide:** That isn't a plant! It's coral. It's actually animals, but they can't move around.

**Mariam:** What does coral eat?

**Guide:** It eats tiny fish and plants in the water. A lot of animals can be seen near coral, like sea turtles and sometimes even octopuses.

**Ahmad:** What's that colorful fish over there?

**Guide:** That's an angelfish. It's very thin and bright. Can everybody see it?

**Several voices:** Oh, yes! Look! Wow!

**Mariam:** I can see a starfish!

**Guide:** Yes, a starfish is easy to see because it looks like a star. And can you see the seahorse?

**Hassan:** I can! It's over by the angelfish.

**Amad:** Excuse me! Why are all the fish swimming away?

**Guide:** Oh! There's a shark!

**Mariam:** What do sharks eat?

**Guide:** Um, fish!

TRACK 88

**Unit 8, Vocabulary**

**B Listen, say, and number the pictures in A.**

1 dolphin
2 clownfish
3 coral
4 angelfish
5 starfish
6 jellyfish
7 seahorse
8 octopus
9 shark
10 whale
11 sea turtle

TRACK 89

**Unit 8, Vocabulary**

**C Close your eyes. Listen, visualize, and say.**

Dolphin. Imagine you are in the sea, swimming with a dolphin. Hold on tight! Is it friendly? Say "dolphin."

Clownfish. Imagine a clownfish hiding on the ocean floor. What three colors is it? Say "clownfish."

Coral. You're swimming at the bottom of the sea. Look at the beautiful coral. Is it soft or hard? Say "coral."

Angelfish. Imagine a blue angelfish swimming in the coral. What shape is it? Say "angelfish."

Starfish. You're holding a starfish. Count its arms. How many are there? Say "starfish."

Jellyfish. You see a lot of jellyfish floating in the water. Do you go close, or stay away? Why? Say "jellyfish."

Seahorse. You're watching a seahorse. Does it really look like a horse? How big is it? Say "seahorse."

Octopus. Imagine an octopus swimming in the sea. How many arms does it have? Say "octopus."

Shark. There's a shark in the water! What do you do? Say "shark."

Whale. A big black whale jumps out of the sea. There's a huge splash! Do you get wet? Say "whale."

Sea turtle. You see a big turtle swimming in the ocean. It has a smooth, hard shell. Say "sea turtle."

TRACK 90

**Unit 8, Vocabulary**

**E Listen and complete. Then watch and sing.**

*Under the Sea*

*What do you see under the sea?*
*Look down through the glass and describe it to me!*
*We take care of living things under the sea*
*So they can keep growing, alive and free!*

I see a whale as big as a truck
And dolphins having fun.
I see some jellyfish floating nearby
Yellow and pink like the sun!

I see a seahorse swimming along,
And a starfish down on the sand.
I see a clownfish, orange and white,
Keep going! I'm not ready to go back to land.

TRACK 91

**Unit 8, Explore Language**

**A Listen and read. What's the word for a group of fish that swims together?**

**Ahmad:** Is that a coral reef?

**Guide:** Yes, it is. Lots of different kinds of coral grow here.

**Guide:** The reef is a shelter for small fish. They often swim into the coral and hide from sharks and other large fish.

**Ahmad:** Look at those angelfish! They're swimming through the coral right now! Why are the fish swimming together like that?

**Guide:** It helps them stay safe. It's called a school of fish.

**Ahmad:** That's a school? Cool! I like their uniforms.

TRACK 92

**Unit 8, Explore Language**

**D Listen and say.**

1 They're swimming through the coral right now!
2 It doesn't usually go near the big fish.
3 The small fish are hiding in the coral reef.
4 They often swim away from big fish.
5 Does the jellyfish always float like that?
6 That shark isn't looking for food right now.

TRACK 93

**Unit 8, Global Citizenship**

**A Listen to Anya and Dean talk about fish. Why are they different shapes and colors?**

**Anya:** Welcome to the New City Aquarium! Are you excited to begin the tour?

**Dean:** Yes! There are so many kinds of fish, and they all look different! Where do we start?

**Anya:** Let's begin with the striped fish. These clownfish are orange with white vertical stripes that go up and down.

**Dean:** What are those fish with horizontal stripes that go across them?

**Anya:** Those are angelfish. They're flat like a piece of paper, but some fish are round like a balloon!

**Dean:** And some fish are spotted instead of striped, right?

**Anya:** Yes, you're right. These special shapes and colors are very important: they protect the fish. All these fish match different plants and rocks under the sea. Then big fish like sharks can't see them.

**Dean:** And jellyfish are clear. You can see through them. That protects them too.

**Anya:** Yes, it does. And did you know that aquariums can also help to save fish and other sea creatures? In some parts of the world, the ocean is very dirty, so the fish are safe in aquariums.

**Dean:** They get all the food they want too! Lucky fish!

TRACK 94

**Unit 8, Global Citizenship**

**B Listen, say, and number the pictures in A.**

1 striped
2 spotted
3 vertical
4 horizontal
5 flat
6 round
7 clear
8 save
9 protect
10 aquarium

TRACK H

**Unit 8, Global Citizenship**

**Close your eyes. Listen, visualize, and say.**

Striped. Imagine you are wearing a T-shirt with stripes on it. What color are your stripes? Say "striped."

Spotted. Imagine you're wearing a shirt that is covered with spots. Are they big or small? Say "spotted."

Vertical. Which direction do your stripes go? Imagine they go from the top to the bottom. Draw these stripes with your hands. Say "vertical."

Horizontal. Now imagine your stripes are horizontal. They go from left to right. Draw these stripes with your hands. Say "horizontal."

Flat. Imagine you have a small box. Mime putting it on the floor and stepping on it! Now it's flat. Say "flat."

Round. Mime holding a huge ball in your arms. Is the ball flat? No, it's round. Say "round."

Clear. Imagine a window with clear glass. Can you see it? Say "clear."

Save. Imagine you see a wave come onto the beach. It leaves a fish lying on the sand. Quickly help the fish back into the water. You saved it! Say "save."

Protect. Think of a mother and a baby. The mother looks after the baby and keeps it safe. She protects it. Say "protect."

Aquarium. Now imagine you're going to a building to look at fish. There are many rooms with many very large tanks full of fish. Say "aquarium."

TRACK 95

**Unit 8, Global Citizenship**

**D Now listen to Yasmin and Li Li. What's special about their aquariums?**

**Yasmin:** My name's Yasmin, and I live in Dubai, in the UAE, the United Arab Emirates. The Dubai Aquarium is the one of the biggest aquariums in the world! In the middle is an enormous space where the sharks live. There is a huge window where I can watch the sharks. I love watching them! Every morning at 11:00, you can watch the divers feed them. Sharks actually don't eat very much, and they never eat people! A shark attack is usually a mistake. It happens when the shark thinks the person is another fish! My aquarium teaches the *real* facts about sharks.

**Li Li:** My name is Li Li and I'm from Shanghai, China. The aquarium in my city, the Shanghai Ocean Aquarium, has one of the longest underwater tunnels in the world! The tunnel goes deep under the water, but it's clear, so you can see all the fish above you. It's amazing! The aquarium protects many kinds of fish from the Yangtze River in China. They can't live in the river anymore because the plants and food they need are gone. But now the fish are safe in the aquarium.

TRACK 96

**Unit 8, Explore Language**

**A Listen and read. What are the boys going to do?**

**Ahmad:** There are dangerous fish here.

**Daniel:** Lionfish? How are they dangerous?

**Ahmad:** People brought them from far away. Now, they live here and eat everything!

**Daniel:** What will happen to the fish that live here? Will they have food?

**Ahmad:** No, they won't. The lionfish will eat it all!

**Daniel:** Hey, this poster says we can help!

**Ahmad:** How?

**Daniel:** We'll catch some lionfish! Then, there won't be so many.

**Ahmad:** But that sign says "No Fishing."

**Daniel:** This is different! We won't catch any other fish—only lionfish!

TRACK 97

**Unit 8, Explore Language**

**D Listen and say.**

1 Will they have food?
2 The fish will be safe in the future.
3 Will the boat be here next summer?
4 We'll catch lots of lionfish.
5 We won't catch any other fish.

TRACK 98
**Unit 8, Take the Stage**
**Pronunciation. Listen and say.**
/h/ heavy huge hard
/w/ whale were worried

## Unit 9

TRACK 99
**Unit 9, Vocabulary**
**A Listen and find. What's the matter with number three?**
**Doctor:** Play a game! Spin the wheel and pick a number!
**George:** OK!
**Spinner toy:** Four!
**George:** I got four. What do I do?
**Doctor:** Look at picture number four and guess what's wrong.
**George:** Number four has an earache. His ear hurts!
**Doctor:** Great! You get a prize!
**Heather:** Let me try!
**Spinner toy:** One!
**Heather:** Number one has a … cough?
**Doctor:** Sorry, that's not right. She isn't coughing.
**Heather:** Hmm … Is something wrong with her neck? Wait, I know. Number one has a sore throat.
**Doctor:** Good! You get a prize too. Next?
**Boy:** Me!
**Spinner toy:** Two!
**Boy:** Let's see—number two. He looks tired and hot, and he's lying down … Oh, I know! He doesn't have a cold. He has a fever.
**Doctor:** Right. He's sick, so he needs to rest. One more person!
**Girl:** Not me. I feel dizzy!
**Daniel:** I'll go!
**Spinner toy:** Three!
**Daniel:** OK, Number three has, uh, is going to, a …
**Doctor:** Number 3 is going to sneeze?
**Daniel:** No, Number three isn't sneezing! She has a headache. Her head hurts.
**Doctor:** Great, that's corr–Oh, excuse me, are you OK?
**Daniel:** No. I ate too much!
**Doctor:** I think you have a stomachache.

TRACK 100
**Unit 9, Vocabulary**
**B Listen, say, and number the pictures in A.**
1 cough
2 sneeze
3 sore throat
4 cold
5 headache
6 earache
7 stomachache
8 dizzy
9 fever
10 sick (British English: ill)

TRACK 101
**Unit 9, Vocabulary**
**C Close your eyes. Listen, visualize, and say.**
Cough. Mime coughing. What do you do with your hands when you cough? Say "cough."
Sneeze. Pretend to sneeze. Can you sneeze with your eyes open? Say "sneeze."
Sore throat. Imagine you have a sore throat. Put your hands where it hurts. Say "sore throat."
Cold. Imagine you have a bad cold. Do you cough or sneeze or both? Say "cold."
Headache. Mime having a headache. What do you do when your head hurts? Say "headache."
Earache. Imagine you have an earache. Point to the ear that hurts. Say "earache."
Stomachache. Mime having a stomachache. Hold your stomach. Do you feel better? Say "stomachache."
Dizzy. Imagine you stood up very quickly. Mime feeling dizzy. Say "dizzy."
Fever. Mime having a fever. Your head feels hot but your body feels cold. Your body's shaking. Say "fever."
Sick. Imagine you feel sick. What's the matter? Mime how you feel. Say "sick."

TRACK 102
**Unit 9, Vocabulary**
**E Listen and complete. Then watch and sing.**
*What's the Matter?*

*What's the matter? Are you OK?*
*I don't feel well. I'm sick today.*

What's the matter? You don't look well.
I have a bad cold
I'm coughing and sneezing
I have a headache.
I need a break!

What's the matter? You look sad.
I feel really dizzy and have a stomachache
I ate a lot in town, and I need to lie down!

What's the matter? Do you feel bad?
Yes, I have a fever, I don't know what to do,
Because I also have an earache and a sore throat, too!

TRACK 103
**Unit 9, Explore Language**
**A Listen and read. What happened to the sign and the skeleton?**
**Daniel:** George, are you OK?
**George:** I feel dizzy. What happened?
**Daniel:** I was standing over there when I heard a loud noise!
**George:** I heard it, too! I was standing next to those balloons when they popped.
**Daniel:** What were you doing when that sign fell down?
**George:** I was listening to the doctor when it fell down. It hit me and I fell down, too!
**Daniel:** Were you holding the skeleton when the sign hit you?
**George:** No, I wasn't.
**Daniel:** You weren't holding it when you fell, but you're holding it now!
**George:** Haha!

TRACK 104
**Unit 9, Explore Language**
**D Listen and say.**
1 I was standing next to the balloons when they popped.
2 The boys were coughing when the doctor came in.
3 You weren't feeling well when you went to the party.
4 Were you sitting beside the man when he sneezed?
5 What was she doing when she fell down?

TRACK 105
**Unit 9, Global Citizenship**
**A Listen to a nurse who works at a community clinic. When do people go to the hospital?**
**Nurse:** Why do people come to see a doctor at our community clinic? Well, there are three main reasons.
The first reason is that a lot of people try to see a doctor once a year. They're not sick, but they want the doctor to check them. The doctor checks their eyes, ears, and mouth. Often the doctor checks their blood, and sometimes the person needs a shot. Then the doctor or a nurse tells them about being healthy, for example how to eat and sleep well.
The second reason people come is because they're sick. Usually, sick people need medicine. The doctor decides what's wrong, and gives them medicine to make them feel better, and get rid of germs. Germs are tiny living things that can make people sick. The medicine helps our bodies fight the germs until we're well again.
The third reason people come to the community clinic is when they have an emergency, like a cut on their finger. We can put bandages on cuts, but we can't put a cast on a broken arm or leg. We usually have to send these people to the hospital. There are special doctors at the hospital who can help them.
Oh, and there's a fourth reason—sometimes people come to say thank you! We like that!

TRACK 106
**Unit 9, Global Citizenship**
**B Listen, say, and number the pictures in A.**
1 shot (British English: injection)
2 broken arm
3 cast
4 nurse
5 medicine
6 germs
7 blood
8 bandage

TRACK 1

**Unit 9, Global Citizenship**

**Close your eyes. Listen, visualize, and say.**

Shot. Imagine the doctor is giving you a shot. Do you watch? Say "shot."
Broken arm. Imagine a bone in your arm is broken. Does your arm hurt? Say "broken arm."
Cast. Mime wearing a cast on your arm. What color is it? Say "cast."
Nurse. Imagine the nurse is asking you questions. Is your nurse a man or a woman? Say "nurse."
Medicine. Mime taking some medicine. Does it taste good? Say "medicine."
Germs. Mime washing your hands. Does this kill the germs? Say "germs."
Blood. Imagine you cut your finger. Is there a lot of blood? What color is it? Say "blood."
Bandage. Imagine the nurse puts a large bandage around your ankle. What color is the bandage? Can you keep it clean? Say "bandage."

TRACK 107

**Unit 9, Global Citizenship**

**D Now listen to Jorge and Olivia. Which museum has nurses' uniforms and hospital beds?**

**Jorge:** I'm Jorge, and I live in Quito, in Ecuador. There's a lot of history in my city. Today, I went with my class to the Ecuador National Museum of Medicine. It's a museum inside an old hospital. They have lots of information there about the history of medicine in Ecuador. I learned about plants that were used as medicine in my country a long time ago. They have some old medical instruments that were used in the past by doctors, nurses, and dentists, too. Some of them were a little scary, but it was really interesting

**Olivia:** My name is Olivia, and I live in London, England. Last week my class visited the Florence Nightingale Museum here. Florence Nightingale was a famous nurse. She started the first school for nurses in London in 1860. Florence Nightingale believed that sick people needed gentle care, nice rooms, and healthy food to get better. She taught nurses to wash their hands and keep the hospital very clean because she wanted to stop germs from spreading. At the museum, we watched a play about Florence Nightingale. We saw nurses' uniforms and hospital beds from those days too.

TRACK 108

**Unit 9, Explore Language**

**A Listen and read. How long was Heather sick?**

**Nurse Hayes:** Heather, how are you?
**Heather:** I'm feeling better, thanks. I was sick for three days.
**Nurse Hayes:** What was wrong?
**Heather:** I had a fever. I was feeling hot and cold while I was helping you at the clinic. When I went home, I felt really sick.
**Nurse Hayes:** Were you feeling sick while you were working with the children?
**Heather:** A little. While we were working, I was washing my hands a lot.
**Nurse Hayes:** Well, that's good!

TRACK 109

**Unit 9, Explore Language**

**D Listen and say.**

1 I was feeling hot and cold while I was helping you at the clinic.
2 My mom was reading a book while we were waiting for the doctor.
3 She was sitting in a chair while the nurse was getting her medicine.
4 Were you crying while the nurse was putting the bandage on your foot?
5 While the nurse was talking, the students were listening.

TRACK 110

**Unit 9, Talk About It**

**Pronunciation. Listen and say**

/kw/ quite quiet quickly
/kr/ crash crazy cream

# Unit 10

TRACK 111

**Unit 10, Vocabulary**

**A Listen and find. What does the machine make?**

**Owen:** Wow. This machine is cool!
**Machine Operator:** Thanks!
**Owen:** How does it work?
**Machine Operator:** I start it over here. I pull this lever.
**Owen:** OK. Then what happens?
**Machine Operator:** Watch and see!
**Kareem:** OK. The lever turns that gear … And that makes the huge wheel go around.
**Machine Operator:** Right. And that wheel turns all these other wheels.
**Kareem:** I see! Then a ball comes out of there … it falls down and pushes a button.
**Ting:** And that opens a door! Look, something's coming out!
**Owen:** What is it?
**Kareem:** It's paper! Look at the colors!
**Daniel:** Hmmm. I wonder what happens when you push this button.
**Hassan:** Oh, please don't … Uh-oh. What's that?
**Jake:** Everything's shaking! Something's wrong!
**Alec:** Can you stop the machine?
**Nurse Hayes:** Oh no! Let's see … is there an "off" switch?
**Carla:** This is paint! Look at me! I'm green!
**Millie:** And I'm pink! And Jake's yellow!
**Alec:** The paint's coming from there! How can we stop it?
**Nurse Hayes:** Everybody, stand back!
**Machine Operator:** Sorry. I guess I still have some work to do!
**Millie:** That was exciting!
**Carla:** Can you make a machine to help wash off this paint?
**Machine Operator:** Of course!

TRACK 112

**Unit 10, Vocabulary**

**B Listen, say, and number the pictures in A.**

1 button
2 push
3 lever
4 pull
5 switch
6 flip
7 wheel
8 turn
9 gear

TRACK 113

**Unit 10, Vocabulary**

**C Close your eyes. Listen, visualize, and say.**

Button. Imagine a computer. How do you turn it on? Put your finger on the button. Say "button."
Push. You push the button. What happens? Say "push."
Lever. Imagine you're sitting on a seesaw. What happens when your friend gets on the other side? Say "lever."
Pull. Imagine a big, long rope hanging from a tree branch. Pull it hard! What happens? Say "pull."
Switch. Think of the switch on your classroom wall. What is it for? Say "switch".
Flip. Put your finger on the light switch. Flip it! Did you flip it on or off? Say "flip."
Wheel. You're riding a bicycle. How many wheels does it have? Say "wheel."
Turn. Now you need to turn left. Do your wheels turn quickly or slowly? Say "turn."
Gear. Think of the metal gears on your bike. They look like wheels with teeth. How many are there? Say "gear."

TRACK 114

**Unit 10, Vocabulary**

**E Listen and complete. Then watch and sing.**

*This Huge Machine*

*How do you work this huge machine?*
*It's easy! Watch and see what I mean!*
*You're right! It's easy! I see what you mean!*

First you pull the lever and flip the switch
Then you push the button and wait!
You turn the gears that turn the wheels
And fill the machine with paint!

Then the paper comes out and the colors are great
And you pull the lever again.
The wheels stop moving and the gears slow down
And your time with the machine is at an end!

TRACK 115

**Unit 10, Explore Language**

**A Listen and read. What does Ting want to know?**

**Carla:** Ting, this machine's as big as that house!

**Ting:** It's really interesting, Carla.

**Carla:** This machine's even bigger than the first one.

**Ting:** It's more complicated, too. It has more parts. Look! This little one's more interesting than those big ones!

**Carla:** It's very small. It isn't as exciting as the big machines.

**Ting:** Cool! It makes tiny frogs. I wonder how it works.

**Carla:** Well, it's quieter than the big machines, but … it isn't as strong.

**Ting:** Bigger isn't always better! I think it works perfectly!

TRACK 116

**Unit 10, Explore Language**

**D Listen and say.**

1 This machine's as big as that house!
2 My machine isn't as loud as yours.
3 This wheel is bigger than that one.
4 Your machine is more complicated than mine.

TRACK 117

**Unit 10, Global Citizenship**

**A Listen to Lily talking to Grandpa José. What's special about his chair?**

**Lily:** Grandpa José, I love your chair!

**Grandpa José:** Thanks, Lily! I made it myself.

**Lily:** Really? That's amazing! How did you make it?

**Grandpa José:** The seat is made from cotton, and the legs are metal. At first, I used wood for the legs, but they broke.

**Lily:** What about those straps? Are they leather?

**Grandpa José:** Yes. The straps need to be strong.

**Lily:** Why did you decide to make a chair?

**Grandpa José:** Well, I wanted a chair that I could fold. I wanted it to fit in my backpack. I like going on bike trips, and I always stop for lunch. But I don't like sitting on the ground. It hurts my back.

**Lily:** And this fits in your backpack?

**Grandpa José:** Yes! Watch. I take out the legs, like this, and fold it up. Then I tie it all together with the straps. There!

**Lily:** Wow! That's great! Can you make one for me? I'd like a plastic seat cover for mine. I don't want my seat to get wet when it rains!

**Grandpa José:** That's a good idea! I can't sew plastic very well, but I can try. What about wool? Wool is nice and warm. It will be good when the weather is cold! Now let's finish this birdhouse, Lily.

**Lily:** Thanks, Grandpa!

TRACK 118

**Unit 10, Global Citizenship**

**B Listen, say, and number the pictures in A.**

1 cotton
2 wool
3 leather
4 gold
5 silver
6 metal
7 plastic
8 wood

TRACK J

**Unit 10, Global Citizenship**

**Close your eyes. Listen, visualize, and say.**

Cotton. Imagine a T-shirt. It's made of cotton. Do you wear it in winter or in summer? Say "cotton."

Wool. Imagine a wool sweater. What animal does wool come from? Say "wool."

Leather. You're at a shoe store. Can you find shoes made of leather? Say "leather."

Gold. Imagine you have some gold jewelry. What color is it? Say "gold."

Silver. Now imagine you have silver jewelry. What color is it? Say "silver."

Metal. Think of your bicycle. What's it made of? Is it light or heavy? Say "metal."

Plastic. Think of something made of plastic in your classroom. What is it? Say "plastic."

Wood. Think about your room. What is made of wood? Say "wood."

TRACK 119

**Unit 10, Global Citizenship**

**D Now listen to Laura from Colombia. How old were the kids that she talks about?**

**Laura:** My name's Laura and I'm in a Maker's Club at my school in Bogotá, Colombia. Every week, we talk about how to fix problems in new ways. I like hearing stories about other kids' inventions. Here are my favorites. They are both true!
A girl named Cassidy was doing an art project and saw all her crayons were broken. She thought about it. Crayons always break so easily. So she invented crayon holders! These are clear plastic holders for crayons. She found a company to make them, and now you can buy crayon holders. Cassidy was only 11 years old when she invented crayon holders.
Another story is about a boy named CJ. CJ saw a commercial for an exercise video on TV. He thought that someone should make one for kids—so he did! His cousin helped him make the first video, with CJ in it. Then, they found a company to help them. Now CJ is "The Workout Kid." You can watch his videos online or buy his DVD! CJ was nine years old when he made his first exercise video.

TRACK 120

**Unit 10, Explore Language**

**A Listen and read. What kind of wheels does the machine have?**

**Millie:** We have to move this machine to the gym today! Can it fit through the door?

**Carla:** Yes, and I'm happy that we don't have to take it apart!

**Millie:** The machine needs a switch to start and stop. Where could I put it?

**Kareem:** You could put it there.

**Millie:** No, I can't. There's no room.

**Daniel:** What about this wheel?

**Alec:** We shouldn't use plastic wheels. They aren't very strong. You should find a metal wheel.

**Daniel:** OK, I think I see one.

TRACK 121

**Unit 10, Explore Language**

**D Listen and say.**

1 You should find a metal wheel.
2 He shouldn't use plastic wheels.
3 They don't have to paint the machine.
4 The team has to finish the machine.
5 We could make the machine really big.

TRACK 122

**Unit 10, Take the Stage**

**Pronunciation. Listen and say.**

**/br/** branches breakfast bright

**/fl/** flat floor flag

## Play 1 Units 1–5

TRACK 123

**The Grassland Orchestra**

**Narrator:** Faruk, Amelia, and Isabella are at a table in the library. Marco looks at books on the shelves. He chooses a thick, old book and puts it on the table.

**Marco:** Look at this old book!

**Faruk:** It looks like a geography book.

**Amelia:** Could it be an adventure story?

**Narrator:** Isabella opens the book. The four friends aren't in the library any more. The children fall off their chairs and onto the floor. Isabella holds the old book in her hands.

**Faruk:** What happened?

**Amelia:** I think we're in the book!

**Narrator:** They stand up and look around.

**Faruk:** But where are we?

**Isabella:** We're in the grassland. The ground's covered with tall grass and flowers.

**Marco:** What was that crash?

**Faruk:** Look, a cheetah! Watch out! It's dangerous!

**Narrator:** Cheetah comes running through the grass up to the children. They are afraid.

**Cheetah:** Hello! Don't be frightened. Many animals are more dangerous than I am.

**Amelia:** It's nice to meet you, Cheetah. Where are the other animals?

**Cheetah:** They're busy. You see, we have a complicated problem here. The grassland's very dry. We need water. So we're going to build a lake.

**Isabella:** Wow! Are lakes expensive?
**Cheetah:** Oh, yes. We need a million dollars—but we don't have any money.
**Faruk:** So, what are you going to do?
**Cheetah:** The Grassland Orchestra is going to have a performance! I'm the conductor, but I also play the cello.
**Marco:** I play the drums, and Isabella plays the piano. Can we help you?
**Cheetah:** Yes! Then you have to come to our rehearsal. We shouldn't be late.
**Narrator:** Cheetah runs off and the children follow him. Finally, the rest of the orchestra arrives. They are all animals.
**Cheetah:** Hello, everyone! I'm glad you're on time. We have some new performers. They're going to join us. Let's tell them about the performance. When's it going to happen?
**Animals:** Tomorrow at noon!
**Cheetah:** Where are we going to perform?
**Animals:** On the stage!
**Cheetah:** How are we going to play?
**Animals:** Together! Loudly! Quietly! Quickly! Slowly! Proudly!
**Cheetah:** Right! Let's begin. Do you have your instruments?
**Animals:** Yes, we do!
**Amelia:** No, we don't.
**Cheetah:** WHAT? YOU DON'T HAVE YOUR INSTRUMENTS?
**Marco:** Well, we were reading… We weren't playing our instruments, …
**Cheetah and Animals:** ROAR!
**Narrator:** The animals come towards the children angrily.
**Amelia:** Isabella, where's the book?
**Isabella:** Right here.
**Faruk:** Close it! Now!
**Narrator:** Isabella closes the book. The children are back at their table in the library.
**Isabella:** That was exciting!
**Narrator:** Marco goes back to the shelf and pulls out another book.
**Marco:** Let's try this science fiction book next.

## Play 2 Units 6–10

TRACK 124

**Into the Future**

**Diego:** Is this your time machine?
**Jin:** Yes. This is the machine that's going to take us into the future.
**Diego:** Cool! I'm ready.
**Jin:** What are you going to do in the future?
**Diego:** Me? I plan to look at sea life. I want to know about the coral reefs. Will people save them?
**Jin:** That's important. Go in!
**Chorus:** Thanks for coming. Step inside. Into the future! Let's go for a ride!
**Narrator:** Diego enters the machine. Then Noor walks over to the time machine. She is dressed as a doctor.
**Jin:** Hi, Noor! What are you going to do in the future?
**Noor:** I plan to talk to nurses and doctors. I want to find out about medicines that help people feel better.
**Jin:** Excellent plan! Go in.
**Chorus:** Thanks for coming. Step inside. Into the future! Let's go for a ride!
**Narrator:** Noor enters the machine. Next, Eli comes over. He is dressed like a rescue worker, and is carrying a big bag of tools.
**Eli:** Cool machine!
**Jin:** Thanks! I enjoyed building it. Why are you bringing all this?
**Eli:** I want to help rescue workers in the future. But what emergencies will I find? An earthquake, a hurricane, a forest fire? I have to be ready for everything!
**Jin:** Good luck! Go in.
**Chorus:** Thanks for coming! Step inside. Into the future! Let's go for a ride!
**Narrator:** Eli brings all his tools into the machine. Then Laura appears. She is dressed like a chef.
**Jin:** Laura, what are your plans for the future?
**Laura:** I love cooking, so I want to learn about food in the future. What will people eat? Will they eat more protein? Will they still need to use a fridge or a stove?
**Jin:** That's interesting. Go in.
**Chorus:** Thanks for coming! Step inside. Into the future! Let's go for a ride!
**Narrator:** Laura enters the machine. Jin looks around and checks the time.
**Diego:** Let's go, Jin!
**Jin:** But there's one more person who should be here…
**Narrator:** Jin starts closing the door. Then he sees Kelsey running toward him.
**Kelsey:** Wait!
**Jin:** You're late.
**Kelsey:** Sorry! I was walking through the park when a huge bird flew down and took my warm wool hat!
**Jin:** A bird took your hat?
**Kelsey:** Yes! I tried to catch it, but it flew faster and faster. And while it was flying, it was eating my hat! My hat's gone.
**Jin:** That's too bad. But we have to go now. Are you ready for the future?
**Kelsey:** Yes! I plan to study materials. I want to find out if people will still use things made from cotton or leather.
**Jin:** Sounds good! Go in.
**Chorus:** Thanks for coming. Step inside. Into the future! Let's go for a ride!
**Narrator:** Kelsey starts to climb into the machine. Then she turns back to Jin.
**Kelsey:** Maybe I'll get a new hat!
**Jin:** Sorry, you can't bring things back from the future.
**Kelsey:** Hmmm… I think you're wrong. I'm going to bring something back!
**Jin:** What?
**Kelsey:** Ideas! We're all going to bring back ideas that will save the world!
**Narrator:** Kelsey and Jin both enter the machine. Jin pulls a lever and the door closes. He pushes a button that says START.
**Chorus:** We stepped inside! Into the future! We're going for a ride!

# Literacy Book

## Literacy Review

### TRACK 1

**Literacy Review, Fiction, *Don't Move***

**Suzie:** A strong wind blew through the trees and our tent shook like a sail. Mom and I were the only two people out on the forest trail that night. I felt very alone. I wished we were at home and I was sleeping in my own bed.

**Suzie (as her mom):** Camping out here will be worth it, Suzie,

**Suzie:** Mom said with a smile.

**Suzie (as her mom):** We'll get some amazing butterfly photos in the morning.

**Suzie:** Just then, from outside the thin walls of the tent, I heard a grunting noise. I jumped. It was some kind of animal. The creature started moving around the tent. One moment, the grunting was next to our heads. Then, it was by our feet. "What is it?" I whispered.

**Suzie (as her mom):** It's looking for food. Stay close,

**Suzie:** said Mom.

**Suzie (as her mom):** And don't move.

### TRACK 2

**Literacy Review, Phonics, Final –*st* and Initial *tr*-.**

**Listen and unscramble. Then find more words ending with *st* and beginning with *tr* in the reading.**

**1** fast
**2** train
**3** nest
**4** travel
**5** trash
**6** best
**7** first
**8** true

### TRACK 3

**Literacy Review, Nonfiction, *The Monarch Butterfly's Journey***

Every fall, in the mountains about 97 km. northwest of Mexico City, something amazing happens. Millions of monarch butterflies arrive at the same small part of the forest. Some monarch butterflies travel more than four thousand km. from North America to escape the winter and to mate. Every year in this forest, there are so many butterflies that the trees turn orange. Branches bend under the weight. In spring, the forest fills with the fluttering of tiny wings, as the monarchs get ready to make the long journey back home.

This part of the forest is now a UNESCO World Heritage Site. Scientists believe this place is important for the planet and for the monarch butterfly species. People take care of this forest. The trees here cannot be cut down.

### TRACK 4

**Literacy Review, Phonics Final –*nd*. and –*ng*. Listen and complete with *nd*. and *ng*. Then find more words ending with *nd* and *ng* in the reading.**

**1** send
**2** find
**3** stand
**4** wrong
**5** thing
**6** sing
**7** strong
**8** sound

## Unit 1

### TRACK 5

**Unit 1, Fiction, *The Beginning of Alice's Adventures***

**Narrator:** Alice sat by the river. Her sister read a novel. Alice was bored and hot. She felt sleepy, and she wondered what to do. Suddenly, a rabbit ran past her. The rabbit was white with pink eyes. He wore a yellow waistcoat.

**Alice:** Goodness me!

**Narrator:** said Alice.

**Alice:** What's that? A rabbit in a waistcoat!

**Narrator:** She was very surprised.

**Alice:** Rabbits don't wear waistcoats!

**Narrator:** The rabbit stopped and took a watch out of his pocket.

**Rabbit:** Oh dear, oh dear, I'm going to be late,

**Narrator:** he said. The rabbit ran off. Alice got up, quickly, and chased after him.
The rabbit jumped down a very big hole.
Alice jumped in after him.
Alice fell—down, down, down—for a very long time.
As she fell, Alice could see shelves of interesting books and things on the sides of the hole.

**Alice:** I wonder if I'm near the center of the Earth,

**Narrator:** she said.
Down, down, down.

**Alice:** I might go right through the Earth and end up in New Zealand,

**Narrator:** said Alice. She knew all about the geography of the Earth from school.
Then, suddenly—*thump!* Alice landed at the bottom of the hole. She saw the White Rabbit run around the corner.
Alice ran after him as fast as she could.
Alice came to a room full of doors. But where was the White Rabbit? She couldn't see him, and all the doors were locked.
Then Alice saw a little golden key on a table. She picked it up.

**Alice:** I wonder which door this key opens?

**Narrator:** This was just the beginning of Alice's exciting adventures in Wonderland. But she didn't know that!

### TRACK 6

**Unit 1, *The Beginning of Alice's Adventures*, Words in Context**

**Find these words in the reading. What do you think they mean?**

sleepy
chased
fell
shelves
corner

### TRACK 7

**Unit 1, Nonfiction, *Learning and Your Brain***

*The Lobes of the Brain*

Your brain works hard all day. There are four lobes, or parts, of the brain. They do different things, but they all work together.
Part of your brain helps you understand what you taste and touch. Can you find it?
Another part of your brain helps you see. Can you find it?
When your teacher reads to you, part of your brain helps you hear the words. It also works when you read silently. Can you find it? Part of your brain helps you speak. It also helps you understand what you are reading. Can you find it?
When you do different things, the lobes of your brain work together like a team. Using the different parts makes them stronger. Reading is a good way to exercise your brain and give it a workout.
Scientists use a special machine to see which parts of the brain we use at different times. During each activity, the red areas show the parts we're using the most, the blue areas show the parts we're using a little bit, and the black areas show parts we aren't using much at all.

*Neurons Make Connections*

Your brain is made up of billions of special cells called neurons. Each neuron has a body with fibers that look like the branches of a tree. These fibers join together, connecting neurons so they can send each other messages or information.
The more you read, the stronger these connections become.

*Reading Helps Your Imagination*

When you read, your brain helps you visualize, or imagine, what the story might look like. Scientists think reading improves the imagination because it makes the connections in our brains stronger. This makes us more creative.

*Your Brain and Other Subjects*
In P.E., you run and kick a ball. Goal! You use this part of your brain.
How much is one plus one plus one plus one plus one? What about 10 minus one? How about two times two? This part of the brain helps you solve math problems.
When you listen to music, this part of your brain is working.
Keep reading and learning to keep your brain in good shape.

### TRACK 8
**Unit 1, *Learning and Your Brain*, Words in Context**
**Find these words in the reading. What do you think they mean?**
lobes
workout
cells
fibers
messages
connecting
creative

### TRACK 9
**Unit 1, Spelling Pattern, Final *–er*.**
**Listen and write. Then check your answers.**
1 computer
2 water
3 answer
4 flower
5 river
**Now check your answers.**
1 computer, c-o-m-p-u-t-e-r, computer
2 water, w-a-t-e-r, water
3 answer, a-n-s-w-e-r, answer
4 flower, f-l-o-w-e-r, flower
5 river, r-i-v-e-r, river

## Unit 2

### TRACK 10
**Unit 2, Nonfiction, *Two Different Forests***
*Deciduous Forests*
Deciduous trees grow all over the world. They grow in parts of North America, Europe, and China. These places have four seasons in the year: spring, summer, autumn, and winter. In the autumn, the leaves of deciduous trees fall to the ground. But before they do, the leaves change color. They go from green to orange, brown, and red. Some people think autumn is the most beautiful season.
Oak trees and apple trees are deciduous. In the spring, they have small flowers. These flowers become fruit and seeds in the autumn. In the winter, the trees have no leaves. Then the leaves and flowers grow back again in the spring.
There are a lot of animals in the deciduous forest biome. They eat plants, fruit, and the seeds from the trees. Some of them hibernate. They sleep all winter when it's cold and there isn't much food.
*Coniferous Forests*
Like deciduous trees, coniferous trees grow all over the world. Many of them grow in places that have longer and colder winters. This means that the summers are shorter and cooler, too.
We call these forests coniferous because the trees have cones instead of flowers or fruit. They also have thin dark green leaves all year round. These leaves don't change color in autumn, so we call coniferous trees evergreen.
Not many animals can survive in the very cold winters of the coniferous forests. Most of them hibernate. Many of them change color in the winter so they can hide in the snow. Some of them have thick white fur, not brown fur. This is one way they adapt.
The trees and animals in these two types of forests are very different, but they must all adapt to changes in their biomes to survive.

### TRACK 11
**Unit 2, *Two Different Forests*, Words in Context**
**Find these words in the reading. What do you think they mean?**
deciduous
hibernate
coniferous
survive
adapt

### TRACK 12
**Unit 2, Fiction, *A New Friend***
**Narrator:** Every spring, a swallow built its nest under Go Ne's roof. Go Ne loved all animals, but the swallows were his favorite.
**Go Ne:** Spring is the best season.
**Narrator:** This spring, there were two baby swallows inside the nest.
**Go Ne:** They're so tiny!
**Narrator:** One day, one of the baby swallows fell out of the nest. Go Ne's father climbed up and put the baby bird back in its nest. The mommy bird was really happy and gave Go Ne a strange, gold seed. He planted it in a pot.
The plant grew bigger. It had a dark green stem and the most beautiful leaves.
**Narrator:** After a few weeks, there was a big, round fruit.
**Go Ne's Mom:** Let's cut it open!
**Narrator:** Go Ne's mom said. It was full of gold coins. They were rich!
**Go Ne's Dad:** Now we can fix the roof!
**Narrator:** Wen Shu saw the gold coins. He had an idea and ran to the nest.
**Wen Shu:** I want a seed, too!
**Narrator:** He shouted. He pulled his slingshot back and let go. A stone sailed through the air. It hit the swallows' nest. It scared the baby birds and one fell.
**Wen Shu:** Oh, no!
**Narrator:** Wen Shu ran to the little bird to put it back in the nest, but it didn't move. Go Ne heard Wen Shu and ran to help. He put the bird in his bike's basket and rode away.
**Narrator:** Wen Shu followed Go Ne. He felt really sorry about the baby bird now. The two boys waited and waited.
**Wen Shu:** Please make the baby bird better!
**Narrator:** After a long time, the vet came out with the baby swallow. It was OK!
**Go Ne:** Thank you so much!
**Narrator:** Go Ne paid the vet with some of the money from the gold seed.
**Go Ne's Dad:** Go Ne, why did you spend that money? Now we don't have enough to fix the roof!
**Narrator:** Later that day, Wen Shu went to Go Ne's house. He left a special gift so they could fix the roof. Go Ne and his family were very happy. And Wen Shu was, too.

### TRACK 13
**Unit 2, *A New Friend*, Words in Context**
**Find these words in the reading. What do you think they mean?**
swallow
roof
hit
slingshot
paid

### TRACK 14
**Unit 2, Spelling Pattern, *ai*.**
**Listen and write. Then check your answers.**
1 rain
2 mountain
3 paint
4 train
5 chair
**Now check your answers.**
1 rain, r-a-i-n, rain
2 mountain, m-o-u-n-t-a-i-n, mountain
3 paint, p-a-i-n-t, paint
4 train, t-r-a-i-n, train
5 chair, c-h-a-i-r, chair

## Unit 3

### TRACK 15

**Unit 3, Nonfiction, *The History of Money***

Thousands of years ago, people didn't use money. Instead, people bartered for things they wanted. Around 6000 BCE, if someone wanted to buy a new goat, he paid for it with grain. But it took time to agree how much things were worth.

Then, in 1200 BCE, people started using cowrie shells as money. The shells were easier to carry than goats or bags of grain.

After that, around 1000 BCE, the Chinese started using metal money. At first, they used small metal knives and spades. But this money was difficult to carry and to use.

Later, probably between 400 and 300 BCE, people started to use round metal money with holes in the middle.

However, around 600 BCE, one of the kings of Lydia, which is part of modern-day Turkey, made the first true coins. These coins had pictures of plants and animals on them. Everyone knew how much each coin was worth.

Soon, many countries made their own coins from valuable metals like silver and gold. This made buying and selling easier.

The first paper money came from China between 800 and 900 CE. It was easier to carry than metal coins. European countries didn't start to use paper money widely until around 1600 CE.

After that, money didn't change for many centuries. Then, in 1958, there was the first credit card. People didn't have to use paper money or coins. Instead, they could use a small plastic card.

Today, in the 21st century, many people use electronic money. Because it's very easy to move around, people often use it to buy things on the internet.

What type of money do you think is going to be next?

### TRACK 16

**Unit 3, *The History of Money*, Words in Context**

**Find these words in the reading. What do you think they mean?**

bartered
metal
valuable
credit card
plastic

### TRACK 17

**Unit 3, Fiction, *The $100 Bill***

**Nina:** Hey, Paige, what's your phone number?
**Narrator:** asked Nina after school. Paige shook her head.
**Paige:** You know I don't have a cell phone.
**Jodie:** Oh, Paige! You really should get one!
**Narrator:** Jodie laughed hard. Nina laughed too.
**Narrator:** Paige walked through the park on her way home. In her head, she could hear the girls laughing.
Then Paige saw something in the leaves. She picked it up. A hundred dollars! The bill was wet and dirty. Who did it belong to? There was no one to ask and no way to return it.
Paige didn't know what to do. Was it wrong to keep it? Suddenly, Jodie was next to her.
**Jodie:** What are you doing?
**Narrator:** Jodie asked.
**Paige:** Nothing,
**Narrator:** said Paige. She quickly put the money in her pocket.
**Jodie:** See you tomorrow, Paige!
**Narrator:** said Jodie. On the other side of the park, there was a cell phone store. Paige looked in the window. There was a beautiful black phone.
Paige touched the bill in her pocket. She could buy a cell phone now.
**Paige:** Ninety-five dollars …
**Narrator:** she thought.
**Paige:** That's expensive, but … No more laughing from Jodie and Nina!
**Narrator:** Paige went into the store.
**Salesperson:** Can I help you?
**Narrator:** the cashier asked. Paige touched the bill in her pocket again.
**Paige:** Um, no, thank you,
**Narrator:** Paige answered.
**Paige:** I should save the money,
**Narrator:** she thought.
Paige's dad sat in the kitchen. He looked really tired.
**Dad:** Hi, honey,
**Narrator:** He said, and gave her a hug.
**Paige:** Dad? I have an idea,
**Narrator:** said Paige.
**Paige:** Let's go out to a restaurant.
**Dad:** Oh, Paige, I'd like to, but you know money is tight right now,
**Narrator:** he answered. Paige smiled.
**Paige:** You don't have to pay, Dad!
**Dad:** Where did you find that?
**Narrator:** he asked.
Paige told him about finding the money in the park.
**Dad:** There's no way to give it back,
**Narrator:** her dad said.
**Dad:** OK. Let's go. I'm hungry!

### TRACK 18

**Unit 3, *The $100 Bill*, Words in Context**

**Find these words in the reading. What do you think they mean?**

belong to
return
pocket
restaurant
money is tight

### TRACK 19

**Unit 3, Spelling Pattern, *ar*.**

**Listen and write. Then check your answers.**

**1** barter
**2** carrot
**3** warm
**4** lizard
**5** garden

**Now check your answers.**

**1** barter, b-a-r-t-e-r, barter
**2** carrot, c-a-r-r-o-t, carrot
**3** warm, w-a-r-m, warm
**4** lizard, l-i-z-a-r-d, lizard
**5** garden, g-a-r-d-e-n, garden

## Unit 4

### TRACK 20

**Unit 4, Nonfiction, *Teamwork Makes the Dream Work***

WNBA is short for the Women's National Basketball Association. It's a professional women's basketball league in the United States that started in 1996. There are twelve teams in the WNBA. Some of the teams are the Minnesota Lynx, the Los Angeles Sparks, the Dallas Wings, and the New York Liberty. They play 34 games each season in front of huge crowds all over the country.

In a basketball game, ten players are on the court—five from each team. Each team has a basket at one end of the court. A player has to get the ball into the other team's basket to score points, but all the teammates have to work together to make this happen. Most baskets are worth two points, but from far away, they're worth three.

In one of the championship games, the Los Angeles Sparks were playing against the Minnesota Lynx. The game was almost over, and the Los Angeles Sparks were losing by five points. Chelsea Gray, a Sparks player, was in the air shooting the ball. And she scored a three-pointer! But three points weren't enough, and the Minnesota Lynx won the game. That didn't stop the Sparks, though. They worked even harder and won the championship that year. Winning is important, but it isn't everything. Working together is part of playing the game. Some of the players from the Sparks and the Lynx talk about teamwork.

*Chelsea Gray*
"My team needed me."

*Candace Parker*
"My teammates and my coaches were always there for me."

*Maya Moore*
"No matter what we're feeling that day, we have to do our best …"

*Lindsay Whalen*
"As a group we have to do it, but everybody has to bring it."

These WNBA players know that teamwork makes their dream work. Their dream, of course, is to win the championship next year.

TRACK 21

**Unit 4, *Teamwork Makes the Dream Work*, Words in Context**

**Find these words in the reading. What do you think they mean?**

league
court
basket
score
shooting

TRACK 22

**Unit 4, Spelling Pattern *or.***

**Listen and write. Then check your answers.**

1 storm
2 history
3 airport
4 forest
5 alligator

**Now check your answers.**

1 storm, s-t-o-r-m, storm
2 history, h-i-s-t-o-r-y, history
3 airport, a-i-r-p-o-r-t, airport
4 forest, f-o-r-e-s-t, forest
5 alligator, a-l-l-i-g-a-t-o-r, alligator

TRACK 23

**Unit 4, Fiction, *Late for the Show***

**Narrator:** It's Friday afternoon. It's the last rehearsal for the only performance of *Twelfth Night* at Woodlands School.
**Mr. Williams:** And … the end. Well done, everyone! Now, remember, the show starts at six o'clock tomorrow night, so please be here at quarter past five. And please remember to bring your costumes!
**Harry, Riya, Arush, and Lynn:** Yes, Mr. Williams.
**Harry:** How did I do?
**Mr. Williams:** Great! Don't be nervous, Harry. It's your first time on stage.
**Narrator:** The next day…
**Harry's dad:** Harry! It's time to go!
**Harry:** Coming, Dad!
**Harry's mom:** Don't worry, Harry. There's plenty of time.
**Harry's dad:** Oh, no!
**Harry:** What's wrong, Dad?
**Harry's dad:** Look at all the traffic! OK, Harry, you and Mom take the Underground! I'll stay here.
**Harry:** What time is it, Mom?
**Harry's mom:** Quarter past five. We're a bit late, but don't worry …
**Loudspeaker:** Ladies and gentlemen, there's a problem with the train. Please stay calm.
**Narrator:** Five minutes later, the train is still not moving.
**Harry:** We're never going to get there!
**Loudspeaker:** Ladies and gentlemen, please get off the train and wait on the platform. We're fixing the problem.
**Harry:** Arush! You're here!
**Lynn:** Me too … and Riya!
**Riya:** Look. We're too late!
**Harry:** The show should be happening now… but we're not on stage!
**Lynn:** Wait a minute … Why don't we perform the show here, now?
**Harry:** Good idea!
**Riya:** We have our costumes and an audience!
**Arush:** Yes, let's do it!
**Lynn:** Viola wakes up on a beach after a storm. She was traveling on a ship with her brother Sebastian, but the ship sank. Now, Viola is alone, and she can't find Sebastian.
**Riya:** Sebastian! Where are you? … Oh, I'm so frightened.
**Harry's mom:** That's my son. He's the tree! Isn't he great?
**Riya:** Sebastian! You're alive!
**Arush:** Viola! My sister!
**Mr. Williams:** Bravo! Fantastic! Well done! Great teamwork! You were fantastic! I'm so proud of you.
**Harry:** That was our best performance!
**Riya:** Yes! We did it together.
**Loudspeaker:** Ladies and gentlemen, thank you for waiting. We fixed the problem. Please get back on the train.
**Harry:** It's too late now!

TRACK 24

**Unit 4, Late for the Show, Words in Context**

**Find these words in the reading. What do you think they mean?**

show
calm
platform
sank
alive

# Unit 5

TRACK 25

**Unit 5, Nonfiction, *The Art of Sound***

A knight runs through a castle, and a man chases after him. Their heavy boots thud on the floor. They pull out their swords. They fight. Their swords crash together with a loud smash.

But this isn't a real castle. It's fake. This is a movie. The swords are made of plastic. The castle is made of wood. So why are the sounds so realistic?

This is the job of a Foley artist, a person who puts special sounds into movies. A Foley artist is a sound artist.

Often when people make a movie, they only record the actors' voices. It is sometimes too noisy outside to record every sound, like a bee buzzing or a dog barking. But these sounds are important. Foley artists record new sounds that are louder and clearer.

Foley artists work in a special studio. They watch the movie and pay attention to what the actors are doing. When the actor walks on a wooden floor, the Foley artist makes the sound of footsteps. When the actor breaks a window, the Foley artist records the sound of real glass breaking. Is there going to be a storm in the movie? The Foley artist can make the sound of thunder by moving a thin piece of metal.

But are the footsteps going to be soft or loud? How much glass is going to break? How loud should the thunder be? Foley artists have to make everything sound realistic. They have to listen to how things sound in real life. Then they have to be creative to make new sounds.

In a Foley studio, there are many tools. The artist uses different things to get the right sound.

There are different kinds of floors, shoes, and books. An old chair can make a loud squeak. Two pieces of coconut banged together can make the sound of a horse walking. Keys can make the sound of a knight marching. A head of lettuce can make a soft crunch. And a big book closing quickly can sound like a punch!

These are just a few of the sound artist's tricks.

TRACK 26

**Unit 5, *The Art of Sound*, Words in Context**

**Find these words in the reading. What do you think they mean?**

knight
swords
realistic
artist
record
voices
studio

TRACK 27

**Unit 5, Spelling Pattern *ou*.**

**Listen and write. Then check your answers.**

1 touch
2 house
3 cousin
4 proud
5 young

**Now check your answers.**

1 touch, t-o-u-c-h, touch
2 house, h-o-u-s-e, house
3 cousin, c-o-u-s-i-n, cousin
4 proud, p-r-o-u-d, proud
5 young, y-o-u-n-g, young

TRACK 28

**Unit 5, Fiction, *Beethoven's 9th***

The orchestra waits—violins, drums, and flutes.
Singers hum—women in dresses, men in suits.
They wait for Beethoven, the great composer
The time for his music comes closer and closer.

Beethoven's new music took him ten years,
At his piano, after lots of hard work and tears.
At last! He's on stage, his hair wild and gray,
There with the orchestra while they play.

The famous composer lifts his arms high,
And brings them down, like an eagle that flies.
The music floats through the air, soft and sweet,
Filling the room—front row to back seat.

Beethoven waves his arms here and there,
Light shines in his eyes, the wind's in his hair.
First, he stands tall, then bends down on his knees,
Like a small boat sailing on stormy seas.

Beethoven wrote the music, so he knows every note.
He stands proudly on stage, in his red scarf and coat.
Trumpets play loudly. Drums boom, voices cry,
The audience wonders how the time flies by.

At last it is finished, the crowd gets to their feet,
They clap and throw flowers. What a wonderful treat!
They shout Beethoven's name, their hands in the air,
But he cannot hear them. For him, they're not there.

Then a kind singer turns him to look at the cheers,
The sad truth is, the composer can't hear.
Beethoven is deaf, his hearing long dead,
But the music is there, still alive in his head.

Beethoven sees the people, and now it is clear.
His heart is happy, his eyes fill with tears.
They like his music, Beethoven feels proud.
He bends down low, thanking the crowd.

Beethoven can remember hearing well.
But now, his ears can no longer tell.
The musician is deaf, his hearing long dead,
But the music is there, still alive in his head.

TRACK 29

**Unit 5, *Beethoven's 9th*, Words in Context**

**Find these words in the reading. What do you think they mean?**

composer
eagle
bends
knees
deaf

# Unit 6

TRACK 30

**Unit 6, Fiction, *Little Chef***

**Helene:** Welcome to *Little Chef*!

**Mark:** And welcome back to Marisa, Carlo, and Amy! You have one hour to prepare the best dessert.

**Helene:** Good luck! Your time starts now. Well, ladies and gentlemen, Carlo, Marisa, and Amy are cooking already. Let's find out what they're making!

**Mark:** What are you making, Carlo?

**Carlo:** I mixed together this "Too Much Chocolate Cake." It's a chocolate cake with dark chocolate in the middle and white chocolate on the top.

**Mark:** It sounds delicious!

**Helene:** Amy, what's your dessert called?

**Amy:** "The Frozen Tree." It's made with pineapple ice cream, fresh strawberries, and lemon juice. It's shaped like a tree.

**Helene:** Mmmm! I'd love to try it!

**Mark:** Marisa, it looks like you are making caramel on the stove. Tell us about your dessert.

**Marisa:** It's called the "Caramel Tower." It's going to be very tall and filled with cream. I also want to add cookie people climbing to the top.

**Mark:** Wow! I can't wait to see that!

**Helene:** We have only 20 minutes left, and everyone is working hard. Uh, oh! There's something wrong with Marisa's tower!

**Marisa:** Oh, no! It's falling apart. I need to start again, but there isn't time. I don't know what to do. It's a disaster! Do I throw it out? My grandpa always says, "When life gives you lemons, make lemonade." Hmm … I know what to do!

**Mark:** It looks like Marisa has a plan. Marisa, only 15 minutes left.

**Marisa:** OK! I just need to add some more caramel and some salt.

**Helene:** … and time's up! Stop cooking everyone! Please carry your desserts to the table.

**Mark:** Well done! You all finished your desserts on time.

**Helene:** Now we have to decide which is the best. Marisa, what happened to your Caramel Tower?

**Marisa:** Oh, I decided to change it. It's now called … "Lemonade."

**Mark:** How interesting!

**Helene:** And the winner is …

**Mark:** Marisa! Congratulations! You're our new "Little Chef!"

**Helene:** Your "Lemonade" was the most delicious and creative dessert. Where do you get your ideas?

**Marisa:** Oh, I got some good advice from my grandpa.

TRACK 31

**Unit 6, *Little Chef*, Words in Context**

**Find these words in the reading. What do you think they mean?**

delicious
frozen
caramel
winner
advice

TRACK 32

**Unit 6, Nonfiction, *Too Young to Cook? True Stories of Young Chefs***

Mikaila Ulmer and Fraser Doherty love cooking. They both had great ideas that made them successful. Here are their stories:

*Mikaila's Lemonade Story*

Mikaila was only four years old when she wanted to make a product for a children's business competition. But how did she decide what to make?

A few things helped Mikaila make a decision. First, she knew that she wanted to make something for Austin Lemonade Day. Then, a bee stung her twice. Mikaila didn't like the bee stings, but she became interested in bees and honey.

Then, Mikaila's great granny Helen sent her family a cookbook that included an old, special recipe for flaxseed lemonade.

Mikaila decided to make a product that helped the honey bees and used her great granny Helen's recipe. She came up with Me & the Bees Lemonade: a cold drink made from lemons, flaxseed, and local honey.

Today, Mikaila has a big company. She sells her lemonade and gives money to organizations that help honey bees. In 2016, she made an $11 million deal to sell Me & the Bees Lemonade in 55 stores across the USA.

*Fraser's Jam Story*

One afternoon when Fraser Doherty was 14, his grandmother taught him how to make jam.

Fraser began to make jam in the evenings and on weekends. He sold his jam in his hometown, Edinburgh. Then he experimented with his grandmother's recipe, trying many different ways to make the jam. In 2006, he discovered a way to make jam with fruit but no extra sugar.

Fraser he called his jam "SuperJam." He worked hard to design an interesting logo and found a factory to make his jam. In 2009, a large grocery chain agreed to sell his jam in their stores.

In 2010, Fraser wrote The SuperJam Cookbook. He also started organizing free "SuperJam Tea Parties" for elderly people, like his grandmother, who live alone. They dance, have tea, and of course, eat SuperJam! Today, people can buy SuperJam in stores all over the world.

The kitchen is a fun place! Maybe one day, you can start a business just like Mikaila and Fraser.

TRACK 33

**Unit 6, *Too Young to Cook? True Stories of Young Chefs*. Words in Context**

**Find these words in the reading. What do you think they mean?**

successful
flaxseed
cookbook
experimented
discovered
elderly

TRACK 34

**Unit 6, Spelling Pattern, Final *old*.**

**Listen and write. Then check your answers.**

**1** gold
**2** cold
**3** told
**4** hold
**5** fold

**Now check your answers.**

**1** gold, g-o-l-d, gold
**2** cold, c-o-l-d, cold
**3** told, t-o-l-d, told
**4** hold, h-o-l-d, hold
**5** fold, f-o-l-d, fold

## Unit 7

TRACK 35

**Unit 7, Fiction, *What Happens Next?***

**Ken:** It was story time. Everyone in our class loved story time. Mr. Carlson, who is our favorite teacher, always brought books to life.
Just then, my desk started to shake. But it wasn't only my desk, it was my chair, too. The shaking was gentle at first, but it got bigger and stronger.
Then, the whole classroom started moving from side to side. Pencils rolled off desks. Books fell off shelves.

**Mr. Carlson:** It's an earthquake! You know what to do, class. Let's move!

**Ken:** Of course, we remembered what to do in an earthquake. We often practiced: stay calm, get on the ground, and crawl under something strong.
Soon, we were all under our desks. Everyone was scared. I looked at my twin sister Aiko, who was holding onto the legs of her desk. I smiled to help her feel less scared.
Then, Mr. Carlson did a strange thing. From under his desk, he started reading again.

**Mr. Carlson:** Sophie climbed into the hot-air balloon and cut the rope that was keeping it tied to the ground. The balloon flew high into the air. She looked down at the city below …

**Ken:** I closed my eyes and listened to Mr. Carlson.
I was in the hot-air balloon—flying through the sky. I could feel the wind on my face. I could see some birds that were flying near me. I was lost in the story. Then we heard the principal's voice on the loudspeaker.

**Principal:** The earthquake is over. It's safe to leave the building.

**Ken:** Suddenly, I was back in our classroom. I looked around. Everything was still. The classroom wasn't shaking anymore.

**Mr. Carlson:** OK, class. It's safe to come out now.

**Ken:** We climbed out from under our desks. Everyone was still scared. Aiko smiled at me.

**Mr. Carlson:** I'm proud of you, class. That was very scary, but you all stayed calm. Good job! Now we need to evacuate the building and assemble outside.

**Ken:** "But what happens next in the story, Mr. Carlson?" I asked. The class laughed. Mr. Carlson laughed, too.

**Mr. Carlson:** Don't worry. We're going to finish it later, Ken.

TRACK 36

**Unit 7, *What Happens Next?*, Words in Context**

**Find these words in the reading. What do you think they mean?**

gentle
crawl
hot-air balloon
rope
loudspeaker

TRACK 37

**Unit 7, Nonfiction, *Animals to the Rescue***

After a natural disaster, rescue workers have to work very quickly to find people who are hurt. They need to save people's lives. But when a building falls down, how do the rescue workers find the people who are trapped underneath? One solution is to use special "search and rescue" dogs.

People who train search and rescue dogs are called dog handlers. They train the dogs for two to three years. Dogs can smell very well. They can use their noses to find things, other animals, and people.

Dogs can fit into very small spaces so they can search in rubble more easily than people can.

The handlers take the dogs to the disaster zone and watch carefully to see where they go. The dogs really like finding people.

In April 2015, there was a huge earthquake in Nepal. Many people died. Search and rescue dogs worked hard to find survivors. Five days after the earthquake, dogs helped to find a 15-year-old boy who was trapped under a building and couldn't get out. He was still alive!

Dogs aren't the only animals that help humans in an emergency.
Sometimes after a big emergency, cars and trucks can't reach the disaster area. One solution is to use search and rescue horses. Horses can travel a long way over difficult ground. They can see well, and they can hear and smell better than humans. The rescue workers watch their horses carefully. Sometimes, the horses find survivors before the people do.
Horses can also carry radios and other useful things. When the rescue workers arrive, they can help survivors and bring them to safety.
Wild animals can be heroes, too.
In 2009, a swimmer in China was stuck underwater. She couldn't move her legs, and she had no air. A whale pushed her up and saved her life.
In 2004 in New Zealand, some dolphins swam around a group of swimmers and saved them from a shark.
In an emergency, sometimes animals can help. They can even save lives.

### TRACK 38

**Unit 7, *Animals to the Rescue*, Words in Context**

**Find these words in the reading. What do you think they mean?**

search
train
rubble
survivors
trapped
safety
stuck

### TRACK 39

**Unit 7, Spelling Pattern, Final *–ly*.**

**Listen and write. Then check your answers.**

1 family
2 friendly
3 quietly
4 early
5 happily

**Now check your answers.**

1 family, f-a-m-i-l-y, family
2 friendly, f-r-i-e-n-d-l-y, friendly
3 quietly, q-u-i-e-t-l-y, quietly
4 early, e-a-r-l-y, early
5 happily, h-a-p-p-i-l-y, happily

## Unit 8

### TRACK 40

**Unit 8, Nonfiction, *Coral Reefs***

*A World of Tiny Animals*

There are fish, sharks, and whales in the world's oceans, but did you know there are also animals that look like mushrooms, trees, brains, and fingers? These are all coral!
There are two types of coral: soft and hard. Both are made of tiny animals called polyps. Polyps are like jellyfish, but they don't swim. They stick to rocks, and after hundreds of years they grow together, and make a coral reef.
Coral get their bright colors from algae, very small plants that live inside the polyps. Algae need sunlight to grow, so they can only live in shallow water.

*Reefs as Shelter*

Fish and other creatures such as sea turtles, starfish, and urchins need coral for food and shelter. The coral reefs protect small fish. The reef is their home. Some fish find food there when they are young, but leave the reef when they're old enough to swim away.

*Are Coral Reefs in Danger?*

Today, all around the world, Coral reefs are in danger. Here are three of the reasons:

- The sea is getting warmer. For coral to be healthy, the seawater can't be too cold or too hot. When the water is hotter than 28°C, the algae leave the reefs. This is why the coral are losing their color. When coral become white, they can die.
- The waste from big cities, including dangerous chemicals, often goes into the sea.
  Then the seawater becomes dirty and the coral don't get the sunlight they need.
- People who visit the reefs can touch the coral and damage them.

*Protecting Coral Reefs*

In many parts of the world, however, people take good care of coral reefs. In the city of Abu Dhabi, people protect the nearby Ras Ghanada reef. In Cuba, the coral reefs in "The Gardens of the Queen" are in a marine park. This means that no one can go fishing there and very few tourists can visit. Without protection like this, the coral reefs will die.

### TRACK 41

**Unit 8, *Coral Reefs*, Words in Context**

**Find these words in the reading. What do you think they mean?**

stick
shallow
creatures
waste
damage
marine park

### TRACK 42

**Unit 8, Spelling Pattern, Final *–ight*.**

**Listen and write. Then check your answers.**

1 night
2 right
3 tight
4 fight
5 light

**Now check your answers.**

1 night, n-i-g-h-t, night
2 right, r-i-g-h-t, right
3 tight, t-i-g-h-t, tight
4 fight, f-i-g-h-t, fight
5 light, l-i-g-h-t-, light

### TRACK 43

**Unit 8, Fiction, *The Lost Camera***

**Fin:** It was a normal day under the sea. Mom and Dad were going to work. My sister and I were swimming to school. Everyone was in a hurry.
Everyone ... except the divers up near the surface. One of them needed a better photo of an angelfish.
*Click!*
But suddenly the camera slipped out of her hand. It fell down, down into the dark water of the ocean ... and into our world! *Thud!* The camera landed on the ocean floor, but nobody saw or noticed it ...
**Fin:** ... except Sandy and me.
**Sandy:** Where did this come from?
**Fin:** Sandy asked. I pointed up. "From divers up there." I looked at the tag on the camera closely. "Where's Mexico?" I asked.
**Sandy:** There! I told you Mexico was real,
**Fin:** Sandy whispered. "I'd like to see this world," I told Sandy.
Then she had an idea.
**Sandy:** Let's take the camera back to Mexico!
**Fin:** "But how can we get there?" I asked. "Dollie! Take us to the surface, please!" I shouted. Dollie swam and swam. Up and up we went.
**Fin:** "Say starfish!"
The surface was so exciting. It was our first time there. Suddenly, we saw something. It was a boat. There were people on it. Divers!
**Sandy:** "Quick, Fin! Let's swim to the boat!"
**Fin:** Sandy shouted. Thump! The camera landed on the boat.
**Man:** "Did you hear something?"
**Fin:** one diver asked.
**Woman:** "Hey, my camera!"
**Fin:** said another diver.
**Woman:** "I was looking everywhere for that."
**Fin:** Sandy and I wanted to see some more. Mexico was amazing! "Wow! Those buildings are so tall!" I said.
**Sandy:** "What are the children making?"
**Fin:** Sandy asked. I didn't know, but it looked cool! We were having a great time until ...
**Sandy:** "I'm feeling sick,"
**Fin:** Sandy said. "Me, too," I said. We were on the surface for too long and breathed too much air. "Quick, Dollie! Take us home. Sandy is sick," I shouted.
**Mom:** Hello, Dr. Crab?
**Dad:** Fin, what's wrong with your sister?

**Fin:** Dad asked me. I didn't want to tell him. I thought he would be angry with us.
**Dr. Crab:** "You're airsick, Sandy. Just rest a little and you'll be fine,"
**Fin:** Dr. Crab said.
**Dad:** Airsick? Where did you go?
**Fin:** Dad asked.
**Mom:** "Tell us what happened, Fin—*everything!*"
**Fin:** Mom said. "It's a long story," Mom, I said.

### TRACK 44

**Unit 8, *The Lost Camera*, Words in Context**
**Find these words in the reading. What do you think they mean?**
divers
surface
slipped
noticed
tag
everywhere

## Unit 9

### TRACK 45

**Unit 9, Nonfiction, *Take Your Medicine***
Most of us don't like being sick. Visiting the doctor's office, taking medicine, getting shots, and staying in bed—it isn't fun, is it? But you should be happy you aren't living in the past, when doctors had some very different ideas about how to cure sick people.
Let's take a trip into the past and look at some old treatments.

*3300 BCE*
For cuts and scrapes, people didn't use a bandage made of cloth or plastic. Sometimes, they used moss.

*2500 to 2000 BCE, Ancient Egypt*
A patient with sore bumps on his neck got interesting medicine made from the blood of birds and flies. For toothaches, the ancient Egyptians took medicine made from dead mice.

*2000 BCE, Ancient Mesopotamia*
Do you grind your teeth while sleeping? The ancient Babylonians had a cure: sleep with a human skull next to you for a week and you'll stop biting down on your teeth while you sleep.

*800 to 100 BCE, Ancient Greece*
Do you feel some pain? In ancient Greece, healers put big, wet sponges on the places that hurt.

*20 BCE to 400 CE, Ancient Rome*
The ancient Romans thought that opposites were good treatments. If a patient had a fever, a healer put cool cucumbers on the patient's body. If a patient felt cold, a healer told the patient to eat hot peppers.

*200 to 300 CE, China*
To stay healthy and live forever, the treatment was to eat or drink some gold.

*1300s, Europe*
There were many strange treatments for the plague, a terrible disease which killed millions of people. Sick people sometimes wore dead toads around their necks, or put chicken feathers on their sores. They thought this made the plague leave their bodies.

*1800s, Britain*
For a sore throat, the treatment started on the feet. The sick person put a really dirty sock around their neck!
The patient tied a cooked potato to their head to cure an earache.
And doctors used leeches for all sorts of problems.
Dirty socks and dead mice? Bird blood and leeches? Yuck! Aren't you glad you see a nice, friendly doctor when you're sick?

### TRACK 46

**Unit 9, *Take Your Medicine*, Words in Context**
**Find these words in the reading. What do you think they mean?**
cure
treatments
patient
grind
opposites
disease

### TRACK 47

**Unit 9, Spelling Pattern, *ur*.**
**Listen and write. Then check your answers.**
1 fur
2 curtain
3 surfing
4 turn
5 purple
**Now check your answers.**
1 fur, f-u-r, fur
2 curtain, c-u-r-t-a-i-n, curtain
3 surfing, s-u-r-f-i-n-g, surfing
4 turn, t-u-r-n, turn
5 purple, p-u-r-p-l-e, purple

### TRACK 48

**Unit 9, Fiction, *A Surprise Cure London, 1928***
**Spider:** My friend, Alexander Fleming, is a scientist. I work on my web, and he works long and hard in his laboratory.
What is he doing? Well, Dr. Fleming wants to find a way to fight germs called bacteria. He keeps bacteria in little dishes and studies them. I keep flies in my web … for dinner.
You see, while Dr. Fleming was working in hospitals, he saw many people die because of bacteria. Now, as a scientist, he wants to stop it, so it doesn't happen anymore.
**Fleming:** I have to find a cure. I have to!
**Spider:** But now it's summer, and Dr. Fleming is going on vacation with his family. What a mess! He isn't always the neatest scientist.
**Fleming:** Leave everything. I'll clean up when I get back.
**Assistant:** Of course, Dr. Fleming.
**Spider:** I've been looking after the lab for Dr. Fleming. When I looked in the dishes, something strange was happening. I saw some mold growing.
**Mold:** Look—it's bacteria! Time to get to work. Attack!
**Bacteria:** Run away!
**Spider:** Hey, Dr. Fleming is back!
**Fleming:** I should clean up those dishes.
**Spider:** Aha, he sees the mold!
**Fleming:** That's funny. There's mold growing on the dishes! How did it get here?
**Mold:** Check it out. We beat the bacteria!
**Spider:** Well done, Mold!
**Assistant:** Where are the bacteria?
**Fleming:** Something in the mold was stopping them. Look, there's some liquid in the dish. Mold juice! I need to find out more!
**Assistant:** That's a very good idea, Dr. Fleming!
**Spider:** Dr. Fleming is a lucky man. Sometimes you find things when you aren't looking for them!
**Fleming:** Aha! This is penicillium mold. I'm going to call the "mold juice" penicillin. Penicillin kills bacteria. It can cure sick people. I have to make it a medicine. I have to share this discovery!
**Spider:** While the scientists were trying to make penicillin into medicine, they worked hard. They had to be sure it was safe.
Today, penicillin is one of the world's most important medicines. It has saved many, many lives. Some people say it has saved around 80 million lives so far!
And it all started because Dr. Fleming didn't clean up before he went on vacation!

### TRACK 49

**Unit 9, *A Surprise Cure*, Words in Context**
**Find these words in the reading. What do you think they mean?**
scientist
bacteria
laboratory
mess
attack
liquid
penicillin

# Unit 10

TRACK 50

**Unit 10, Nonfiction, *Moving Machines***

*Parts of a Machine*

Machines have lots of different moving parts. Looking at the inside of a clock can show you how many parts there are. There are four basic parts inside many of these machines—cranks, gears, levers, and pulleys.

A crank is made from a handle, a thin rod, and supports. When you turn the handle, the rod moves. Many machines use cranks, including mechanical pencil sharpeners, bike pedals, and sewing machines.

Gears are like wheels with teeth. When the gears turn, the teeth connect to make them move. Gears can make something move faster or slower. Clocks, multi-speed bikes, and music boxes all use gears.

A lever is a strong, straight object that sits against a support. When either end of the lever is pushed down, the other side moves up. There are several types of levers. Scissors and seesaws are both examples of levers.

A pulley is a machine made from a wheel and a rope or chain. The rope or chain is pulled over the wheel and it helps lift heavy objects easily. Elevators and wells use pulleys.

*Automata*

Most machines only move when someone uses them, but automata can move on their own. In the past, automata were simpler. Some were even toys! Cuckoo clocks and wind-up dolls were popular automata before robots and automatic cleaning machines. People could turn a key or pull some strings and see the toys give a performance!

The designers were usually clock makers or inventors because they understood how the machines worked. Designers had to use their imaginations to make the machines look and move like real people or animals. It often took many people and a lot of hard work to build one.

This silver swan is at the Bowes Museum in England. It is made from many pieces of silver and gold. The river is made from glass rods. When someone turns the crank, the machine starts. The gears under the swan turn the glass rods, so it looks like moving water. Then, the swan turns its head and pulls a silver fish from the water. It even plays music.

Some automata need someone to press a button or put a coin in the machines to make them work. They can be very interesting to watch. There are automata in many places in our lives: in art museums, toy stores, and homes. These machines can be useful, fun, or both.

TRACK 51

**Unit 10, *Moving Machines*, Words in Context**

**Find these words in the reading. What do you think they mean?**

basic
rod
support
either
wind-up
swan

TRACK 52

**Unit 10, Fiction, *Searching for Sterling***

**Ed:** That was a hard day!
**Narrator:** Ed shouted to the cowboys.
**Ed:** Time for some food!
**Narrator:** They were moving the cattle south. It was almost winter, but they were almost home.
**Ed:** How's your new horse, Jules?
**Narrator:** Ed asked his son.
**Jules:** Oh, Sterling's great. When I push the Go to Sleep button, it shuts down,
**Narrator:** Jules explained.
**Jules:** OK, you can laugh. But it's better than all your horses,
**Narrator:** he said.
**Jules:** You'll see.
**Narrator:** Very early the next morning, Silas woke everyone up with his shouting.
**Silas:** Jules, come quickly! Sterling is gone!
**Jules:** Oh, no! Did I forget to shut it down last night? I have to find Sterling!
**Narrator:** Jules decided to ask Sheriff Ada for help.
**Jules:** Sterling isn't a normal horse, Sheriff,
**Narrator:** said Jules.
**Jules:** I need your motorcycle to catch it.
**Sheriff Ada:** Sure, you can borrow it,
**Narrator:** Sheriff Ada said.
**Sheriff Ada:** To start and stop, you pull this lever. But you have to bring it back tonight!
**Narrator:** she shouted.
**Sheriff Ada:** It's powerful. Be careful with it.
**Narrator:** Jules loved the motorcycle. It was faster than Sterling! He drove it for kilometers through the desert.
**Jules:** I still have to look for Sterling,
**Narrator:** he thought.
Jules was tired. He wanted to keep looking for Sterling, but it was too dark. He stopped to rest and fell asleep under the stars.
Later that night, Jules awoke to a strange sound. A coyote was eating all of his food!
**Jules:** Hey, get away from there!
**Narrator:** Jules shouted.
Jules was upset.
**Jules:** I lost my horse, my food is gone, and it's getting cold. What a tough day!
**Narrator:** he thought.
**Jules:** What do I do now? The motorcycle! I promised to bring it back to the Sheriff yesterday!
**Narrator:** He jumped on it and pulled the lever to turn it on.
**Jules:** Giddy-up!
**Narrator:** Jules rode back to Snowmore as fast as he could. He was very tired, very hungry, and very sad.
**Jules:** I'll never find Sterling,
**Narrator:** he thought. Then he saw Chayton outside the restaurant.
**Jules:** Have you seen Sheriff Ada?
**Narrator:** he asked.
**Chayton:** I haven't seen her today.
**Narrator:** Chayton said.
**Jules:** I brought her motorcycle. Sheriff Ada! Sterling!
**Sheriff Ada:** Good morning, Jules!
**Jules:** How did you find it?
**Narrator:** Jules asked.
**Sheriff Ada:** It showed up here last night,
**Narrator:** said Sheriff Ada.
**Sheriff Ada:** You pressed the Go Home button, not the Go to Sleep button!
**Jules:** You really are the best Sheriff in the West!
**Narrator:** said Jules.

TRACK 53

**Unit 10, *Searching for Sterling*, Words in Context**

**Find these words in the reading. What do you think they mean?**

cowboys
cattle
shuts down
motorcycle
fell asleep
tough

TRACK 54

**Unit 10, Spelling Pattern *ough*.**

**Listen and write. Then check your answers.**

**1** cough
**2** rough
**3** thoughtful
**4** dough
**5** though

**Now check your answers.**

**1** cough, c-o-u-g-h, cough
**2** rough, r-o-u-g-h, rough
**3** thoughtful, t-h-o-u-g-h-t-f-u-l, thoughtful
**4** dough, d-o-u-g-h, dough
**5** though, t-h-o-u-g-h, though

# Video Scripts

## Language Book

The video scripts for the songs in the **Language Book** are exactly the same as for the audio scripts and the text on the page. Please refer to the relevant unit in the Audio Scripts on TB pp. 213–228.

### Unit 1

CONVERSATION

*At the Bookstore*

**Natalia:** Rania, I can't decide!

**Rania:** Let me help. I read a lot last summer. Ask me anything! Oh, why don't you get this book, Natalia? *Lily B on the Brink of Cool.*

**Natalia:** What kind of book is it? Is it scary?

**Rania:** It's not scary; it's funny. It's a novel. It's the diary of a girl named Lily.

**Natalia:** It sounds great. OK, I'll get it. What kinds of books do you like?

**Rania:** Well, I like novels, and I like history.

**Natalia:** How about this book? I read it at school.

**Rania:** Maybe. What's it about?

**Natalia:** A little girl grows up and becomes a queen.

**Rania:** I don't know. It doesn't sound very interesting.

**Natalia:** I agree, it wasn't very exciting. OK, what about this one? *Sarah, Plain and Tall.* It's about a girl on a farm. She works hard, but she has adventures, too.

**Rania:** Did you like it?

**Natalia:** Yes, and it has a happy ending!

**Rania:** Perfect! I love happy endings! OK, let's get it.

### Unit 2

PRESENTATION

*The Sun Forest*

**Rania:** I'm Rania, and this is my dream biome—the sun forest. I'm going to talk about its climate, plants, and animals.

In my sun forest, the climate is hot and wet. It rains every night, so the grass and plants are very green and grow happily. During the day, it's *always* sunny—there are no clouds at all!

There are a lot of plants in my sun forest. There are very tall trees with huge leaves. And the biggest flowers in the world! They're called *super-sunflowers*.

All the animals sleep in the trees at night. One special animal is the *sunkey*. They look like monkeys, but they lie quietly in the sun like cats. They're very friendly, so you can get close and play with them.

I like my biome best because it's the sunniest place of all. The plants and animals in the sun forest are the happiest of any biome in all the world. Thank you.

### Unit 3

CONVERSATION

*My Sister's Birthday*

**Stephen:** Can I help you?

**Anya:** Yes. I'm looking for a birthday present for my sister. She's going to be seven.

**Stephen:** OK. You could get her a doll. These pretty dolls are popular. Look how she drinks milk! Does your sister like dolls?

**Anya:** Not really. She likes games and puzzles. And she likes to draw.

**Stephen:** You could buy her this animal puzzle. It has 500 pieces.

**Anya:** Hmm, maybe.

**Stephen:** Or you could get her this video game. She can drive any car! It's for ages five and up.

**Anya:** That's a good idea. What do you think?

**Stephen:** I think you should buy her the video game. It's way more fun!

**Anya:** Perfect! She's going to be so surprised. Thank you very much!

**Stephen:** You're welcome. That will be $30, please. Have a nice day!

**Anya:** You too!

### Unit 4

PRESENTATION

*When I Perform*

**Natalia:** I'm Natalia, and I'm a folk dancer. Today I'm going to talk about folk dancing. Do you like my costume? I started dancing when I was five. My family is Polish, and folk dancing is part of Polish history and life. My parents love dancing, so they wanted me to learn Polish dancing, too.

I go to dance class once a week. Practicing is fun, but I think performing is even more fun! There are three things I like about performing. The first is the music. We dance to traditional Polish music.

The next thing I like is the teamwork. We work hard together and we help each other. The third thing I like is the audience. They always clap and shout. They look happy and this makes me happy, too! I love dancing, and I love performing. Come and see me dance. Then try it yourself!

### Unit 5

CONVERSATION

*Math or Music?*

**Lewis:** That was such a fun music class, Otis!

**Otis:** Yeah! I love music. It's my favorite.

**Lewis:** I like it, too. But I think math is much more important.

**Otis:** Really? Why?

**Lewis:** Well, music is fun, but we learn more important things in math.

**Otis:** I disagree, Lewis. In my opinion, music is the most important class.

**Lewis:** Really? Why do you think that?

**Otis:** Because we have to work with each other as a team in orchestra. We watch each other and the conductor, and we learn to think fast. Those are all important skills.

**Lewis:** Huh, that's true. I didn't think about that.

**Otis:** And, music uses math. We have to count all the time!

**Lewis:** You're right. Music is important!

**Otis:** So, do we agree?

**Lewis:** Yes, math and music are both important!

## Unit 6

### CONVERSATION

*The Friendly Tomato*

**Rania:** Welcome to The Friendly Tomato! My name's Rania. I'm going to be your server. Here's our menu.
**Stephen:** Thanks.
**Rania:** Is this your first time here?
**Stephen:** Yes! I read about it on a food blog.
**Rania:** You're going to have fun! Do you want some water?
**Stephen:** Yes, please!
**Rania:** Now, at The Friendly Tomato, you only have one choice for dinner: salad. But you can choose everything in it!
**Stephen:** OK!
**Rania:** First, choose your main green vegetable. There's lettuce, spinach ...
**Stephen:** Lettuce, please!
**Rania:** Now, choose three more vegetables.
**Stephen:** Tomatoes, corn, and ... mushrooms.
**Rania:** Next, choose a protein. We have chicken, nuts, black beans...
**Stephen:** I want to try black beans!
**Rania:** Now, choose dairy—that's cheese. Or you can have fruit.
**Stephen:** Cheese, please!
**Rania:** Next, choose a salad dressing. That's your healthy fat. You can choose from blue cheese or honey mustard. And then you're done!
**Stephen:** Thank you! But what about carbohydrates?
**Rania:** Here's some bread. Now, you have the healthiest lunch in town!
**Stephen:** And the biggest!

## Unit 7

### PRESENTATION

*When I Grow Up*

**Otis:** Hello, My name's Otis. I'd like to be a rescue worker when I grow up because rescue workers are very important people in an emergency. Here are my reasons why.
First, rescue workers help people in many different ways. They're usually the first people who come and help in a disaster. They travel by ambulance, helicopter, or fire truck, and they go straight to the emergency.
Next, rescue workers know a lot about the body. They're not doctors, but they can help a lot. They know exactly what to do, and they take people to hospitals or shelters.
Finally, rescue workers are calm and kind. They don't get stressed, and they try to help other people stay calm, too. They're strong and brave, and they help people feel safe in emergencies.
Rescue workers help people in disasters all over the world. They're my heroes. That's why I'd like to be one, too. I want to help the world.

## Unit 8

### PRESENTATION

*Blue Whales*

**Anya:** That was the sound of a blue whale, the biggest animal on Earth. My presentation today is about blue whales and how people saved them.
A blue whale isn't blue—it's blue-gray. It's as heavy as twenty elephants, and as long as three school buses. It's huge!
A long time ago, there were lots of blue whales. People didn't see them because they lived deep in the oceans. Sometimes people tried to catch them, but it was very hard. They're fast and strong. In those days they were safe from people.
But then people with fast boats learned how to catch whales. Whale-hunting became popular. People sold the meat and oil. They made lots of money.
Soon there were almost no blue whales left. Many people were worried and worked hard to protect them. As a result, people stopped catching whales. So their numbers began to grow again. Today, we protect whales. We enjoy watching them, not catching them! Thank you.

## Unit 9

### CONVERSATION

*A Bad Headache*

**Rania:** Natalia, are you OK? You don't look well.
**Natalia:** Not really. I have a bad headache. Every noise sounds like a loud crash.
**Rania:** Oh, I'm sorry. Are you drinking a lot of water?
**Natalia:** Yes, I am. But my head still hurts like crazy!
**Rania:** OK, first, you should put a cold, wet towel on your head. That always helps me.
**Natalia:** Really?
**Rania:** Yeah. You could also put ice in a towel and put it on the back of your neck. That works, too. Or you can buy a special cream with medicine in it.
**Natalia:** So, do you get headaches, too?
**Rania:** Yeah, quite often. But I usually just go home and lie down in a quiet room and close my eyes.
**Natalia:** I'm going home to do that right now. And I'm going to try putting ice on my neck, too.
**Rania:** I hope you get better quickly.
**Natalia:** Thanks!

## Unit 10

### PRESENTATION

*My Treehouse*

**Lewis:** I'm going to tell you a story about something I made.
I have four noisy sisters and sometimes I wanted to get away from them!
There was a big tree with strong branches in our yard. I liked climbing it. After breakfast one day, when I was sitting in the tree, I had a bright idea. I decided to build a tree house!
I climbed down and found some flat pieces of wood. I wanted to climb back up with the wood, but it wasn't safe.
I had to ask my dad to help. Together, we built my tree house. We put the wood across the branches to make a floor, and we made some walls and a roof. I made my own flag, too. I loved my treehouse! It was my special place.

# Literacy Book

The video scripts for the **Literacy Book** reading texts (fiction and nonfiction) are mostly the same as for the audio scripts and on the pages of the book. Occasionally, some narrator's lines have been cut to work better with the animation; these altered scripts are shown here.

## Unit 1

FICTION

*The Beginning of Alice's Adventures*

**Narrator:** Alice sat by the river. Her sister read a novel. Alice was bored and hot. She felt sleepy, and she wondered what to do. Suddenly, a rabbit ran past her. The rabbit was white with pink eyes. He wore a yellow waistcoat.

**Alice:** Goodness me!

**Narrator:** said Alice.

**Alice:** What's that? A rabbit in a waistcoat!

**Narrator:** She was very surprised.

**Alice:** Rabbits don't wear waistcoats!

**Narrator:** The rabbit stopped and took a watch out of his pocket.

**Rabbit:** Oh dear, oh dear, I'm going to be late,

**Narrator:** The rabbit ran off. Alice got up, quickly, and chased after him. The rabbit jumped down a very big hole. Alice jumped in after him. Alice fell—down, down, down—for a very long time. As she fell, Alice could see shelves of interesting books and things on the sides of the hole.

**Alice:** I wonder if I'm near the center of the Earth,

**Narrator:** Down, down, down.

**Alice:** I might go right through the Earth and end up in New Zealand,

**Narrator:** She knew all about the geography of the Earth from school. Then, suddenly—thump! Alice landed at the bottom of the hole. She saw the White Rabbit run around the corner. Alice ran after him as fast as she could. Alice came to a room full of doors. But where was the White Rabbit? She couldn't see him, and all the doors were locked. Then Alice saw a little golden key on a table. She picked it up.

**Alice:** I wonder which door this key opens?

**Narrator:** This was just the beginning of Alice's exciting adventures in Wonderland. But she didn't know that!

## Unit 2

NONFICTION

*Two Different Forests*

Audio Track 10 TB p. 231

## Unit 3

NONFICTION

*The History of Money*

Audio Track 15 TB p. 231

## Unit 4

FICTION

*Teamwork Makes the Dream Work*

Audio Track 23 TB p. 233

## Unit 5

NONFICTION

*The Art of Sound*

Audio Track 25 TB p. 233

## Unit 6

FICTION

*Little Chef*

Audio Track 30 TB p. 234

## Unit 7

NONFICTION

*What Happens Next?*

Audio Track 37 TB p. 235

## Unit 8

NONFICTION

*Coral Reefs*

Audio Track 40 TB p. 235

## Unit 9

FICTION

*Take Your Medicine*

Audio Track 48 TB p. 237

## Unit 10

FICTION

*Searching for Sterling*

**Ed:** That was a hard day!

**Narrator:** Ed shouted to the cowboys.

**Ed:** Time for some food!

**Narrator:** They were moving the cattle south. It was almost winter, but they were almost home.

**Ed:** How's your new horse, Jules?

**Narrator:** Ed asked his son.

**Jules:** Oh, Sterling's great. When I push the Go to Sleep button, it shuts down. OK, you can laugh. But it's better than all your horses. You'll see.

**Narrator:** Very early the next morning, Silas woke everyone up with his shouting.

**Silas:** Jules, come quickly! Sterling is gone!

**Jules:** Oh, no! Did I forget to shut it down last night? I have to find Sterling!

**Narrator:** Jules decided to ask Sheriff Ada for help.

**Jules:** Sterling isn't a normal horse, Sheriff. I need your motorcycle to catch it.

**Sheriff Ada:** Sure, you can borrow it. To start and stop, you pull this lever. But you have to bring it back tonight! It's powerful. Be careful with it.

**Narrator:** Jules loved the motorcycle. It was faster than Sterling! He drove it for kilometers through the desert.

**Jules:** I still have to look for Sterling.

**Narrator:** Jules was tired. He wanted to keep looking for Sterling, but it was too dark. He stopped to rest and fell asleep under the stars. Later that night, Jules awoke to a strange sound. A coyote was eating all of his food!

**Jules:** Hey, get away from there!

**Narrator:** Jules was upset.

**Jules:** I lost my horse, my food is gone, and it's getting cold. What a tough day! What do I do now? The motorcycle! I promised to bring it back to the Sheriff yesterday!

**Narrator:** He jumped on it and pulled the lever to turn it on.

**Jules:** Giddy-up!

**Narrator:** Jules rode back to Snowmore as fast as he could. He was very tired, very hungry, and very sad.

**Jules:** I'll never find Sterling,

**Narrator:** he thought. Then he saw Chayton outside the restaurant.

**Jules:** Have you seen Sheriff Ada?

**Chayton:** I haven't seen her today.

**Jules:** I brought her motorcycle. Sheriff Ada! Sterling!

**Sheriff Ada:** Good morning, Jules!

**Jules:** How did you find it?

**Sheriff Ada:** It showed up here last night. You pressed the Go Home button, not the Go to Sleep button!

**Jules:** You really are the best Sheriff in the West!